June 1967 Family Bookshelf.

3cc

Lincoln's Mothers

Dorothy Clarke Wilson

A Doubleday-Galilee Original
Doubleday & Company, Inc., Garden City, New York
1981

Permission to quote from the following sources is gratefully acknowledged:

To Macmillan Publishing Company, Inc., for the selection from "The Lincoln Child," taken from *Monday Morning and Other Poems* by James Oppenheim (New York: Macmillan, 1919).

To Ethel Barnett de Vito for her poem, "Lincoln's Foster Mother," published in *Ladies' Home Journal* in February, 1950.

LINCOLN'S
MOTHERS

PART ONE

The color of the ground was in him, the red earth;
The snack and tang of elemental things:
The rectitude and patience of the cliff;
The good-will of the rain that loves all leaves;
The friendly welcome of the wayside well;
The courage of the bird that dares the sea;
The gladness of the wind that shakes the corn. . . .

From "Lincoln, the Man of the People":
Edwin Markham

— *1* —

Who was she?

As she grew out of childhood into girlhood, the question became increasingly perplexing, baffling, disturbing.

She had a name. She was Nancy Hanks. She was part of a family. There were Grandfather Joseph and Grandmother Nannie. There were uncles, five of them—Thomas, Joshua, William, Charles, and Joseph, only three years older than herself. There were aunts— Elizabeth (Betsy), Mary Polly, and, strangely enough, another Nancy, almost exactly her own age. Nannie, the family called her, the pet name Grandfather had given long ago to his wife, who was also Nancy.

Perhaps it was the presence of this other young Nancy, exuberant, confident, a little bold, which made her feel like an echo, a shadow of something real and vital. Nannie belonged. She was loved. She had a mother and father to whom she was the wonder child of their later years and in whose eyes she could do no wrong. Not so, Nancy. No matter how hard she tried, she could never elicit from Grandmother more than grudging approval.

"There, child, you see? You *can* spin a decent thread if you try hard enough, though look now, you've broken it!" . . . "Can't you even lug a bucket from the spring without sloppin'?" . . . "Not bad, child. You got the corn meal and water mixed right well, but gracious me! Can't you turn a hoecake on the shovel without makin' such a mess?"

Grandmother was not happy here in the small cabin on the Rolling Fork in this far western county of Virginia beyond the mountains. She lamented the loss of her more luxurious home back in the

Patterson Creek Valley of Hampshire County where a family of ten or sometimes more people had not been crowded into one fourteen-by eighteen-foot room, where there had been neighbors whom she had known from childhood, broad fertile fields all about instead of dark forests full of lurking dangers, where one could go down to the "crick" or even to neighbors' cabins without fear of being ambushed and perhaps scalped.

Such fears were by no means groundless. The hordes of pioneers who, during those years of the 1780s, streamed down the Ohio River from New York and Pennsylvania, or swarmed through Cumberland Gap and along the Wilderness Road from Virginia and the Carolinas in the wake of the intrepid Daniel Boone, came at peril of their lives. The territory of Kentucky had belonged for countless generations to the Indians—the Cherokee, Choctaw, Creek, Wyandotte, Shawnee, and Iroquois. It was their beloved hunting ground. Like the ancient Hebrews, Indians believed that land, like air and water, was free, to be used but not owned, and the white man's idea of ownership of land they found incomprehensible. Any arrangement that implied the "sale" of their beloved domain, with its clear streams, its gushing springs, its salt licks, which attracted herds of buffalo, could not be considered permanent. Each tribe had fought off encroachment by others through the centuries. Naturally this new white alien invader could be no exception.

Kentucke . . . Kentake. The white man, who borrowed the name, was never quite sure of its meaning. "Fair land of tomorrow" or "Dark and bloody ground"? In his experience it was often the latter. Pilgrims were ambushed and slain along the Wilderness Road. Horses were stolen, children taken captive, cabins burned, their occupants slaughtered. But retaliation could be equally savage, resulting in mass murders, enforced exiles, unjust treaties designed to cheat and exploit.

"Kaintuck!" Grandmother repeated the word with a shudder. "No wonder the Indians named it 'dark and bloody ground'!" She resented the fact that Grandfather had sold his fine farm of one hundred eighty acres back in the fertile valley for a ridiculously small sum, only twenty-one pounds and nine shillings. And what did they have now? One hundred fifty acres of forest with only the doubtful promise of a deed! Why had he been so foolish?

Grandfather, always close-mouthed, usually met such complaints with grim silence. Only once did Nancy hear him respond with outspoken vigor.

"You know why. Wasn't it you what kep' sayin' we had to move, you couldn't stand the talk, the neighbors lookin' down their noses at us, the way they'd hush up when they'd see us comin'? And all on account of the child!"

Nancy, looking up from the small loom where she was painstakingly learning to weave a piece of linsey-woolsey, was startled to see the eyes of both grandparents fixed on her, then turned hastily away. The shuttle fell from her fingers. Though her stool was close to the fire, a shiver passed through her thin body. A child, Grandfather had said. Then both of them had looked at her. Why? Was she to blame for their leaving that place called "Virginny" and coming here to "Kaintuck" where Grandmother had to work so hard and was so unhappy? But—how could she be? What had she done? She had been just a baby when the family had made the terribly long journey over the mountains, and what could a baby do?

Aunt Betsy, who had been a big girl when they made the journey, told her and Nannie about it.

"We traveled the same trail Daniel Boone did long ago. There was nary even a path when he went fust, just thick forest, and Injuns mebbe hidin' behind every tree. But by the time we come along there was a fair decent trail, wide enough for a wagon. We took horses. Polly and I rode on one. Father and the boys rode another, turn about, two ridin' while the others drove the cattle and hogs on ahead, and Mother and Joseph and you two Nancys rode in the ox wagon. We rode and rode, for days and days. And when nights came—" She shivered.

Nannie's eyes shone with avid anticipation, for both children had heard the story before. "When nights came, you made a fire to cook supper and frighten off the wild beasts, the bears and buffalo and wild cats and mebbe even snarlin' wolves." She recounted the roster with relish. "But sometimes you didn't dare to make fires for fear of Injuns."

Nancy shivered in sympathy with Aunt Betsy. Unlike Nannie, who thrilled to every sort of excitement, she hated this part of the story. She experienced it all too vividly, heard the crackling of bushes, the prowling feet, saw the red eyes reflecting the firelight, felt the terror of lurking unseen shapes.

"But the nights could be beautiful too, like the days," assured Aunt Betsy.

It was Nancy's eyes that shone now, for she could picture it all—the green valley of the Shenandoah, the trail winding up, always up, through the Cumberland Gap, with mountains so high they were lost in purple haze, blazing sunsets, huge stars shining under the canopy of an ox wagon. And then the ecstasy of coming down, down into Kentucky in the spring! How could anybody call it a "dark and bloody ground"? She had no need to imagine it. She reveled in the springtime, the rushing of waters in the Rolling Fork, the bursting into bloom of the wild honeysuckle, the creams and crimsons of the tulip and Judas trees, the flashing of bluebirds, robins, cardinals.

"I was there, wasn't I?" chattered Nannie. "I can almost remember it."

Aunt Betsy gave her little sister a hug. "Of course, pet. Right there with all your brothers and sisters. Do you think Father would have his little Nannie anywhere else? And during most of the trip you were in Mother's arms."

Nancy felt the ecstasy drain from her body. Brothers . . . sisters . . . Father . . . Mother . . . Of all the people who filled the little cabin to bulging she was the odd one. Yet to all her questions she encountered a wall of diversion or silence.

"Don't I have a mother?" she once asked Grandmother timidly. "Don't bother me, child. Can't you see I'm busy? I've got to get these deerskin britches done before your grandfather catches his death. Now see what you've gone and done! Made me jam the needle so hard it pricked my finger." Grandmother sucked the offending member, inspected it for nonexistent damage, and returned it to her pursed lips, apparently to gain time for thinking. Finally she drew the child awkwardly to her side, one of the few times Nancy remembered her displaying affection. "Yes, of course you had a mother—and a father. Everybody does, child. And—I'll tell you this much—she loved you very much." Her voice, which had softened, resumed its usual brisk tone. "But let's forget about it, shall we? And remember this, child. Your mother is not to be mentioned in this house."

But Nancy, usually compliant to the point of subservience, became suddenly bold. "You said—I *had* a mother," she persisted. "Is—is she dead?"

"And I said forget about it," snapped Grandmother. "And don't never let your grandfather hear you ask such questions."

She loved you very much. The words lulled Nancy to sleep as she cuddled next to Nannie under the buffalo skin on the trundle bed. They sang in the breezes that ruffled her hair when she went down to the stream to help with the washing or to draw water. Sometimes they seemed accompanied by a vague memory of arms enfolding her. It came especially when she was on the edge of sleep, and she would rouse, expecting to see a half-remembered face close to her own, its features warm and soft in the candlelight. But of course there was nothing there.

"Did you know my mother?"

Aunt Betsy, startled, interrupted the rhythmic beat-beat of her pestle. Nancy, squatting beside her feeding corn into the wooden mortar and a little frightened by her own temerity, let some of the precious gold kernels slip through her fingers to the ground. "Did you—know my mother?" she repeated faintly.

Betsy took a hasty glance at the cabin to make sure no one was listening. "Yes," she said, almost in a whisper. "She was my oldest sister."

"Please—tell me about her."

"I—shouldn't. I'm not supposed to even speak her name. But—" Again Betsy looked over her shoulder, then the words came in a rush. "She was warm and bright, like sunlight. An' always laughin' or singin' or dancin'. It seemed like she could never keep still. And she was pretty, full of life, like Nannie. And smart. Over in Virginny she went to school. She could even read and write."

"You said 'was.' Is she dead?" demanded Nancy.

"I dunno. Mebbe. After we come here, to Kaintuck, she went away." Betsy began to pound vigorously. "Come now. We got to get this corn ground."

Pretty, like Nannie. When she had washed one of Grandmother's pewter plates and polished it with clay, rubbing and rubbing until it shone, Nancy could see her face reflected in it, long and thin and sober, skin a little too sallow, dark hair looking dull and lifeless. Certainly not like Nannie, with her round cheeks and full red lips and curling hair. She was unaware that the reflected eyes, a clear hazel, could be bright and sparkling as well as sober, that the dark hair was soft and fine like spun silk and the high forehead bespoke unusual potential of intellect. No, she did not look like her mother—whoever she was.

It would be pleasant to be pretty like Nannie, but . . . *She could read and write!* These were the words she repeated hungrily to herself, over and over. Oh, to be able to read! She listened enthralled while Grandfather, halting frequently and stumbling over every difficult word, read a few verses each morning and night from the Book, which was kept wrapped in a linen cloth and placed on a high shelf. Once when she was alone in the cabin Nancy dragged one of the three-legged stools under the shelf, climbed on it, and terrified by her daring (yet determined), took down the heavy bundle. Seating herself on the stool, she reverently unfolded the wrappings. It was a moment to be remembered always, the first time she had held or even touched a book. Her fingers caressed the rough surface, traced the gold markings which, Grandfather said, spelled the words THE HOLY BIBLE. Still aghast at her temerity and heart beating hard, she opened it, not to the first half or even three quarters—there were the stories which could be rather frightening—but to the last part, which told about the loving Jesus. She had watched Grandfather and knew almost exactly where it must be. Again her fingers traced the strange markings, black now instead of gold, her eyes achingly intent, as if by straining hard they might decipher the mysteries. Perhaps under her fingers were some of the words she loved best. At least she could imagine . . .

" 'Come unto me, all ye that labor and are heavy laden . . .' " She repeated the words softly, picturing Grandfather and the uncles coming in dead-tired from the fields, herself and Aunt Betsy toiling up the bank with back-breaking buckets.

"What are you doing?"

She was so startled she almost dropped the book. "I—I—"

But to her surprise Grandmother was not angry. "You know your grandfather sets a great store by that book, don't allow nobody else to touch it. But I reckon as long as he ain't around to see, there's no harm done."

"I—I wisht I could read it," blurted Nancy.

"I know. But readin' and such like larnin' ain't for us womanfolk, leastwise not in this Godforsaken country. Come now. Let's put it back. And Grandfather will never know."

It was one of the rare ecstatic moments of her childhood. She and

Grandmother had a secret. For a little while she had a warm feeling of belonging.

She heard others beside Grandfather read from the Book. Whenever a circuit rider or a traveling preacher came into the area, people gathered at the Hanks's farm for religious services, for Grandfather had been a devout Baptist back in Virginia, and the preachers depended on him to secure for them a hearing. To Grandmother's dismay, for she was mortally afraid of marauding Indians, he would send the older boys into the sparsely settled country along the Rolling Fork to invite the settlers. The boys were overjoyed. Each rode his favorite horse, Joshua on the gray mare called Bonney, William on another gray that he had christened Gilbert, Charles on the gentlest of the five owned by Grandfather, a roan called Dove. Joseph, disconsolate at being too young to go, had to content himself with following to the edge of the fields on his own favorite, a sorrel called Bald.

People came from long distances by horse or oxcart. Preachers were eloquent in their appeal to sinners, denouncing, pleading, threatening. Their stentorian rhetoric was frequently interrupted by shouts of "Amen!", "Praise the Lord!", "Yes, Lord!", "Blessed be Jesus!" As emotions surged, speech merged into action—clapping, swaying, weeping, waving of arms, embracing.

"Come, brothers, sisters, yes, and you young'uns too. Come to the waters, drink, wash away your sins! That's right, shout. Show the Lord that you've laid holt of His glorious salvation!"

Nancy's child body tingled with excitement. She envied Aunts Betsy and Polly, who could abandon themselves, shout, jump up and down, sway to imagined celestial rhythms. Even little Nannie aped their exuberance, leaping and waving and cavorting about. Nancy's own arms, tensed with latent energy, stayed straight at her sides. Her small bare feet remained rooted to the ground. Again she was the odd one. What made her different? She could fill to bursting with ecstasy—over a new-blossomed magnolia or a flaming sunset or a little newborn calf—and still give no outward sign. It was something to keep inside, too precious to share. And always for some reason there was a vague unrest mingled with the ecstasy—sadness perhaps, knowledge that the magnolia would die, the sunset fade, the darling sprightly calf grow into a stodgy cow. Or was it desire for something even more satisfying which lay beyond—always beyond—and which she might never find?

Her childhood world widened slowly. At first it was very small, the cabin, the stream, the fields Grandfather had wrested from the forest, the family, the few neighbors infrequently seen. One knew vaguely that there were other realms out "yander," a big surrounding area known as Nelson County, beyond that another something called Washington County, all in this "dark and bloody ground" which was "Kaintuck." And beyond that lay "Virginny," Grandmother's Garden of Eden.

She knew little of the distant worlds outside or of the portentous history being made. Almost coincident with her birth in 1784 a nation was being born. When she was three its Constitution was being conceived, perilously gestated with constant threat of miscarriage, and finally, when she was four, brought to birth with great uncertainty and travail. She was five when its first President, George Washington, was inaugurated in far-off New York. She had heard of the "Revolution" and knew that Uncle Thomas, Grandfather's oldest son, who had not come with them to Kentucky, had fought in it. She knew the name of George Washington too, for the Hanks family had lived not far from his ancestral estate in Virginia. But he was far less a hero than Daniel Boone, with whom Uncle Abraham, Grandfather's brother, had trekked west and helped chart the perilous trail for other pioneers to follow. And in the territories beyond the thirteen new states politics were of slight importance compared with problems of sheer survival.

Only once in her young childhood did Nancy travel beyond the narrow limits of the farm. Grandfather and the uncles sometimes forded the Rolling Fork and rode some fifteen miles west to the settlement in the Severn's Valley to be known later as Elizabethtown. A church had been founded there in 1781, known as the Regular Baptist Church of Severn's Valley. Grandfather, one of its members, attended its official meetings. To one of these he decided to take some of his family. William would stay with Grandmother and look after the farm. Grandfather would take with him the other three boys, Elizabeth, and Polly.

"And little Nannie," he decided, his eyes resting lovingly on his youngest.

Nancy's small body tightened. Her lips compressed. Only Aunt Betsy noticed the bleak misery in her eyes.

"If Nannie goes," she said firmly, "Nancy should go too. I'll take keer of her."

"Very well." Grandfather consented with obvious reluctance.

Never had she known such exquisite adventure. Fording the Rolling Fork, riding in front of Aunt Betsy on big gray Gilbert, riding through valleys among oaks and sycamores and willows with steep wooded hills surrounding her on every side—how often had she wondered, looking toward the west, what lay beyond! She could not know, as the trail wound along the foot of that huge pile of forested limestone known as Muldraugh Hill, that she came perhaps within a stone's throw of the spot where she would spend the happiest and most fulfilling years of her life.

The settlement in Severn's Valley was already a thriving community. A few years earlier, in 1780, it had consisted of three forts with blockhouses and stockades, each built on high ground, about a mile apart. Now, with attacks by Indians becoming less frequent and the forts to protect them, pioneers were pouring into the valley, clearing away the dense growths of poplar, walnut, cherry, maple, building their cabins beside the clear waters of Severn's Valley Creek, preparing the rich soil for their first crops of corn.

There was no church building. Meetings were held outdoors since the weather was still warm. In winter they would be in some cabin. People had come long distances, some from as far as the settlement called Louisville, over forty miles away. Awed by the crowd, more people than she had ever seen, Nancy clung to Aunt Betsy, while her eyes and ears absorbed every sight and sound. Except for the strangeness of place and numbers, it was like the meetings at Rolling Fork, the men in leather leggings and moccasins, hats made of splinters rolled in buffalo wool and sewed together with deer sinews, shirts of buckskin, the women dressed like herself and the aunts in coarse linsey-woolsey cloth and sunbonnets, all barefoot. The men, ever alert to danger, sat with rifles propped at their sides. There were the same long sermons, fervent appeals, ardent physical response.

It was not the meetings which Nancy remembered most. It was the home in which Grandfather and his family, being respected guests, were entertained, and especially one member of the household. Christopher Bush was an early settler in Severn's Valley. Burly, hard-working, of thrifty German stock, he was fast becoming a successful farmer. His wife, red-cheeked, bustling, efficient, welcomed the influx of guests into her already crowded cabin with the cheerfulness and aplomb of a hostess with a dozen rooms and a panoply of servants.

"Come right in and make yourselves to home. We'll be packed in like kernels on a right healthy ear of corn, but nobody'll mind. The boys and menfolks kin sleep in the loft. There's plenty of fresh boughs and buckskins. There's beds in two corners for us womenfolks and girls, and you two young'uns kin sleep in the trundle with my baby."

The cabin seemed full to bursting, but there was a warmth about it, a brightness, which contrasted with the one at home. Perhaps it was the candles supplementing the blaze in the huge fireplace. Grandmother was frugal with her candles. More likely it was the cheerfulness of the hostess which created an atmosphere of well-being. But Nancy, separated in the melee from Aunt Betsy, felt timid and alone. She was almost glad when Grandfather, introducing his family, stopped with Nannie.

She shrank back against a wall, attempting to hide herself. The round logs felt hard against her back, making the linsey-woolsey of her dress scratch against her skin. It was hot inside the cabin but she shivered, as if the cracks so carefully chinked by Christopher Bush had been left open. She felt timid, yes, but there was also that sense of separation, of aloneness, of sadness in the presence of gaiety. She could hear Nannie, already thoroughly at home, chattering merrily and Grandfather laughing with proud appreciation.

Suddenly she felt a small hand tucked into hers. She looked down into the face of a child two or three years old, a lively, attractive face framed by dark curls.

"Me Sally," said the child, eyes sprightly curious. "Who you?"

"I—I'm Nancy." She felt warmth stealing through her fingers, up her arms, coursing through her body.

"You're nice," said the child. "Sally likes you."

Before she realized what was happening Nancy was pulled away from the wall, drawn around the groups sitting on stools and benches and around a table, and led to the woman down on her knees stirring something in a big iron kettle.

"Look, Ma. Nancy, my new friend."

Mrs. Bush turned, her red cheeks an even brighter crimson from the fire. She was a tall woman, and her eyes, kindly and shrewdly appraising, were almost on a level with Nancy's. She reached out an arm and drew the child to her. "Nancy. A nice name. I'm right glad to meet you. Funny I didn't see you before. This here is my baby." She circled her own child with her other arm and gave them both a motherly hug. "Her real name is Sarah, but we all call her Sally. I reckon you'll be good friends. Now get along with you, while I finish cookin' for this crowd."

Nancy no longer felt alone. She had a friend. For the rest of the time spent in Severn's Valley Sally was her constant companion, her shadow. She sat beside her on the hard split log benches at meetings, at meals in the Bush cabin. Her small warm body was curled against her in the trundle bed which they shared with Nannie. And when she left for home Nancy took with her the memory of a small figure dancing up and down and waving, of a flopping sunbonnet pushed carelessly back to reveal a fringe of curls, trembling lips, blue-gray eyes blurred with tears.

"That cute little Sally sure took a fancy to you," commented Nannie. "Follered you round like a shadder. But didn't you git tired of her, such a baby? Me, I liked her sister Hannah better, so much prettier and nearer our age."

Nancy received all such quips with good-natured silence. Nobody could lessen the joy of this, her first friendship. Someone had sought her out, showed her affection. *Nancy and Sally.* She repeated the names sometimes to herself. They seemed to belong together.

Not for many years would she see Severn's Valley again. Once more the boundaries of her life contracted, enclosing her in the tiny neighborhood along the Rolling Fork, but occasionally there were incursions from the world beyond. Some twenty miles to the east, over on Beech Fork in Washington County, lived Grandmother's sister, Rachel Shipley Berry, and her family. Grandmother never visited them. She shuddered at the thought of mounting a horse and traversing the miles of "dark and bloody ground" that lay between. But Uncle Richard and Aunt Rachel came more than once to the cabin on the Rolling Fork.

"You're all afeared for nothin'!" Aunt Rachel would taunt cheerfully. "Here we traveled all the way and never saw nothin' more fearsome than coons and possums and that deer Richard shot and brought in for your kittle. No Indians, not even a shadder of one. And with the crowds of new settlers pourin' in all the time along the Wilderness Road, Kaintuck'll soon be as civilized as old Virginny." But on one visit, the year Nancy was six, Aunt Rachel arrived looking pale and troubled. She warned her sons to stay close to the cleared fields near the cabin, not even to go down to the creek unless their father went with them with the gun. The story the Berrys had to tell was one of ambush, murder, terror.

"You mean you folks ain't heard? But, then, news can be slow comin', and you're off the main traveled trails."

Gathered about the newcomers in the cabin, Joseph and his family listened to the tale of tragedy. Another of Grandmother's sisters, Naomi, who had married Robert Mitchell, had been traveling from North Carolina up through the Cumberland Gap and along the Wilderness Road into Kentucky. They were planning to buy land and settle on the Beech Fork near the Berrys. They had almost reached the Crab Orchard Fort, but at a place about twenty-five miles away called Defeated Creek, they had been set upon by a wild band of Potawatomi Indians.

"Oh!" moaned Grandmother. "God help us! Naomi—"

"She was struck down." It was Richard who continued the story that his weeping wife was unable to finish. "Robert stood bravely over her with a spear, and he and other men of the party managed to hold the attackers at bay until they finally ran away. Naomi was not dead. Robert carried her the twenty-five miles to the Crab Orchard Fort, but—she died the next day."

Though it was still daylight outside, it was dark in the windowless cabin. Nancy, crouched on a stool, watched the play of firelight on the anguished faces, redness where the light struck, blackness wherever they were shadowed. Vividly she could picture the terror of creeping figures, flashing spears—but not death. Not, that is, for a person, one called Aunt Naomi. Was it like the stiffness, the terrible stillness of the deer Uncle Richard and his sons had brought in, which just a few hours before had been beautiful and proud, leaping through the forest?

"That's not all," continued Uncle Richard. "Their little daughter Sarah, you know, the eleven-year-old—"

"Not—not dead?" gasped Grandmother.

"Worse," mourned Aunt Rachel. Sarah had been taken captive by the Indians. Her father had followed, trying to find and bring her back. In attempting to cross the Ohio River in pursuit, he had been drowned.

In spite of the atmosphere of tragedy, with the cabin full of guests there was also an air of festivity. Grandmother spent much time cooking. There was a bit of pride, even jealousy, in her attempt to provide the best hospitality, for Richard Berry's land holdings were known to be much larger than Joseph's, at least six hundred fifty acres. He owned several slaves, and, though she had never visited it, she knew her sister's cabin was far more luxurious than her own. She saw to it that her table was loaded with all kinds of game—venison, wild turkey, squirrels, as well as roast lamb and veal from their own flock and herd—bacon, corn pone, dried beans cooked with pork from the smokehouse.

Nancy, as usual, remained shy and inconspicuous. It was not until the second day of her visit that Aunt Rachel, distraught and preoccupied by the sad news she had brought, gave her more than scant attention.

"Mercy sakes!" she exclaimed. "How the child has grown! I reckon she's goin' to be tall like—like—"

Nancy waited curiously for her to finish, but the words trailed off into silence. "Who am I goin' to be tall like?" she dared to ask.

"Oh, nobody special," replied Aunt Rachel vaguely. "I just meant like some of the rest of the Hankses."

Nancy saw the look she and Grandmother exchanged. What had Aunt Rachel started to say? And why did they always say "the child" when they talked about her instead of calling her by name as they did Nannie? It was as if—as if they thought she didn't have a name!

It was by accident that she heard Grandmother and Aunt Rachel talking that same day. She had been out in the field with Nannie, weeding corn, and since the sun was hot, had come back to the cabin for her sunbonnet. Slipping in soundlessly on her bare feet, she saw the two women seated in front of the fireplace.

"Of course you want to know more about *her,*" Aunt Rachel was saying. "Now that Joseph's not here to shut our mouths, we can really talk."

"Yes," said Grandmother. "You can't guess how it's been all this time, not knowin'. No matter what she's done, after all, she's my daughter."

"I know. And you can't tell me she was really as bad as they say, spite of her bein' charged in the court of Mercer County last year for fornication."

"Fornication!" Grandmother echoed in a shocked whisper. "Did—they really use that awful word?"

"Yes, but I don't believe they had any proof. There's an old busybody over there who always believes the worst of people. She probly heard about what happened back in Virginny, about the child, and started the rumor all over again. Somebody's always quick to see fire where there's a bit of smoke, and you know how gay and pretty and sprightly-like *she's* always been."

"Yes," said Grandmother. "I know. It was the war, I've always thought, and all its excitement that caused the trouble back there. It turned all the girls' heads. But—you know I never did blame her so much. Joseph would be shocked to hear me, but—he was such a handsome and brave soldier and seemed so—so trustworthy. And she was such a child, only seventeen. Whoever would have thought he could have made such promises, and already married! They say he's a big plantation owner now."

"Anyway," said Aunt Rachel, "I reckon her troubles may be all over now."

Grandmother sounded suddenly eager. "You say this good man has taken out a license for a bond of marriage?"

"Yes. Last April. His name is Henry Sparrow. He was in the war, then he came with his folks from Virginny to Kaintuck over in Mercer County, where *she's* been livin', and since his father died last year he's been carin' for his mother and sister and brother. A right good respectable man."

"He must really love her," said Grandmother, "and believe in her."

The two women were silent for a few moments, then, "Does the child know?" asked Aunt Rachel. "Does she have any idea—who she is?"

As noiselessly as she had entered, Nancy slipped out of the cabin. She did not go back to the cornfield. Instead she ran to a little secret shelter she had found, where the branches of a Judas tree grew close to the ground, making a little tent into which one could crawl. Her head swam. Of course she could not understand all they had said, but certain words raced through her mind with inescapable meaning. *The child . . . does she have any idea . . . who she is?*

There it was, put into words, like a shadow turned into a shape lurking behind a tree—the loneliness, the difference, the separation which even a child could instinctively sense, yet be unable to express. *Who was she?*

She could not know that nearly two hundred years later the same question would still be asked and would remain unanswered.

=2=

Death! So this was it. Not like the other times she had known it, the deer and buffalo and bear brought in from the forest cold and motionless, the beautiful wild turkeys with their wings forever stilled, especially the little bull calves she had tended and fondled and wept over when they had to be sacrificed for food. This was Grandfather, who, just a few weeks ago, had been vigorously chopping down trees, clearing away stumps, planting corn, shouting orders to his sons, laughing uproariously over a joke, caressing his beloved Nannie, stumblingly reading from the Bible, holding steady the carcass of a greasy two-hundred-pound hog while his neighbors stripped off the bristles.

In the crowded confines of a cabin, death was an intimate reality. Even the youngest, Nancy and Nannie, participated in the washing and dressing of the body (not in good clothes, which must be kept for his sons), the placing of it in the crude wooden box made from one of the trees he had been cutting, the storing of it in a tight outhouse built to keep ice, for the weather was still cold enough to allow time for a funeral service. They saw the departure of one of Joseph's sons for Beech Fork to alert the only relatives within traveling distance and of another to Severn's Valley, hopefully to secure the services of an itinerant preacher or at least of a church elder.

They helped Betsy and Polly prepare food for the neighbors and relatives soon to arrive, for Joseph's wife was too stricken to be of use. She could only wring her hands and moan.

"If only we hadn't left Virginny! It's this dark and bloody ground that made him ailin'. He'd still be alive, I know. Oh, heaven help us pore critters, God have mercy on us!"

It was 1793, and Nancy was nine years old. She was growing tall, as Aunt Rachel had predicted, much taller than Nannie. They were unlike each other in both looks and temperament, Nannie blue-eyed and fair, a bit chubby, pert nose slightly upturned, a gay composite of smiles and bobbing curls; Nancy slender, dark of skin, usually more grave than smiling, a hint of sadness—or was it yearning?—in the hazel eyes. Aunt Betsy had tried more than once to roll Nancy's hair into curls, like Nannie's, but it was no use. Straight and fine, it slid back into its usual dark cloud.

The relatives came, drawn by that loyalty which drew pioneer families together in any unusual experience, but especially a wedding or a funeral. The Berrys arrived with their sons. Some of Joseph's cousins came from over on the Kentucky River, though most of his immediate family, his brothers Turner and Abraham, and his oldest son Thomas, were still in Virginia, too far either to get the news of his death or make the journey. There being no preacher in Severn's Valley, one of the church elders came and read the funeral service.

Perhaps Joseph had been forewarned of the sickness which had so suddenly sapped his strength, for in January he had made his will, making his mark and having it signed and sealed in the presence of three neighbors who acted as witnesses. At the court held for Nelson County in May the will was produced and sworn to. It was a simple document. To each of his five sons he bequeathed a horse—to Thomas the sorrel called Major, to Joshua the gray mare, Bonney, to William the gray named Gilbert, to Charles the roan named Dove, to Joseph the sorrel called Bald. To Joseph also, perhaps because he was the youngest and less able to provide for himself, as well as being his namesake, his farm of one hundred and fifty acres.

For his daughters there was a bequest of yearling heifers, the one named Gentle to Elizabeth, Lady to Polly, and to Nannie the little one she had nicknamed Peidy. All of his other property was to belong to his wife as long as she lived, and she with his son William was to be the executor of his will.

"You must come to Beechland," Aunt Rachel told her firmly. "Richard has land a-plenty. We will build a cabin for you close to ours, and there will be room for all of you who want to come."

"No!" For the first time since Grandfather's death Grandmother awoke from the lethargy into which grief had plunged her. She would have nothing more to do with this "dark and bloody ground." "Fair land of tomorrow" it might be for some people, but not for her. She had not wanted to come here in the first place and now, like Naomi in the Bible, she would return to her own country. Her children could go with her or not, as they chose. Her oldest son Thomas had had the good sense to remain in Virginny, and she would go and join him. Though she shivered at thought of the journey, better to run the risk of being ambushed, even scalped, like that poor Chenowith woman who had managed to escape her captors, bare-skulled, than to live here in mortal fear for the rest of her life. She would stay until after William's wedding to that good respectable girl Elizabeth Hall. Then she would take her younger children and go back home.

Her younger children. Nancy knew that this did not include her. In the days that followed, after Aunt Rachel and her family had returned home and Grandmother was making plans for departure, she felt lonelier than ever, wondering what was to become of her.

One day in early summer she was sitting on the ground in front of the cabin knitting skeins of flax into a piece of linen cloth. Looking up, she saw two horses approaching, one bearing a man and a very small boy, the other a woman, one arm wrapped about a bundle which might contain a baby. Not neighbors. She had never seen them before, yet, since travelers were always welcomed in the settlers' cabins, she rose and curtsied politely. The strangers alighted and came toward her. Something in the woman's face drew Nancy's gaze. She was looking at her with a painful intensity, lips parted, eyes so brightly probing they reminded Nancy of an eager squirrel's. Beautiful eyes they were, big and dark, lustrous even in the shadow of the arching sunbonnet. Thrusting the bundle—it *was* a tiny baby—into the man's arms, she came running toward Nancy, her long skirt almost tripping her. "My dear, tell me quick," she gasped. "What is your name?"

"I—I'm Nancy."

The child felt arms go around her, enveloping her, drawing her so close she was conscious of the woman's heartbeat. Words, half spoken aloud, half breathed, filled her ears. "My dear—my own—dear child—my very own dear child!" Nancy's pulses leaped and tingled in response. She had a strange sense of reliving an experience of well-being long past, as if she had known the solace of these same arms before.

The man laid a restraining hand on the woman's shoulder. "Wait. You don't know yet, wife. Remember, you told me there were two Nancys almost the same age. You don't know—"

"But I do know," she replied. Giving the child a final hug, she rose to her feet.

Suddenly, there was Grandmother in the door of the cabin, shading her eyes to peer at the newcomers, then, face alight with joyful recognition, stumbling toward them. In another moment the two women were clasped in each other's arms.

"Lucy! My darling! After all these years—"

"I had to come, Mother. When I heard Father was gone, I hoped— You *are* glad to see me?"

"Yes, oh, yes! And I believe Joseph, toward the end, was sorry— but you know him, he was so stubborn—"

"Mother, this is my husband, Henry Sparrow, and these are my two babies. And this—" The woman turned expectantly toward Nancy.

Grandmother's manner suddenly changed. Her eyes lost their softness, became narrow and speculative. She hesitated, but only for a moment.

"This," she said, "is my granddaughter Nancy. And this, child"— once more she hesitated briefly before continuing firmly—"this is your aunt Lucy."

The woman drew a quick breath, which might have been either a gasp or a sigh.

"I see," she said. "So that's the way you want it. Well, I—I reckon mebbe it's the best way."

The man put the baby in her arms. "It is, my dear," he said. There was relief as well as gentleness, together with a hint of sternness, in his voice. "I'm right sartin it's the best way, for all of us."

The woman clasped the baby tightly, holding it with a rocking motion against her breast, but over its head she kept looking at Nancy as if she could not take her eyes away. "She's—beautiful," she murmured.

Not me, thought Nancy, she can't be talking about me, even though she is looking straight at me. It must be the baby that she thinks is beautiful. She gazed from one to another in bewilderment —Grandmother, who could change so quickly from joyful tenderness to cold severity; the man, eyes gentle and kindly but lips set firm and chin stubbornly square; the woman— She was the most puzzling of all. Nancy could still feel the arms about her, holding her tightly, as they were now holding the baby. She had been so sure she had felt them long ago, that this was the mother she had always dreamed of. But if she was, then why didn't they say so? Why must she call her "Aunt Lucy"? Years would pass before she fully understood.

The days that followed were the happiest Nancy had known. Henry Sparrow and his family were staying until after William's wedding, and again the cabin was full to overflowing. Whatever the relationship between Lucy Sparrow and Nancy—aunt and niece? mother and daughter?—the bond between them was as firm and binding as the oneness of two strands of flax and wool in a linsey-woolsey garment. But if Nancy believed firmly that "Aunt Lucy" was her mother, she was equally sure, with a shrewdness beyond her years, that Henry Sparrow was not her father. Sometimes she found him looking at her, if not with distaste, at least with the same coolness and detachment she had detected in Grandfather's eyes.

The cabin bustled not only with the confusion of occupants but with the flurries of imminent change. The family of Joseph Hanks was about to scatter. Grandmother had found reliable parties with whom she could make the journey to Virginia. Cheered and energized by the prospect, she was sorting her possessions, choosing, discarding, constantly changing her mind about the limited contents of two saddlebags. Joseph, now twelve, was going with her. The older sons, William, Joshua, and Charles, were able to fend for themselves. In addition to other land he was planning to purchase near the Falls of Rough over in Grayson County, William would assume responsibility for the acres left to Joseph in their father's will. Polly and Nannie would make their home with one of the three brothers. Watching the preparations, listening to the plans, Nancy was both hopeful and apprehensive. She seemed still to be the odd one. What was to become of her? Was it possible—? But there was another one left out of the discussed plans, Elizabeth.

"You and I," Aunt Betsy told her near the time of the wedding, "are going back with the Sparrows. Your—your aunt Lucy needs someone to help her with the children, especially with another one coming. We'll stop on the way with Aunt Rachel and Uncle Richard."

Nancy's heart leaped. So she *was* wanted and by the one whose touch and words of endearment assured her of what must be a mother's love!

Time passed swiftly, and the wedding day came. They all traveled to the bride's home several miles away, witnessed the ceremony, participated in the "infare," complete with crowds of neighbors, riotous merriment, and huge quantities of food. Exciting though it all was, Nancy was glad when it was over. Soon she would be starting on another journey, eastward, toward the rising sun and a new life with the two people she loved best and who loved her, Aunt Betsy and the woman with the softly shining eyes and the tender enfolding arms whom she had to call "Aunt" but wanted so much to call "Mother."

She rode in front of Aunt Betsy on William's gray horse, Gilbert, her few possessions stowed in one of the saddlebags—a linsey-woolsey dress for winter, her buckskin moccasins for weather too cold to go barefoot, a doll made of corncobs with a dried apple face and long tresses of corn silk for hair, an extra sunbonnet, and her most precious possession, a little shawl which Aunt Betsy had knitted for her out of real wool, soft as thistledown, not like the heavy scratchy garments woven of wool, brittle nettles, and flax. Her eyes under the flopping sunbonnet were bright and eager, unlike the wariness of her elders', alert to a possible lurking shape behind each tree, but avidly absorbing every new detail—a crimson burst of sumac, the flash of a red-winged blackbird, a scurrying rabbit, too quick, she was thankful, for Uncle Henry's swiftly leveled gun, a white shaft of limestone so bright in the sunlight that it made one blink. She could hardly wait to see what lay behind each turn of the trail, beyond each hilltop.

They had started so early in the morning that they reached Uncle Richard's cabin before sunset. Nancy caught her breath. It was the biggest cabin she had ever seen. And when she went inside she could not believe her eyes. Two big rooms instead of one! Real chairs, not three-legged stools, and a table around which a dozen people could sit without crowding! A floor made of half logs instead of earth, and bright woven mats covering part of it! Even the Bushes' cabin in Severn's Valley had not been so fine and beautiful.

"Welcome, my dear." Aunt Rachel enfolded her in motherly arms. "I hope you'll be very happy here."

Nancy was puzzled. Uncle Henry had said he must get home immediately. He could stay with the Berrys only a single night. Why should she not be happy for that short length of time?

So big was the cabin that everybody did not have to sleep in one room. There was a loft upstairs to which the boys climbed by a ladder. Nancy slept with Aunt Betsy on a bed of boughs covered with a buffalo skin in the room with the big fireplace. It was all so strange that she found it hard to sleep.

"Do we have to start early in the morning?" she asked, conscious that Betsy also was restless.

There was a long silence. Perhaps Aunt Betsy was asleep, after all. But, no. Turning over, she gathered Nancy in her arms. "Didn't they tell you, pet? You're not going with us, you know. You're staying here with Uncle Richard and Aunt Rachel."

Though the room was still hot from the fire, Nancy felt suddenly cold. "But—" she whispered, "I thought—she wanted me."

"She does want you," comforted Aunt Betsy. "But—Henry thought it was best—it would be hard to explain, a child so much older than theirs, and—and there had already been talk—he was afeared— Oh, someday when you're older, you'll understand." Her arms tightened. "You'll be happy here. And if I ever get married and have a home, I'll have you come and live with me. I promise."

Nancy lay tense and wide awake, long after Aunt Betsy was asleep. She watched the flickers of light from the smoldering fire chase each other endlessly over the walls until they disappeared in the shadows of the cracks between the logs. When she did fall asleep it was to dream that she was running through a dark wood, trying to escape from something, she didn't know what. Somewhere ahead there was light between the trees. She could glimpse it faintly but whenever she seemed to be approaching it, it either vanished or moved farther away.

Henry Sparrow was up early, anxious to be on his way. There was great bustle in the cabin and outside, Aunt Rachel superintending the cooking of a hearty breakfast of corn bread and bacon, giving orders to her two black slaves, Nan and her daughter Hannah. The oldest Berry son, John, and one of the daughters came from their neighboring farms to bid the guests good-by. Horses were being fed and saddlebags repacked. There was much last minute exchange of invitations, advice, warnings.

"Come agin when you kin stay a longer spell."

"Be keerful when you cross the Chaplin. Water'll be low, but sands kin be treach'rous."

"Come now, we don't need all that journeycake. We're goin' less'n twenty miles."

"Keep your eyes peeled. Remember, all the Injuns in Kaintuck ain't dead yet."

Nancy stood withdrawn from the confusion, silent and remote. She watched the horses being loaded, heard the good-bys being said. "Remember my promise," assured Aunt Betsy, giving her a farewell hug. Then once more she felt those other half-familiar arms around her, drawing her close, a cheek wet with tears close to hers, but she did not return the caress, and her eyes remained dry. She watched the woman named Lucy mount the horse, saw her husband put the baby in her arms. Still dry-eyed and silent, thin shoulders drooping, she saw the little cavalcade ride away. The woman kept turning and looking back at her, waving her hand, but Nancy did not wave back. Then they were gone, disappearing into the woods at the top of the hill.

"There, they're gone!" said Aunt Rachel cheerfully, drawing the child into her motherly embrace. She was a large woman, and through the stiffness of her linen waist Nancy could feel the softness of her bosom against her dry cheek. "I'm right glad you're goin' to stay with us, my dear. You know, my girl young'uns are all gone now, married, and I miss 'em. You'll take their place." With a final little pat on Nancy's shoulder, she turned briskly toward the cabin. "I've a heap lot of work to do this mornin', child, and you kin help me. Come when you git ready."

Nancy still stood looking toward the hill where the horses and their riders had disappeared. Though the sun had long since risen, it had not yet topped the line of trees. As she watched, it slid into view, and she turned to face it, seeing it mount steadily, bright and blinding. She drew a long breath. Her shoulders straightened.

The question she had been asking half-consciously all her life sprang into new perspective, not as doubt and uncertainty, but as hopeful, if grim, challenge. *Who was she?* She knew suddenly that there could be only one answer. *She was herself.*

Turning again, she ran toward the cabin as fast as her tough bare feet could carry her.

⸻ *3* ⸻

For five years Nancy lived in the Berry household, long enough to grow from childhood almost to womanhood. They would be the most comfortable and least burdened, if not the happiest, years of her life.

Old Richard Berry, as the neighbors called him to distinguish him from his oldest son, was more prosperous than many pioneers. Unlike Nancy's Grandfather, he had been able to sell his lands in Virginia at sufficient profit to purchase six hundred acres on Beech Fork, a branch of Salt River, which in its meandering way made a great curve through the hills of Washington County, setting apart a huge section of fertile soil known as Beechland. Since then he had entered a second land warrant of two hundred more acres not far from his home. His son Richard, Jr., had built a cabin on a tract taken from his father's original acreage and just a year after Nancy came to stay in the Berry home, in October 1794, he took his young bride, Polly Ewing, there to live.

Nancy could scarcely believe the luxury and ease of her new life. The cabin seemed like a palace. There were soft feather beds to sleep on, a cupboard for the pewter cups and plates, two spinning wheels. And, strangest of all, Uncle Richard's womenfolk were expected to do no heavy work. The carrying of water buckets, grinding of corn, washing of clothes, scouring of the three-legged iron skillet and "kittle"—all such work was done by the two slaves, Nan and her daughter Hannah, whom the Berrys had brought from Virginia when they had journeyed here. Other slaves assisted with the farming, though Uncle Richard and his sons were equally hard-working.

Slavery. Nancy knew about it. Grandfather and his Baptist associates had belonged to a section of the church which severely denounced it. He had been shocked and grieved when Kentucky was admitted to the Union as a state in 1792 under a constitution whose Point Nine assured the right of settlers to keep slaves.

"You mean," Nancy ventured to ask Aunt Rachel, "they belong to you, like—like your cows and horses? They couldn't go away even if they wanted to?"

Aunt Rachel laughed indulgently. "I reckon that's right, child. If they took it into their heads to run off, Uncle Richard could go after 'em and bring 'em back like as if it was his filly Rosy. But the last thing they'd do is hanker to leave. Why, Nan has been with us since a child and Hannah was born in our house. They have plenty to eat and wear and a good outhouse to sleep in. What more would they want?"

"I—I don't know," replied Nancy. Still she was not quite satisfied.

Though hard work was at a minimum there was no dearth of activity. She spent many hours spinning, becoming increasingly skillful, to Aunt Rachel's keen delight. "I declar, child, those long slim fingers of yours work magic. None of my girls ever spun thread that long and fine. If you keep on, you'll bear the palm at all our spinnin' parties."

But Nancy's joy in pleasing her aunt was nothing beside her satisfaction in another achievement. She was actually learning to read! It all started one day when Uncle Richard found her poring over his Bible, the one book in the household, which he had neglected to put up on the top of the cupboard after family prayers. Guiltily, remembering the reprimand from Grandmother on a similar occasion, she closed it hastily and looked up at him, fear in her eyes. "I—I'm sorry—"

"My dear, why should you be sorry? I'm delighted that you wish to look at, to touch the sacred book."

"If—if I could only read it!" Nancy blurted.

Uncle Richard's eyes sharpened with keen interest. "There isn't any school in our neighborhood yet," he said regretfully. Then, after a pause, "But, I tell you what, child. I'll teach you myself."

She was half frightened, half ecstatic. It had to be done after supper, for Uncle Richard worked in the fields or woods all day. Aunt Rachel, surprised but indulgent, set a candle on the table. The Bible was produced, opened with proper ceremony, and the lesson began. After the first nervous tension, when her lips felt dry and her heart beat like a hammer, Nancy proved an apt and eager pupil. Cousins Francis and Ned, at first amused and somewhat derisive ("Whoever heard of a girl hankerin' to read?"), soon treated her efforts with respect, even admiration.

"The—Lord is—is my—sh—shep—shepherd." It was a triumphant day when, slowly and laboriously, partly from memory, she was able to read the familiar psalm, finger pointing out each syllable with meticulous care.

Nancy was ten when the whole state of Kentucky was plunged into great excitement. Though the southern half of the state had been largely cleared of threats by Indians, the northern half still lived in constant fear of occasional ambushes and attacks. In 1792 Washington had appointed "Mad Anthony" Wayne, hero of the Revolution, to command the western army. In 1793 he failed in an attempt to establish a treaty with the Indians to permit white settlements beyond the Ohio River. Now, in 1794, having advanced to Greenville on a branch of the Great Miami, he was calling for volunteers from the Kentucky militia. Uncle Richard's sons were fired with excitement and wanted to enlist, but their father, always cautious, discouraged them.

"Tom Lincoln's joinin' up," Ned announced enviously, "and he's only sixteen."

Nancy had heard of Thomas Lincoln, the son of a neighbor, Widow Bersheba Lincoln, who with her sons Josiah and Thomas and her two daughters lived with her oldest son, Mordecai, on the Beech Fork perhaps a mile from the Berrys. Nancy had been to the Lincoln home and knew Thomas' two sisters, Mary and Nancy, one nine years older, the other four years older than herself. But since Thomas spent much of his time away from home finding work wherever he could with neighboring farmers, she had not yet met him.

News of the western struggle kept coming. By July of 1794 Wayne's army had been reinforced by some 1,600 Kentucky volunteers and had advanced to Fort Defiance on the Miami River. Then came the decisive battle of Fallen Timbers, which brought final defeat to all the Indians east of the Ohio. In August of 1795 Wayne negotiated the Treaty of Greenville, bringing peace and freedom from fear at least to Kentucky. It brought also to the home of Richard Berry the child who five years before had been taken captive by Indian assailants.

Aunt Rachel wept when she heard the news. "My sister's child— little Sarah—still alive? Oh, God be praised!"

A miracle it seemed. The child's grandmother, Mary Mitchell, had written Governor Isaac Shelby back in 1793, when Wayne was attempting to make a treaty with the western Indians, in the vain hope that information might be obtained about her lost granddaughter. Two years later the information came, like a thunderclap. The family was even more excited when it was learned that the child was coming to the Berry home to live.

The household was agog with anticipation. For Nancy there was also apprehension. A new girl cousin, older than herself, a stranger. "It'll all be queer for her," said Aunt Rachel. "I reckon it's up to you to make her feel ter home."

Two horses rode into the yard, on the first a soldier from one of the forts, on the other a strange-looking figure riding bareback, straight as an arrow, skin so dark it was almost black, long dark hair hanging in two braids, a doeskin tunic with a wrap of animal skins thrown over the shoulders. The family was all there, neighbors having run ahead of the little cavalcade and alerted the men working in the fields. The soldier alighted and went back to help his companion, but she did not wait for him. Springing lithely down, she stood looking at the little group in front of the cabin, eyes defiant, almost hostile. She was not at all what they had expected, a poor abused refugee from terror and long suffering, eager to be restored to her family. She was a stranger, an alien of another race, aloof, proud, wary, looking very much alone.

No one moved, not even Aunt Rachel. Nancy was distressed. Wasn't anybody going to do anything, give her a welcome? It was the aloneness she noticed, not the pride or the defiance. She knew what it was like to feel alone. Suddenly she ran and put her arms around the girl.

"You're Sarah," she cried out, "and I'm Nancy, your cousin. We're glad you've come!"

The ice was broken. The others rushed forward, crowded around. "My dear!" It was Aunt Rachel, her big motherly arms enfolding the girl. "I knew you when you were just a young'un back in Virginny. Remember—your aunt Rachel?"

Sarah's readjustment to white family life was long and slow, sometimes painful. She had been in her eleventh year when taken captive, and the five ensuing years had fully conditioned her to a new culture. Even language was a barrier, for she seemed reluctant to return to the English she had learned as a child. At first she spoke hardly at all, then slowly, mostly at Nancy's urging, there came a word or two at a time, as if she were learning the language all over again.

It was a constant struggle between two cultures. Lying beside Nancy on one of Aunt Rachel's plump feather beds, she would turn and toss; then, with a muttered "Ugh! Much bad soft!" she would get up, wrap herself in one of the skins they used for "kiverlids," and lie on the puncheon floor. Scorning the single garment of rough linsey-woolsey which Aunt Rachel provided, she insisted on returning again and again to the tunic of soft doeskin which she had worn on arrival. "My best," she told Nancy proudly. "This other much rough, scratch."

"It's beautiful," agreed Nancy, fingering the soft pliant leather and tracing the intricate pattern of dyed porcupine quills adorning the bodice. Why, she wondered, had they always thought and spoken of Indians as "dirty savages" when they could make lovely things like this?

Sarah was reluctant to talk about the tragedy which had resulted in her capture, though the cousins, especially Ned, kept questioning her curiously. Only after many days did she consent to share some of the details. Yes, it had been frightening. The Indians had come whooping wildly and striking with their tomahawks. She had seen her mother fall. Her brother had seized her hand and run with her, one of the Indians in pursuit. They had come to a deep stream, and he was going to lead her over a log, but she had been too frightened. She had stood like a log herself, and he had gone on without her. She had never seen any of them again, and she knew that her father had drowned trying to find her. Yes, of course she had expected to be killed herself, would have been if an Indian woman had not first hidden her, then taken her into her tepee—the girl's eyes softened—and become her mother.

"And what then?" demanded Ned. "Where did you go?"

Many places they had gone, into the north country called Canada, on the shores of great lakes near a settlement named Detroit, where she had heard the guns of a great battle. Later she had seen her people come back from war—her eyes glowed with triumph—with much booty and prisoners because for once they had been able to conquer their enemy the white man.

"St. Clair's defeat," muttered Ned, who had heard stories of those crucial battles of 1791. "Tell me, cousin," he challenged. "Those savages killed your parents. They took you prisoner. Yet you don't seem to hate them. Why?"

The girl's eyes flashed. All at once she became again the proud aloof stranger. She was wearing the doeskin tunic, and for the moment she was all Indian. "It was you whites," she replied scathingly, now fully in command of her native language, "who took away our land, who made us promises and broke 'em, who kep' drivin' us back an' back an' back. You kill our papoose with guns and call yourselves heroes. We kill yours with tomahawk, and you call us devils. Who should I hate, I ask you?"

Sarah and Nancy became inseparable. In spite of the difference in age, Nancy often seemed the older. In the cabin she was the teacher, the patient instructor in spinning the buffalo wool and flax and weaving them into cloth, in sewing buckskin breeches for the men, in mixing the corn meal and water in just the right consistency for the johnnycake. She had even learned how to toss the cake into the air from the frying pan when it had cooked brown on one side, catching it deftly on the other side when it came down.

"But you ain't really learned how," Aunt Rachel told them with tongue in cheek and a sparkle in her eye, "unless you can toss it up the chimney, run out of the cabin, and catch it in your fryin' pan t'other side up when it comes down!"

"Let's see you do it!" the girls demanded in frank disbelief. Aunt Rachel confessed that, while she might have attempted it once, she was now much too old and slow-moving.

Outdoors, however, Sarah was the teacher. She taught Nancy to mount a horse with a running jump and ride bareback with her along the paths skirting Uncle Richard's fields, Nancy on the gentle sorrel filly Rosy, herself on the more lively Blueskin. She knew where to find the wild strawberries, grapes, pawpaws, and in the autumn all the nut-bearing trees—chestnut, beech, walnut, hickory. She collected "yarbs"—various roots, leaves, bark, weeds—and brought them to Aunt Rachel with directions for their use in stomach ailments, head injuries, snake bite, and other infections. But Aunt Rachel, who distrusted any remedies not her own, especially those of superstitious

Indians, thanked her, then quietly disposed of them. Wild verbena or wild mint for a stomach ache? Nonsense. For stomach ache one should take the comb of a hornet's nest, scorch it before the fire and make a tea of it, cover the patient with a blanket or buffalo robe and make him sweat. One could use sage tea instead of the hornet's nest, but it wasn't as good.

Sarah was finally persuaded, regretfully, to store her beautiful doe-skin tunic in the chest, and save it for special occasions, donning the serviceable but scratchy linsey-woolseys, but the sunbonnet she scorn-fully rejected. Firmly tied under her chin by Aunt Rachel before an outdoor excursion, it would soon be dangling from her neck or waist, her face fearlessly exposed to sun, wind, or rain. No blinders for her! She had known freedom too long. Nancy envied her the ability to flout custom. She herself had never been able to see far enough, high enough, wide enough to suit her.

Sarah was not the only one to startle the Berry family with a tale of dark adventure and tragedy. One day when Nancy was about twelve Ned brought a young man to the cabin. "My friend Tom Lin-coln," he announced. "He's back from away workin'. I reckon you know everybody, Tom, except these here girls, my cousins. This is Sarah Mitchell, and this here young'un is Nancy Hanks."

Young'un. Nancy resented the word, which implied she was just a child. She regarded the newcomer curiously. Thomas Lincoln was about eighteen. Though not of unusual height, he was so strong and rugged of build that he seemed to tower above his friend Ned. His eyes, a dark gray set deeply under heavy brows, held a whimsical gleam as they moved slowly from one person to another. In fact, all his movements were slow and measured, as if carefully considered beforehand. Seating himself deliberately in a proffered chair, he ran a big calloused hand through his thick shock of black hair, already disordered as though buffeted by a high wind. Certainly not a hand-some man, thought Nancy, but somehow you wanted to keep looking at him, the way you couldn't take your eyes from an eagle soaring above the trees on heavy but effortless wings. She felt a ridiculous urge to go and smooth that unruly thatch into some kind of order.

"Tom's father knew old Dan'l Boone," Ned interjected eagerly. "Came into Kaintuck long before we did. Tom was only a young'un when his folks moved here from Virginny, how old, Tom?"

"Four." The reply came slowly, after some thought, as if Thomas

Lincoln wanted to make sure he was right before answering. "Yes, four."

"His father was a rich man in Virginny, owned all kinds of land," went on Ned with the pride of a loyal friend, "and he entered a heap of land here in Kaintuck up on the Green River, as much as 3,000 acres. I reckon he'd be one of the most important men in Kaintuck if he hadn't . . . You tell 'em, Tom. Tell 'em what happened."

"Aw, they don't want to hear that old yarn." Embarrassed, Tom Lincoln twisted on his chair, but a gleam in his eyes belied the modest disclaimer. "Anyhow, they must have heard it."

"I have," said Uncle Richard. "Your brother Mordecai told me. And no doubt your mother, Bersheba, told Rachel. But the girls don't know. See how they're all perked up, curious?"

"Wal, I sure remember the day it all happened," Tom drawled softly, almost apologetically. "It come sudden, like a thunderclap. There we was, my father, Abraham, and my two brothers, Mordecai and Josiah, and me. We was up on our land in what we called the Beargrass Country on Green River, six miles below Green River lick. It was near Hughes Station, where there was a sort of fort. We was workin' not far from our new cabin, clearin' with the oxen, haulin' logs down to the crick. That is, they was workin'. I wasn't much help, bein' only six, but I went along. Mord, he was a big feller, Josiah a little younger, about thirteen. Mother and the two girls, Mary and Nancy, were back at the station, livin' in one of the eight cabins there. All at once it happened. We heard a blood-curdlin' yell, then a rifle cracked. I looked for Father, but he wan't there. He was lyin' on the ground—shot."

Warming to the stimulus of shocked, excited faces, Thomas Lincoln was no longer drawling or apologetic. He seemed all at once a different person, charged with the afflatus of a born storyteller. Eyes shone. Slouching body straightened. Words became pictures, sounds, emotions. Yet he still spoke slowly and without raising his voice.

"'Injuns!' yelled Mord. 'Run for the fort,' he told Josiah, then Mord, he run for the cabin like sixty. Me, I knowed I ought to run too, but I couldn't leave Father lyin' there on the ground. I knelt down by him, tried to make him move, but I guess I knowed he was dead. All at once I looked up and there was a big Injun standin' right over me, holdin' a knife. I knew what he was goin' to do, scalp Father. I was half crazy. 'You git away!' I yelled, but he jist laughed, picked me up and threw me, then turned back to do his scalpin'. Then all of a suddint, *bang!* Another rifle shot, and that Injun dropped like one o' the big oaks we'd been fellin'. You know what happened?"

The responsive gasps were gratifying. "Wal, Mord got inside the cabin, took down Father's rifle from the wall, and stuck it out one o' the cracks. Soon's I was out of the way he aimed it at a silver thing danglin' from that Injun's breast, and bing! He hit the target right on the nose! That Injun was as dead as Father. There were some others off in the woods, but I guess seein' him dead scairt 'em off. Anyhow, help come from the fort in time to save the rest of us."

Nancy drew a deep breath. Her eyes had not left the visitor's face since he started talking. So intense had been her participation in the tragedy, her sense of identity with the terrified six-year-old that, now it was over, she felt drained of emotion.

That had meant the breakup of Tom's family, he continued with his former unassuming, deliberate manner. His mother, Bersheba, had been afraid to live in that wild area alone, and she had moved here to Washington County where Hananiah Lincoln, her husband's cousin, had settled. Mordecai, as the oldest son, had been given control of the property. And since then he had hated all Indians like poison, had killed every one he could see within shooting distance, even going out and hunting them like deer or possum, shooting every one on sight, not waiting to find out if it was friend or foe.

Suddenly Sarah moved out of the shadows where she had been sitting crouched on a stool. Her bright eyes, aglow in the firelight, seemed disembodied flecks in her brown face, like those of an animal caught in a flare of lantern light.

"And what about you, Tom Lincoln?" she demanded. "Do you hate all the Indians too? Would you like to kill them?"

Nancy gasped. How did she dare? Young girls were not supposed to thrust themselves forward. But Aunt Rachel, though she made a reproving gesture, remained silent. The visitor, surprised, regarded Sarah thoughtfully. Then his sober features broke into a transforming smile. "No," he replied, "I don't hate Injuns. Some of 'em are bad and some are good, like white folks. I reckon if I'd been done wrong to the way we've done to them, I'd feel like doin' just what that big Injun did."

Sarah nodded with satisfaction and slipped back into the shadows.

For some reason Nancy felt a queer stabbing of envy. For the first time she was realizing how young she was beside Sarah—Sarah, who was already seventeen and old enough (startling thought!) to be ready for marriage; Sarah, at whom this stranger was looking with such obvious understanding and, yes, admiration; the admiration, she sensed, of a young man for a young woman, while in his eyes, no doubt, she, Nancy, was just a "young'un," a mere child. But she did not feel like a child. And if expertise in homemaking—spinning, weaving, sewing, cooking—was a measure of maturity, she was older at twelve than was Sarah at seventeen.

Aunt Rachel continued to be proud of Nancy's skill at spinning, which had won her prizes at many of the spinning parties in the neighborhood. It was soon after Tom's visit that one of these parties was held at the Lincoln cabin. Was it because of the possibility of Tom's presence that Nancy looked forward to this event with both anticipation and trepidation? For some reason she had been unable to forget him. In her dreams she saw the small boy standing over his dead father, felt his terror and anguish. The young oak spreading its sturdy branches outside the cabin door reminded her of his rugged strength. In the beat of the pestle on the grinding stone she heard the slow measured tones of his voice. She was haunted by the memory of his sober face lighting up when he answered Sarah's question.

"Would you—would you like to marry him?" she suddenly dared to ask Sarah when they were out gathering hazelnuts.

"Marry? Marry who?" Sarah, down on her knees, stared up at Nancy in amazement. "Oh!" she laughed. "You mean that Tom Lincoln. You've talked and thought of nothin' else since he was here. Marry him? No, I should say not! He's too slow and easygoin'. I reckon he'll never amount to much." Returning to her task, she vigorously swept up a handful of shining brown nuts and deposited them in her already brimming apron.

Nancy, who liked to pick her nuts one by one and store them more deliberately, stopped to consider. "He looked kind," she remembered, "and he had a nice twinkle in his eye."

Sarah sat back on her heels, shaking with laughter. Then she sobered, her eyes lighting with swift tenderness. "Speakin' of marryin'," she said, "I want you to know, if I ever have daughters, the first one will be named Nancy."

"And if I ever have one," promised Nancy, "I'll name her Sarah."

Two spinning wheels were taken to the Lincoln cabin on the ox-cart. The girls carried their distaffs. Fortunately it was a good day, so much of the contest could be held out of doors. About a dozen girls had gathered from neighborhood farms, including Bersheba's two daughters, Mary and Nancy Lincoln. Nancy Hanks was one of the youngest. Loading the distaff with the long fibers of flax and attaching it to the wheel, Nancy placed her foot on the treadle. At a given signal all the wheels were put in motion.

Nancy was not one of the fastest spinners, but she was meticulous and accurate. Her hand pulled the long wet fibers of flax from the distaff, feeding them onto the spindle. With the other hand she tested each fiber expertly to get it of uniform and finest possible size, spinning the wheel at just the right speed to make the thread firm and long and very fine. She had little interest in winning the competition except to please Aunt Rachel, yet every movement was pure joy. She loved the sounds of gentle whirring, like a musical chorus, the feeling of the soft fibers running through her slender fingers, the fine texture of the hanks of "linnen" yarn. None of the rough coarseness of lin-sey-woolsey here! That was for winter. This was for summer with its smooth coolness. Only once was the rhythm of her motions interrupted.

"Wal, if it ain't the young'un from Old Richard Berry's! Whar did you larn to spin like that, in the cradle? They tell me you walk off with all the prizes at these here parties, and I don't wonder. You'll take the palm today, I reckon."

Nancy's cheeks flamed. Her fingers lost their rhythm, tightened about the slender thread she was sizing so that it almost broke. No need to look up to know who was standing by her side. The voice was enough. She could picture the rugged features with the whimsical gray eyes and heavy brows, the shock of lively, unruly black hair. After the momentary hesitation her fingers continued their steady skillful motion.

"I do the best I kin, Mr. Lincoln," she said composedly.

"And if you ask me," he rejoined in his slow measured manner of speech, "you sure do a purty good job at spinnin' for a young'un."

He moved away, stopping briefly to observe the work of his two sisters, longer at the side of Sarah Mitchell, who, thanks to Nancy's tutelage, had almost compensated for her lost five years in the art of spinning. Nancy heard them laughing together. Then he went on to help his mother, Bersheba, who was laying a long puncheon table in preparation for the feast which always accompanied such parties. The competition finished, it was Nancy's reel of unusually fine-spun linen thread which won the prize, a new distaff of dogwood, "made by my son Tom," Bersheba told her proudly. "He's right handy with tools. I'm sure goin' to miss him now he's goin' away agin."

"He's goin' away?" repeated Nancy, trying not to show her disappointment.

"Yes, over to Hardin County. There's a big new town over there called Elizabethtown. They jist give it a name last year. It's in a place called Severn's Valley. They say there's a lot of work there, and he's set his mind on goin'."

Walking home beside Sarah, Nancy hugged her prize to her breast. It was a simple implement, a short staff with a clef at one end for holding the long fibers of flax or the strands of carded wool ready for the hand to draw out in spinning, but for years it would be her most precious possession. Her fingers stroked its polished golden surface. He must have worked on it for hours, she thought, and with what patience, to make it so straight and round and smooth, without a single groove or splinter! And he was going away. She might never see him again.

She was still a "young'un," yes, her slender body almost as childish and uncurved as the new distaff. But the emotion she felt that night was not that of a child, but of a woman.

= 4 =

For a second time she stood beside an open grave, listening to solemn words which meant the end of one life and, it was believed by the fervent preacher, the beginning of another. Jesse Head, the young preacher, had moved a year or two ago to Kentucky.

"Dust to dust, ashes to ashes," intoned the preacher piously. Then, lifting his head so that his bright red hair caught the sun's rays and streamed backward like a banner, he continued triumphantly, "Yet if the earthly house of our tabernacle be dissolved, we have a building from God, a house not made with hands, eternal in the heavens."

Nancy tried to picture such a house. Not a log cabin, of course, the only kind of house she had ever lived in. No, he was talking about the body, Uncle Richard's body, which was lying in the box in the ground but was going to turn into something shining and wonderful, perhaps like the angels one saw in pictures, always playing their harps? No, not Uncle Richard. She hoped wherever he was going there would be fields to till and corn to plant and children to teach. That would be his idea of heaven.

She mourned his loss as she had been unable to mourn Grandfather's. He had been more than uncle—guardian, supporting and protecting; mentor, revealing the wonder of written words; kindly friend and companion; the father she had never known. Like Grandfather, he must have quietly anticipated his last brief illness, for only the preceding summer he had made a will.

In December 1798 it was entered for probate, and Mordecai Lincoln, their neighbor, was one of the appraisers of the estate. The property, which was considerable, was apportioned to his wife and children—several black slaves, feather beds, household furniture, including table, chairs, and a cupboard, two spinning wheels, kitchen utensils. As in Grandfather's will, the horses were listed by name, Blueskin, Cherriot, Rosy. He had owned a dozen head of cattle, an unusually large herd for a frontier farmer. His lands, of course, went to his three living sons. John, the eldest, had died three years before.

For Nancy, as well as for Uncle Richard, his death meant an end and a beginning. She was fourteen, a competent housekeeper and seamstress, even-tempered, beloved by all the Berry family. More than one home was open to her.

"Of course you'll be stayin' on with me," assumed Aunt Rachel. "Francis will be marryin' soon, but Ned will be with us still. And Sarah would be lost without you. You've been more like sisters than cousins."

"We want you to come with us," young Richard insisted. "I have been named your legal guardian in place of my father. Polly wants you and needs you, now that the children are coming."

It was hard to choose. Aunt Rachel did not really need her, with

Sarah there and two slaves to do all the heavy housework. Nancy liked Polly Ewing Berry and knew she could make herself useful in Richard's household, but there again she was not actually needed, for Cousin Richard had already acquired several slaves. The presence of slaves in her uncle's house had always made her uneasy. It didn't seem right somehow for one person to *own* another. Jesse Head denounced slavery with an eloquence as vigorous and fiery as his flaming red hair, even though it was said he had once owned slaves himself. No, she wouldn't really feel at home in Cousin Richard's home.

Then came a happening which dispelled all doubts. A man and woman rode into the yard, each on a horse, another horse led behind them. Nancy took a startled look at the woman, then rushed to meet her. "Aunt Betsy!"

It was a joyful reunion. Elizabeth introduced her husband, Thomas Sparrow, whom she had married two years before, a brother of her sister's husband.

"I didn't send word," she explained to Nancy after the guests had been welcomed, fed, and hospitably settled. "I wanted to wait until I could keep my promise. Remember, I told you sometime you'd come to live with me, and when I heard Uncle Richard had died, I knew this was the time." She had come hoping to take Nancy back with them to their farm in Mercer County.

Mercer County. The Sparrows. Instantly a face sprang into her mind's focus, eager, loving, with beautiful dark lustrous eyes. She felt arms enveloping her, a voice breathing, "My dear—my own dear child." Surely in Mercer County she would be close to the woman she had been taught to call "Aunt Lucy." But this was not the only reason Nancy felt a stirring of anticipation. She knew suddenly that Aunt Betsy, not the woman named Lucy, had been the mother-figure of her childhood. They belonged together.

The farewells were painful. The cousins seemed genuinely sorry to see her go. Cousin Richard assured her that he would remain her guardian and his home would always be hers. Aunt Rachel wept. Sarah clung to her with wails of "My best friend, what will I do without you?" though Nancy knew that already her role of comrade and confidante was being usurped by a certain John Thompson, who had recently come from Virginia. It was over at last, her possessions stowed in two saddlebags, and she rode away toward the east, in this third chapter of her life—no, the fourth, for back beyond memory there was that hazy foretime of beginnings, ending in a journey along the Wilderness Road. She wondered, would it always be so? Was she destined to keep forever moving, always looking for something beyond each horizon and perhaps never finding it?

Nancy felt completely at home in the new life. It was almost as if the preceding five years of sheltered and comfortable living had never been. With no slaves to assist she fell easily into the old routine of carrying water from the nearby creek, pounding corn until the palms of her hands became as calloused as the tips of her fingers from spinning, frying venison in the three-legged skillet or roasting it over the coals on spits until her cheeks smarted and turned as red as the raw steaks.

The farm of Henry Sparrow was, as she had expected, close by. She looked forward to her first visit there with both excitement and trepidation. Would she be received as a daughter? Would Henry Sparrow resent her presence in the neighborhood? To both questions she soon had an answer.

"My dear child!" Lucy Sparrow embraced her tenderly, but with one eye on the tot pulling at her skirt and, Nancy suspected, the other on the baby crying in the cradle.

"Welcome, my dear." Henry Sparrow's greeting was genial, if restrained. "Your aunt Lucy has been looking forward to your coming. Come, James." He motioned to a child of seven or eight. "Why don't you introduce the rest of our family to your new cousin Nancy?"

Aunt Lucy. *Cousin* Nancy. So that was still the way it was to be. If she felt a stab of disappointment and a painful recurrence of the loneliness of childhood, she gave no sign. Smiling, she acknowledged the introduction by grave little James to her "cousins," Thomas, Henry, George, Elizabeth in the cradle, and, she could not help observing, another was soon to arrive. Perhaps it was better this way. She could never be anything but an outsider in this family, unhappy reminder of an episode everyone wanted to forget. At least in the household of Aunt Betsy and Uncle Thomas Sparrow she was *wanted*. And if the embraces of Lucy signified an affection more tender than that between aunt and niece, no one but themselves would ever know.

Nancy was not the only member of Joseph Hanks's family to find

sanctuary in the home of Thomas and Elizabeth. It was sometime in
the summer of 1799 that Nannie once again entered Nancy's life.

She came riding into the yard one day with Aunt Polly, and Nancy
and Elizabeth ran out joyfully to greet them, helping them down
from their horses. This was a far different Nannie from the one
Nancy remembered, a petted child, beautiful, coddled, gay, a little
bold and overconfident. Her eyes were red from weeping. Her hair,
once shining and carefully curled, tumbled in dull strands beneath
her sunbonnet. Her shoulders sagged. And she carried a small bundle
which emitted lusty infant sounds. Any jealousy or resentment Nancy
had ever felt was washed away in a flood of love and sympathy.
"Nannie, darling!" She gathered both the girl and her bundle into her
arms.

Releasing them, she took the bundle, pushed aside its wrappings,
and looked into the puckered red face of a baby not more than a few
weeks old. "He's beautiful, Nannie," she said eagerly. "I reckon it's
a boy, with that manly voice."

Nannie's eyes brightened. For a moment she was her old gay self.
"He's a boy all right, and his name," her head lifted with defiant
pride, "is Dennis *Friend* Hanks."

Betsy and Polly went away to talk. Only later did Nancy learn the
story as Polly told it to her sister—her husband Jesse's anger on the
discovery of Nannie's pregnancy, his chagrin at finding that the
offender had been his own brother Charles, and his insistence that he
be made to marry her, Nannie's obstinacy in refusing such a forced
relationship when the other party was obviously reluctant, the birth
of the child in their cabin on Nolin Creek.

"She wanted to come to you, Betsy. You were always her favorite
sister. And she certainly doesn't find our home congenial any more.
You will take her?"

"Of course." Elizabeth's reply was unhesitating. "And the child
too, if she wishes. For good, I mean, especially since we don't seem
to be having any of our own."

Thomas Sparrow rode back with Polly to Hardin County. Such a
long journey was unsafe, he insisted, for a woman traveling alone. It
had been bad enough for two coming together. Besides, he wanted to
explore the possibilities of land in that more settled area.

Though Nannie and Nancy were in closer intimacy than in former
days, Nannie remained uncommunicative. Only once did she let her

emotions break through the stubborn shell of reticence. "It was awful," she confessed, shuddering. "Jesse so angry and all the neighbors liftin' eyebrows, pursin' lips, turnin' their backs. And the preacher came and told me I had to stand up in meetin' and confess my sin or I'd be put out of the church and go to hell. But I didn't. I know now it was wicked, what I did, but I didn't know then. Nobody ever told me."

Nancy ached in sympathy. She's just my age, she thought, only fifteen, yet already she's lived a lifetime of trouble. I know now what my mother must have suffered.

Relieved of some of her burden, Nannie slowly reverted to a semblance of her former self, careful of appearance, lighthearted, a bit irresponsible. Except for necessary intervals of nursing she was glad to relinquish all care of little Dennis to Elizabeth and Nancy, both of whom gladly welcomed the duty. In fact, from the moment of his arrival in her home to the end of her life, Elizabeth, who would have no children of her own, was accepted as the mother of Dennis. Nancy, assuming much of his care, felt a joy which even her exultation in the new life of spring was unable to inspire. Gently washing the squirming little body, wrapping it in the shirts of soft yellow "flannen" which she had spun and woven herself, she wondered as she hugged the tiny bundle to her breast if she would ever be clasping such a precious little son of her own.

The years spent in Mercer County were a time of waiting, of transition. Thomas Sparrow returned from his trip to Hardin County with glowing accounts of its superior opportunities. Unlike most of the other numerous Sparrow-family members, who had migrated from Mecklenburg County in Virginia about 1788 and were perfectly satisfied with their new nests along the Chaplin River, Thomas had the wanderlust. Already he was making plans to move to this more desirable farm land to the west, and during the ensuing months he made several trips in search of land either to rent or purchase.

Severn's Valley. Elizabethtown, or E-town, as it was often called. Nancy's mind leaped back to her visit there, and a figure sprang into memory, a child laughing, gray-blue eyes wide and trusting, black hair in curls. Sally had been her name, Sally Bush. Nancy wondered what she was like now. If they moved to Severn's Valley and the Bushes were still there, she might find out. And Elizabethtown! It was the place where Thomas Lincoln had gone to find work.

It was 1801 before Thomas found a farm to suit him. He would rent it first, with the option of later purchase. So for the fifth time in her seventeen years Nancy set forth on pilgrimage into a new life, this time to the country very near the scenes of her childhood. She was anxious to go. Even the parting with "Aunt Lucy," while affectionate and tearful, was for neither of them painful. Perhaps Nannie was most loath to leave, for they were returning to the neighborhood where her moral lapse was well known and rigidly condemned. With her carefree optimism, in this new environment she had been able to relegate the unhappy episode, including regret and guilt, to a half-remembered past. It was Elizabeth or Nancy who kept watchful eyes on bouncing, excited Dennis, held him when he slept. They traveled by horse-drawn wagon, piled high with household goods and accompanied by the considerable miscellany of other horses, cattle, and hogs which Thomas Sparrow had accumulated. It was February, a good time for moving, to avoid the spring mud and arrive before planting season.

They stopped at the Berry farms where Cousin Ned was still living with Aunt Rachel in the original cabin. Sarah was no longer with her aunt, having married John Thompson just a year before.

"You come jist in time," Aunt Rachel greeted them joyously. "You must stay for the wedding."

The following day, they learned, Aunt Rachel's grandson, William Brumfield, was being married to Nancy Lincoln, youngest daughter of Bersheba. The ceremony would be at Bersheba's cabin and the infare at Mordecai's. Since both families were among the most prominent in the community, it was to be a festive occasion.

Nancy felt a stirring of excitement. A wedding at the Lincolns! All the family would be there, surely, including . . . Five years had gone by since she had seen Thomas Lincoln, and then she had been only twelve. In another few days she would be seventeen. Had the feeling aroused in her then been mere childhood infatuation? Whatever it was, certainly it had not been returned, for his attention had been all for Sarah. If she could meet him now, talk with him, she would no doubt discover that she had been a moonstruck, susceptible child and laugh at her foolishness.

She did see him at the wedding ceremony, but only at a distance. The Lincoln cabin was so crowded that there was barely room to move, and Nancy, always shy, pressed herself obscurely against an outer wall. His head, with its shock of unruly black hair, was unmistakable. Once she got a clear view of his face.

"He's not a bit handsome," she thought with faint disappointment. His features were too rugged, eyes too deep-set under craggy brows, nose rather prominent and blunt, and he didn't seem nearly as tall as she remembered. Had she been idealizing his memory all these years?

The infare following the wedding was a riotous affair, and the crowds attending it must have come from as far away as Springfield. Though it was early February and still winter cold, tables were set for the feast out of doors and loaded with all kinds of game, as well as roast beef and mutton, breads, sweets. The wedding had been at sunset, and the festivities lasted far into the evening, enlivened to roistering merriment as the supplies of whiskey, always an accompaniment of pioneer gatherings, grew steadily lower. Again Nancy shrank back into the outskirts of the crowd, still inside the circle of light cast by the flaring pine-knot torches, yet having no wish to join in the lively, often riotous dancing.

"Wal, if it ain't the young'un," a voice drawled close to her ear, "all grown up into a young woman, and a right purty one too, I've been noticin'."

Nancy turned, her pulses pounding. "Oh! It's you. Good evening, Mr. Thomas Lincoln."

"Good. You do remember me. It's been so long it 'peared you might have forgot."

So he had remembered her. "No, I hadn't forgotten." She returned his gaze gravely. "How could I, when you made that six-year-old boy so real and so pathetic?"

"Aw," he smiled shamefacedly, "me and my storytellin'! But why ain't you out there dancin', Nancy Hanks, a purty young thing like you?"

"I'd rather stay here and watch." Her dark eyes caught the torchlight glow and sparkled. "And why ain't you out there, Tom Lincoln, a big strong thing like you?"

"I'd rather stay here an' talk with you, Nancy Hanks. I hear you all are movin' on toward Elizabethtown in the mornin', and this may be our last chance for a while."

It was Tom who did most of the talking, and Nancy was a good listener, enjoying the sound of his slow measured voice, the whimsical gleam in his deep gray eyes, prodding him with an occasional question about his life in the last five years. Yes, he had lived in Elizabethtown for a while, working at building, for he was a sort of carpenter. Then he had gone to Tennessee for a year, helping on his uncle Isaac's farm on the Watauga, but he had been back with his mother for the last couple of years. He liked the country around Elizabethtown. In fact, he was trying right now to persuade his mother and sister Mary, who was getting married later in the year to a fine young fellow named Ralph Crume, maybe also the new bride and groom, to move over that way. He might buy some land in the Severn's Valley and settle there. They talked of the wedding, laughed over the booming voice of the officiating Jesse Head, whose blessing of the couple could surely have been heard a mile away at the Berry cabin, Tom's eyes softening with tenderness as he spoke of his baby sister, Nancy.

"He jist better be good to her. If he don't—" A big hand knotted suddenly into a fist bespoke not only an excess of strength but a possible reserve of temper, even of violence if sufficiently aroused. "But thar!" The fist splayed out into sinewy but relaxed fingers. "He's a kind man, William Brumfield. You know, he's your cousin." He laughed. "I reckon that makes us sort o' relatives, don't it?"

"Hey, Tom!" someone shouted. "Where are you?"

"Here!" he called back.

"C'mon, boy, what we waitin' for? Time to put the bride and groom to bed!"

Nancy felt her hand encased in a warm, firm grasp. "Good night, young'un all grown up. See you agin mebbe, sometime."

Walking home to the Berry cabin in the moonlit dark she had no new distaff this time to hug to her breast. She did not need one.

"Why didn't you dance?" demanded Nannie as they moved along the path, guided by the lantern of Cousin Richard, who walked ahead, swinging it cautiously about in quest of lurking rattlesnakes. "I had such a good time, better than I've had since—since—" She hesitated, then rushed on. "I saw you talkin' with that Lincoln man, the one that's so dark and stodgy-lookin'. You could have danced with some lots handsomer ones if you'd come out where I was. Whatever did you find to talk about so long?"

"Oh—we just talked," replied Nancy, her eyes reflecting the flickering light of the lantern. No, Thomas Lincoln was not handsome. Neither were the gnarled trunks of the huge trees beside the path, their roots thrust deep into the red Kentucky earth. But like them he was strong. Slow of speech and movement, yes, but slowness meant patience, like the gentle growth of winter into spring. Somewhere in the ground under her feet life was already stirring. He was kind, too, for he had been concerned that the new husband should be good to his little sister. And, best of all, there were whimsical gleams in the eyes under the heavy brows, like glimmers of sunlight on deep forest pools.

Cousin Richard and Polly were anxious for her to stay with them rather than go on to Severn's Valley with Aunt Betsy. "You can help with the children," Polly had urged, "and you and I were always such good friends!"

"I'm your guardian, you know," Richard had reminded. "You'll be getting married before long, and of course it should be from my house."

Should she stay? She must make up her mind, for Uncle Thomas was determined to move on. It was a tempting prospect—a comfortable home without the rigors of a pioneer cabin; slaves to perform all menial work; pleasant tasks of child care, spinning, needlework; and, just a mile away—her pulse beat quickened—the Lincoln cabin. "See you agin mebbe sometime," he had said. Surely if she lived so near . . .

"If only I didn't have to go back there," moaned Nannie, "at least not yet! Everybody will remember. They'll look at me queer, and turn their backs."

"Would you—would you like to stay here for a while?" asked Nancy.

"Oh—yes! If I only could!"

Nancy was very quiet the rest of the way to the Berry cabin. Her eyes, bent on the path, no longer reflected the light of the lantern. Lying beside Nannie on the soft feather bed, she stared at the shadows chasing each other endlessly across the whitewashed walls. Once Nannie stirred and laughed softly in her sleep, probably dreaming of the good time she had had dancing.

"You will stay, won't you?" asked Polly the next morning. "We do want you."

Nancy drew a long breath. The time had come for decision. "Why not let Nannie stay in my place," she suggested, "at least for a visit?

She would help with the children, and you'd like her. Would you mind very much?"

"Why—no. Of course we'd rather have you. In fact," Polly's frowning face brightened, "there's room for you both. Frank's wife Elizabeth would like a helper and companion. Their house is even larger than ours, two stories with a kitchen annex. Please!"

Nancy shook her head. Aunt Betsy would need her if Nannie did not go. There would be no slaves in the wilderness cabin, work enough for two strong women, even without the lively Dennis to care for. So . . . it was decided. The wagon was loaded, the animals herded. Aunt Betsy would drive, while Uncle Thomas walked ahead to drive the cattle. Nancy, on the seat beside Betsy, held Dennis in her lap. Good-bys were said. Nannie, staying behind, was all smiles, no tears at parting from her son. Already he was Betsy's child more than hers. They lumbered away, taking the road toward Bardstown, almost passing the Lincoln cabin.

"Should we stop and say good-by?" asked Aunt Betsy.

"No," said Uncle Thomas. "We've stayed too long already. Must git on."

See you agin mebbe sometime. Meb-be some-time . . . Meb—be some—time.

The words echoed in Nancy's ears to the rhythms of hoofbeats on the hard ground. She knew suddenly that she had fallen in love with Thomas Lincoln, no childish, fleeting infatuation, but a steady maturing emotion which would dominate all the remaining years of her life.

= 5 =

It was a journey back into her childhood. Coming into the valley of the Rolling Fork, they passed within a few miles of the cabin where she had lived with Grandfather Joseph. Leaving the valley the road wound tortuously over the steep wooded ridges of "Old Muldraugh," so huge it was called Bigg Hill, with two "g's," then down into another valley through which ran Nolin Creek. Uncle Thomas's rented farm was not far from the waterfall where Robert Hodgen had built a mill in 1788. Already a settlement was growing up at Hodgen's Mill, to be incorporated seventeen years later into the town of Hodgenville. As they passed through the thriving little community on their way to the farm, Uncle Thomas pointed out some of its features with pride.

"A real mill where we kin take our corn, one of the first in Kaintuck, and only a mile or two from our cabin! And look yander! That big house is Hodgen's ordinary (he pronounced it "ornery"), a right popular tavern. Why, they say an exiled prince who later became King of France, Lafayette's country, stopped there only four years ago!"

Nancy was properly impressed. Though she had no idea of the location of the fabulous France, the name Lafayette was almost as familiar a symbol of national freedom as Washington.

She was returning home in more ways than one. Some of the Hanks uncles and aunts lived not far away. Uncle William, who had married Elizabeth Hall in 1793, had bought land over in Grayson County near the Falls of Rough, as he had planned. Still nearer, on Nolin Creek, was Aunt Polly, who in 1795 had married Jesse Friend. It was with her that Nannie had been living when Jesse's brother Charles had unhappily entered her life.

Nancy was thankful she had come when she saw the rented farm. The cabin had been neglected. The cracks between the logs were big enough to let in snakes and other "varmints." While Uncle Thomas prepared the ground for planting, in time to get the corn growing well by the time the leaves of the oaks were "the size of a mouse's ear," she and Betsy mixed clay with little pieces of split wood and chinked the cracks. They brought sand from the creek bank and spread it on the earth floor. Spring had moved into the valley with all its bursting vigor before the cabin was in order and the first seeds planted.

"Now," announced Uncle Thomas with satisfaction, "we can take time to go to town and git what things we need."

A good road, wide enough for a wagon, had been laid out between Hodgen's Mill and Elizabethtown. It ran for some twelve miles among knobby limestone hills before entering the fertile valley watered by Severn's Creek. Nancy's first trip to the town after some ten years was a revelation. It had grown from a tiny settlement with three crude protecting forts into a flourishing center, named after the wife of Colonel Andrew Hynes, one of the fort builders. In 1793 it had been laid out into streets and alleys, and public buildings had been erected, including a new jail of thick oak planks, well spiked, complete with stocks and whipping post, plus a ducking stool for scolding women. While most of the homes sprawled along the flanks of towering Muldraugh Hill were still one-room cabins, Uncle Thomas showed her a house built two years before by Samuel Haycraft, another of the town's founders, a magnificent structure of yellow poplar timbers with a stone chimney which "took more than a hundred wagon loads to build!" That same year of 1801 a brickyard was being opened by Major Benjamin Helm, another of the three founders.

"And they say he's goin' to build a real brick house," Uncle Thomas marveled, "with a deep cellar walled with huge stone!"

He pointed out the courthouse, built in 1795. "John Crutcher built it, they give him sixty-six pounds. All hands hove to, anybody that could fell trees, hew with a broadax, cut plank with a whipsaw, or make shingles with a drawin' knife. And it was a grand raisin', with skids and hand-spikes and pushin' dog-forks all ready. Up she went. And Sam Haycraft's wife sarved the dinner, roast shoats, chickens, ducks, potatoes, roast beef with cabbage an' beans, baked custard. Folks still talk about it." He chuckled. "But what a fight there was before! Both the Valley and Hodgen's Mill wanted to be the county seat. Been hot blood between 'em ever sence. Still fights at every election, mebbe fifty of 'em in the last seven years."

But it was another improvement that made Nancy sit up straighter in her saddle and stare with brightening eyes.

"And there yander's the mill Sam Haycraft built," indicated Uncle Thomas as they forded the Valley Creek. "And if I ain't mistook, one of his workers was a nigh neighbor of yours over on Beech Fork, young Tom Lincoln. You know him, I reckon."

Nancy's pulses quickened. "Yes," she agreed. "I know him—a little." She gazed at the mill race and its substantial building with a sense of personal pride. Which, she instantly reminded herself, was not only presumptuous but stupid! Just because Thomas Lincoln had been kindly attentive for an hour . . . *See you agin mebbe sometime.* For some reason the clear spring sky over Elizabethtown had faded into a dull blue-gray.

But soon afterward it again brightened. "There's a man I want to see," said Uncle Thomas. "He's one of the early settlers here, owns several lots, and knows somethin' about land titles. A man has to be keerful if he's even thinkin' of buyin' land. His name is Christopher Bush."

"Oh, we know him!" Betsy exchanged a knowing glance with Nancy. "Remember? That's where we went with Father long ago."

Did Nancy remember! The child who had drawn her out of solitude into warm and intimate friendliness!

It was just as she had seen it long before, the Bush cabin with its atmosphere of coziness and cheer. Mrs. Bush was still red-cheeked, bustling, hospitable. "I remember you," she greeted Nancy. "You were a sober, shy young'un, and now you've grown into a right purty young woman. Remember my daughters, Hannah, Rachel, and Sally?"

Nancy looked eagerly from one girl to the other, her eyes lingering on the youngest, who was seated at a loom deftly slipping a bobbin between long warp strands of yarn. Many years had gone by, but Sally Bush at thirteen was still the lively, wide-eyed bundle of tossing curls and friendly smiles that she had been at three.

"I'm sure you don't remember me," Nancy said doubtfully, hopefully, "but we used to be friends."

The curls bobbed, the smile deepened. "Seems as if I do—a little." Carefully placing her bobbin on the piles of linen and nettles with which she was forming the woof, Sally rose and took both of Nancy's hands in a firm grip, interlocking capable short fingers with long slender ones. "Anyway, you look nice. I like you." They were almost the same words the child had used years before. "We'll be friends, shall we?"

"Oh yes," said Nancy gratefully.

It would be a peculiar friendship, based on a feeling of affinity which neither could quite define. There was disparity in their ages, four years' difference. There was diversity of appearance and temperament—Sally fair-skinned and curly-haired, sprightly, talkative, carefree, demonstrative, extremely practical; Nancy dark of both skin and hair, shy, introspective, keenly sensitive, alert more in mind than body, joy always tinctured with a hint of melancholy. Perhaps it was this very disparity which made their friendship more significant, one complementing the other, making them a subtle blending of sunlight and shadow.

They met occasionally in the months that followed. Before 1803 there was no church on Nolin, and the good Baptists at Hodgen's Mill, which included most of the inhabitants, were a part of the Severn's Valley congregation. In fact, Nolin Creek was supposedly named for this preacher, whose name was Lynn. One day, the story went, he had wandered away from his party while hunting and been killed, it was thought, by Indians. The hunting party had reported sadly on their return, "No Lynn!"

"So you accent the name Nolin on the second part," Uncle Thomas explained, "as if you were sayin' 'No Lynn.' "

Elizabethtown had a new church building of hewed poplar logs on the hill northeast of the courthouse where services were held once a month, and always Nancy and Sally managed to sit together on one of the hard backless benches patiently absorbing, both morning and afternoon, the two-hour bombardments of threats, admonitions, and inspiration. Then in August 1801, they spent four whole days together at a huge camp meeting marking the climax of a great revival which swept through the scattered settlements of Kentucky with the vigor and soul-scorching intensity of a forest fire. It was held at Cane Ridge, some thirty miles from Nolin, and it was said afterward that between twenty and thirty thousand people attended it.

There was no good road to Cane Ridge, so they traveled on horseback by forest trails which led among giant trees—sycamores, chestnuts, oaks, walnuts, their branches so interlaced overhead that for long stretches one could not see the sky. It was like moving through dark tunnels. Nancy marveled at the hugeness of the trees, some six, eight, even ten feet in diameter.

"That's nothin'." Uncle Thomas recalled stories of early pioneers who had found hollow sycamores so large that whole families could camp inside them while they cleared ground and built their cabins.

The whole state of Kentucky, it seemed, must have congregated in a frenzy for its soul's salvation. Some settlers had traveled a hundred miles. Around a huge tent erected in the center, families set up housekeeping in smaller tents, built fires to cook the food they had brought, turning the valley into a mammoth camping ground. Families long separated were reunited. Uncle William had brought his family from Grayson County, and to Nancy's surprise Uncle Joseph, returned from Virginia, was there with them, grown into a sturdy young man of twenty. In Virginia he had served as a carpenter's apprentice and wanted to ply the same trade in Kentucky. When Nancy saw Cousin Richard Berry and his family, with Nannie, she felt sudden eagerness. Had the Lincolns come too?

"I know who you're lookin' for," taunted Nannie with affectionate amusement, noting her roving eyes. "That Lincoln man with the black hair like a hedgehog's coat. No, the Lincolns didn't come. We're the only ones from Beech Fork."

The Bushes with others from Elizabethtown camped near the group from Nolin Creek, and Nancy spent much time with Sally. Side by side on the halves of split logs, backs aching, eyes strained with nervous tension, hands sometimes clasped in terror, they listened hour after hour as preacher after preacher described the tortures of hell for all who participated in the commonest pleasures—cards, horse racing, drinking, fornication, fighting. At night, with the pine torches flaring, licking helplessly at the interminable darkness beyond, the warnings assumed the literal aspect of fire and brimstone.

"Why," wondered Nancy, "can't they talk sometimes about the beauties of heaven instead of the tortures of hell?"

But heaven was far from the actual experience of these pioneers, and the warnings were pertinent. Whiskey peddlers on the outskirts of the camp were more numerous than the preachers, and even recent converts were tempted to blackslide, and did. Fights were easily provoked, and guards were constantly on the alert to prevent young people from wandering out of bounds.

But one night there came another preacher with a different message. He talked about the love of God instead of his anger over people's sins, about the young Galilean who had gone about the country saying to all who were willing to listen, "Follow me . . . Come unto me, all ye that labor and are heavy laden. . . . Behold I stand at the door and knock." That night when the usual invitation was given Nancy found herself joining the group moving down the aisle toward the "mourners' bench," Sally clinging to her hand. Shy, self-conscious at first, she feared everybody was looking at her. Then, kneeling there in the sawdust, the other kneelers, the vast crowd, even Sally, were forgotten. She might have been completely alone, except that there seemed to be One close beside her, a presence enveloping her in comforting warmth, radiant light. She went back to her tent in a glow of exaltation. The stars seemed brighter, closer to earth. If she lifted her arms high, she felt she could surely touch them. She knew she would never feel completely alone again.

As the weeks progressed, emotions, kindled by months of the great revival, fanned now by currents of fiery preaching and contagious zeal, rose to white-hot heat. There were singing and shouting. Convicted sinners rushed from their seats to fall on their knees in the sawdust at the "mourners' bench." Such common responses at religious services as "Praise the Lord!" "Blessed be Jesus!" "Hallelujah, I'm saved!" were enhanced by physical expressions of ecstasy. And all rose to a climax on the last night, which became an orgy of conviction and repentance. Some leaped in the air or fell writhing to the ground. Others "spoke in tongues," emitting sounds like gibberish. There was "holy laughter." People kissed and embraced. One man, embracing another, shouted at the top of his voice,

> "I have my Jesus in my arms,
> Sweet as honey, strong as bacon ham."

In the midst of the confusion Nancy saw a young woman, hair unbound, tears streaming down her face, weaving her way toward the platform, throwing herself into the straw. "It's Nannie," she whispered. Always sensitive and impressionable, she felt her own emotions stirred to almost unbearable tension. Not like the emotion which had stirred her on that other night, which had brought comfort, light, peace. Fear? Guilt? Yearning for that unattainable something which always seemed to lie just beyond? She could not have told. She had risen from the bench and was about to follow Nannie when a firm hand drew her back.

"No," said Sally, "that ain't for you."

Nancy sat down again, slowly, and met the gaze of clear, calm eyes on a level with her own. "It ain't for me neither," continued Sally, her voice low yet audible amid the confusion. "We're diff'rent, but we're the same about some things. We keep what we feel deep inside of us. This ain't like the other night. We already told God about our sins and got forgiven. Nobody kin scare us with talk of hell. And we ain't goin' to give people the idea we are afeared—of anything."

Nancy looked wonderingly into the clear calm eyes. This girl, so much younger than herself, hardly more than a child—what had made her so wise? How had she known that an act of emotional extravagance which could bring spiritual release to one like Nannie would violate another's secret and preciously guarded intimacy with the Unseen? Nancy sank back on the bench and gratefully squeezed Sally's hand.

Nannie had indeed found release. Lying beside Nancy that night in the little tent of sewn deerskins, she confided her plans. "I'm not goin' back to Beech Fork. They were good to me, but it waren't home. I'm goin' home with Polly and Jesse. People kin talk if they want to. I don't care. I know God has forgiven me for what I did wrong, and"—her whisper was suddenly defiant—"and I ain't sure it was *so* terribly wrong when I look at little Dennis. It will be wonderful seein' him sometimes agin, though it's better he don't know I'm his mother."

"Yes," Nancy agreed humbly. How little one person understood another! She had thought Nannie completely indifferent to Dennis, when in reality . . . "And it will be wonderful," she whispered, "having you nearby agin."

The camp meeting ended, and the thousands returned to their lives of rigor and drudgery, most of the new converts reverting to the proscribed "sins" they had temporarily renounced—whiskey, gambling, card games, dancing—postponing further renunciation until the next camp meeting should bring another impulse for repentance. Recreation was meager in their pioneer life and temptation to seize it in any possible form irresistible.

One of the most popular and harmless diversions was "play parties." They were held in all sorts of places, cabins, "orneries," Robert Hodgen's mill, out of doors. Nancy attended some of them on Nolin Creek, at the Hodgens', the Larues', the Kirkpatricks'. At first she felt shy and awkward, unlike Nannie, who participated in the games with joyous abandon. She shrank back against the wall, watching the lines of players, refusing all offers of partners. It was Uncle Thomas who finally initiated her.

"Come, child. Don't be afeared. It's easy."

She found herself facing him at the head of the two lines of players. The game was called "sheep stealing." It began with every person pointing a finger at Uncle Thomas and singing to a rollicking fiddler's tune:

> *"There's the man that stole the sheep,*
> *There's the man that stole the sheep,*
> *There's the man that stole the sheep,*
> *He stole it while we was all asleep!*
> *He helt the salt in his right hand,*
> *He helt the salt in his right hand,*
> *And bid the sheep, 'C'Nan! C'Nan!' "*

Then to her dismay all the fingers were pointed at her!

> *"There's the lady that fried the meat . . .*
> *She fried it while we was all asleep;*
> *She helt the knife in her right hand . . .*
> *And turned it over in the frying pan!"*

Now once more it was Uncle Thomas' turn to be accused.

> *"Irish potatoes, tops and all,*
> *Irish potatoes, tops and all,*
> *Kiss her now or not at all!"*

Uncle Thomas crossed over, gave her a smack on the cheek, and whirled her down the line. To her surprise she found herself yielding to the gay rhythm, feeling the intoxication of combined music and motion, loving it. After that she was almost as much at ease at such parties as Nannie. She had no dearth of partners. Some would have been glad to follow the casual kiss with extended attentions, but a wall of reserve discouraged all further intimacies. Only one person possessed the magic which could penetrate that wall.

She had been living on Nolin Creek more than a year when Uncle Thomas came home from Elizabethtown with news which set her pulses racing.

"Remember that neighbor of the Berrys, the widow Lincoln? She's moved here to Hardin County with some of her family. Her daughter Mary married a Ralph Crume, and they've bought a farm on Mill Creek north of Elizabethtown. I hear the other daughter, the one we saw married to Brumfield, has come too and is livin' in the same place."

Nancy waited in an agony of suspense, but no further information seemed to be forthcoming. "Did—did any other members of the family come?"

"Yes. That Thomas I told you about, the one that helped Sam Haycraft build his mill. He's livin' with his mother and sister and workin' around Elizabethtown, doin' carpenterin'. He's right clever with tools, they say, helpin' to build cabins and makin' furniture."

Though he was less than ten miles away when working in Elizabethtown, it was months before she saw him. Church services were now held each month at Nolin, so the family worshiped nearer home. Dennis, a lively three-year-old, together with household duties, kept both Nancy and Betsy confined. Then in 1803, when Nancy was nineteen, Uncle Thomas returned from Elizabethtown with an invitation. He had visited the Bush cabin, and Mrs. Bush, Hannah, and Sally had begged him to bring Nancy for a visit. There was to be a big play party on a certain day in the new house of Major Benjamin Helm, to which all the young people were invited.

"Of course you must go," insisted Betsy. "You're young, and you've done nothin' but work for months. Besides," she smiled archly, "you should be meetin' more likely young men."

Was it the possibility of seeing Thomas Lincoln or the certainty of seeing Sally which made the sky bluer, the autumn air more heady, as she rode beside Uncle Thomas to Elizabethtown? Even her horse seemed infused with her exhilaration, for she held her head jauntily and climbed the steep hills with little slackening of pace.

Mrs. Bush greeted her like a mother, and Sally . . . Nancy stared at her friend in delight. Sally had become a woman, a beautiful one. A mature fifteen, she had grown taller, more dignified. Still straight as a pine sapling, round face framed by black curls, cheeks a delicate pink, not red like her mother's, she exuded health and happiness.

"You're lovely!" Nancy exclaimed, giving her a warm hug. "You're all aglow."

"Maybe she's in love," teased Hannah. "She has half the swains in town dancin' around her at every play party. And now there's another one what keeps comin' here, a dark, broody sort of fellow."

Sally laughed. "Nonsense, Hannah! Tom Lincoln don't come to see me. He's our brother Isaac's friend, and you know it."

"Mebbe he was fust," Hannah retorted. "But I've seen the looks he gives you."

"Anyway, he's old. He must be at least twenty-five. And he's slow. Look how long it took him to build that cupboard."

"And not handsome, neither," agreed Hannah, "like that Dan'l Johnston who's been moonin' over you since you was no bigger'n a little newborn calf."

"You're both wrong," put in Mrs. Bush. "Tom Lincoln comes to see me. I'm the one what hired him to put in that corner cupboard, and a right good one it is, too. I hear tell he's doin' a lot of carpenterin' for folks in town, even buildin' houses."

"Yes," agreed Hannah, "and they say he's bought a piece of land up on Mill Creek near where his folks live, two hundred acres, paid for it with cash he'd saved, more'n a hunderd pounds. That's more'n Dan'l Johnston's likely to do. What money he earns is spent instead of saved."

"Mebbe Tom Lincoln is slow," said Mrs. Bush, "but he's right dependable. If he weren't they wouldn't have hired him to guard that counterfeiter James Wilson at the jail. Watched him for six days, he did. And they've made him a juryman, too. When your brother Elijah was plaintiff and they decided the suit in his favor, and agin when Isaac brought that suit against the Shaws for assault and battery. Only folks well thought of and dependable are put on the jury."

Nancy listened, flushed with excitement, her mind fully absorbing only one disclosure in the conversation, that Thomas Lincoln was still in town. No, two, for her eyes flew to the cupboard indicated, noting with satisfaction that it was sturdy and of good workmanship. Later, when no one was looking, she ran her fingers over the fine-grained cherry wood, finding it smooth to the touch. And there were decorations, fluted strips attached to the jamb facings, with a six-pointed star inlaid at the top of each one.

"Is that all you brought, that gray linen?" demanded Sally as they made ready for the play party. "You need more color with your dark complexion. Here! Wear this waist I dyed yellow with peach leaves and smartweed, and this skirt. I colored the yarn green with bark of blackjack and added a nubbin of alum before dousin'. There! You look like a blossom of yellow flag. You'll have all the young men crowdin' round like honey bees. See, look at yourself!"

Nancy gazed into the shining pewter plate held in front of her. Distorted though it was, the face looked not unattractive. The hazel eyes were sparkling, and the dark hair circled the thin cheeks and

high forehead like a cloud of fine-spun silk. She didn't want all the
young men to look at her with admiration . . . only one.

Major Helm's house was breathtakingly splendid. Fifty feet long
and twenty wide, it had two high stories of brick. It had been two
years in the building, and the major had ridden on his horse to Lex-
ington, ninety miles, returning with a pair of saddlebags filled with
thirty pounds of wrought single nails. The room where the party was
held was wainscoted with black walnut, its floors laid on massive
beams of blue ash. Its walls, plastered an inch thick, were so smooth
you could see your face in them. But Nancy saw little of its splendor.
She was searching its swarming occupants, looking for a figure, a
face, a shock of black unruly hair. He saw her first.

"Wal, I been wonderin' whar you been keepin' yourself. Seen your
uncle, and he told me you was livin' with them out at Nolin. Looked
for you at all the play parties since I come here. Where you been?"

"I—I've been busy," Nancy replied faintly.

The fiddlers started another rollicking tune, and the play resumed.
Nancy recognized the game, called "Skip to My Loo." It was natural
that Tom Lincoln, standing by her side, should swing her into line.
Every young man had a partner except one, who was "It." All sang
the song as they went through the motions.

> *"Pretty as a red bird, skip to m' loo,*
> *Pretty as a red bird, skip to m' loo,*
> *Skip t' m' loo, my darlin'.*
> *Come again, skip t' m' loo,*
> *Come again, skip t' m' loo,*
> *Skip t' m' loo, my darlin'."*

Stocky though he was, Tom Lincoln was light and graceful in motion. Nancy felt herself spun about, lifted off her feet, helpless as a
leaf blown by a strong wind. Her head swam dizzily but whether
from the whirling motion or the pulsing consciousness of the firm
hands holding her own, she could not have told. Finally the moment
came when it was time for the young man who was "It" to steal his
bride.

> *"I'll get another one, skip t' m' loo,*
> *I'll get another one, skip t' m' loo,*
> *I'll get another one, skip t' m' loo,*
> *Skip t' m' loo, my darlin'."*

Her hands were dropped, and there was a wild scramble for new partners, leaving the unsuccessful stealer as "It." Nancy found her hands held, but this time not in a strong grip which sent currents of warm vibrations pulsing through her body. She moved through the sequences mechanically. Tom Lincoln, she noted, had chosen Sally for his new partner.

The games continued. There came one in which two chairs were placed side by side but facing in opposite directions. A girl was seated in one of them, and the music began, the crowd circling about her.

> *"There was a young lady sat down to sleep,*
> *Sat down to sleep, sat down to sleep,*
> *There was a young lady sat down to sleep,*
>   *So earlye in the morning.*
> *She wants a young man to keep her awake . . ."*

The girl whispered a name in the ear of a "confidante," and the song continued.

> *"Mr. Dan Johnston his name shall be,*
> *His name shall be, his name shall be,*
> *Mr. Dan Johnston his name shall be,*
>   *So earlye in the morning."*

A handsome young man took his place in the empty chair, and after a brief interlude of music the girl left him, and the game went on, Daniel Johnston without a moment's hesitation choosing Sally. But, Nancy noted with a queer sense of relief, Sally did not choose Tom Lincoln. She was excited but horrified when her own name was called.

> *"Nancy Sparrow her name shall be . . ."*

The young man calling her name was from Nolin, where she was often known as "Sparrow." Blushing with discomfiture, she took her seat in the chair beside him.

> *"There was a young lady sat down to sleep . . .*
>
> *She wants a young man to keep her awake . . .*
>
> *Oh, write his name down and send it by me,*
> *And send it by me, and send it by me,*
> *Write his name down and send it by me,*
>   *So earlye in the morning."*

Blindly Nancy reached out and chose the nearest girl as her "confidante." Her mind again whirled, and there was an embarrassing pause. Dared she choose him? Perhaps he would consider her too bold. She tried to think of another name but could not. Finally she whispered in the girl's ear, and the game went on.

>*"Mr. Tom Lincoln his name shall be . . ."*

"Good," he said, sitting down beside her. "I been hopin' somebody'd be foolish enough to choose me. Gives me a chance to choose."

The musical interlude ended, she escaped, cheeks burning with the embarrassment of feeling all eyes upon her. Fleeing to the edge of the circling players, she came face to face with a dim image of herself, reflected in the smooth plastered wall. It was her first experience of seeing herself so, from head to foot, for few pioneer cabins possessed mirrors, and she caught her breath in wonder. Yes, she did look like a blossom of yellow flag, the golden petals rising out of long slender green leaves. She felt the tension ebb out of her body as if a cooling breeze had risen from the wet land where the flags grow. Words of the song came from a distance.

>*"There was a young gentleman sat down to sleep,*
>   *Sat down to sleep . . .*
>
>*He wants a young lady to keep him awake . . .*
>   *So earlye in the morning. . . .*
>
>*Oh, write her name down and send it by me . . ."*

But then she quickened to attention.

>*"Miss Sally Bush her name shall be,*
>   *Her name shall be, her name shall be . . ."*

So Tom Lincoln had chosen Sally.

= 6 =

The years 1803 . . . 1804 . . . 1805. They meant for Nancy only a passing of time, a waiting, but for what she did not know. When Uncle Thomas decided in the autumn of 1803 to move back to Mercer County, she felt as if winter with its intense cold and dreariness had already arrived. She had come to love the country around Nolin Creek, its friendly neighbors, its monthly church services, its play parties, cabin-raisings, husking bees—and especially its proximity to Elizabethtown. Even the prospect of seeing Lucy Sparrow again aroused only slight anticipation. The bond that united them had been cut long ago at her birth. There were others with whom she had much stronger ties.

But she was not to go to Mercer County, after all. On the way they stopped at the farms on Beech Fork to visit Aunt Rachel, still living with Ned in the old home, and the other Berry cousins. Richard begged her to stay.

"You should never have left us," he insisted. "Remember, I'm your guardian, and Beech Fork should be your home. Mother needs you. She says the house has never been the same since you left. And you can see she's failing."

Nancy yielded gratefully. Dennis, now four, was no longer in need of her care, and she had long worried over her dependence on Uncle Thomas. Embarked on this new venture he would find it difficult enough to support a family of three. Parting with the Sparrows was painful. They were the closest to parents she had ever known. Yet even with them, as in all other relationships, she had no sense of actual belonging. She stayed with Aunt Rachel until her death in 1804, then made her home with Cousin Richard and Polly.

They were contented, if not happy years, and they brought the satisfaction of full independence from charity. Her reputation as skilled spinner, weaver, and seamstress soon spread beyond the Berry households, and her services were in demand throughout the neighborhood. Occasionally she was hired by a family for a week or longer, to spin and weave, sew wedding or funeral clothes. It was discovered also that she had other talents. Thanks to Old Richard Berry, she could read. Where there was a Bible or some other book in a household she often gathered the children around her and read to them, even attempting to teach them their letters. To her delight there were books in many of the homes. Cousin Richard had his father's Bible. Joanna Brumfield was proud of the Bible she had bought back in 1800, boasting that she had paid a whole pound, four shillings, and sixpence for it. In 1804 Cousin Francis brought home a dictionary which he had purchased for sixteen shillings, the only book in evidence at a sale he had attended. Nancy pored over it for hours, exulting in every new word and trying to absorb its meaning.

Among the homes where she worked were those of the Lincolns, Mordecai and Josiah, and of her cousin Joanna Brumfield, whose son William had married Nancy Lincoln. She looked forward eagerly to such visits, for they often yielded news of their Elizabethtown relatives. Like the Berrys, all these families were prosperous, with excellent farms, comfortable homes, some with two stories, and a fair amount of property, though, unlike the Berrys, the Lincolns did not own slaves. Mordecai, who had married Mary Mudd, daughter of a well-to-do settler, was becoming an important man in Washington County, serving it as sheriff. He had three sons and three daughters, whose clothing needs kept Nancy engaged for weeks at a time.

Bersheba, she learned, was still living with her daughter Mary Crume on Mill Creek, near the Brumfields' farm. Thomas also had bought land on Mill Creek, as perhaps Nancy knew, since he had made the purchase before she left the neighborhood.

"Yes," murmured Nancy, sucking the finger she had suddenly pricked, careful that the blood should not soil the fine linen on which she was working. She waited tensely, hoping for more news but hesitant to ask. It came.

"But he's not livin' on his farm, I hear. Too busy doin' carpenterin' in Elizabethtown and other places. And I hear he's got a partner now, our cousin Joseph Hanks, who came back from Virginny. Your uncle, Nancy. You must have known him well."

"Yes," said Nancy. There! The finger seemed to have stopped

bleeding, and bending her head low to hide her hot cheeks, she continued her meticulous, even stitching.

"It's funny," commented one of Mordecai's daughters, "that Tom don't get himself married. He must be at least twenty-five, and I reckon he earns enough with his carpenterin' to support a family."

Occasionally during the three years Tom Lincoln came to visit his brothers, and always, if he did not find her at one of the Lincoln homes, he would turn up wherever she happened to be staying. "It isn't that he comes to see me." She was careful to stifle each surge of hope. "Or if he does, it's because he's kind and knows I'm homesick for news of Nolin and Elizabethtown." He came in the spring of 1805 when the land was struggling to emerge from the throes of an exceptionally cold and devastating winter.

"Wal," greeted Cousin Richard, at whose home Nancy was then staying, "the carpenterin' must be a right good business to deck you out so handsome."

Tom gave a sheepish laugh. "I s'pose you mean the new beaver hat and mebbe the suspenders. I reckon I spent more'n I should—$8.75 for the hat and $2.19 for the suspenders. But we've got a good store in E-town, and I got tempted."

"Looks like it," Cousin Richard returned dryly. "*Silk* suspenders! City wear! We don't get stuff like that in Springfield."

"Our merchants are right busy," agreed Tom with obvious pride. "Bring teams over the mountains to Pittsburgh, then float the goods down the Ohio on a flatboat, landin' at the mouth of Salt River. Then they send off a messenger to the clerk callin' for eight or ten wagons, and you should see the excitement when the stuff arrives. You remember the store, Nancy, log house at corner of the public square, Bleakley and Montgomery's? They come about 1801, been in the Irish rebellion, in prison. Had to flee Ireland to save their skins."

Nancy nodded. She always felt tongue-tied when Tom arrived. Cousin Richard grinned. He looked slyly from Tom to Nancy. "*Silk* suspenders! Mebbe preenin' yourself like a lovebird, lookin' for a mate. And about time, I should say."

"No, no," disclaimed Tom hastily, his round cheeks turning fiery red. "Nothin' like that, sir."

"Oh, please don't, Cousin Richard!" Nancy wanted to cry out. "You'll frighten him away so he won't come again. You think he comes to see me, but he doesn't. There's a girl, a beautiful girl, that I think he's in love with back in Elizabethtown."

"Tell us what's been happenin'," she urged Tom in a swift attempt to change the subject. "Did—did you have a hard winter like we did?"

Did they! Tom needed no further invitation to launch into a story. His big body lounging on a stool, rough buckskin trousers and linsey-woolsey shirt in odd contrast to the bright silk suspenders, he was soon regaling the family with a droll account of one winter day. Remember that Friday, did they, when it was so cold some cows froze to death? "Wal, Sam Haycraft's sons, young Sam and his brother, was sent down in their basement to beat a mess of hominy, that bein' their cookin' department with a fireplace near seven feet wide. They was dividin' the work atwixt 'em, usin' a pestle with an iron wedge inserted, a hundred licks to each boy. Corn was in water. They kep' pourin' in more water, hot, but it froze soon as it hit the corn, hard as a hunk of ice. Next day they cut it with an ax, put it in a pot over the hot fire, boiled it for two hours, and only then could they put it in the mortar an' finish it."

Tom had news of his own too, divulged with mingled modesty and pride. At the March term of court he had been appointed one of the patrollers for the northern district of Hardin County, to serve for three months. He had to hurry home to assume this responsibility. Christopher Bush was to be captain of the patrol.

"And how are the Bushes?" asked Nancy eagerly.

Tom looked self-conscious. He reverted to his usual slow measured speech. Hannah was married to Ichabod Radley, a man from the East, right well educated so he taught school. Rachel, Hannah's sister, was likely to marry Samuel Smallwood. His own friend Isaac— Here Tom's speech quickened, presaging another story. Nancy knew how strong and bold all the Bush men were, never shunned a fight or cried "Enough." Well, Isaac had got into a quarrel with Elijah Hardin and got himself shot. The doctor had had to cut out the bullet. And what did Isaac do? Let himself be tied? Not he. He had lain down on a bench with a musket ball in his mouth, and he'd chewed the ball to pieces while the doctor cut a hole in him nine inches long and an inch deep before they got to the bullet. And would you believe it, he had never once cried out or winced!

"And—and Sally?" asked Nancy quietly after the exclamations of shock and admiration had subsided.

She had her answer in his sudden flush and brightening eyes even before he spoke. Sally was fine. He had seen her just a day or two ago. And she was more beautiful than ever. She had sent her love to Nancy and wanted very much to see her.

Thomas Lincoln did not come to Beech Fork again that summer. As Nancy went from one Lincoln house to another, spinning, weaving, sewing, fingers growing calloused as the fine linens of summer gave place to the coarse linsey-woolseys for the coming winter, she listened eagerly for mention of his name. It came finally when the William Brumfields came to visit. It was autumn, the time for visiting, when crops had been gathered, potatoes and beans "holed up," corn stored, cabin cracks rechinked—the brief hiatus in activity before winter snow and cold made traveling difficult.

Nancy Brumfield was full of news. Her mother Bersheba was well and living with them on Mill Creek on the farm Tom had bought. Mary and her husband Ralph Crume had moved to Breckinridge County. Cousin Joseph Hanks was doing well carpentering in Elizabethtown with her brother Tom, and Tom himself . . . Nancy's heart seemed to stop beating while she waited.

"Tom," the voice continued, "is buildin' himself a cabin, a right good one, in E-town. Looks as if he's fixin' to git himself married, and it's about time, him bein' twenty-seven or more. Folks say he's courtin' the daughter of a farmer nearby named Christopher Bush, a pretty girl and smart, but she seems sort of young for Tom, not more'n seventeen."

Winter came. Perhaps for Nancy it started at that moment, though, as with the sewing of the linsey-woolseys, she had been long preparing for it. Not that winter had ever been an unhappy time. She loved its whiteness, its sparkle, the snugness of a cabin with its glowing fire, even the buffeting winds that taxed every gasping breath and straining muscle. She was not unhappy now. Day followed day, each with its allotment of duties. The only thing lacking was a sense of waiting, a looking forward to spring.

But spring came, its forerunners bringing February mists and rushing waters and mud and the smell of wakening earth, bringing also, by a horseman who was passing through, a letter. "You mean—it's for me?" Nancy regarded the strange object in disbelief.

"That's your name on the envelope," assured Cousin Richard. "Why don't you open it?"

She did so, hands trembling. The paper inside was covered with meaningless black marks. Though she could read printed words, she had never learned to write, even her own name, and script like this was unintelligible.

"Here. Let me read it to you. It's from your friend Sally."

"Sally?" Nancy was even more bewildered. Sally could neither read nor write.

" 'Dear Nancy,' " read Cousin Richard, " 'Hannah's husband Ichabod is writing this for me. I want you to know that I am being married on the thirteenth of March. I wish you could be here, for you are my best friend. I would like you to stand up with me, but I suppose that is impossible. I am very much in love. I hope you will be as happy sometime as I am. Your friend, Sally.' "

"Obvious," he commented with a smile, "that they are Ichabod's words, not hers. Sounds like a schoolteacher." He gave the letter back to her. "Queer they didn't mention the name of the groom. But perhaps you know that."

"Yes," said Nancy. "I do know." It did not once occur to her that any woman loved by Thomas Lincoln could fail to return that love. She was not jealous of Sally. She did not begrudge Tom his happiness. She loved them both too much for that.

But spring that year was a time for brooding, not for awakening. Never had she felt so apart from others, so alone. Not that she was unwanted. Aunt Betsy, who had moved back to Nolin with her family, had urged her to join them. The Berry households, as well as the Lincolns and other neighbors, were constantly begging her services, and the amounts they insisted on paying, though small, assured her a life of independence. But she was not really needed. The Berrys' slaves could have done the work, if not as expertly, at least passably. She could have mounted her horse and ridden off into the mists of some early morning and, after a brief flurry, never have been missed.

In rare moments of leisure she liked to walk down the path to the river fork where the slaves went to draw water and do the washing. There was a flat rock where she could sit and look through a gap in the trees to distant hills whose limestone flanks could change excitingly from white to blue to purple, sometimes, most beautifully, to pink and rose-red when the sun was right. She went there one day in early March and sat there for a long time, yet not once looking toward the hills. The swollen stream curling through endless meanderings, moving restlessly yet never seeming to know where it was going, seemed more in accord with her mood than hills one would never have a chance to climb.

Looking up, she saw a figure coming down the path, the figure of a man moving slowly, deliberately but purposefully, as if, unlike the stream, he knew where he was going. Her quickened pulses told her his identity even before she could see his features.

"Hello, Nancy Hanks," he said. "They told me I might find you here."

"Hello, Thomas Lincoln," she returned, her voice, she hoped, coolly steady. He had come, she supposed, to tell his brothers and their families about his coming marriage, and he had obviously dressed for the important occasion, for he was wearing the expensive hat, yes, and the silk suspenders, price two-nineteen. She smiled shakily.

Swinging himself to the flat rock beside her, he removed the hat, his black hair instantly springing into lively disorder. A sweep of his blunt fingers only added to its disarray. "I—I decided to come," he began in similar confusion. "I—wanted to get it off my mind before—before—"

Nancy took pity on him. "I know all about it. Sally sent me a letter. And—and I want to congratulate you on your good fortune. I"—her own voice broke a little—"I'm so happy for you."

He looked bewildered. "You mean—you know about the trip, about Isaac and me goin' to N'Orleans?"

It was Nancy's turn to look surprised. "No. About your marriage to Sally."

"But—it ain't me that's marryin' Sally. She's gittin' married right soon, yes, but not to me. To Dan'l Johnston. I reckon she's been sweet on him all the time."

"Oh! I'm sorry!" Her first upsurge of emotion was not relief but sympathy. She wanted to console him for his loss. "I understand how you must feel. It ain't easy, lovin' somebody and not bein' loved back." She almost added, "I know."

His big hands fidgeted, turning the wide-brimmed hat round and round. "I reckon," he said slowly, "what happens is sort of—intended, and we shouldn't try to change it or want to. The preachers

say so. Not that Jesse Head that comes here. He's a Methodist. But
our Regular Baptist ones. 'What's meant to be,' they say, 'will be,
and nothin' you do kin change it.' You know. You've heard 'em."

"Yes," she said. "I know." There was a word for it, a long one,
which Cousin Richard had told her. Pre—predestination.

There followed an uneasy silence into which a whole lifetime of
waiting seemed compressed. The birds were hushed. Even the rushing stream seemed to stand still. Tom cleared his throat.

"I—I been thinkin'. You and me—we've known each other a long
time, since—since you was a young'un. Mebbe—mebbe it's sort of intended—"

He had been hired by Bleakley and Montgomery's store, he continued, still haltingly self-conscious, to go to New Orleans with some
merchandise. It would get him—well, quite a lot of money. He had
already built him—them, that is—a house in Elizabethtown. When he
got back they could mebbe—well, get—get *married*. He finally managed to blurt out the word. That is, if she—if she—

"Yes," said Nancy. "Oh yes!" The stream started rushing again.
Lifting her face, she saw that the sun was just right to turn the distant
hills into a shimmer of rose and gold.

Tom reached out his hand and awkwardly fingered a strand of her
hair. It was one of the few moments in his life when he would wax
almost poetic. "I—I've allers liked your hair. It—it's like cobwebs or—
or mebbe the soft downy feathers of a little bird I once had for a
pet."

Nancy held her breath. And she had envied Sally her crisp curls!

As they walked up the path together, again he reached out in an
awkward gesture and took her hand. There had been little of romance in the halting proposal or the trifling intimacies which followed it, but Nancy had no sense of deprivation. Suppose she was his
second choice. It did not matter. She had love enough for both of
them.

The families, both Berrys and Lincolns, rejoiced at the news.

"So you woke up at last, and about time!" This from brother Mordecai. "Thar she's been right before your eyes, a right purty plum to
pick if I ever saw one, and you never once lookin' up the tree!"

"We'll miss you," mourned Polly but with excitedly sparkling
eyes. "I don't know what we'll do without you. But—how wonderful!"

"As your guardian," approved Cousin Richard, "I give my heartiest blessing. Even though you're of age and no longer my legal ward, I still feel a responsibility for your happiness."

"A June wedding!" exulted Elizabeth Berry, Francis's wife. "And only three months to get ready for it! We must get to work at once." For the first time in her life Nancy found herself the center of attention. Instead of spinning, weaving, sewing for others, she was expected now to use all her skills in preparations for herself. Not without help! All the women of both families were involved in plans and bustling activity. Feather beds must be made and filled for the new cabin, "kiverlids" woven, a whole new wardrobe assembled for the bride. Nancy herself did much of the sewing, but not her wedding dress. That was made by Mary Litsey, a neighbor whose skills rivaled those of Nancy. And with the coming of June, as the red earth turned green with corn shoots, the potatoes blossomed, and the last turnip seeds were in the ground, all, both men and women, plunged into food preparation. Outdoor ovens were cleaned, "kittles" scrubbed, the fattest sheep chosen for roasting. The men went hunting for deer, ducks, wild turkeys. For the wedding of Tom Lincoln and Nancy Hanks was to be the year's big event on Beech Fork.

Meanwhile Tom was making his preparations. Returning from New Orleans about May 1, with about $150 credited to his account at Bleakley and Montgomery's, he proceeded to spend almost the whole amount during ensuing weeks on items designed to bedeck a fastidious young man for his approaching marriage: twenty-two yards of cloth (linen, jeans, Brown Holland, Cassimere, red flannel, plus a quarter yard of Scarlet); thirteen dozen buttons; seventeen skeins of twist, silk, and thread, two yards of tape. On June 2 he bought a new bridle for his horse. Worthy complements to the hat and silk suspenders! Perhaps some of the items were for his mother and sisters and their families, for he had persuaded them to travel the long distance from Mill Creek to Beechland for the wedding.

He arrived at Mordecai's a few days before the wedding, for arrangements must be made. It was necessary for the groom and a relative of the bride to sign a bond with the clerk of the county where the bride lived, giving oath that there was no legal obstruction which might prevent the wedding. On Tuesday, June 10 Tom and Richard Berry rode together to Springfield and set their hands to this bond for "a full sum of fifty pounds current money" with the condition that "there is a marriage shortly intended between the above bound

Thomas Lincoln and Nancy Hanks." The bond was attested by Thomas and by Richard, who signed his name as Nancy's guardian ("garden," he wrote it).

"Now," Tom worried, "we have to git ourselves a clergyman."

That turned out to be easy. By a curious coincidence, Jesse Head, the Methodist local deacon, happened to be in the courthouse that very morning, come to sign a court order in a lawsuit, one of his functions as chairman of the trustees of the town of Springfield. Yes, he would be delighted to officiate at the wedding on June 12. Since he lived only a mile from the Berrys, it would be a simple matter for him to ride over on his old gray mare. Though Tom would have preferred a Baptist, Jesse Head, who was not only a preacher but, like himself, a carpenter and cabinetmaker, had been his good friend and neighbor for many years. Though they might differ in theology, Tom had deep admiration for this fiery zealot, whose hatred of sin and ability to combat it, with fists as well as texts, were equaled only by his love of human kind. At camp meetings Tom had seen him take a rowdy by the collar and hurl him from the tent, then later kneel beside him in the sawdust and pray with him. The wicked feared but respected him. All, enemies and friends alike, poked fun at his salient features.

> "His nose is long and his hair is red,
> And he goes by the name of Jesse Head."

The county court was in session that week. Several of Nancy's and Tom's relatives were involved in its activities. Mordecai Lincoln was defendant in two cases called for the wedding day. Others were serving on juries. And, since both the Lincolns and the Berrys were prominent in the county, the court was recessed from Wednesday to Friday.

The day dawned, Thursday, June 12, 1806, fair, hot—too fair and too hot, for there had been almost no rain that spring. The corn, already twice plowed, was withering, and there was fear that, if prayers and fasting for rain did not soon bring results, it could remain dwarfed and shriveled, certainly not "knee high by the Fourth of July"! But the flax fields were in blossom, every shade of blue from pale robin's egg to deep cobalt. And the roses were riotous with their pinks and corals and crimsons.

Though the wedding was scheduled for late afternoon, activity began long before dawn. For almost the first time in her life Nancy was not permitted to lift a finger. It was a strange feeling, finding herself the center of attention, the object of solicitude—yes, and the butt of bawdy jests, for the rough and ready life of the pioneer did not encourage refinement of language. But there was no place to retreat with her blushes. The cabin was filled with bustling women, scrubbing, frying hoecakes, plucking and dressing ducks and turkeys, peeling potatoes, chattering; the yard was full of men setting up puncheon tables, digging pits for the barbecue, placing in spots accessible but not too obvious the full kegs of whiskey which were the necessary adjuncts to pioneer hospitality—occasionally sampling them.

Nancy faced the day with dread, partly because of shyness, more because she knew what such festivities entailed. A wedding, she felt, should be a solemn sacred occasion, not the boisterous ribald affair frontier society had made of it. But she almost forgot her uneasiness when the guests began arriving—the Sparrows, Betsy and Thomas, with Dennis, now a husky boy of seven; Uncle Joseph, Tom's partner in building; Polly and Jesse Friend and family; Nannie, now married to Levi Hall, a tailor in Elizabethtown; William Hanks and his wife Elizabeth, who had traveled the long way from the Falls of Rough with their four-year-old son John; and, best of all, Sarah Mitchell Thompson, who was to be her bridesmaid. Sparrows, Hankses, Mitchells, Thompsons, Berrys—they soon filled the cabin, yard, barns, pastures to overflowing.

But these were only the beginning. By mid-afternoon the whole county, it seemed, whether friends or strangers, was pouring in, for a wedding drew these drudging, fun-starved pioneers like bees to clover. Some came in oxcarts, but most on horses, which, relieved of their saddles, were tethered to the limbs of the many beech trees. Nancy eagerly scanned the faces of all new arrivals, wondering, hoping . . . but the face she looked for was not there. This was a day when even a much loved pseudo-mother like Betsy could not quite take the place . . .

Several times she ran down the path to the stream, where travelers crossed Beech Fork by the ford, partly to get away from the crowds, partly to watch for approaching guests. She was there when she saw them, quite a company, a man, a woman, and several children riding tandem on three horses.

Nancy watched them come, the horses stopping to drink, then moving slowly, relishing the coolness of the water against their hot flanks. Her heart beat faster as they approached. It had been a long time, years, since they had seen each other, but she saw the woman's eyes light with recognition. Her own were blinded with tears. As soon as they reached the bank the woman dismounted, ran toward her, and once more Nancy felt the half strange, half familiar arms enfold her.

"My dear! My own dear child!" The words were the same she had heard long ago, awakening the same warmth, the same sense of belonging. There were more children, eight in all—James, Thomas, Henry, George, Elizabeth, Lucy, Peggy, Polly. Brothers and sisters? No, she must not call them so. Cousins. They went up to the cabin, where the groom's family had joined the guests, coming from Mordecai's and Josiah's. "My—my aunt Lucy and uncle Henry Sparrow," Nancy introduced the newcomers.

The traditional wedding rites began. The young men of the neighborhood set off for the Lincolns' to conduct the groom and his attendants to the bridal house. This was a hilarious jaunt, with the companions putting every sort of obstacle in the way, piling up brush in the path, tying vines together. When they were a short distance from the cabin the "race for the bottle" began. Two young horsemen were chosen to compete for the prize. At the yelled signal away they went, and the first one to arrive won the bottle of whiskey, returning to his fellows to share its contents.

But the solemn moments came at last. Jesse Head arrived at the appointed time on his gray mare, recognizable county-wide as the circuit rider's mount. Dismounting, he yielded the docile old animal into willing hands for tethering and, red head turned into a flaming beacon by the setting sun, led the way to the cabin. Though the space inside was crammed to the walls merely with the bridal party and their immediate families, the deacon's stentorian voice reached to the farthest bounds of the crowd outside.

"Dearly beloved, we are gathered together here in the sight of God and in the face of this company, to join together this man and this woman in holy matrimony. . . ."

Standing beside the man she had loved almost from childhood, thin dark face aglow, eyes sparkling in the light of a profusion of candles, slender hand enclosed in his strong hard grasp, Nancy

Hanks repeated the vows that made her the wife of Thomas Lincoln.

"I Nancy take thee Thomas to my wedded husband . . . for better for worse, for richer for poorer, in sickness and in health, to love and to cherish, till death do us part."

"Forasmuch as Nancy and Thomas have consented together in holy wedlock . . . I pronounce that they are man and wife, in the name of the Father, and of the Son, and of the Holy Ghost. Amen."

It was over. The couple had been "joined together in the Holy Estate of Matrimony agreeable to the rules of the Methodist Episcopal Church."

The cabin where the wedding took place, while sumptuous for its time and situation, was typical of pioneer dwellings, built of stout hewn logs carefully dovetailed, its cracks chinked with lime and wood splinters, rafters of sapling poles, chimney and roof of split "shakes," battened door hung with leather hinges, rough floor but of sawed logs, not puncheons. How amazed the couple would have been had they known that over a hundred years later it would be taken down and replaced, not in Beechland but in Harrodsburg some fifteen miles away, to be enclosed afterward in a beautiful brick church; that on its rough log surface a bronze plaque would declare to its thousands of fascinated visitors that "In this cabin at Beechland Thomas Lincoln and Nancy Hanks, parents of Abraham Lincoln, were married by the Rev. Jesse Head, June 12, 1806"!

The solemnities were finished, not the festivities. Out in the yard the barbecue pits were exuding tantalizing odors of roasting lamb and veal. Great slices of hams from the smokehouse were being loaded on salvers. "Kittles" were steaming. And soon the guests were being served dinner around the puncheon tables. One chance guest was Christopher Columbus Graham, a naturalist who traveled through Kentucky studying wild life and happened to be in the vicinity looking for roots, and so attended the feast. Many years later he would immortalize its details in a sworn statement.

"I was at the infare. We had bear meat that you can eat the grease of, and it does not rise like other fats; venison, wild turkey, and ducks; eggs wild and tame (so common that you could buy them at two bits a bushel); maple sugar strung on a string to bite off for coffee and whiskey; syrup in big gourds; peach-and-honey; a sheep that the two families barbecued whole over coals of wood burned in a pit and covered with green boughs to keep the juices in; and a race for the whiskey bottle."

After the dinner came dancing, to last until dawn. There were fiddlers, spelling each other with reels, squares, jigs, danced to such rollicking tunes as "The Girl I Left Behind Me," "Turkey in the Straw," "The White Cockade," "Sugar Gourd," "Moneymusk." As the contents of the kegs outside diminished, spirits heightened, ribaldry increased. Nancy felt herself blushing at the pointed compliments, the hearty toasts. "Here's to the bride, thumping luck and big children!" She noted gratefully that Tom barely put his lips to the gourds that were brought to him, and when he swung her in the dances his big hands were gentle, his eyes kindly and understanding.

Relief or apprehension when the climax of the frontier wedding sequence came? A little of both. Late in the evening some of the young women surrounded her, bore her away, propelled her up the ladderlike approach to the loft in the cabin, undressed her, and put her in the carefully prepared marriage bed. Soon a similar group of young men, but far more boisterous and uproarious, performed the same service for the groom. There, while the stout cabin resounded with the sounds of hilarity and stamping feet, the marriage was consummated.

The next day they mounted two horses and rode west toward Elizabethtown, the wedding revelry, including its finery, left behind. Nancy wore her usual linsey-woolsey and sunbonnet, Tom his buckskin breeches and rough hunting shirt, the fine-woven wedding dress, the jeans, and silk suspenders packed in their bulging saddlebags. Both knew that in the life ahead there would be little use for finery. Since Tom rode ahead, leading the way over the rough terrain, Nancy felt free to look about her, to rejoice in bright birds, wild flowers, little scuttling animals. But whenever they emerged from the high overhanging trees, she lifted her face toward distant hills and skies.

For the first time in her life she felt that now she was really journeying beyond the far horizon.

"This ain't like what you're used to." Tom was apologetic. "It's sure a pore sort of place side of the Berry houses."

He was right. The cabin in Elizabethtown to which Thomas Lincoln brought his bride was minimal in both structure and contents. While it conformed to the requirements attending the sale of lots beginning in 1797—a house of framed or hewed logs at least sixteen by eighteen feet with a brick or stone chimney and shingle roof—it still had no floor, the window openings were covered with greased paper, and there were no furnishings except a pole bed fastened in one corner, a rough puncheon table, and a few three-legged stools.

"It—it's fine," said Nancy, her voice choked with emotion. Always she found words inadequate to express her deepest feelings. How could she make her new husband understand that this rough bare cabin was the fulfillment of all her dreams, that here for the first time in her life she belonged, was really wanted, that it was the first place in the world she could call her own?

Tom mistook her emotion for disappointment. "I wisht it was better. I've jist been so busy—this trip to N'Orleans—but we'll fix things, you'll see."

"Oh, but it's fine!" Still she was unable to find adequate words. "It —it's a wonderful house."

Slowly, with loving hands, she turned the bleak emptiness into a home. The contents of the saddlebags—feather bed, "kiverlids," mats for the floor, a dyed linen cloth for the table, candles—effected immediate magic. A trip to Bleakley and Montgomery's at the corner of the public square on the following day, June 14, opened to her excited gaze such a wealth of luxuries as she had never imagined, for she had not been in a store before—cloth (not only linens and wools, but silks, cottons, velvets), threads of different colors, cooking utensils, groceries.

"Pick out anything you keer for," said Tom with grandiose largesse.

She chose only the barest necessities, a three-legged skillet to set on the fire for frying, a larger skillet with a lid for corn pone, and two pewter plates, but Tom insisted on adding a half set of knives and forks for five shillings and three skeins of real silk for three pence, all charged to his credit. The other essential equipment for the household, a spinning wheel and loom, he would provide with his own hands, working in the evenings by late sunlight or candlelight, for his days were employed in building cabins and doing carpenter work for people in the town and surrounding area.

As spring burgeoned into summer and the tall poplar outside the cabin finished sewing its tufted seeds and its restless leaves ripened into deep green, Nancy also felt life coming to fruition, not only in the deep recesses of her body but in mind and spirit. If growing up meant emerging self-confidence and independence as well as the sobering prospect of motherhood, then at last she had become a mature woman.

"If it's a boy," Tom once ventured shyly, "s'pose we could call him Abraham after my father—that is, ef you don't mind?"

"Of course," agreed Nancy. And if it's a girl, she thought, we'll name her Sarah, as I promised. But, oh, let it be a boy, for I know every man wants a son!

One of the joys of life in Elizabethtown was the presence of Sally Johnston, who was living close by in a cabin built on one of the lots owned by her father, Christopher Bush. With Tom away nearly every day Nancy would have been lonely indeed without Sally. True, Aunt Betsy was only nine miles away on Nolin Creek and Tom's sisters as far to the north on Mill Creek, but she saw them seldom. And, while Uncle Joseph was often in Elizabethtown engaged in carpentering with Tom and it was a comfort to see him often, it was not like having a woman friend.

Had she been of an envious nature, Nancy might easily have felt jealous of Sally. Not only had she presumably been Tom's first choice for a wife, but the luxury of her home accentuated the bare simplicity of the Lincolns'. Sally was the pampered baby of a prosperous and indulgent family. The cabin she lived in, the property of her father, while built of hewed logs, had a brick chimney, a puncheon floor, and real glass in the windows. And its furnishings!

Sally's six brothers, William, Samuel, Isaac, Elijah, Christopher, and John, all scions of a respected and well-to-do family which for years provided the jailers, patrollers, and sheriffs for the county, had outdone themselves in providing for their little sister. One of their wedding gifts was a bureau of polished cherry wood with gleaming brass handles and wide deep drawers. "It cost forty whole dollars!" Sally's mother disclosed with pride to Nancy. Sally also possessed a set of real chairs with backs, a clothes chest, pewter dishes and flatware, and kitchen utensils which demoted Nancy's precious two skillets almost to pauper frugality. But she felt not the slightest envy. When Tom proudly bought her a half dozen spoons in August, she would not have exchanged them for all of Sally's shining pewter.

She noted shrewdly, moreover, that none of these luxuries seemed to be provided by the labors of the handsome and debonair Daniel Johnston, whom Sally had chosen in preference to Thomas Lincoln. Here also the Bush brothers attempted to provide for their youngest sister by giving her husband varied means of employment, seemingly without much success.

"That Dan'l Johnston's give up his job agin." Was there a tinge of smug satisfaction in Tom's announcement of this news? "Isaac hired him to break ground on some land he bought on the South Fork down in Nolin, but Dan'l decided the work was too hard for him. Spite of his big handsome body he's always been sort o' spleeny. I s'pose now one of the brothers will have to find somethin' easy for him to do, mebbe like sittin' in the jail and watchin' the prisoners."

But Nancy never heard Sally complain. If she had regretted the choice she had made, she gave no sign. Together the two young brides, both expectant mothers, met in one or the other of their cabins and made their preparations, knitting the little shirts of soft yellow "flannen" which were requisites in the layette of every pioneer baby, weaving the warm "kiverlids" which would keep small bodies warm in late winter or early spring, and of course sharing their mutual joy and wonder in the mystery of creation. How strange and marvelous that their babies would be born almost at the same time! Would they come to know each other, grow up to become friends? If one were a boy and the other a girl, might they perhaps . . . ? But each hoped, of course, that it would be a boy, because every man wanted his firstborn to be a son.

If Nancy had felt even a smidgen of jealousy of Sally Johnston, it would have been swept away that first autumn of her marriage. Tom was a sociable person and liked to participate in all community activities, both religious and secular—camp meetings, play parties, cabin-raisings, apple peelings, log-rollings, hoedowns, and, by no means least, cornhuskings. One of these was held in Christopher Bush's barn at the end of harvest. While Nancy disliked such affairs, with their boisterous frolicking and rough jests, their whiskey, she pretended enjoyment for Tom's sake. Fortunately he never embarrassed her by an overindulgence in liquor.

A cornhusking was a jolly occasion, a happy contrivance of pioneers to get work done as amusement instead of labor. The men and boys were divided into equal groups, chosen by two captains. The corn, pulled from the stalks, was piled in a long oval in the middle of the barn floor, a rail in the center separating it into two sections. The captains drew lots for choice of the two ends, and the fortunate captain chose the end he considered the smaller. At a signal each team set to work, trying to be first to reach the rail. The winners would be waited on by the losers in the feast that followed. There was an additional bonus for an individual. If a shucker found a red ear he was permitted to kiss the girl of his choice. The judges walked around the pile several times, examining it carefully to make sure the two heaps of ears were as evenly divided as possible, and the teams took their places.

"Ready! Go!" shouted old Christopher Bush, and with wild whoops the shuckers attacked the pile, ripping off husks, tossing the golden ears to one side, all to the accompaniment of rollicking fiddles, strumming banjos, and exuberant cheers from the bystanders.

Nancy stood near the rail on the side where Tom's team was competing, her eyes following the stalky figure topped by the shock of black hair. Though his movements were measured, as always, his powerful hands were swift at tearing off the husks, and he easily kept pace with his mates. Once he looked up, met her gaze, and grinned. Sally, Nancy noted, was standing on the other side of the rail, cheering the opposite team of which Daniel Johnston was one of the most boisterous members. His sensitivity to hard physical action obviously did not extend to sports. Sally was looking especially pretty, cheeks pink with excitement, eyes sparkling, black curls dancing as she jumped up and down shouting encouragement to her husband's side. Occasionally someone would shout, "Red ear! Red ear!" and all motion, including the music, would stop while the lucky competitor sought out some blushing objective and claimed his privilege, to the accompaniment of much hilarity and applause. All females were fair game in this coveted sport, and, while a courting swain usually chose his sweetheart, a husband almost never bestowed the favor on his own wife. It was too good an opportunity to indulge in a bit of respectable philandering. After the riotous interlude, again would come the signal, and the competition would resume.

The piles were diminished by perhaps a half when another shout went up.

"Red ear! Red ear!" In the hush that followed Nancy saw Tom holding one of the prized specimens aloft. Even from where she stood she could see its redness, like a banner.

"Tom! Tom Lincoln!" Other shouts followed. "Come on, Tom, do your pickin'!" "Now's your chance!" "Bet we know who you'll be pickin'!" "Ef you can't git 'em one way, git 'em another!" "Come on, Tom, let's see you pick the purtiest!"

Nancy felt her cheeks burn. She wished she could shrink back out of sight, but she was in the front line, and there was no room to move. If only Tom hadn't insisted on her getting this place! She knew they all expected him to choose Sally, for his courtship of her must be a matter of town gossip. Of course he would. She had never felt jealous of Sally before, but suddenly all the unconscious frustration of knowing herself to be second choice flared into flame. She wished desperately she had not come. She wanted to sink through the floor.

"So I'm s'posed to pick the purtiest, am I?" demanded Tom. "That's right easy. There's only one gal looks purty to me."

Her heart gave a sudden lurch, for there was Tom coming straight toward her, a broad grin on his face but a look in his eyes she had never seen there before, the look he must surely have given many times to Sally. To her intense embarrassment—or was it delight?—he gathered her into his arms and kissed her, no peck on the cheek, like many of the more bashful swains, but boldly, possessively, a public act of husbandly devotion which would hereafter silence all such sly taunts of wagging tongues. Then amid more than the usual loud cheers and clapping he ran back to his place on the team.

Embarrassment? Yes. But certainly delight. It was as if she had been married all over again, and in a ceremony even more holy, for this time it was consecrated by love. "Dearly beloved . . . in the

sight of God, and in the presence of these witnesses . . ." No blessing of Jesse Head's, no wedding night, no stirring of new life within
her body, could have sealed her marriage as Tom had just done, not
by his embrace or kiss, but by the look of love in his eyes.

It was an isolated incident in their marriage, for Tom was not a
demonstrative man. In the months that followed he showed his devotion in more practical ways, insisting that she leave such heavy tasks
as water- and wood-carrying for him to perform after his day's work,
bringing home little gifts to aid in her housekeeping and approaching
confinement. In January 1807, two months before the baby was due,
he attended a sale of the personal property of Thomas McIntire,
recently deceased, and bought some dishes, a basin, some spoons,
and other flatware, all for $8.92.

"And mebbe I shouldn't," he confessed shamefacedly, "but I went
an' bought this old sword. Paid three dollars for it. Thought it was a
right good bargain, for another one had jist sold for over seven.
Thought I could make it into a good drawin' knife."

Tom was proud of his tools, which, as Nancy well knew, were one
of the best sets in all of Hardin County. It was the use of these tools
and his reputation as a carpenter which caused Denton Geoghegan to
offer him a contract. The oldest son of Ambrose Geoghegan, a well-
educated engineer and surveyor who had come to Elizabethtown the
year before, Denton had already established an honorable reputation
as a farmer of considerable wealth. He wanted Tom to help in the
construction of a new mill on Severn's Creek just over the original
boundary of Elizabethtown, hewing timbers for a wooden aqueduct
raised to the top of the mill wheel and carried back sufficiently to
meet the water at its highest point. It was the first time Tom had ever
considered such a contract, preferring to do work at his own pace,
which, like his manner of speech, was slow and painstaking, and, it
must be confessed, often erratic. But it was an attractive offer, not
only for the good pay but because the timber could be cut in the immediate vicinity, making it possible for him to come home each
night. With the prospect of an increase in his family and a desire to
be near Nancy during the last months of her pregnancy, it offered irresistible inducement. He agreed to hew thirty-five pieces from nine
to forty feet in length at one and a half pence a foot and to do the
work "in good workmanlike manner." Joseph Hanks, Nancy's young

uncle, who worked with him on many projects, refused to join him in this one.

"Not me. Not for that Denton Geoghegan." As yet unmarried, Joseph kept his residence in Grayson County at his brother William's home and stayed at Samuel Haycraft's "ornery" when in Elizabethtown, but he spent much time in the Lincoln cabin. "I hear tell he's a hard man to work for. Penny pinchin'. No wonder he kin afford to build a mill. I'm afeared you ain't goin' to like workin' for him, Tom."

"I'll risk it. It's work I kin do, and he pays good money."

Tom began fulfilling his contract in December and reckoned that the job would take about three months, ending just about the time the baby was due. It was hard cold work during those winter months, and Joseph's prediction proved correct. Denton Geoghegan was a hard man to work for, not only a "penny pincher" but a stickler for exactness, insisting that every timber should conform to his specifications, to the fraction of an inch. He even looked displeased when during the coldest weeks of December and January Tom insisted on slipping home during the day to replenish the wood and assure himself of Nancy's welfare.

"Is it your wife or your son you're worried about?" she teased him.

"Both," he returned promptly, warning her for at least the dozenth time not to lift heavy wood or to leave the cabin when the lane was icy.

It was fortunate that he formed the habit of returning often, for one day in February, a month before the child was due, he came back to find Nancy already in labor.

"I reckon—he's comin'—our son," she gasped. "You better—go—git help."

He made her as comfortable as possible, then rushed away, first alerting one of the nearest neighbors, then hurrying to the cabin of the most helpful and capable woman he knew, Sally Bush's mother. Yes, of course she would come. Swiftly assembling all the articles she considered necessary, she hastened to the Lincoln cabin as fast as her considerable bulk could carry her.

Many hours and much agony later Nancy looked up into the smiling familiar face with its reassuring eyes and bright red cheeks. "My —my son?" she murmured.

"My dear, you have a lovely healthy little girl. Have you decided what you're going to name her?"

"Sarah," replied Nancy without hesitation.

Mrs. Bush nodded with satisfaction. "After my Sally, your friend. She'll be so pleased."

Nancy did not disillusion her. It was a happy coincidence that her two best friends should both be named Sarah.

Tom did not seem disappointed that their first child was not a son. In fact, he became such a doting father that he begrudged the time spent at work away from the cabin. At first wary and reluctant to handle the tiny bundle, his big awkward hands were soon as tenderly skillful as a woman's. He never tired of rocking the cherry wood cradle he had made, even after its small occupant was asleep.

"She's gonna look like you," he said with satisfaction. "Same sort o' brownish eyes and fuzzy dark hair like—like feathers." Nancy smiled to herself. She did not tell him that eyes often changed color or that the first growth of fuzzy hair would likely be shed long before color or texture was determined. She wanted to savor his pleasure in the belief that the child was a small replica of herself.

It was the beginning of March, when the big poplar was flinging its lacy catkins to the spring breezes and the world was wakening to new life that she noticed Tom had turned silent and brooding. He seemed more reluctant than usual to leave for his timber cutting and when at home paid less attention to the baby, spending more time moving restlessly about than working on the loom he was making for her. Perhaps, after all her hopes, was he tiring of the extra burden, especially of a daughter instead of a son?

"Is—is anything the matter?" she ventured at last.

At first he evaded the question, then, "It's that Denton Geoghegan," he blurted. "He makes out the logs I been hewin' for him ain't up to what we agreed on. And he won't pay me the rest of the money he owes me."

"Oh!" exclaimed Nancy in sympathy. She knew he had not enjoyed the work and understood why. Joseph on one of his visits had put it into words. "Tom ain't what you'd call lazy, but he's easygoin', and he likes to take his time doin' things. Ef he wants to sit down and tell a story to make folks laugh when he's makin' a cupboard or take a day off huntin', he does it, and most people like him for it. But not folks like Geoghegan."

She understood from experience, too. The cabin was still without the promised floor, the window openings still covered with greased paper, and the loom he had been working on for months so slowly and painstakingly remained unfinished. But these things did not matter. The floor would be laid in time. The windows would have glass. The loom would be of the finest, smoothest workmanship. And meanwhile, except for this present unhappy involvement, he was a cheerful, patient husband, a loving father.

"He says my timbers ain't square and some too short." It was a bitter blow. It was not so much that Tom needed the money as that his reputation as a good workman was questioned.

"I'll have to take it to court," he decided at last. "Ain't no other way."

He did so, the case coming up in a magistrate's court on March 27, and to his relief Tom received judgment for the amount due. His entire bill came to six pounds, one pound and eleven shillings of which he had already been paid, leaving a balance of four pounds and nine shillings, the amount he had sued for. Still Geoghegan refused to pay the remainder, managing at least to postpone payment by appealing the case to the county court.

It was the vindication that mattered to Tom. Possessions meant little to him so long as his family had a roof over their heads and enough to eat. Once more he was the old Tom, and Nancy breathed a prayer of thanksgiving.

That summer she began to feel herself a part of the pulsing, thriving life of Elizabethtown, took pride in its burgeoning growth. Walking through the now familiar streets, she recognized cabins which Tom had helped to build, or, taking the path along the creek, watched with fascinated interest the erection of the new mill whose timbers he had hewed. In the town's three glamorous stores— Bleakley and Montgomery's, Crutcher's, John James Audubon's—she fingered the alluring merchandise, chose the few necessary articles, chatted with the proprietors, especially with Mr. Audubon, who knew so much about birds. Like Sally, who had also given birth to a little daughter, Elizabeth, she was one of the town's matrons, expected to participate in women's activities. The two often attended such affairs together—sewing circles, quilting bees, spinning parties— sometimes taking the babies, at other times leaving them with Mrs. Bush, who played doting grandmother to both.

There was time for gaiety, and Tom, freed from worry, drew her into the many recreations of the lively frontier town. In July a number of active citizens petitioned for use of the courthouse to celebrate the anniversary of American independence. It was a gala occasion, with speeches, toasts, dances, games, and a magnificent barbecue—all frowned upon by the more rigid members of the Severn's Valley Baptist Church, which Tom and Nancy faithfully attended. The Reverend Warren Cash, a severe disciplinarian who had moved to town in 1806, spurred the congregation to condemn such worldly pursuits.

"Is it right," the minutes of the church recorded, "for the members of our church to visit barbecues on the Fourth of July? No."

In spite of such prohibitions on levity and their threatened eternal punishments, Elizabethtown continued to enjoy itself. There was a dancing master, Archibald McDonald, who doubled as the town tailor. Even the respected and dignified Samuel Haycraft wore knee breeches at play parties and excelled in lively action. Perhaps it was the rigidity of these doctrinal pronouncements that kept Tom and Nancy from becoming members of Warren Cash's church while they lived in Elizabethtown.

Months passed. Autumn . . . winter . . . another spring. The two babies, Sarah and Elizabeth, grew into healthy, amiable toddlers, delighting in each other's company, to the joy of their young mothers.

"Imagine their bein' so near of an age and size! Though I reckon your Elizabeth is taller."

"Mebbe a leetle. But your Sarah is stronger. Look how she lifted that heavy stick and carried it across the room. She takes after your Tom, I'm thinkin'."

"Yes." Nancy nodded with satisfaction. "Wouldn't it be wonderful, Sally, if the two of them could only grow up together!"

But separation was soon to come, at least for a time. Tom's carpenter work often took him away from Elizabethtown, and in this spring of 1808 he agreed to do some building on the farm of George Brownfield some five miles below Hodgen's Mill to the south. "I don't want to leave you and the young'un here," he told Nancy. "There's a cabin in the crick bottom there, mebbe not much, but it's warm in summer, and we kin git along. I want you with me."

Nancy gladly agreed. Though she would have been perfectly capable of managing alone in Elizabethtown and had during many of

Tom's absences, this promised to be a longer assignment than most, and the fact that he wanted her with him filled her with delight. Besides, the Brownfield farm was only a few miles from Aunt Betsy's home on Nolin Creek, and until now their visits together had been infrequent.

Packing a minimum of baggage into the saddlebags—clothes, a cooking pot and "kittle," "kiverlids" for cool nights—they set out on Tom's two horses, stopping overnight at the Sparrows'. It was a joyous reunion with Aunt Betsy, featuring many exclamations over the charms of chubby little Sarah and the physical prowess of nine-year-old Dennis.

"Isaac Bush owns a farm near here somewhere," remarked Tom as they rode away. "Bought it from a man named Vance. Queer sort o' place, I hear, cabin 'most on top of a big cave, with some fine water they call 'Sinkin' Spring.'"

"Mebbe not much," Tom had said about the cabin on the Brownfield farm, and he was right. It was a makeshift shelter, earth floor, cracks unchinked, but, oh, its surroundings! Nancy caught her breath in sheer delight. It was set in the midst of a wild crab apple orchard, and the trees, every shade of blossom from pale pink to the deepest crimson, were in full bloom. The fragrance, sweet as the most precious perfume, was overpowering. Bless the cabin for its cracks, since even at night, lying on the bed of hemlock boughs which Tom gathered from the creek bottom, the spring breezes wafted the scent through, turning the bare little shelter into an enchanted bridal bower! It was on one of these nights, always to be remembered, that a child was conceived.

But a serpent crept into the paradise, for one day in early May a message came calling Tom back to Elizabethtown. The lawsuit again! He was summoned to appear in county court on May 8 to answer the appeal of Denton Geoghegan to have the previous decision revoked. "I shouldn't be gone long," he told Nancy, "but if you don't like to stay here alone, I'll take you and the young'un with me."

"Oh no!" Nancy was reassuring. She would be quite safe here, with the Brownfields so near. She might have added that the very thought of Elizabethtown with its crowds of cabins, dusty lanes, rumbling carts, noisy mill, dirty brickyard, even its friendly neighborliness, aroused only distaste. Until now she had not realized how much she had missed high trees, broad fields, the songs of birds, and

sounds of little scampering life. To leave this place now she would
have felt like Eve being thrust out of Eden.

Tom returned, jubilant. Once more the suit had been decided in
his favor. Geoghegan's claim that seven of the logs hewed were not
exactly to specification, four being six inches too long and three six
inches too short, that he had overpaid Tom by ten dollars and been
damaged to the amount of a hundred, had been completely disclaimed. Even had it been true, a sawmill would not have demanded
such accuracy. The court order read: "Denton Geoghegan vs.
Thomas Lincoln on an appeal from a Magistrate judgment. The
court being fully advised of and concerning the premises, do consider
and order that the said appeal be dismissed, and the Magistrates'
judgment be and hereby is confirmed, and that the defendant recover
from the said plaintiff the sum of four pounds and nine shillings, and
four shillings and six pence cost, and also the cost of this appeal."
Grudgingly Geoghegan had at last paid him the money due, but with
the blunt warning that "You haven't heard the last of it!"

It was true. Again Geoghegan brought suit in the Hardin County
Circuit Court in June for one hundred dollars in damages, still claim-
ing that Tom had done his task in "an unworkmanlike manner." At
the July, August, and September terms of court the case remained in
the docket and at each hearing was continued until next term. But on
October 3 Geoghegan yielded. He sent a letter to Benjamin Helm,
the clerk: "I have agreed to have the suit brought by me against
Thomas Lincoln struck off the docket. I will pay you the costs.
Yours, D. Geoghegan."

A stubborn man. Tom would have found it hard to reconcile his
experience with the appraisal of the estimable Samuel Haycraft, who
years later in his *History of Elizabethtown, Kentucky* called Denton
Geoghegan "a large farmer, clear headed, honorable in all dealings,
noted for punctuality."

Tom was called to Elizabethtown again in June to do jury service
and to guard a prisoner, but Nancy continued to stay on the
Brownfield farm. It was one of the happiest times of her life. With no
spinning wheel and no loom, housework was soon finished. While
Tom worked for George Brownfield, she and little Sarah ran in the
fields, waded in the creek, hunted wild flowers, listened to the songs
of birds, sat under the wild crabs while Nancy told stories or sang
hymns and lullabies, as much to the child growing in her body as to

the one enfolded in her arms. The swelling of the bright red globes of fruit above her head seemed to keep pace with the growth of new life within her. Surely this would be a boy! What would he be like? Little Sarah had Tom's sturdy, stocky body but her hazel eyes and soft cloud of dark hair. Would he have black hair whose liveliness no comb or hand could quell, that always seemed buffeted by the wind? Would he have the strength of his father like the rugged cliffs springing from this red Kentucky earth? Would he grow tall and tough like the Brownfields' corn, which made sounds like laughter when rustled by the breeze? Would he be unafraid of climbing, like the white-bellied ospreys that soared high enough to escape the hunter's gun? And, oh, she hoped he would have his father's liking for a bit of a yarn and a good laugh when the going got rough!

The work for George Brownfield finished, it came time to return to town. Nancy dreaded the day. She wished her son could be born here, close to the red earth and green fields and trees that would keep bursting into bloom. Then Tom returned from a trip to Elizabethtown looking sheepish and apologetic.

He cleared his throat. "Would—would you mind much if—if we didn't go back to the old cabin? Sence that trouble with Geoghegan I ain't so keen about workin' for folks in town. Thought I might like to try farmin'. There's that farm Isaac Bush owns on Nolin Creek, the one by that Sinkin' Spring. He'd sell it for two hunderd dollars. Fact is, I—I told him we'd rent it for a while till I decided. That is"—he looked even more worried—"ef you don't mind too much."

"No," said Nancy, "I don't mind." Then for once she managed to find the right words to match the heightened color of her cheeks and the swift shining of her eyes. "I—I think it will be jist wonderful!"

PART TWO

Frail Mother of the Wilderness—
How strange the world shines in,
And the cabin becomes a chapel
And the babe lies secure—
Sweet Mother of the Wilderness,
New worlds for you begin,
You have tasted of the apple
That giveth wisdom sure. . . .

Do you dream, as all Mothers dream,
That the child at your heart
Is a marvel apart,
A frail star-beam
Unearthly splendid?
Ah, you are the one Mother
Whose dream shall come true,
Though another, not you,
Shall see it ended.

From "The Lincoln-Child," James Oppenheim

= 1 =

They moved to Sinking Spring farm in October of that year, 1808. The harvests were gathered. Tom had raised a crop of corn on the Brownfield farm for winter. The countryside was aflame with color. The big oak beside their new cabin was a blaze of gold-bronze splendor. The cold, ever-flowing spring in the cave down below was an assurance of continuing bounty even in the poverty of winter. And already in her body Nancy could sense the virile motion of new life.

"This is where my son will be born," she thought as she entered the cabin.

It was a humble place, less pretentious even than the one in Elizabethtown, a bit smaller, perhaps sixteen by eighteen feet, but its notched logs were well chinked, its earth floor tamped hard and smooth. The door, two long wide slabs fastened together, was hung with stout leather hinges, and the small opening in the front wall was well protected with greased paper. The roof of clapboards split from good straight-grained oak, overlapped and held firm with heavy poles, was sure protection against wind, rain, and snow. The cat-and-clay chimney, as it was called, was well lined with stones to make it fireproof and safe. The fireplace, wide and deep, had an immense stone hearth and was topped with a fine stone mantel. Inside, Nancy noted with satisfaction, were plenty of hooks fitted into the stonework and a long crane from which to hang her "kittle." What more could any woman want?

"We'll soon have it right livable," Tom assured.

He set to work immediately with more than usual swiftness and concentration. Driving a crotched pole in the floor on which the ends of a long and short pole could rest, he thrust the other ends between the logs at the side and back of the cabin. Then across this frame he placed rough slats and soon had the bed built, the customary pioneer convenience, luxurious comfort with the addition of Nancy's feather bed and "kiverlids." This time he fashioned real chairs instead of stools, making them from hickory poles with backs, their seats of woven strips of bark. A puncheon table, and Nancy's spinning wheel and loom completed the furnishings.

There was nothing unusual about the cabin. A hundred more like it could have been seen along the banks of Nolin Creek. And the farm was not the best of Kentucky land, being on the edge of "the Barrens," a treeless stretch of land despoiled by fires started by Indians to open fields where the buffalo could graze. But to Nancy its rolling hills and grassy hollows, its great spreading oak above the cabin, its hilltop view of treetops bordering Nolin Creek a half mile away—all were beautiful. And the farm had one treasure that surely could not be matched anywhere else in Kentucky, perhaps in the world.

"Look, darling, it's fairyland!" she exclaimed to little Sarah the first time they went down the path to the "Sinking Spring."

At the foot of the rocky hill on which the cabin stood the rocks curved, making a sort of cave or grotto, its sides covered with gray and green mosses and clinging vines. Out of an aperture in the limestone rock flowed a clear stream which ran through a short horizontal channel, then, dropping into another rounded opening, disappeared. The overhanging rocks were high enough so that one could stand upright and drink from the clear sparkling water. It was indeed a fairy grotto.

"We'll come here every day," Nancy promised the child. And they did, after the household chores were finished, as long as the lingering heat of October made the cool shade a welcome change from the stuffy cabin and the sun-baked grassy knolls around it. But with the coming of November's chill winds and, soon, the onset of winter, Tom insisted that she no longer travel the steep path, even to bring up a bucket of water. The big oak shed its leaves, and the countryside turned brown and dead, but the water from the spring, unlike "crick" water which turned brown and sluggish, remained crystal clear and sparkling. Neighbors from all along the creek almost to Hodgen's Mill, three miles away, came to fill their buckets, and in spite of her shyness Nancy knew them as friends—Enlows, La Rues, Walters, Kirkpatricks, Keiths.

But it was the nearness of Aunt Betsy, only two miles away, which gave the crowning touch of joy to her new home. Perhaps it was because he sensed her need of family that Tom had chosen to settle here rather than on his more fertile land on Mill Creek where his mother and sister, Nancy Brumfield, had been living. Always sensitive and understanding, he had known that no relatives of his could give her the assurance and support of this pseudo-mother. Now they could see each other often. When Tom went to Hodgen's Mill to get his corn ground, Nancy and Sarah would often ride part way on the other of the two horses and stop at the Sparrows' while he was at the mill. Dennis spent almost as much time at the Lincolns' as at home, and in spite of his robust friskiness proved as patient and careful a protector of little Sarah as a woman. To Nancy's delight the Sparrows were sending Dennis to an A.B.C. school held in the old Baptist church at Nolin during the winter months when he was not needed on the farm. Already he was learning to read and write.

On December 12 Tom, who had been renting the farm, completed the deal with Isaac Bush for three hundred acres of land, paying him two hundred dollars in cash. Where did he get the money for this transaction? Many years later the question would puzzle skeptical researchers who persisted in the belief that Thomas Lincoln was a "vagabond," a mere "wandering laboring boy" in his youth, and in his manhood a "ne'er-do-well," lazy, poverty-stricken, an indifferent workman, even such a sorry specimen of manhood that he was incapable of fathering a worthy son. In reality the sole evidence of tax records of Hardin County was ample refutation of such conjectures. In the following year he was listed as owning not only the three hundred acres just purchased but two hundred more acres on Mill Creek, at least two lots in Elizabethtown, and two horses, a year later three.

January passed, bringing relief to Nancy, for she had feared that this baby also might be premature. It was February 11, with just a hint of spring in the air, when she felt the first sharp demands of life ready to be born.

"It's time," she said to Tom late that afternoon. "You'd better go and git the granny-woman."

"B-but"—In his excitement and concern Tom was almost inarticulate—"I hadn't ought to leave you. S'pose—"

"Nonsense." Nancy laughed. "I'll be fine. It may be hours yet."

Tom rushed out. The local midwife lived less than a mile away. When he reached the road he saw a horse and rider coming and to his relief recognized Abraham Enlow, the young son of the midwife, "Granny Enlow," evidently returning from Hodgen's Mill with bags of corn just ground. "Sartin sure," he told Tom cheerfully, "I'll tell Mother, and if she can't come, I'll git my sister Peggy. Don't you worry none, Meester Lincoln. You go back and tend to your wife."

It was Peggy, young wife of Conrad Walters, who came, riding behind Abraham on his horse. She was a fresh-faced girl about twenty who had assisted her mother at many births and, having married young, had given birth to a child of her own. She took charge efficiently, keeping water boiling in the iron "kittle," feeding little Sarah her supper, giving Tom, far too distraught to eat, errands to keep him occupied.

"Should I go and git Betsy?" he inquired once of Nancy.

"No." She smiled wanly up at him. "Not yet. Let's wait—until he's really here."

Long afterward Peggy Walters, herself a "Granny," as the midwife was called, would tell the story of that night, decrying those same skeptical researchers who, relying on traditions, would have made the snug cabin a beggarly shanty, the child's father a neglectful ne'er-do-well.

"They was pore folks, yes, but we all was. They didn't lack things they needed. Nancy had a good feather bed underneath her, not goose feathers, but good hen. She had 'kiverlids.' There was a little girl there, two years old. She went to sleep before much of anything happened. There ain't much to tell of a thing like that. She had as hard a time as most women, I reckon, easier than some, mebbe harder than a few. It came along kind o' slow, but everything was regular and all right. The baby was born just about sunup on Sunday.

"Oh, yes, and I remember one other thing. After the baby was born Tom come and stood beside the bed and looked down at Nancy lyin' there so pale and tired, and he stood there with that sort of a hang-dog look that a man has, sort of guilty like but mighty proud, and he says to me, 'Are you sure she's all right, Miz' Walters?' And Nancy kind of stuck out her hand and reached for his and said,

'Yes, Tom, I'm all right.' And then she said, 'You're glad it's a boy, Tom, ain't you? So am I.'

"No, you can't tell much about the birth of a baby except that you were there and the baby was born. But you can tell whether folks wants a baby or not. I tell you I never saw a prouder father than Tom Lincoln and I never saw a mother more glad than Nancy was to know her baby was a boy. And Nancy says to Tom, says she, 'Now we can use the name we couldn't use before.' And Tom says, 'Yes, Nancy, and it's a right good name. This here baby boy,' says he, 'is named Abraham Lincoln.' "

It was Dennis Hanks, telling of the event long afterward, when he was an old man in his nineties, who gave the sequel to Peggy's story.

"I ricollect Tom comin' over to our house one cold mornin' in February an' sayin' kind o' slow an' sheepish, 'Nancy's got a boy baby!' Mother got flustered an' hurried up her work to go over and look after the little feller, but I didn't have nothin' to wait fur, so I jist tuk an' run the hull two miles to see my new cousin. Nancy was layin' thar in a pole bed lookin' purty happy. Tom'd built up a good fire and throwed a b'ar skin over the kivers to keep 'em warm. You bet I was tickled to death. Babies wasn't as plentiful as blackberries in the woods o' Kaintuck. Mother come over an' washed him an' put a yaller flannen petticoat an' a linsey shirt on him an' cooked some dried berries with wild honey fur Nancy, an' slicked things up an' went home. An' that's all the nuss'n either of 'em got.

"I rolled up in a b'ar skin an' slep' by the fireplace that night, so's I could see the little feller when he cried an' Tom had to git up an' tend to him. Nancy let me hold him purty soon. Folks often ask me if Abe was a good lookin' baby. Well, now he looked jist like any other baby at fust—like red cherry pulp squeezed dry. An' he didn't improve none as he growed older. Abe was never much fur looks."

Nancy would never have agreed to that. To her he was beautiful. The wizened little face looked far more like a tight rosebud than a dried-up cherry, and the ruddy lips tugging at her breast reminded her of a full-blown blossom. Delightedly she found that the tufts of coarse black hair gave promise of being exactly like Tom's, springing back into disorder no matter how much she smoothed them. And when people marveled at the length of the small legs protruding from the yellow flannel petticoat, she smiled with secret triumph. Made to climb high, she might have told them.

She kept only one memory of that night's haze of pain. The stars had been shining.

"Are there stars?" she had asked Peggy Walters, rousing from one bout of agony. Peggy had gone to the door and looked out. Yes, dear, there were stars. It was a bright clear night, no moon so the stars were all the brighter. Nancy was glad he had been born just as a new day was dawning.

Abraham Lincoln. She repeated the name sometimes to herself, thinking of the man who had borne it, who had been young and virile when death took him so suddenly. Then there was that other Abra-ham, pioneer of old, for whom she had also secretly named him. Some day she would read him the story out of the precious Book Tom had bought her at one of the sales he was always attending. She liked to think that the child had been named for both of them, the man who had boldly traveled the Wilderness Road to his death and the one long ago who had heard a Voice and journeyed to a far country.

She was amused to learn that young Abraham Enlow thought the baby had been named for him, out of gratitude for the service he had rendered in hustling after the midwife. "Silly fool!" Tom spluttered. "I'll soon put that idea out of his crazy head!"

"Oh, let him think so if it gives him any pleasure," soothed Nancy. "I reckon it won't do no harm." She wanted everyone possible to rejoice in the birth of their son. She would have been less amused could she have foreseen that some of those avid scandalmongers of the future would pounce on the rumor and deduce that the sixteen-year-old neighbor must have been the father of her son!

Spring came, turning the red earth into a medley of green, the dog-wood along the creek bottom into ribbons of creamy beauty. Tom put in a crop of corn, but it was by no means above ground by the time the oak leaves were "the size of a mouse's ear."

"It ain't the best land," he complained. "I'd ha' done better to go back to my farm on Mill Creek."

But no infertility of land could mar Nancy's joy in this spring of all springs which had brought to herself and Tom such fertility of life. The growth of a field of corn seemed unimportant beside that of a child. As spring turned into summer she marveled at his sturdiness, his lusty appetite, the increasing, sometimes painful vigor of the lips

tugging at her breasts. She seemed to imbibe strength from his growing. She exulted in all her daily tasks—the kneading of corn into
cakes, the baking of them in her three-legged skillet at the open
hearth; the milking of the cow Tom had bought to provide milk for
Sarah and herself; spinning and weaving; sewing big and little garments of linsey-woolsey; making soap; drying peaches, apples,
plums, wild grapes.

But she found time for a few snatched moments of leisure. Sitting
on one of Tom's new chairs with Sarah on a stool beside her, she
rocked the baby. Though the chair had no rockers she tipped it
gently backward and forward on its stout legs, singing to its rhythmic
motion. Usually it was religious songs she sang, sometimes hymns
she had learned from the Methodist Jesse Head, hymns which
brought comfort to souls fearful of the dangers and privations of the
wilderness.

> *"If in this darksome wild I stray,*
> *Be Thou my light, be Thou my way;*
> *No foes, no violence I fear,*
> *No fraud while Thou, my God, art near.*
>
> *If rough and thorny be the way,*
> *My strength proportion to my day;*
> *Till toil and grief and pain shall cease,*
> *Where all is calm, and joy and peace."*

Such hymns she sang when her shoulders ached from carrying
heavy buckets, her eyes burned and her head throbbed from kneeling
before the hot fire holding the cakes of corn pone on the shovel, or
sewing by dim candlelight.

> *"Jesus is a rock in a wearye land,*
> *A wearye land, a wearye land;*
> *Jesus is a rock in a wearye land,*
> *A shelter in a time of storm."*

She sang songs heard at camp meetings, appeals to sinners, not,
however, those holding threats of damnation!

> *"He now stands knocking at the door*
> *Of every sinner's heart;*
> *The worst need keep Him out no more*
> *Nor force him to depart."*

It was those telling of love that were always her favorites, and she sang them like lullabies, softly, when the baby was drifting into sleep.

> *"O Love divine, how sweet thou art! . . ."*
> *"Love divine, all loves excelling. . . ."*

But there were secular songs too, rounds sung at games, old ballads, country airs which abounded in the pioneer settlements, like the song of Fair Eleanor and the Brown Girl, which ended in tragedy for both hero and heroine, as poignant as the denouement of *Romeo and Juliet.*

> *"And bury fair Eleanor in my arms,*
> *And the Brown Girl at my feet."*

Some of the old ballads she avoided, such as "Wicked Polly," who persisted in pursuing pleasures condemned by the church, like play parties and dancing, saying, "I'll turn to God when I get old, and He will then receive my soul," but punishment overtook her and she declared to her mother on her dying bed, "When I am dead, remember well, your wicked Polly screams in hell." Nancy wanted her son and daughter to hear no such dire prophecies of eternal punishment while they were yet too young to understand them!

When she was not too tired she would take Sarah and the baby down to the Sinking Spring. With Abe lying on a bed of moss and little Sarah playing in the coolness of the grotto, she would feel a contentment which banished all weariness. Dipping up gourds of the fresh sparkling water, she would hold it to the children's lips, pour it over their dusty feet, making Sarah beg for "More, more!" and little Abe gurgle with delight.

"If them legs o' his keep growin'," Tom marveled with paternal pride, "I reckon he'll be nigh up to my waist when he gits to walkin'. I sure wisht my corn would grow like that!"

When Tom had to go to Elizabethtown to pay his taxes or make purchases he often took Nancy and the children with him, Sarah on the horse in front of him, Nancy holding the baby on the other horse. The road ran through Hodgen's Mill and to the west of Muldraugh's Hill, about fifteen miles in all. Once they went on to Mill Creek to visit Tom's mother and sisters, and Bersheba wept joyfully over her new grandson. Another Abraham Lincoln! To Nancy's satisfaction she commented on his resemblance to her son Thomas. Nancy knew he was not a handsome baby, not round and dimpled and rosy as Sarah had been. "Scrawny, kind o' funny-lookin'," she had over-heard Dennis remark with ten-year-old frankness, "sort o' like a plum with the juice squeezed out. I reckon he won't never amount to much." But Bersheba's admiration left nothing to be desired.

Of course Nancy visited Sally in E-town, a strangely subdued Sally, her usually sleek black curls untidy and a harried look in her eyes. But her tall, slender body was still straight as an Indian's, and her eyes brightened at sight of the baby. She and Daniel also had an-other child just a few months younger than little Abe, another girl whom they had named Matilda.

"How wonderful that you have a son! Tom must be right pleased." She looked a bit wistful. "I know Dan'l would like one too, but so far we have only our darling Elizabeth and Matilda. Mebbe next time . . ."

The two little girls, shy of each other at first, were soon playing with corncob dolls. After seeing Nancy comfortably seated Sally re-turned to her loom. "You won't mind, will you, dear, if I keep on -with this while we talk? It's a 'kiverlid' that I promised to finish for Miz' Haycraft right soon. Of course Dan'l don't want I should do sich things, but the money helps out."

Tom had business with Isaac over the farm he had bought from him, and on the way home he imparted news of the family. "The Bush boys are sure gittin' tired o' handin' out money to git that Dan'l Johnston out o' debt." Was there a hint of smug satisfaction in his voice as he patted the bulging saddlebags containing the new mer-chandise he had purchased at Bleakley and Montgomery's? "They wouldn't mind if it was jist for Sally, but he goes and keeps runnin' into debt jist for stuff he wants, like a new gun to go huntin'!"

His pride was so obvious and, yes, pardonable, that Nancy could not help smiling to herself, but for Sally she felt only sympathy un-tinged by self-satisfaction. She was so happy in her marriage to Tom that she wanted others to be equally blessed.

There was one flaw in her life at Sinking Spring farm. She missed the church services they had been able to attend in Elizabethtown. True, the South Fork Baptist Church, established at Nolin as a sepa-rate organization in 1803 with 105 members, was only three miles from their cabin, but in 1808 it had been torn by dissension over the issue of slavery, and from 1807 to 1811 there was no preacher and the church was closed.

Both Tom and Nancy had been exposed from early life to slavery. Tom's Uncle Isaac, with whom he had lived for a year in Tennessee, owned many slaves. His brother Mordecai owned one. Nancy had known slaves intimately at the Berrys'. But both had grown up under the influence of strong antislavery agitation which was splitting many of the Kentucky churches. Their friend Christopher Columbus Graham, the naturalist who had attended their wedding, was to say of them later, "Tom and Nancy Lincoln were just steeped full of Jesse Head's notions about the wrongs of slavery and the rights of man as expressed by Thomas Jefferson and Thomas Paine."

But the fiery Jesse Head, who was known to have kept slaves himself, had not been the strongest influence. "He don't practice what he preaches," Tom had cannily observed. Joshua Carmen, the earliest and most outspoken exponent of antislavery in Kentucky, had been far more persuasive. Both Tom and Nancy had heard him in Washington County as he traveled from his Emancipation Church near Bardstown, and the Severn's Valley church, which he had once served, was permeated with his ideas. Ten years before their arrival in Elizabethtown it had been a hotbed of controversy, with the antislavery faction, thanks to Brother Carmen, playing the major role.

"Is it lawful for a member of Christ's church to keep his fellow creatures in perpetual slavery?" The question, hotly debated by congregations throughout Kentucky, was answered in Severn's Valley by a decisive "No," and slaves had been taken in as members.

Now, at South Fork, Tom and Nancy sympathized with the dissenters. When a new church of these "Separate Baptists" was formed, they would have attended, but the meetings were held three miles beyond Hodgen's Mill, too far to travel each month. However, a preacher came sometimes into the Nolin community, and the Lincolns often entertained him overnight. Nancy accepted the responsibility proudly, giving him the pole bed with its plump feather bed and the best "kiverlids" while she and Tom slept on the floor, serving him her good hog and hominy on a table set with the pewter plates and spoons which Tom had bought for her, better than many pioneer wives possessed. There were chickens, too, which might be sacrificed for his breakfast, and milk for his corn meal porridge. But pride in these amenities was nothing beside her satisfaction in being able to produce the Bible when it came time for him to read the service or preside at family prayers.

Another winter, and Abe was a year old. Summer, and he was toddling after Nancy as she and Sarah went to the spring for water, picking flowers for her to admire, gleefully rolling in the tall coarse grass. Autumn, and he was trotting after Tom, picking up ears of corn tossed to him and putting them in a basket. Winter, and all at once he was two, his legs lengthening so fast that it kept her weaving and sewing frantically to keep him in linsey-woolsey shirts long enough to protect him from the cold.

"I told you he'd be most clean up to my waist, didn't I," said Tom proudly, "soon's he was walkin'! Now look at him. Smart, too. See how he tuk those two pieces of wood I jist cut and fit 'em together jist the way they belong? Reckon he'll be another carpenter."

"Yes," retorted Nancy, "and see how he took them shavin's I jist swep' up and strew 'em all over the floor."

It was during this third winter at Sinking Spring farm that Nancy noticed a growing moodiness in Tom. In the evenings he might put down the trencher he was carefully gouging out of a block of hickory wood and walk restlessly around the cabin. Daytimes, instead of going into the forest to cut wood or hunt he might hoist little Abe to his shoulders and go roaming about the farm. Returning from a trip to Hodgen's Mill to grind a bag of corn, he grumbled about the meagerness of last season's crop, worrying that their supply might run out before the next harvest. Nancy also worried, but more about Tom's unusual mood than the possibility of hunger, for with his cheerful, easygoing nature he was not a man to grumble or worry.

"Vance ain't paid Mather the money he owes yet," Tom told her one day on his return from a trip to Elizabethtown. "I sure wisht I could git that deed from Isaac Bush. Seems as though I'm always havin' trouble with land titles."

Nancy knew what he meant. His difficulties had begun with the purchase of his first farm on Mill Creek, 238 acres as he had thought. Wanting to dispose of it, he had found that the boundaries indicated in the deed covered an area of only 200 acres. So he had had to lose 38 acres just because one word in the survey had been copied "west" instead of "east." It was a common experience of pioneers in Kentucky, for Virginia had neglected to provide for a general survey of the new territory, and original entries made by Daniel

Boone and others had naturally been imprecise. Now all such vague entries were declared null and void, resulting in lawsuits, inevitable losses, and much sorrow. Long before purchasing land himself, Tom had seen his brother Mordecai forced to try to prove their father's right to his big acreage, with resultant loss of much of his heritage.

Now there was a question of Tom's title to this Sinking Spring farm. Isaac Bush had bought it from David Vance, who had purchased it from Richard Mather, an important landholder in Hardin County. Vance had paid Mather all but fifteen pounds, twelve shillings, and four pence of the purchase price, giving his note for the remainder. The debt was still outstanding when Tom had bought it from Isaac for two hundred dollars, so no deed had ever been received. Tom had known of this lien on the property but with his usual confidence in others' integrity, he had assumed that the debt would be paid as promised. But Vance had moved out of the state, leaving the balance unpaid. Of course Tom was worried. Mather might bring suit at any time, demanding that the land be sold for payment of the debt.

"Mebbe," suggested Nancy hopefully, "you could promise to pay what's left yourself, a little at a time?"

"On this pore land?" Tom scoffed. "I already paid too much. All rank grass and gravel, nothin' good about it but that spring. Now over yander, beyond Old Muldraugh"—his eyes brightened—"I hear tell thar's really good land on Knob Crick, whar anybody could grow a right fine crop of corn, rich, not like this here soil."

Nancy's heart sank. So that was the reason for his restlessness. He wanted to move. She felt a swift surge of panic. Leave this spot she loved, with its beautiful rolling hills, its majestic white oak, its flowering shrubs, its fairy-like spring, its closeness to Betsy, its neighbors she was beginning to think of as friends? But there was the old sparkle in Tom's eyes, the eagerness in his voice. If this was the price she must pay . . .

"Then why don't you go there?" she said calmly. "At least you kin find out if it's as good as folks say."

He needed no further encouragement. At dawn the next day he was off on his horse, enough smoked hog meat and corn pone in his saddlebags to last several days, a jaunty set to his sturdy shoulders, the glint of adventure in his eyes. Nancy waved him out of sight. He had wanted her and the children to spend the days of his absence with Betsy, but she had refused. If they must move, she had work to do. But while spinning, weaving, drawing water, milking, pushing the bone needle through tough deerskin "britches," sewing new shirts for the children, singing to them, she was following Tom on his journey, the three miles up the good road to Hodgen's Mill, turning right on the road to Bardstown . . . Road? A rough, hard, narrow trail leading up, up over the huge escarpment which was Old Muldraugh, then down, down, into—what? The future?

It was the children who gave notice of his return a few days later. "Pa's comin'!" "Pa's here, ridin' up the path!"

Tom was jubilant. The soil on Knob Creek was even richer than he had expected. Why, corn would grow there higher than a giant's eye and with half the work! Nancy must remember the country. Her Grandfather Hanks's land had been in the Rolling Fork Valley on the east side of the stream. And Tom had found just the farm he wanted, not more than three miles from where she had once lived. It was on Knob Creek, a beautiful stream fed by many other streams high in the cliffs with fields already cleared and such rich soil that a man could hardly get his seed sown before the corn shoots would be popping out of the ground. He had met the man who owned it and found he could get easy terms.

"Is—is there a house?" Nancy inquired when she got a chance to speak.

Well—no. The tide of enthusiasm suffered a slight ebbing. Right now there was only sort of a half-faced camp there, but that didn't matter. Summer was coming, and they could get along without much shelter, and once the crop was in he would start work on the cabin. It would be even better than this one, he promised, with a good puncheon floor and a window with real glass. She needn't worry.

"Yes," said Nancy.

They were ready to leave by the first of May. Tom had gone to Elizabethtown to legalize the purchase and had made several trips to Knob Creek to prepare the land for planting. To Nancy's relief he borrowed a wagon from a neighbor, so all of their few possessions, including the cradle and the two precious chairs, could go with them. Tom would travel ahead, driving the cow and hogs, while she sat on the wagon seat and drove the two horses, the children safely ensconced on the feather bed under the canopy behind her. But when

Tom started to hoist little Abe into the wagon, with a sudden impulse she stopped him.

"Wait! Please—jist a minute!"

Taking each child by the hand, she led them down the path to the Sinking Spring and into the lovely grotto. Taking the gourd lying on the rock shelf which lined the round aperture where the stream disappeared, she dipped it into the sparkling water and held it to each child's lips.

"Take a good long drink," she told them, "and remember it. For it's the clearest, sweetest water you will ever taste." Then she replaced the gourd, for neighbors and travelers often stopped there for refreshment.

Even when all was ready, the children in the wagon, Tom waiting impatiently with the animals rounded up, before mounting the seat she stopped to look back. There it stood on the little hillock, looking bereft, deserted, the cabin where her son had been born, where she had spent the two, nearly three, happiest years of her life. What would become of it, she wondered. Would some other woman love it as she had, keep its cracks chinked, its earth floor swept, lie on the pole bed in the corner and know the pain and ecstasy of bringing new life into being? Would it be taken down by careless hands, scornful of its meager crudity, eager to build a more pretentious structure on such a beautiful site, under its spreading oak, above its everlasting spring? Would its logs be carried away, burned perhaps, scattered, left to rot away somewhere, be forgotten?

It would be taken down, yes. The logs would be carried away in time, but not burned, not scattered, not forgotten. How her eyes would have widened could they have followed those same logs in their travels over half a century later . . . to a Centennial in Nashville, Tennessee; to Central Park, New York; to an exposition in Buffalo; to the basement of a mansion on Long Island; then a hundred years after the birth of her son, brought back to be re-erected on a hill near where it was now standing!

And surely she would have been even more confused and unbelieving if she could have foreseen the "more pretentious structure" which would be standing there, a granite temple, dignified, heroic, designed by a distinguished architect and consecrated by three presidents; if she could have seen the path of red clay changed to a long flight of granite steps, could have mounted them, passed inside the six noble columns, entered the spacious interior, seen there, carefully enshrined, the humble cabin where her son had been born.

"Come, wife. We've got a right hard road ahead of us. Time to go."

She mounted the wagon, took up the reins, turned to see that the children were comfortably settled on the feather bed, a linsey-woolsey "kiverlid" spread carefully over it to keep it clean. Abe's hair, black and coarse like his father's, was untidy as usual, and she tried to smooth it down, but it sprang back rebelliously, as if every filament had a life of its own. His dark eyes were bright with excitement.

"Whar we goin', Ma?"

"I dunno, son," she returned soberly. "Let's jist say—into the future."

They stopped at the Sparrows' to say good-by, and Nancy clung to Betsy, trying not to let Tom see her tears. Dennis, now a rugged eleven-year-old, gave Abe a last ride around the cabin on his shoulders, the long spindly legs dangling almost to his waist. Both boys were suddenly sober at the thought of parting.

"Anybody'd think we was goin' to the moon," grumbled Tom, "stid of less'n eleven miles."

Another stop at Hodgen's Mill, to say good-by to Mrs. Hodgen, who had taken a fancy to Abe and Sarah. Then up the narrow, rough, tortuous road leading over Old Muldraugh, Bigg Hill. It was this steep, frowning escarpment which to Nancy seemed to separate irrevocably the old life from the new. As the wagon groaned, creaked, reeled its way upward, once on the edge of a sharp thrust of rock slid sideward and nearly overturned, she clung desperately to the reins while Tom, panting and sweating, his great strength sorely taxed, either goaded the frightened animals forward or turned back to pull at the halters of the straining horses. But they reached the top at last, and there below them the road plunged downward, even more winding, dangerous, yet with a prospect so infinitely beautiful that Nancy caught her breath. She pulled sharply on the reins, drinking in the view. On either side great limestone scarps lifted tree-crowned crests into the sky, stretched out long arms to embrace widening green valleys. Somewhere she could hear rushing water. As far as she could see there was nothing but treetops, forests of every shade of green, like the waves of a huge ocean flowing into the distance, mysterious, impenetrable.

"Pretty, Mama, pretty!" cried Sarah.

"Pitty, Ma," echoed little Abe.

Beautiful? Yes. And terrifying. Her hands still tight on the reins, she stared down the winding, shadowy trail, unable to move, like a swimmer poised on the edge of unknown depths. Tom, already at a curve in the road, turned and looked back.

"Come on!" He waved impatiently. "What you waitin' for?"

Nancy flicked the reins, clucked to the horses, and they started down the dangerous descent . . . into the future.

= 2 =

"Look thar!" Tom made a wide gesture, proud as a king displaying his vast and rich domain. "Ain't this better'n what we had on old Nolin? Ain't you glad we came?"

Nancy nodded in humble agreement. She had felt like Eve being ejected from Eden. Instead Tom seemed to be opening to her and the children the gates of Paradise. Just off the road down which they had traveled was a long green valley with two great limestone bluffs reaching out to enclose it within giant arms. Through the middle of the valley ran a stream of clear water, one of the branches of Knob Creek, which ran north about two miles into the Rolling Fork.

"It's ours," Tom boasted, "clear up into the hills, more'n two hundred acres, thirty of 'em on this level land, both sides of the crick. Corn'll grow thar almost without a man's even hoein'. And look at them trees, cedars two foot through and tops mebbe a hundred foot in the air. Oaks, too, and sycamores and willows. Mountain streams teemin' with fish and woods so full of game we'll be livin' on the fat of the land."

And without too much hard labor on your part, thought Nancy with tolerant amusement, by now sympathetically perceptive to both the strengths and weaknesses of her persevering but slow and easy-going husband.

She viewed the new temporary shelter with some dismay, glad that it was May and not November. It was her first experience in a "half-faced camp," though she knew that most pioneers, including her ancestors, had subsisted in such a makeshift place sometimes for months until crops could be put in and a cabin built. It was a sort of lean-to built of poles with three walls, its open side facing south, its roof of poles covered with brush. A fire was kept constantly burning on the open side for cooking and heat, if necessary, by day; for protection from wild animals at night. They had brought live coals with them from Nolin carefully packed in ashes in an iron kettle. Otherwise they would have had to borrow from their new neighbors.

It was Nancy who had to arrange the new shelter, for Tom was busy getting a small field ready to plant. He had no time even to build a pole bed. They would sleep for the time being on animal skins laid on piles of leaves and grass. The precious feather bed would remain carefully stored in its linen bag until the new cabin was built. The two sturdy chairs which Tom had fashioned looked so incongruous in the rude shelter that she could not help laughing.

"It will be fun camping," she told the children. "We'll pretend we're pioneers jist come over the Wilderness Road from old Virginny." Gaily she told them the story of the journey as Betsy had told it to her, stressing its merry adventure, omitting any mention of lurking wild beasts and Indians.

But the day Tom went back to Nolin to return the borrowed wagon seemed the longest she had ever spent. Though the road between Nolin and Bardstown passed close to their farm and travelers occasionally passed, all were strangers and, yielding to her natural shyness, whenever she heard hoofbeats she managed to busy herself inside the camp. Not so, two-year-old Abe. At the first indication of approaching travelers he would run to the cedar tree which she had set as the children's play limit, wave frantically, and shout greetings to every passer-by.

Tom had planned to spend the night at the Sparrows', returning the next day. "You're sure you'll be all right, not afeard?"

"Of course. What is there to be afeard of?"

Dusk came early on Knob Creek, for the towering cliffs hid the sun by late afternoon. Nancy fed the children their supper of corn

pone, with some of the service fruit ("sarvis," they called it) which
they had picked that morning, finding some of the little ripened berries on a bush close by. Sarah screwed up her face in disgust at the
sharp puckery taste, but Abe ate his with gusto and asked for more.
Before putting them to bed Nancy told them their bedtime story, as
usual from the Bible. Why, she wondered afterward, had she chosen
Daniel in the lions' den? To quiet her own unconscious fears—or to
reinforce them? Long after the children were sleeping she lay tense
and watchful, heart beating hard, eyes aching with strain as they tried
to probe the darkness. The fire's red glow, bright though it was,
seemed puny protection from the vast surrounding blackness. Silly,
she knew, to be frightened! This was not the Wilderness Road with its
threat of lurking shapes and red reflecting eyes. There were no more
Indians nearby, certainly no lions, nothing more frightening than a
timid deer or squirrel or rabbit or, at worst, a prowling bear or wild
cat sure to be kept at a distance by the fire. Still in those sleepless
hours she endured all the fears and harassment of every pioneer who
had braved the hardships and terrors of the Wilderness Road.

Then suddenly into the silence came the pounding of hoofs, not
passing, stopping. Her first surge of panic became a swelling of relief
at sound of a familiar voice.

"Ho, thar! Don't be afeard. It's me, Tom!"

"Decided to come back," he told her half apologetically. "Didn't
like to think of you alone. Reckoned you wouldn't be afeard, but—
wal, here I am."

He would have been there earlier, but on the way he had found a
gray mare wandering in the road, evidently lost, and had tried to find
the owner. Not succeeding, he had sent a message by a traveler going
back to Nolin and on to the county seat, asking that it be advertised.
He had brought the mare home with him but didn't want to assume
ownership dishonestly.

The news was advertised as he requested on May 11, a notice to
be on record a hundred years later, its wording indicative of Tom's
keen knowledge of horses. It read: "Taken up by Thomas Lincoln in
Hardin County on the road leading from Bardstown to Nolin a gray
mare, eight years old, fourteen hands high, branded on the near thigh
but not legible, a scar on her off side, a dark spot on her neck on the
off side, under the mane about the size of a dollar, a sore back, trots
naturally, appraised to twenty dollars."

If Tom's early return from Nolin resulted in the acquisition of another horse, for the owner never was found, to Nancy it yielded a far greater satisfaction. Not even his choice of her instead of Sally in that play-game long ago had so assured her of his love. Somehow he had sensed her need and cared enough to answer it.

Knob Creek was a more settled community than Nolin, and there were many neighbors, some no more than a mile or two away, but Nancy, always shy, made few acquaintances until Tom was ready to build his cabin. Then, after the custom of pioneers, many came to help, like Jonathan Joseph, Nathaniel Owens, Thomas Price, William Ash. Nancy, of course, furnished meals for the workers with the help of Elizabeth Owens and other wives. It was the first time she had seen a cabin built, and she watched the process with fascination, proud of Tom's skill and competent authority.

First the men cut logs, about twenty of them, a foot through and perhaps twenty feet long, for the sides of the house, then an equal number about sixteen feet long for the ends, for it was to be a large cabin, bigger than any they had lived in before. Shorter logs were cut for the gable ends. Then all were carefully notched. She was almost as excited as Sarah and Abe when the four walls slowly rose, the notched logs fitting together so neatly that they formed solid facings, almost without the need of chinking. Then came the fireplace, a huge one at least seven feet wide, set into an opening cut in the logs at one end of the house. The chimney, of course, was of wood, like those of most pioneer cabins, called "cat and clay." The men made a stiff clay mixed with straw or grass, then split oak timber into laths. First came a layer of clay, then a round of laths, the clay covering the laths inside and out about three inches thick. The first section ran up a little higher than the mantel, then kept narrowing nearly to the eaves, when it was built straight up above the roof in a section about three feet square. When finished the fireplace was lined with stones and heated slowly until it was fully fireproof. A lubber pole set across held pot-trammels on which Nancy would hang her pots and kettles. The roof was of oak clapboards overlapping each other and held in place by poles.

To Nancy's surprise and delight there was to be a real puncheon floor cut with Tom's adz and broadax, tools much admired by his neighbors. But the most exciting feature was a ceiling laid across the top side logs, making a loft reached by wooden spikes set in the back wall to make a ladder.

"When you git big enough," she told Abe, "you kin sleep up there in a real room of your own."

Whereupon Abe promptly demonstrated that at nearly three he was already big enough, hands clinging precariously, spidery legs negotiating the projections with awkward but successful expertise, until to Nancy's profound relief he disappeared through the hole in the ceiling. She ran to get Tom, who arrived just in time to rescue the adventurer from precipitous descent and to administer discipline on a sensitive shirttailed area.

"Thar, you young daredevil! Don't you try that agin without I'm here to catch you." But there was pride as well as warning in the reproof. Tom's eyes shone at every indication that his son had inherited his unusual strength along with his physical appearance.

"Mebbe I'm like that Samson feller you read us about in the Book," he said once to Nancy. "It's my hair what gives me the brawn. And the young'un's sure got it too."

Little Abe's swift progression from long-legged babyhood into curious, forever active, and even longer-legged boyhood reminded Nancy also of Scripture. One day as she watched him climb agilely to the top of a jag of limestone to pick a spray of honeysuckle that she had admired, words sprang to her mind. She murmured, " 'And the child increased in wisdom and stature and in favor with God and man.' " Then, aghast, she clapped her hand over her lips. Compare her son to that Other? The preacher at Little Mount Church would certainly accuse her of sacrilege! And yet—*His* mother had been human, too, and mothers must be all the same, believing that their sons were different from all others, designed for some holy purpose.

Though Nancy was too timid at first to call on her neighbors, she always welcomed them with shy cordiality, served them gourds of raspberry cordial or sassafras tea sweetened with honey, and corn pone, or, if it was near mealtime, a good dinner of pone and bacon, with perhaps slabs of venison or bear or possum. But once they were able to attend church services, she began to feel part of the community.

Little Mount Church had been established by the seceders from Nolin who had differed with the congregation on the question of slavery. The church belonged to a group known as the Salem Association of Baptists. Opposition to slavery was not the only distinctive principle of their denominational creed. Unlike the earlier Baptist churches west of the mountains, which accepted the Calvinistic Philadelphia Confession, dating from 1765, they believed that no creed should control an individual's conscience, even belief in the doctrine of predestination. They had no creed but the Bible. They were fiercely democratic, insisting on complete freedom of the local church from any outside control. Moreover, they heartily disapproved of trained and salaried ministers. Education was considered dangerous and unnecessary. If a man was called to preach, God would fill his mouth with the proper words.

Elder William Downs, however, who came to preach at Little Mount, was fairly well educated, having been a schoolteacher. His denunciations of slavery were sufficiently fiery to suit his fervid congregation, and Nancy's early questionings about the institution were soon crystallized into strong conviction. It was wicked, she decided, for one person to own another. But, though she heartily approved of his preaching, she found his habits offensive. He went into the pulpit with a waistcoat and kerchief stained with food, and when he shook hands with them at the door she shrank from the odor of unwashed clothes and a whiskey-laden breath. Tom's jeans and linsey-woolsey shirt were always freshly washed for Sundays with the strong lye soap she had made herself. And Tom seldom touched liquor, certainly not on a Sunday.

It was another weakness of William Downs that roused Tom's disapproval. "Mebbe he kin preach right well, but look at his corn. More weeds than stalks! If the church folk didn't give him a lot, he wouldn't have enough corn to keep him in whiskey." Having himself been inspired to an unusual display of hard labor since moving to the fertile land of Knob Creek, he felt a righteous scorn for indolence.

Nancy preferred another preacher who was one of their near neighbors. David Elkin was a man of great intellect and natural ability, though barely able to read. When he started to preach, it was said, he had known only one letter of the alphabet, "O," and that because it was round. He could not sign his name. Yet he knew his Bible almost by heart. Extremely poor, he also was careless about his dress and indifferent as a farmer, but "at least he practices what he preaches," approved Tom after listening to the neighborhood gossip, "and don't go round fornicatin' like another one I could name."

The Little Mount Church was three miles northeast of Hodgen's Mill, so the family rode there each month on horseback, Tom and Abe on the roan, Jennie; Nancy and Sarah on the new gray mare, which proved gentle and tractable, commendable traits in the estimation of Nancy, who dreaded each journey over the rough hilly trail. But once they had joined the church, attendance was required, of the whole family at worship services, of Tom at the Saturday business meetings held once a month to settle complaints and render penalties for immorality, gossiping, frolicking, "folsities," intoxication (drinking was not an offense), and other sins.

But Nancy anticipated as well as dreaded the journey, for it often meant reunion with family. Jesse Friend, husband of Aunt Polly, had been one of the fifteen dissenters who had left the South Fork church and founded Little Mount. "Jesse Friend," the South Fork's minutes accused, "forfeited his seat with us for going off and joining a disorderly set of people who call themselves the Separate Baptists." There was also a chance of seeing Aunt Betsy, Uncle Thomas, and Dennis either at the church service or if Tom decided there was time to ride to Nolin afterward.

Sarah found the long preaching services intensely wearisome. Her small body slumped on the hard backless bench, and long before it was over she was leaning against Nancy, sound asleep. But from the time he was three Abe sat bolt upright, eyes fixed on the preacher, ears absorbing earnest dissertations on human conduct, promises of eternal bliss, and fervid threats of fire and brimstone with equal sobriety and interest. And he would apparently ponder the absorbed matter long afterward, as Tom said, "like a cow chawing her cud," until a question might erupt.

"What's s-slavey?" he inquired during one evening meal.

"What's—*what?*" Tom stared, a hunk of corn pone and gravy halfway to his mouth.

"I think he means slavery," said Nancy quietly. "Remember, Parson Elkin talked about it Sunday."

"Sunday!" Tom's bewilderment changed to a frown. "But that was three days ago. Dad blame it, the boy's only three—or is he four now? Anyway, how could he remember?"

"What is it, Pa?" persisted Abe.

"Slavery? Why, it—it's a bad thing, like the preacher said." Tom propelled the dripping hunk of pone into his mouth, the resultant exercise of chewing postponing the necessity of mental exertion. "Anyway, son," he swallowed, then cleared his throat, "it's nothin' you need to worry about, not yet."

"Slavery," said Nancy quietly, who always tried to answer the children's questions, "is sort of like us and our horse Jennie. She belongs to us. She has to do what we say. That makes her sort of our slave. And sometimes people are like that, black people. You've seen them goin' by in the road, never alone, allus with white men, tellin' 'em what to do, makin' sure they won't run away. They—they belong to the white men, the way Jennie belongs to us. Now—don't think about it any more. Eat your pone and bacon."

Obediently he began chewing, but the puzzled look was still in his eyes, and she knew he had not stopped thinking. He kept asking so many questions! Not at all like Sarah, who accepted life placidly, cheerfully, did what was expected of her, never worried about things she could not understand, was a bit slow and easygoing like her father. But, oh, how well Nancy understood Abe! How often she herself had wondered, yearned to know everything possible, strained to find meaning in unfamiliar words, been shunted aside without answers! That must never happen to her son, and yet—how long would she be able to answer his questions?

The Knob Creek farm was on no isolated backwater of pioneer life. Though itself a quiet eddy, it was on one of the mainstreams of western migration. The road from Louisville to Nashville ran close to the cabin, and the life of the wilderness flowed along its narrow, red clay trail—pioneers in covered wagons moving north, south, or west; missionaries bound on errands of salvation to Indian tribes or equally benighted settlers; soldiers traveling to or from the woefully unfortunate War of 1812.

Some of these latter stopped briefly in the cabin, sometimes overnight, and, while filling their empty stomachs with huge platefuls of corn and bacon, Nancy listened to weary recitals of tragic defeats at Detroit and Niagara, or to the patriotic fervors of some of Kentucky's 10,000 volunteers, bound to recover the jeopardized Northwest. To her the struggle seemed far away, but she could see that Tom, always the adventurer, was half wishing himself independent and able to join them, and that four-year-old Abe was all ears and wide-eyed.

One day, when he and Sarah had gone fishing in a little stream that threaded the valley, he came home empty-handed.

"We caught a little fish," Sarah reported aggrievedly, "and was bringin' it home for our supper, and what do you s'pose? As we were comin' along the road we met a soldier, and Abe gave him his fish. Now we don't have any for supper."

Abe looked stubbornly defensive. "Wal," he muttered, "don't Pa allus tell us we should be good to soldiers?"

Nancy smiled. "Of course. That was very kind and gen'rous of you, son."

Many years later when the boy, long since become a man, was asked what he remembered about the War of 1812, he was to reply, "Nothing but this," and he would relate the story of the fish.

But it was another frequent traveler along the road that Nancy welcomed with far greater joy than soldiers, for he talked, not of battles and bloodshed, but of the things she loved best, flowers, trees, stones, the little wild life of field and forest. Christopher Columbus Graham was already becoming famous for his work as a botanist, geologist, naturalist. When he stopped at the cabin, as he always did when passing, Nancy produced her best pewter plates, laid a linen cloth on the table, cooked the finest meal the season afforded, and she and Tom insisted on his sleeping on the comfortable feather bed while they spread skins for themselves on the floor. But she found time also to travel with him and the children up some of the steep paths winding into the hills, where he taught them the names of birds and flowers and trees, showed them animal tracks and snake trails, told them about the marvelous ways of the bees that garnered their honey from the huge growths of honeysuckle, widened their eyes with tales of the ancient turmoils which had shaped Old Muldraugh's jagged limestone cliffs and gorges, caves and pools and stream beds, through the ages.

In the evenings, by candle and firelight, Dr. Graham would show the contents of his sack, display the various stones, leaves, bones, snakeskins, specimens of flowers and butterflies and insects that he was taking back with him to Louisville, probably to write books about them. Even more exciting for Tom and Abe were the stories he told of when he went camping with Daniel Boone, how they would make tracks pointing forward or backward to mislead Indians, of the many times when they had almost lost their lives.

"But I like the evenings when we're alone better," confided Sarah, "and you read us stories out of the Bible."

Abe also admitted that for adventure a Daniel who could successfully encounter lions was not much less exciting than his modern namesake who had triumphed over bears and Indians.

Tom's antagonists, unlike Boone's, were not of the wilderness but of civilization. Land titles! Again in 1813 the problem rose to haunt him. On September 1 he was made the defendant, with David Vance and Isaac Bush, in a suit brought by the original owner of the South Fork farm, to recover payment of that note which Mather claimed Vance owed him. A summons was issued for Tom's appearance in court on September 6. Because Vance had left the area and moved to another state, the suit was postponed, but the threat remained, hovering over the future like a dark cloud.

Nancy's sky was unclouded these days. It was during the preceding spring, when the dead world was beginning to come alive, that she also had once more felt a new life stirring within her. Another son? Or another sweet daughter like Sarah? It did not matter. Tom had his Abraham. If it was a girl, perhaps they could name her Elizabeth, after Aunt Betsy. If a boy, of course he must be Thomas.

Looking at Sarah and Abe, she could not help speculating on this young life to come. Strange, how two offspring of the same parents could be so different! Not like the seeds she had planted that third spring on Knob Creek, cucumbers for pickling, cabbages ("Nothin' like biled cabbage," Tom said, "with a chunk o' salt pork when a man is hog hungry!"), radishes, turnips, sage, red peppers. You knew when they came up and bore fruit that each one would be like every other of its kind. They might vary in size and quality but not in nature. Yet the seed growing to fruition in her body, slowly taking shape into Thomas or Elizabeth—what would this—this *person* be like? Not sex or looks, those didn't matter, but *inside*. Would he be calm and happy and incurious like Sarah? Would she be restless and questioning and never quite satisfied like Abe?

The harvest had long been gathered, and it was winter when her time came, with one of the neighbor women and a midwife attending. The baby was Thomas, not Elizabeth, and he was unlike either Sarah or Abe. His hair, what there was of it, was not coarse and black, not soft like feathers, just a scruff which resembled dried-up prairie grass. His legs were not unduly long, and he had none of baby

Sarah's healthy chubbiness. "A scrawny mite," murmured the mid-wife to the neighbor woman as the latter sat by the fire gently wash-ing the small newcomer and clothing him in the yellow "flannen" shirt which, small though it was, seemed far too big for the tiny body. "Mark my word, Miz' Lincoln's goin' to have trouble raisin' him."

She was right. In spite of Nancy's worried care and frequent feed-ing, little Tommy did not gain, and he cried almost constantly. Seven-year-old Sarah, anxious as his mother, sat rocking his cradle by the hour. Abe kept running in from outdoors bringing offerings—a branch of plump pussy willows, a golden curl of shavings, a bird's nest he had found—and dandled them over the cradle, hoping to at-tract the baby's attention. Tom, though busy with his early plowing, often came and stood silently, staring down at his namesake, eyes brooding, big hands hanging helplessly or stroking the smooth bars of the cradle, as if some of the skill with tools which had fashioned it might build the same strength into its human occupant.

Nancy's own slender body wasted as if in attempt to impart more of its substance to the struggling life it had helped create. She made use of all the "yarbs" and other medicines she had been taught to store as aids in combating fevers, indigestion, "trembles," colic, and many more ailments—mullein, calomel, senna, sage, elder blossoms. She moistened clean rags with sage and sassafras tea and gently forced them between the baby lips, hoping they might make her breast milk more digestible. Spring came with all its burst of buds and blossoms, but for Nancy the bright colors and sweet fragrances were a mockery.

"If only we were in Elizabethtown," she said despairingly, "we might find a doctor to help."

Tom roused himself. "That big Dutchman, Doc Sulcer's thar," he said. "I'll go and talk to him. Mebbe he kin tell us what to do."

Nancy shook her head. "But he'd have to see little Tommy, and I wouldn't dare take him. He's so weak, I doubt if he'd stand the journey."

Nevertheless Tom saddled his horse and was off within the hour. To Nancy's amazement, when he came back the next day, another horseman was with him, a young man she had never seen before. Dismounting, he came quickly into the cabin carrying a black bag.

"Dr. Daniel Potter," Tom introduced him proudly. "Everybody

says he's right smart, a reel eddicated doc." As the doctor went directly to the cradle Tom continued to Nancy, "Insisted on comin' with me, and I already paid him. Folks say he's a right good doctor. He kin help Tommy if anybody kin."

If anybody can. Nancy watched in an agony of anxiety as the young doctor bent over the baby, listened to his heartbeat, gently prodded the small body, turned back the eyelids, then spent long minutes listening again to the heartbeat. It was the first time she had ever seen a doctor at work, and the mummery of an Indian medicine man could not have seemed more mysterious. When he straightened she could tell nothing from his face.

"Kin—kin you make him well?" she asked almost in a whisper.

He smiled, but she noticed that his eyes remained grave. "My dear lady, I can only try."

Opening his bag, he took out of it a small jar of earthenware. Fascinated, she saw him lift out a black, wormlike object perhaps three inches in length, obviously alive, for it squirmed slightly in his hand. Bending again over the cradle, he prepared to place the strange object on the baby's arm.

"Oh—no!" Nancy's own flesh quivered in horror.

The young doctor paused. "Don't worry," he said kindly. "This won't hurt him. It's what we doctors call blood-letting. It seems to be the best cure for many ailments."

Nancy turned away, unwilling to watch. She felt as if the blood were draining from her own body. When she looked again, the doctor had returned the black object to the earthenware jar and was closing his bag.

"There, you see, dear lady? It was quite painless. The child did not even cry. And it may ease the pressure on his heart, which seems none too strong."

Before leaving, he spoke with Tom a long time in the yard, while Nancy watched anxiously from the doorway, little Tommy held close against her breast.

"What did he say?" she asked fearfully when the sound of retreating hoofbeats had died away.

Tom was evasive. "Wal, looks like the babe ain't right husky. Heart don't sound quite right. But—mebbe he'll begin to spunk up soon. Anyway"—his eyes did not meet hers—"what's to be will be."

No need to say more. Nancy knew then what was to be. She held the child almost constantly in her arms, putting him in his cradle only when night came or she had to get meals, sometimes even then holding him in the crook of one arm while she mixed the corn bread in the wooden bowl with one hand, or stirred cabbage and hog meat in the "kittle." Other work was neglected, the weaving of the linsey-woolsey shirts and the sewing of deerskin britches, even the sweeping and scrubbing of the cabin, which she usually kept so spotless. She wanted him to know the feeling of love as long as possible.

Then— "Ma," said Sarah, hanging over the cradle one morning, "little Tommy won't wake up, even when I tickle his feet. And they feel right cold. Should I git him another blanket?"

"No," said Nancy. "I—I'll tend to him."

She picked him up as usual, feeling the coldness of him penetrate the blanket and course through her body. Or did the coldness come from herself? She could not have told. She continued to hold him, putting off the moment when she must tell the children about death. Finally, very gently, she laid him back in the cradle.

"He's asleep," she told Sarah. "Don't try to wake him. He—he must have been very tired."

"I know," said Sarah, always wise and practical, "he's dead, like the bird that flew against the window and the animals Pa brings in for us to eat. He's gone to be with God. We'll miss him, but I reckon he'll be right happier."

Nancy breathed a sigh of relief. Sarah would never have trouble accepting life's exigencies as they came. Her credo was as simple as her father's. What was to be would be. But Abe was different, like herself, probing, wondering about the whys of things. How would she answer *him?*

"What you makin', Pa?" asked Abe, always delighted when Tom started on a carpentering job, for it meant long, curling, golden shavings to play with. This time it was walnut wood, which he liked best of all, the shavings were so soft and brown. Out in the yard where his father was working, the boy kicked at them, rolled in them, tossed them over his shoulder to see what forms they would take when they fell.

"I—I'm makin' a—a box," replied Tom.

Tom had made many coffins in Elizabethtown, gaining a reputation for his work. He had charged a dollar for each foot, and sometimes people had complained of the prices, perhaps three dollars for

a child's coffin, six for a woman's, seven for a man's. Someone would
come to his cabin bringing an alder branch cut to show the length,
and Tom would judge accordingly, allowing an extra inch at each
end. The top plank had to be wider than the bottom, since it must be
fastened at the sides and ends, so it was the top that he measured for
the price. But never had he made one quite so small as this or taken
such pains in making it. Somehow he must be raising more dust from
the wood than usual, for he had to keep wiping his eyes.

"What you goin' to put in the box, Pa?"

"I— It's— Go ask your mother, son. She kin tell you."

But it was Sarah, come out to watch, who enlightened him. "It's a
bed for little Tommy, Abe, that is, not reely for him, jist for the stuff
he's been livin' in. The rest of him's gone away. He's goin' to live
with God now."

Of course Abe was not satisfied, but to Nancy's relief he asked no
further questions. When the little box was finished she lined it with
cotton wool, then took some soft linen cloth she had spun and woven
and made a soft bed. They laid the little body inside. Tom placed
two pennies on the baby's lids.

"Why?" asked Abe, but his father could not tell him why. It was
just something that people did.

Tom rode that afternoon to make arrangements for a grave to be
dug in the Little Mount Church's new tiny cemetery. Then he went
on to the Sparrows' and the Friends' to tell Nancy's relatives of the
baby's death. They started back with him immediately. That evening
they and the neighbors assembled in the cabin, sitting up with the
dead, as was the custom. Occasionally someone would quote Scripture, or start the singing of a hymn celebrating the joys of heaven.

"On Jordan's stormy banks I stand, and cast a wishful eye
To Canaan's fair and happy land, where my possessions lie.
O the transporting, rapturous scene that rises to my sight;
Sweet fields arrayed in living green and rivers of delight."

About once every hour one of the women would take the cloth
lying on the baby's face, dip it in a basin of water mixed with salt-
peter, wring it out and lay it back again. Betsy persuaded Nancy to
lie down, but she could not sleep. She lay dry-eyed, glad that Tom,
for the first time since she had known him, was able to weep.

The next day they rode over Bigg Hill to the cemetery, the small coffin tied to the back of a lead horse, and there, without ceremony, little Tommy was laid in the newly dug grave. There was no religious service. That would come later. The Baptists of their association had voted that funeral processions, attended with singing, conformed too much to anti-Christian customs and ought to be omitted. But when Parson Downs came for his next monthly meeting, he would preach a short funeral sermon.

It was the third time in her life that Nancy had faced death in one she loved, first Grandfather, then Uncle Richard, and now . . . But this was different, for it was part of herself that had died.

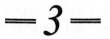

It was a year of close encounters with death. Presently in many parts of Kentucky, including the area around Elizabethtown, a disease called the "cold plague" was raging, resulting in frequent fatalities. The word "cold" was literally applicable, for, starting with chills, the patients soon lost all feeling of warmth and finally seemed to freeze to death. News came that young Dr. Potter, who had come the long distance to visit little Tommy, had succumbed to the illness, and Nancy felt genuine grief as for the loss of a friend. For weeks she was gripped by the coldness of fear, fortunately not that of plague, and she watched Tom and the children constantly for signs of chills or tremors, rising sometimes in the night to make sure the children were warm and well covered. But this too passed, and with the excess of summer heat the epidemic subsided.

It was not the cold plague but an illness presumably less dangerous which brought to the Lincolns near tragedy. Perhaps it was from one of the passing travelers stopping in the cabin that Tom contracted a sickness which almost cost him his life.

It began with measles, which attacked both him and the children at about the same time. Fortunately Nancy had had the disease as a child, so she was able to nurse without interruption. The children soon recovered, thanks to liberal doses of hot sage tea, profuse sweating, and insistence that they remain in the cabin when the weather was wet. But Tom developed high fever and at last became delirious.

"Give him sheep-nannie tea," advised one of the neighbors. "Make him swallow a quart of it at night, and it's sure to cure. Brings out the measles."

Nancy followed directions, and to her relief the dusky red patches did appear in profusion, but the fever did not subside. With the onset of diarrhea he developed what seemed to be bleeding ulcers. Again the kindly neighbor proffered advice.

"Don't give him calomel. If you do it'll unlock the liver and let down bile, and you might as well order his coffin." Here the neighbor stopped, somewhat embarrassed, remembering that Tom himself was the chief purveyor of this appurtenance. "Go out and find a white oak tree and take off a good bit of its inner bark near the root on the north side where the bark is thickest. Put it in an iron pot with a gallon of water, boil it down to a quart, then take out the bark and add a quart of new milk and a lump of sugar size of a duck's egg, boil that to a quart, then give him half a cupful, and keep on givin' him two big tablespoons every two hours."

Nancy listened in amazement. Though she had been brought up on recipes for herbal remedies, this one sounded like sheer nonsense, especially when the neighbor continued, "Some old grannies have a notion that the bark has to be peeled upward and the water dipped upstream, but I don't hold with that. Superstition, I call it."

Nevertheless, Nancy was so anxious she was willing to try any possible remedy, and she followed the neighbor's directions in explicit detail, except for the manner of peeling and dipping. Perhaps the steaming "kittle" was as effective for relief of some of the symptoms as the imbibed concoction. At least, Tom recovered, though it was doubtless as the result of this illness that he was never able to father another child.

As if in compensation, good fortune seemed now to overflow their lives like the tumbling streams which brought fertility to the land. By now Tom had three small fields under cultivation, fourteen acres running up and down the branch of the creek, about forty feet on either side. At least half the farm was on the rich bottoms, the soil formed out of silt and decomposed vegetation fed down by streams from the surrounding hills. True, sometimes the streams went rampant, destroying instead of creating, so the seed, carried away to the creek, had to be planted all over again, but this happened seldom, and corn, beans, and pumpkins grew so luxuriantly that a minimum of effort was required to raise bumper crops.

Abe was old enough now to help both his father and his mother. Big and strong for his age, he could follow after the bull-tongue plow and sow seeds, hoe corn, run errands, carry water, clean the fireplace of ashes, fill the wood box, while Sarah was already adept at the household tasks of spinning, weaving, cooking. Tom, filled with a new sense of well-being and confidence, felt the urge to make this new property more secure.

"I reckon we might sell the Mill Creek farm," he told Nancy, "and put the money into this one. Now the Brumfields have moved, they won't be rentin' it any more."

Nancy gladly agreed. This lovely valley with its encircling mountains and sparkling streams, so clear you could see the bright pebbles shining at the bottom, its oaks and cedars, some stretching a hundred feet toward the sky, its symphonies of birds and rushing waters, its profusions of honeysuckle, roses, snowy daisies . . . it was as near to paradise as one could hope to be in this world.

For the first time in their marriage Tom seemed perfectly contented. He was becoming a well-respected and important member of the Knob Creek community. Early in 1814 he was appointed by the Hardin County court as one of the appraisers of the estate of Jonathan Joseph, together with Joseph La Follette, to be known later as the great-grandfather of a United States senator. Attending the auction sale of the late Jonathan's possessions, Tom bought the best one of three heifers put on the block, paying for it $9.42½, a big price, but it was a fine heifer. At the same time he paid $.63 for a currying comb, accounting no luxury too expensive if it improved the condition of his fine stallion and several mares.

"Now," he told Abe, "it will be your job to keep Jennie and the others as slick and shiny as the trout you fish out o' the crick. And by jiminy, if them legs of yourn keep gittin' longer, you soon won't have to stand on a stool to reach their top sides."

But he was as generous with his family as with his horses. At another sale that year he bought a toy wagon for 8⅓ cents and brought it home to the children, who delightedly filled it with stones, corn-cobs, berries, sticks, whatever, and played game after game—traveling peddler, going to the mill, lumbering, carpentering. Nancy made them a little canopy out of a sheepskin so they could play pioneers going west.

Tom went to Elizabethtown in May to pick up his deed to the Mill Creek farm at the Hardin County Courthouse where he had left it since the purchase in 1803, and in October he sold the farm to Charles Melton, receiving cash from the transaction. He took the family with him when the sale was made, signing the deed of convey-ance by writing his signature, laboriously but legibly. Nancy, required to sign also as his consenting wife, made her mark. (If only she could have learned to write as well as read!)

The long trip on horseback over Old Muldraugh and on to E-town, which Nancy always dreaded, was worth all the hazards and discomforts, for it meant not only a visit with the Sparrows and Friends but, an even rarer privilege, a renewal of friendship with her beloved Sally.

The Johnstons were no longer living in one of Christopher Bush's houses. That very month, October, they had moved into the county jail, for Daniel had just received the appointment of jailer. The fine stone building erected in 1806 was of generous size, forty-two feet long and twenty-one wide. The dungeons were underground, and there were comfortable quarters above for the jailer and his family. Its preceding occupant, Frederick Tull, had died from cholera that same year. Daniel had applied for the position and been accepted.

To Nancy's joy Sally seemed happier than she had ever seen her since her marriage. Proudly she exhibited her new rooms, trans-formed by her fine cherry bureau, her puncheon table, her shining pewter dishes, her woven rugs and curtains, into homelike comfort and beauty. Already she had scrubbed walls, floors, glass windows into a shining perfection which even the immaculate Mrs. Chris-topher Bush had never quite attained. Accustomed to only a single room, Nancy exclaimed in admiration over the space, a separate room for the four-poster bed which, along with the bureau, had been a wedding present from her brothers.

Sally had three children now, and the third, to her great joy, had been a son, born in 1810, only a little more than a year younger than Abe. Named John Davis (the Davis for Daniel's mother's family), he was usually called John D. to distinguish him from Sally's brother John. Nancy could not help exclaiming over his beauty, not so he could hear, of course, but after the two boys, so near of an age and size, had gone outside to play. Fair waving hair, blue eyes with long lashes, finely molded features, he had all the attractive charm of his father, in marked contrast with the lanky, black-haired, sharp-featured son of Thomas Lincoln. They were as unlike as a rough-hewn cedar post and a delicately carved stick of fine cherry. Not that Nancy had even a twinge of envy in spite of her love of beauty! She felt a fierce pride that her son bore not the slightest resemblance to a man like Daniel Johnston.

"If only they lived closer!" she said to Sally as they watched the two playing noisily together. "They might grow up 'most like brothers."

Having lived long years under the shadow of debts, Sally could not help a bit of boasting. "Dan'l's salary," she confided to Nancy, "will be twenty-three whole pounds and five shillings."

"Prob'ly the most he ever earned in his life," scoffed Tom when he heard the news. "And he was lucky to git the job. Wouldn't have 'cept for the influence of the Bushes. And you know what, Nancy, my girl? Dan'l had to git a bond of a thousand dollars to qualify for the job, and, though it seldom takes more'n two persons to go bondsmen, he had to find six to back him before he got the amount guaranteed. And do you s'pose any one of the six was one of Sally's six brothers? No! They'd got mighty tired signin' his notes and gittin' sued for 'em when he couldn't pay. And another thing." Was there in Tom's voice a bit of the rejected suitor's smug satisfaction? "It ain't goin' to be easy for your friend Sally bein' the jailer's wife. She'll be doin' most of the hard work, not only havin' to git all the meals for the pris'ners but keepin' both the jail and the courthouse clean and lighted when candles are needed. The jailer has to find all the fuel, too, and keep the fires goin' at the courthouse. Dan'l may git the wood all right, he'll have to, but I reckon it'll be Sally what keeps the wood lugged and the fires tended."

But Nancy tried not to worry about these problems which, she comforted herself, might well have been magnified by town gossip. She wanted to remember Sally as she had seen her, radiant, sprightly, hopeful, crisp black curls dancing beneath the ruffles of her cap, square capable hands ready to tackle with zest whatever task they might be called to do.

It was toward the end of that year, 1814, when Sarah was seven and Abe was five, that Nancy, usually timid about taking the initiative in decisions concerning the family, became suddenly bold.

"The children," she told Tom firmly, "must go to school. They say a new term is jist startin'."

As she had expected, Tom began making objections. "You mean— send our young'uns to that blab school of Zach Riney's, that—that *Catholic?*"

Nancy slipped her shuttle with its long flaxen weft thread between the divided woolen warp strands stretched on her loom and beat the new thread firmly into position. When there was possibility of tension in the small cabin, she always liked her hands to be busy.

"He'll be teachin' 'em readin', writin', and spellin', Tom, not religion. And you know you like the Rineys. They're our good friends."

"B-but—the school cabin's away up the road, much too far for two young'uns to walk."

"It's only two miles, Tom, and they walk farther'n that lots of times, visitin' neighbors. And there'll be other young'uns goin'. If there's need they kin always take one of the horses."

"But"—now Tom was arriving at his real objection—"what do they need to go to school for? You and I never went, and we git along fine. Book larnin' ain't important for folks like us. Besides, you need young Sarah here at home. She's jist gittin' big enough to help good."

"School don't last long, Tom, only a few weeks in the term, and I kin git along fine without Sarah."

"Wal, Abe don't need to go. He's too young. Plenty of time for him to larn all he needs to."

Another firm stroke of the shuttle, her hands steady though her head was whirling. "He's big of his age, Tom, and he wants to larn. Don't you know how he's always askin' questions, things you and I can't sometimes answer?"

"Then Zach Riney can't. I reckon he never went to school much himself."

"He kin teach him to read, so he kin find out things in books."

Tom gouged his knife deeper into the wooden bowl he was fashioning. It was evening, and the children were asleep, Sarah in the trundle bed and Abe on his bed of straw and skins up in the loft.

"Why can't you teach him to read, girl? You read plenty good out of the Bible."

"Mebbe I could, but it's not the same. And you know I can't write. I don't want our young'uns to grow up havin' to make their marks, like me."

Tom put the bowl aside. Unlike Nancy, he could think better when his hands were idle. "Anyways, I ask you, what good's larnin' goin' to do a lad like our Abe? It won't help him hew trees or plow fields or grow corn and beans or even make cupboards and build houses if he takes to carpenterin'. I tell you, love, larnin' ain't for folks like us."

Nancy's fingers flew. The candlelight, flickering on the threads, seemed to create magical color out of the dull cloth she was weaving. Now, she knew, they had reached the crux of the argument. All the rest had been preliminary.

"Mebbe," she said quietly, "our Abe won't want to be farmin' or carpenterin' all his life. Mebbe he'll want to be a teacher like Sally's sister Hannah's husband, Ichabod Radley, or like that Duff Green at the academy in Elizabethtown. Or—a preacher."

"He wouldn't need larnin' to be a preacher," threw in Tom dryly. "Look at Dave Elkin. Cain't even sign his name."

Nancy might not have heard. The candlelight seemed all at once to play on the strands in rainbow hues like fingers on a harp. "Or—who knows? He might even git sent to the state capital at Frankfort to sit on the assembly, be somebody right important!"

Tom snorted. "I'll be happy if he gits to plow a straight furrow, and he don't need no book larnin' to do that."

Nancy sighed. Her fingers fumbled, and she dropped the shuttle. Tom could be very stubborn. But she still had one shabby thread of argument left which she was almost ashamed to use.

"Aunt Betsy and Uncle Thomas sent Dennis to school at Nolin," she reminded, "when he was as young as Abe. And now at fifteen he kin both read and write. I'd hate to think he was smarter than our Abe."

The children went to school. The cabin set apart for a schoolhouse was two miles away on the road to Bardstown near the junction of Knob Creek and Pottinger's Creek. Zachariah Riney, their first teacher, had bought the farm on the Rolling Fork where Nancy had once lived with Grandfather Joseph. Their second teacher, when they attended a short term the following year, was even better known to the family, a good friend of Tom's, for Caleb Hazel lived on a neighboring farm.

Nancy prepared the children for school each morning with as painstaking care as for church. In fact, the schoolroom possessed for her all the mystery and sanctity of a holy place. Cleanliness, that counterpart of godliness! She insisted that they take a full bath in the wooden tub each morning and made sure that there was a clean shift, the single garment that both boys and girls wore in warm weather for each day, or the heavier linsey-woolseys when it was colder. It took constant weaving and stitching to keep Abe in linsey-woolsey garments long enough to reach his knees. When she wrapped their lunch in a linen cloth—extra corn pone and slabs of bacon or boiled fish in case some of the neighbors might have forgotten theirs—she thought sometimes of the mother who had once sent her boy to a sacred tryst, carrying five barley loaves and two small fishes. If only something she could give *her* son, like that other mother's, could be multiplied to bring blessing to many people, not five thousand of course, but . . . She laughed at herself. How foolish!

"Thar, you see?" grumbled Tom after Nancy had toiled up the hill with a bucket of water. "You'd ought to have Sarah here to help you! She'll be gittin' spiled with all this book larnin'."

He grumbled, too, because Abe was not there to pull weeds or run back to the cabin for a needed tool, but, Nancy noticed, he beamed with pride when the boy took a charred stick and scrawled $A B E$ on the fire shovel, and when one day the whole word $A B R A H A M$ appeared, he produced a thin slab of cedar which he had worked to a smooth surface with his adz. "Write your name on that," he told Abe, and when the boy had done so, he proudly placed the piece of wood with its black uneven scrawl on the mantel above the fireplace, remarking, "Not bad for a boy his age!" That night he told the children the story of his father's long journey along the Wilderness Road, his courage in facing dangers, his untimely death.

"That's who you're named fur," he finished, fixing stern eyes on the boy. "Abraham Lincoln. It's a good name. See that you don't never bring dishonor to it."

But his satisfaction in the children's educational progress suffered deflation when other achievements than writing were demonstrated. "What did you larn today?" Nancy would often ask eagerly, whereupon both children would burst into a high-pitched recital of words they had learned to spell followed by sentences containing them. For, like most schools of that time and place, the method of teaching was that of the so-called "blab school," in which the pupils were required to study aloud, as proof that they were really studying. The one textbook used was a speller, Webster's *Old Blueback*. Along with the words and their illustrative sentences the book contained nature stories about "The Mastiff," "The Stag," "The Squirrel," and Abe, long before he could read, was able to repeat these from memory and did so, at the top of his voice. Tom would endure the barrage as long as he could.

"You mean all you young'uns talk that way, all at the same time? How in tarnation does old Caleb stand it!"

Conscious of Tom's mounting restlessness, Nancy would often forestall his protests. "Come. It's time now for our reading." And she would take the Book from its safe place on a high shelf, remove its linen covers, brighten the fire with spicewood bushes she had cut and hacked on a log, and quietly, slowly, for she had never learned to read with glib confidence, bring the world of the Bible to life in the little cabin. It was not an unfamiliar world. Indeed, it might have been Knob Creek and Kentucky, with its sheep and cattle, its crude plows, its sowing of seed and reaping, its sleeping mats and "kiverlids," its grinding of grain and baking of bread over open fires, its garments of haircloth and animal skins . . . yes, even its pioneer named Abraham, who had come journeying through much peril to a far country.

Sarah listened happily but incuriously, fingers always busy like her father's with some kind of handiwork. It was little Abe who became wholly absorbed in the stories, sometimes squatting on lean haunches at Nancy's feet, long arms wrapped about skinny knees, sometimes leaning over her shoulder reaching with a bony finger to pick out some of the letters and words he was learning, often interrupting with impatient questions. "Why did he do that?" "What does that word mean?" "Read that again, Ma, please?"

Nancy looked forward to such evenings which again brought the family together. Once she had been the children's only playmate. They had roamed the hills, waded in the clear streams, played hide and seek among the huge trees, many of them "three-footers." But school had brought them other playmates, which Nancy approved.

However, she missed the former intimacy. One of Abe's new play-mates was Austin Gollaher.

In 1812 Thomas Gollaher and his family had settled on one of the headwaters of Knob Creek about two miles from the Lincolns. The children of the two families would follow the same road home from school for about a mile, then the Gollahers and others would turn off the main road while the children from the Lincoln neighborhood had another mile to go on the main road. Though Austin was four years older than Abe, they were so near the same size and mentality that they became intimate friends, often visiting each other's homes and roaming the two miles of fascinating playground which lay between—hills and valleys, creeks, caves, trees to climb, animals to chase or (Abe's idea) set free from the traps his father had set.

"We already got enough to eat," he would explain. "Folks hadn't ought to kill more'n they need."

Not that Abe was averse to doing a bit of hunting himself! He and Austin were fond of stalking rabbits with weapons no more formidable than hickory clubs. As with most boys, many of their adventures savored of mischief. One day Abe returned home unable to conceal the evidence of such an escapade. Sheepishly he held out his coonskin cap, its inside badly smeared with a mass of sticky pulp.

"What—!" But before Nancy could finish he had launched into embarrassed but frank explanation. He might seek refuge from naughtiness in silence, and often did, but never in deception.

"Me and Austin," he began, "had been playin' in the woods and huntin' rabbits. We got tired and stopped to rest. After a while I threw down my cap, clumb a tree, and found a nice place to lie atween two limbs."

Abe had inherited his father's love of storytelling, even one at his own expense. His details were graphic. There below was Austin, full length on the grass, apparently sound asleep, his coonskin cap beside him, inside facing up. And in Abe's jacket was a ripe pawpaw recently picked, *very* ripe. What fun to drop it into Austin's upturned cap! So soft and ripe it was that he could hardly get it out of his pocket. Down it went, splash, straight into the cap, sending soft yellow pawpaw spattering all around. What fun to see how mad Austin would get! But—nothing happened. He didn't even wake up. He couldn't be that sound asleep! So—slide down the tree. Surprise! He

hadn't been asleep, after all, and while Abe had been climbing the
tree Austin had changed their caps. So— "Look, Ma, it was my cap
what got messed up, not his!"

Nancy tried to look severe, but her lips quirked. "That's what
often happens," she said soberly, "when you try to be mean to somebody. You find out what it's like yourself. It was naughty, but I guess
you'll be punished enough, havin' to wash your cap in the crick as
well as you kin and then wear it."

It was well for her peace of mind that at least one of the boys' es-
capades never reached her ears.

It was June when it happened, for Nancy a time of joy and a time
of worry. The encircling hills with their crowns of oaks and sycamores and cedars were panoplies of green. To the east one could
sense, if not actually see, a purplish haze where the blue grass was
springing into bloom. The honeysuckle and wild roses turned the valley into a paradise for bees and hummingbirds. And in Tom's three
fields the tender shoots of corn and beans and turnips were promising
swift growth. But the rushing of swollen streams still filled one's ears,
and the dangers of flooding were not past. A heavy rain could bring
water sweeping down over the fields, ruining the crops at a time too
late for good replanting. But this was not her greatest worry. The
swollen streams were treacherous, and a six-year-old boy was often
heedless of danger, especially one bold and adventurous and sometimes careless. The pools where one could usually wade, sail boats,
pick bright stones from the clear water, were now seething eddies.

"Be careful, son," she admonished each time he started off alone
or with a companion. "Remember, you promised . . ." And she
would breathe a sigh of relief when he came running back. But that
Sunday when the Gollahers came to visit and Abe and Austin, as
usual, went off to explore, she did not worry. Austin was ten and reliable. She never knew how close her young son came to death. No
one knew, except Abe and Austin, and as long as they both lived the
secret would be kept. But years later, after his friend's tragic death,
Austin Gollaher would relate the story, again and again.

"Yes, the story that I once saved Abraham Lincoln's life is true.
He and I had been going to school together for a year or more and
had become greatly attached to each other. Then school disbanded
on account of there being so few scholars, and we did not see each
other for a long while. One Sunday my mother visited the Lincolns,

and I was taken along. Abe and I played around all day. Finally we concluded to cross the creek to hunt for some partridges young Lincoln had seen the day before. The creek was swollen by a recent rain, and in crossing on the narrow footing Abe fell in. Neither of us could swim. I got a long pole and held it out to him, and he grabbed it. Then I pulled him ashore. He was almost dead, and I was badly scared. I rolled and pounded him in good earnest. Then I got him by the arms and shook him, the water meanwhile pouring out of his mouth. By this means I succeeded in bringing him to, and he was soon all right.

"Then a new difficulty confronted us. If our mothers discovered our wet clothes they would whip us. This we dreaded from experience and determined to avoid. It was June, the sun was very warm, and we soon dried our clothing by spreading it on the rocks about us. We promised never to tell the story, and I never did until after Lincoln's tragic end."

So to young Austin Gollaher, age about ten, could be credited a small act of heroism which changed the course of history.

= 4 =

There was a restlessness in Tom, heritage of a long line of Lincolns, sometimes named Lincon, Linkhorn, Linkern, Linkhern, and other variants—Samuel, who migrated from England to Salem, Massachusetts; Mordecai, who moved to Monmouth County, New Jersey; John, who journeyed via Pennsylvania to the Shenandoah Valley of Virginia; Abraham, who traveled the Wilderness Road to his death. In Tom it was like the streams that coursed into the valley from Old Muldraugh, for the most part placid, gently nourishing, except when fed into turbulence by a disturbing storm . . . or like the fire banked well for the night but ready to burst into flame at the touch of a poker.

For days, weeks, he would work contentedly, if slowly, plowing, tending his cattle, sheep, horses, cutting wood, carpentering; then something would happen, and his big hands would lie idle on the plow, the restive look would come into his eyes. It was often some little happening that would stir the stream, blow on the embers. A peddler might come along the road, unloading his packs of tantalizing merchandise, bright calicos, silks, spices, buttons, jewelry, knives, razors, weapons, bringing news from distant cities. A covered wagon might pass, or its occupants stop for refreshment or overnight entertainment, eyes bright with the prospect of more fertile lands, free for the taking, farther west, always west. Or his son might ask a simple question.

"Whar does the road go, Pa?"

"Silly question. You know whar the road goes," would have been the natural reply. "North to Bardstown, you've been thar. The other way over the hill to Hodgen's Mill whar we go to git the corn ground." Instead he leaned on the plow or hoe or ax and the look came into his eyes. "The road, son? It goes yander, over Bigg Hill, to a river, and beyond the river there's a place called Indianny, and beyond that—who knows? But people are findin' out."

Or—"Whar does the crick go, Pa?"

"Down to the Rollin' Fork," he might have answered, but instead, "Into the Rollin' Fork, son, then into a bigger stream they call Salt River, then into the still bigger Ohio River, and then into another so big, son, you can't imagine it, so wide you kin scarce see acrost it, and you kin travel down it, forever it seems, past cities bigger even than E-town, till you come to the biggest of all, called N'Orleans."

"Was you ever thar, Pa?"

"Yes, onct. A long time ago, it seems." He sighed as he turned again to the plow, or the hoe, or the ax.

Nancy understood how he felt, for she also had come from a roving pioneer people, had always seemed to be moving, always searching for something beyond the far horizon. But here was the Eden she had always hoped to find. Here in this green valley with its protecting hills, its broad vistas, its ever changing lights and shadows, she would be glad to live and die. Sometimes she wished the long road did not pass so near the cabin. Its ugly narrow red ribbon of clay, hard and cracked or deep with mud or thick with dust, seemed an imprisoning shackle binding one to an inescapable past and an unknown future.

For it was the road and its moving cavalcades that most often brought the restless look to Tom's eyes.

He sometimes traveled the road, on business to Bardstown, the nearest big settlement, to Hodgen's Mill for grinding, though there was a mill nearer the farm, on to Elizabethtown to purchase goods, sell surplus products, obey a court summons, pay taxes. Often he took the boy with him, and Abe would come back, eyes shining with adventure.

"Look, Ma, what Miz' Hodgen sent us, some honey cakes! And she read me a story out of a book Mr. John bought. It's called Ae— Aesop's Fables. She's goin' to read me more stories when I go agin." . . .

"We went clear to E-town, Ma, and in a store we saw a man what wears his Sunday clothes every day, and I sat on a keg o' pickles, and he give me one to eat!" . . .

"See, Ma, we found this little dog whinin' by the road. His leg is broke. Pa says we kin fix it with a piece of wood. He's yaller, so I call him Honey. Pa says I kin keep him if you say so. Kin I, Ma, please, kin I?". . .

"You know that stone house, Ma, this side of Hodgen's? We stopped there today, cus I had a stomach ache. Old Mis' Kirkpatrick, what lives thar, give me some hot water with red pepper in it. An' look, Ma, what else she give me!"

It was a newspaper, several weeks old, printed in Bardstown, and it became one of Abe's most precious possessions. He pored over it by the hour, his long bony finger tracing the letters, his tongue laboring over strange names—Jackson, Napoleon, Madison, Federalists. Curious about the events that were shaking the nation in the wake of the war, he asked questions that his parents were unable to answer. He knew only that "Mr. Madison's war" was at last over, that their young neighbors who had gone to fight the Indians, those still alive, had returned home, and that as a result of the burst of euphoria following the war victories more and more carts, wagons, sleds, travelers on horseback and on foot, with goods slung in saddlebags or over shoulders, were passing by on the road heading west.

Strangely enough, that stone house where Abe acquired his first newspaper was almost the only distant landmark he was to recall from his life at Knob Creek.

Except for journeys to the monthly service at Little Mount Church

and occasional visits to the Berrys on Beech Fork and to the Sparrows and Friends on Nolin, Nancy would have been glad never to
venture on the ribbon of red clay save to cross it on her way to the
creek. But for Tom's sake she traveled it without demur, to play parties and cornhuskings and cabin-raisings and weddings and camp
meetings and funerals. Always after such an outing Tom returned to
the drudgery of farm labor with more zest and contentment. She even
accompanied him to the horse racing held on Martin's Turf on Middle Creek, midway between Hodgen's Mill and Elizabethtown, an annual event which Tom looked forward to all the year. He was a good
judge of horses, and his stallion and brood mares were among the
best in the neighborhood, though he never entered one in the races.
Nancy found these festivities, with their raucous revelry, their bet-
ting, their clouds of red dust and rushing bodies and pounding hoofs,
hardest of all to endure. But for Tom they were meat and drink
which would sate his appetite for days.

Even the camp meetings, for a week in the spring and another in
the fall, were a time to be dreaded, and Nancy felt guilt that this was
so. They were held near the church at the foot of a knob in a beautiful spot known as the "Church of the Maple Trees." A huge maple
overspread the platform and pulpit of poplar logs, its branches interlacing with those of the trees on the hillside, and in front was a
fine grove of smaller trees, their lower limbs trimmed so that the
tallest sinners making their way to the mourners' bench need not
duck their heads.

Nancy was always an active participant in these religious activities.
She entertained guests in the cabin. She prepared huge quantities of
corn pone and stews and hams and dried fruits for the week in camp.
She sent the children to the neighbors to invite the more reluctant
ones to attend. She prayed earnestly that a great revival might take
place. Why, then, when the emotional fervor was at its height, when
the shouts of "Amen" and "Praise the Lord" had reached a deafen-
ing climax, did that inner door of sensitivity, always wide open to
beauty and spiritual truth, seem suddenly to close? It was when she
was alone, out on the hill, with her sunbonnet pushed back and the
wind or sun or rain on her face, or reading to the children from the
Book by candlelight, that she felt closest to God, not here in the
noise and frenzy and—yes, rowdiness.

But many found release here from guilt and frustration, including

Tom. She rejoiced when during one camp meeting he left her side and went to the mourners' bench.

"But I ain't so sure about his bein' cured of sin," Abe remarked soon afterward. "Look how he went and kicked Honey."

Abe, at five or six, was already developing a stern code of conduct, especially for those who professed holiness. When one circuit rider came to conduct a camp meeting, a brother named Gentry, and was crossing the creek, his hat had been blown off and carried away. Since the ford was close to the Lincoln cabin Nancy saw his plight and loaned him Abe's best coonskin cap. When all were assembled at the camp meeting ground and the meetings were due to start, the preacher did not arrive. He never did. It was the missing cap that Abe found most disturbing, not the defection from duty. "He stole it," he maintained stoutly. "He went and stole my cap."

"But he was bareheaded," Nancy reminded him. "We wouldn't want him to catch cold."

"It was stealin'," Abe insisted stubbornly. "And it ain't right to steal."

During the winter when Abe was turning six Tom seemed to enjoy a surcease from unease. It was his favorite season, for there was more time for hunting and trapping, and this year the game was unusually plentiful. The smokehouse was filled with fat hams of deer and bear and even buffalo, which were getting scarcer all the time, and the shed was hung with wolf and coon and mink and beaver skins. He liked the long evenings when Nancy read from the Book and his fingers were busy, fashioning wooden bowls or scooping out gourd cups or shaping an ax handle or whittling toys for the children.

Often neighbors came to the cabin in the evenings, and then Tom was in his element, his love of spinning yarns equaled only by his enjoyment of a good argument. While Nancy and Sarah sat quietly knitting or sewing by the fire and Abe squatted by his father, his lean dark face screwed into a frenzy of concentration, the men's lively discussions rivaled the heat of the fire. Though most of them were unlettered, they were by no means ignorant of the day's current issues and, though they lived in an outpost of the world, a pulsing artery brought its life-blood past their very doors. They seized with gusto on problems pertinent not only to themselves but to the nation —western migration, crops, states' rights, religion, taxes, a national bank, land titles, slavery.

Especially slavery. It was a burning issue in Kentucky, with the state constitution permitting the institution and blacks pouring into the state by the hundreds. Scarcely a day passed when one did not see them moving along the road, pulling wagons, bent beneath heavy loads, sometimes chained together and being driven in gangs. Already over a thousand slaves were listed in Hardin County. Washington County had about 1,500 in a population of some 1,800 white males. There were more than 15,000 slaves in the state. Discussion waxed hot, especially when Abe's two teachers, Zachariah Riney and Caleb Hazel, were present, the former an outspoken supporter of the institution, the latter an implacable foe. On one such evening the arguments were even more furious than usual.

"If slavery ain't wrong," Caleb Hazel thundered, his fist pounding the puncheon table top, "then nothin's wrong. It's a sin not only against God but against the principles on which our nation is founded, that all men are created equal. I tell you, we should all be shouting for emancipation."

Abe pulled at his father's sleeve. "What's he sayin', Pa?" he demanded in a shrill whisper. "What's e-manci—that word he said? What's it mean?"

Nancy held her breath, expecting the sound of a swift and resonant slap, for Tom was a firm believer in the adage, "A child should be seen and not heard." But he was obviously too engrossed in thought to answer. It was Hazel who responded with the kindly diligence of the teacher. "Emancipation, son. And it means freedom. You know what freedom is, the right to belong to yourself, not be owned by somebody else, like a slave." The boy nodded gravely. "It's a right every man should have, son, no matter what color he is, and don't you forget it."

Nancy relaxed, and her wooden needles began again to click. There was a lull in the conversation while Tom refilled the guests' mugs with whiskey, the inevitable stimulant to any pioneer discussion. Then suddenly she tensed to full attention.

"I been thinkin'," Tom was saying. "We've all got a heap of stuff that could bring us good money if we had it in the right place—hams, hides, corn meal, honey, wax, gentian root, whiskey. You know what. And the place to sell it is down river, in N'Orleans. What say I build a flatboat and we git our stuff together, what we kin spare, and somebody run it down when the crick is high?"

Again Nancy held her breath. Somebody? Himself? But at his next words she once more relaxed. "Of course I shouldn't be the one to go. Somebody young, without a wife and young'uns. But I'd build the boat and help collect the stuff."

There was concerted interest. Dissension was forgotten. Matters of graver import, like war and slavery, even crops and taxes, were relegated to future sessions of disagreement. All were united in making plans for a project which promised mutual profit.

Tom immediately began building his flatboat, starting it in the shed which he used for a carpenter shop, but soon moving to the bank of the creek, which, when the boat was finished, would be swelled by the spring freshets enough to float it. The children came to watch, and for once he did not say, "Run along, young'uns. You have your chores to do." Neighbors came too, and passers-by stopped to investigate and comment. Like the observers of Noah and his ark, they were not always complimentary. "You're building it too high," some scoffed. "Too narrow," said others. But, like Noah, Tom continued with his slow, painstaking work, matching his timbers as neatly as if they were the fine cherry facings of a corner cupboard, cheerful in the face of all criticism. It would travel faster built like that, he told them.

By the time the creek rose it was ready for floating, and the neighbors came again, to assist and admire. But none offered to pilot the bulky and unwieldy craft. If any of the younger and more adventurous sprouted interest, their elders swiftly nipped it in the bud. They were "needed to help with spring plowin' and plantin'," or "too young, wait another year," or "it was a good idea, but the trip was too dangerous."

Dangerous it was, as all knew, for it meant poling down the swollen creek into the Rolling Fork, down the Rolling Fork twenty-odd miles into Salt River, down Salt River another ten miles into the Ohio, and down the Ohio, nobody knew how far, to the Mississippi, with its treacherous hundreds of miles, imperiled all the way by snags, shoals, deadheads, rocks, shallows, sand bars, whirling eddies, to say nothing of pirates and marauding Indians.

One day Tom returned from a trip to the mill with a familiar figure astride the horse behind him. "Dennis!" They greeted the newcomer with delight.

The Sparrows' adopted son was now about sixteen, husky, taller than Tom, broader of shoulder. Tom lifted the bag of ground corn from the horse's back and gave it into Abe's waiting arms. "Dennis is goin' to stay," he announced with studied casualness, "while I'm gone to N'Orleans. He's good at farmin' and kin manage the plowin' and plantin' if I don't git back in time." He turned then to Nancy, regarding her anxiously, pleading with her to understand. "You—you don't mind much, do you? I couldn't find nobody else. You kin see I have to go."

Nancy hesitated only a moment before answering. "Yes," she said quietly. "I kin see you have to go."

"I tried to find somebody else. You know I did."

"Yes. I know."

She helped him get ready, packed extra buckskin trousers, heavy socks, linsey-woolsey shirts, and a second coonskin cap, for the nights would be cold, even though the swelling streams were chattering of coming spring (Would it be summer when—*if* he returned?). She fried great hunks of bacon to wrap in linen packets with what seemed a month's supply of corn pone (How many months for those hundreds of miles? Two? Three?). She lay beside him on the pole bed, listening to his even breathing (No restless tossing now!), counting the nights remaining, already feeling the emptiness ahead. And when the flatboat was loaded and the neighbors were all around to wish him and their produce God-speed, she spared him the embarrassment and chagrin of her tears, conscious that already he felt enough guilt and shame for the exuberant eagerness he was trying to hide.

A month passed . . . two . . . three. Never had days crawled by so slowly. The honeysuckle blossomed, the roses, and the streams subsided into murmuring ripples and clear limpid pools. Dennis (the children were soon calling him "Denny") plowed the three small fields, the largest containing seven acres, and Abe did the seed-dropping, remembering to put the pumpkin seed, as his father had taught him, into every third hill along with the corn. Later they cultivated with the bull-tongue plow, Abe riding the horse carefully between the rows. Denny was a hard worker, kindly, good-natured, and the boy soon became his faithful shadow. Since he had gone to school at Nolin and had learned the basic three R's, Abe was constantly teasing him to practice his skills, especially writing, so that the red earth outside the cabin became scored with stick scrawls, and the fire shovel needed constant wiping to make room for all the words the boy kept demanding. For while Abe had learned his letters in the short weeks with Riney and Hazel, script was still an unknown art. But since Denny, like most pioneers, was an indifferent speller, the exercise that "Aprail" was at times a "rite pore" supplement to Abe's "eddication."

They look a little alike, thought Nancy, seeing the two heads bent over the shovel in the glow of the fire. There were the same high cheekbones, broad forehead, wide mouth, deep-set eyes. But Abe's chin was squarer, the line of his jaw stronger, the brows more outthrust over the dark probing eyes. It was as if one face had been carved out of granite, the other out of soft limestone. A mother's fond conceit, no doubt, and Denny was certainly handsomer. But—it was like comparing a pretty green knoll with the rugged if ungainly strength of Old Muldraugh.

In the third month she began watching the road, doing as much work as possible outside the cabin, so, whether spinning or washing at the creek or keeping the ashes wet in the hopper for making soap or cooking over the outdoor fire, she could glance up frequently. Like all the hundreds of river runners who took produce to New Orleans, he would sell his flatboat at the end of the journey and return some other way. But it was late evening and she was not watching when he came, appearing suddenly in the door when she was reading to Denny and the children. She rose so suddenly that the precious Book dropped unnoticed to the floor. It was Abe who, before going to greet his father, picked it up and carefully smoothed out the rumpled pages.

"Wal, I'm home." As always, Tom's inadequacy of speech belied his depth of emotion, but as he folded Nancy in his arms, almost stifling her, words were unnecessary. She knew not only that he was glad to be home, that he was unutterably tired, discouraged, but also that, for the time at least, all restlessness, zeal for change and adventure, had burned itself out like a guttered candle.

"What happened, Uncle?" demanded Denny, who had always thought of Nancy as aunt instead of cousin. "Did you come back rich, as you hoped?"

"No," said Tom wearily, "not rich. Pore." But he managed a smile. "I guess it's jist that luck is agin me."

Not for a long time did they learn the details of his unfortunate trip. He had used the money from the sale of his flatboat plus some from the sale of his Mill Creek farm to reimburse the neighbors at least in part for the products entrusted to him. It was assumed by most either that his boat had met with rough water and overturned ("We told yer it was too high and narrer!") or that he had encountered river bandits.

But in time he told a few people something of the story, so that many years later his son was able to impart some of the details to an interested listener.

"Father often told me of the trick that was played on him by a pair of 'sharpers.' It was the year before we moved from Kentucky to Indiana that Father concluded to take a load of pork down to New Orleans. He had a considerable amount of his own, and he bargained with the relations and neighbors for their pork, so he had quite a load. He took the pork to the Ohio River on a clumsily constructed flatboat of his own make. Almost as soon as he pushed out into the river a couple of sleek fellows bargained with him for his cargo and promised to meet him in New Orleans where they arranged to pay him for the price agreed upon. He eagerly accepted the offer, transferred the cargo to the strangers, and drifted down the river, head filled with visions of wealth. Thought he was going to accomplish what he set out to do without labor or inconvenience. He arrived in New Orleans and waited several days, but his whilom friends did not turn up. At last it dawned on him that he had been sold, and all that he could do was to come back home and face the music."

He was at home and glad to be there. To Nancy that was all that mattered. In his travels he had seen no other land so rich and productive, and he plunged into the farm work with zest. Thanks to Dennis, the season produced a bumper crop, and the family faced the winter with abundance in store—not only corn for bread but "holed-up" potatoes and onions, dried beans to "bile" with the fat hams hung in the smokehouse, dried fruits and berries, maple syrup and sugar, bees' honey, gourds hanging from the rafters filled with medicinal herbs or seeds for spring planting. That year of 1815 Tom listed for taxation four horses, one of them a stallion. His herds of cattle, swine, and sheep were increasing each year. Never had he seemed so contented nor had Nancy been filled with such a sense of well-being.

Yet before winter came she felt the approach of an even more ominous coldness. Tom came home from Elizabethtown one day grave and silent.

"What is it?" she asked anxiously. "Something is the matter."

He hesitated, opened his lips to explain, closed them. "Don't worry," he said at last. "It's nothin' you need to bother your pretty head about."

"Is it more trouble about the farm?" she persisted. "The Sinkin' Spring one you bought from Isaac Bush?"

"That agin, yes," he admitted. "Looks as if Mather's bound to git his money either from Isaac or from me, mebbe both. But—that ain't what's worryin' me. Looks as if we may be driven off the farm here." He drew a paper from his pocket. "This here says how if I cain't show a right to the title to these acres I jist bought and the ones I been payin' for, I'll be turned out, and not only me but ten others."

"But"—Nancy felt the coldness mounting through her body, stiffening her lips—"you bought the land. We signed the paper, you and me. They give you a deed."

"No deed. Not yet. We bought it, yes, from George Lindsey, but—it's jist my luck for somethin' to be wrong with the title. This'd be the third time."

His worst fears were realized when eviction papers were served on him on December 27. Since he had no deed to the land, it was claimed that he was only a tenant and that Lindsey, now living in Breckinridge County, was his landlord. He was sued as a trespasser, even though he had paid Lindsey cash for at least part of his 230-acre farm, was paying taxes in Hardin County on the property, and was making further payments according to his agreement. It was Lindsey's title which was in dispute. And unless Tom could show his own claim to the title, he would be turned out of possession.

The farm was part of a tract of ten thousand acres, surveyed in 1784, and patented by a Thomas Middleton. Tom was not the only alleged squatter. He was one of ten. The plaintiffs were men named Stout, Sheridan, and Rhodes, who claimed to be heirs of Middleton's. It was another result of the defective land law system in Kentucky whereby each pioneer had been allowed to locate where he pleased and was required to survey at his own expense. Even Daniel Boone, pioneer of all pioneers, had lost his land and been forced to leave the state.

When neighbors gathered in the cabin that winter one subject dominated the discussion. *Land titles.* They worried it helplessly like a dog struggling with a fossilized bone. Some of the neighbors were among the nine other settlers being sued along with Tom, including the La Follettes, Will Brownfield, Clark Tucker, Peter Minges, Job Dye, George Redmond, William Ash, and Ignatius Strange. Tom's suit was being made a test case by the plaintiffs. On February 12, 1816, Abe's seventh birthday, it was filed by Samuel Haycraft and listed for the next term of court.

But as the weeks passed another word reared its head persistently in the discussions.

"What's Indianny, Pa?" asked Abe. "Why do you keep talkin' about it?"

The restless look, Nancy noticed with a sinking heart, was once more in Tom's eyes. "Indianny, son? It's a place whar you don't need to worry none about whether the land belongs to you or not, where they can't take it away from you after you've paid good money and worked your fingers to the bone cuttin' trees and broke your back plowin' and seedin' and weedin' and harvestin'. And it's good land, better even than this, nice rich black soil. Yes, and it's a place whar there ain't no slaves, neither white nor black. I reckon it's what the good Book says, a right Promised Land."

"Then why don't we go thar, Pa?"

"Mebbe we will, son. Mebbe we will."

Tom's frustration was all the greater because in January Richard Mather, who had a claim on the property at Sinking Spring, had begun to press his suit.

"Luck's jist agin me," he complained hopelessly.

In spite of possible impending disaster he plowed his three fields as usual and planted corn in what they called the "Big Field," which contained seven acres. Abe walked behind him dropping pumpkin seeds, as his father had taught him, two seeds in every other hill and every other row. It was a Saturday afternoon when they finished. That night Nancy was awakened by the sound of rushing waters. No sound of rain on the roof, but this was what often happened. Rain would fall in great sheets on the surrounding hills and send torrents rushing down through the gorges into the valley. She lay tense and wakeful for hours, listening, knowing that the cabin, which was on higher ground between two of the fields, could not be touched, but feeling as if all the foundations of her happy life were being swept away. In contrast with the tumult outside, the cabin remained quiet, all its other occupants asleep.

Sunday morning they opened the door on bright steaming sunshine and a scene of devastation. Red earth from the cultivated fields, together with rocks, branches, dead leaves, fragments of honeysuckle bushes redolent with fragrance, yes, and the freshly planted seeds—all had washed, were still washing, down the valley slopes, across the road, into the creek.

"Bad luck agin." Tom ruefully eyed the denuded field, adding with cheerful resignation, "Wal, the Book says, 'The Lord loveth whom he chasteneth.' Accordin' to that, I reckon he must love us a turrible lot."

But when the freshets had subsided he replowed, replanted the field, and once more Abe went behind him dropping the pumpkin seed. Strangely enough, it was one of the few vivid memories he was to take with him of Knob Creek and share with companions in a far different milieu nearly a half century later.

Indiana. The road past the cabin with its constant flow of life led inevitably in that direction. Pioneers with wagons piled high stopped briefly to share their glowing hopes before moving eagerly on up the steep scarps of Old Muldraugh.

Abe and his friend Austin found one such pioneer couple camping beside the road on a knoll. They were sitting on a quilt spread on the ground, and there were some books on the quilt.

"Is one of those *Robinson Crusoe?*" asked Abe.

"No," the woman replied with a friendly smile, "they are readers. My husband and I are teachers. We are going to Indiana hoping to open a school."

"Couldn't you stay here and have a school?" pleaded Abe.

The woman shook her head. No, this part of the country was not sufficiently settled. There would not be enough pupils to make it worth their while. There would be more opportunities in Indiana. But—she smiled again—she did have the book *Robinson Crusoe* in her bag, and she would be glad to read it to him.

Abe took them home, and Nancy welcomed them, urging them to remain as long as they wished. She watched joyfully yet yearningly while the visitor, Mrs. Dawson, read from her fascinating book, Sarah listening politely, head bent over her sewing, but Abe crouched at her side, enthralled, long bony legs tucked under his scanty shirt, lips parted, eyes bright as a ferret's beneath his shock of black hair. To his disappointment the couple left before the book was finished. He stood by the road and looked after them until they were out of sight. Nancy watched him turn back, slowly, reluctantly, thin shoulders drooping.

She sighed. The restlessness was in his eyes, too. Already, like his father, he was yearning to be on the way toward some Promised Land. Abraham. They had named him well, and not only for his pioneer grandfather. Words sprang to her mind from the only book she could share with him.

By faith Abraham . . . went out, not knowing whither he went.

It was then, perhaps, that she made her peace with destiny. Like Tom, she came from people who were in the Calvinist tradition. What was to be would be. If she must forfeit this paradise, then she would do so without rebellion, even without regret.

By faith Nancy . . .

= 5 =

Tom's poor luck in land transactions by no means affected his reputation as a good citizen in either the neighborhood or the county. He served on juries, signed marriage bonds. He was a respected communicant at Little Mount Church and raised his voice in many of its meetings, especially when the discussions involved slavery. And in May of that year 1816 he was given a responsible position, supervision of that part of the road leading from Nolin to Bardstown between the "Bigg Hill" and the Rolling Fork. Though he was appointed "surveyor" the word "overseer" more clearly defined his responsibility. Others were to "assist Lincoln in keeping said road in repair." There was a penalty on the "surveyor" to keep the road open, which was no mean task on this most difficult of all the road's sections, with its frequent washouts on the stony descents of Old

Muldraugh. It was also his job to keep at the forks of the road a stone or tree sign with plain lettering directing to the most important places. Tom assumed the responsibility with conscientious zeal.

Nancy was relieved, hopeful. For the present fear of losing their land seemed to have receded. At the March term of court the case had been continued that a deposition might be taken. At the June term George Lindsey, from whom Tom had bought the land in good faith and to whom he had made partial payment, was made a co-defendant, and the plaintiffs ordered a survey. Perhaps the case would be decided in Tom's favor. At least he seemed more contented, and both he and the neighbors were too tired after grueling days in the fields to spend time together chewing and worrying over problems.

Never had the corn grown so tall and luxuriantly green, its ears so fat, the pumpkins and potatoes and beans so plump, so jewel-bright and luscious. "Gold and ivory and emeralds," she exulted as she and Sarah washed them at the creek and prepared them for the kettle. The rushing waters which had seemed so destructive had instead brought new richness to the soil. Perhaps it would be the same with this storm-cloud which hung over the future.

But the cloud only darkened. At the September term of court the case was again continued. The plaintiffs attached two hundred bushels of the fine corn, half the whole crop, and George Lindsey brought suit to recover this attached corn. The jury would eventually decide the suit in his favor. The restlessness was back in Tom's eyes, this time a driving, relentless turbulence.

"We'll never be safe here," he told Nancy. "Jist work our fingers to the bone and nothin' in the end to show for it, nothin' to call our own, nothin' for our young'uns. But over yander, over in Indianny . . ."

When he started to build another flatboat down by the creek Nancy knew the decision had been made. So be it. She was used to moving. One circumstance made her even happy at the prospect. The day Tom began to build the boat a man passed by on the road riding in a wagon drawn, not by horses or oxen, but by a cordon of slaves. They were fastened to the shafts by ropes. She could see their black backs and shoulders dripping with sweat, straining almost double under the heavy load. When one of them faltered the driver uttered an oath and struck him with a long whip. Sickened, she ran into the cabin, the sound of his shouts and the lash resounding in her ears. At least there would be no slaves in Indiana. This very year it was to enter the Union as a free state.

1816

"Shall I bring Dennis?" Tom inquired when he was almost ready for an exploratory trip.

"No," said Nancy firmly. "I will git along fine. And you won't be gone long—I hope."

"No longer'n I need to. We'd ought to git moved before dead of winter. There'll be land to clear and mebbe a cabin to build before spring."

Nancy regarded him with mounting wonder. He was not a man who welcomed hard labor and this land he was leaving had yielded abundance with the least possible exertion. Yet here he was, eyes eager, shoulders squared, facing the torturing conquest of a new wilderness with boyish optimism.

"They say the land thar's black and deep and rich," he told her, eyes already focused toward the west, "not like this red stuff. And thar's places whar thar's no trees at all to be cut, jist grass. We'll do well thar, you'll see."

Nancy nodded. She could understand how he felt, for she also had been forever searching for something just over the horizon, yearning for a new earth, not one of blacker, richer soil but one of the spirit, a sense of identity, of belonging, of oneness with beauty, of becoming part of the enduring work of creation.

"Are we goin' to Indianny, Ma? Are we?"

"Yes, son. I reckon we are."

Again Nancy gazed wonderingly into an eager face, old for its seven years, its bright eyes already turned toward another world. And what would he be searching for along this new Wilderness Road? What would the move mean for him?

"Do you s'pose, Ma, we might find the lady, the one with the books?"

Her heart sank, even while it leaped suddenly with joy. So that was the goal of his yearning! But how tell him that instead of books his hands would be holding an ax, a hoe, an ox goad, a carpenter's drawknife and knife froe, gripping the handles of a plow, splitting fence rails? She ran her hand through the thick shock of hair, so like his father's, yet sensing that beneath it surged far different thoughts and dreams and conflicts and aspirations. For nine-year-old Sarah she had no fears. She would spin and weave and pat corn into cakes and fill the soup kettle and bear children as cheerfully there as here. But for this boy . . .

"I reckon, son," she said gently, "we'll all find in the new country jist the kind of world we want to make of it."

With his neighbors' help Tom tugged and pushed and heaved the finished flatboat into the sunken waters of the creek. He had invested his earnings from his surveyor's work in several barrels of whiskey, always the pioneer's best medium of exchange. These he loaded into the boat, along with his chest of fine tools, and all the clothes and food which Nancy insisted on his taking. He tried to appear sober and regretful as he took leave of his family and friends but could not hide his exuberant eagerness at the coming adventure. Amid the half skeptical, half envious God-speeds of his neighbors he poled off, turning to wave at the sharp bend in the stream where it was joined by a fork from the hills and the waters had cut a deep pool through the limestone rock. Nancy watched until the overhanging sycamores, elms, and willows cut him off from sight, then turned slowly back to the cabin.

There was less to worry about this time. No dangers of the Mississippi with its rocks and shoals and brigands. No rushing torrents of spring. Only a short journey down the creek to the Rolling Fork, into the Salt River, then to the Ohio, and down the Ohio to—where? But there was no time to wonder. When one's roots were being torn up, like nerves being laid bare, there was much to do.

While Abe gathered nuts and herbs and berries for storing and drying, she and Sarah spun and wove and sewed linsey-woolsey garments and fashioned deerskin jeans and moccasins and coonskin caps, sufficient to last through the winter. For who could tell whether there would be a place for spinning wheel and loom? And certainly there would be no time until spring to build a new ash hopper.

It was Abe who helped her make a fresh supply of soap, filling the funnel-shaped wooden hopper with ashes, then drawing water from the creek to cover them. After the water had leached through, running into the tub at the open end of the wooden trough at the bottom, he ran to a neighbor's house for the big iron kettle used by all the neighboring housewives, a heavy load even for an outsized seven-year-old. Then they boiled the dark lye water mixed with hog grease over the outdoor fireplace. Nancy was not satisfied until she had enough of the strong soft soap to fill a small kettle.

It was Abe too who fed and curried the four horses, tended the swine. But Sarah did the milking. They had only one cow now, which Tom had bought with her calf for ten dollars. There was still feed for her to gather by ranging in the woods, but she came home at night to her calf. Then Sarah would drive her into a fence corner, lead the calf out of its pen, and let it begin its meal. When the milk flowed freely she would lead the reluctant calf back to its pen and, standing beside the cow, milk the stream into a gourd held in her left hand, stopping occasionally to empty it into a bucket. Then, when she had secured enough for the day's use, she would bring back the calf.

Weeks passed, and it was November. In spite of her worry over Tom's long absence Nancy felt relief. Surely it would be too late now to move before spring! There would be a few months' respite. Then suddenly, when no one was watching for him, Tom appeared in the doorway. His hands were empty. His buckskin trousers were shrunken and badly soiled, his shirt torn. But his eyes under the heavy brows were as bright as the glowing mussel shells visible along the creek bottom in low water.

"Tom!" Nancy's swift burst of relief changed to an exclamation of dismay as she eyed his forlorn appearance, especially the width of bare shins between pant bottoms and moccasins. "Oh, Tom! What happened to you?"

He looked down at his jeans, grinning sheepishly. "You mean them? Nothin' much. Jist a bit of a wettin', is all."

He related this, the discouraging part of his adventure, first. He had floated safely down the Salt River and into the Ohio, but there suddenly he had got caught in a whirlpool and his boat had capsized, tipping all his cargo into the river. Fortunately, through quick action, he had been able to recover some of his load and bring it to land, first the precious tools, then some of the whiskey. With the help of passing boatmen he had succeeded in getting the flatboat righted and proceeded down the river, where he had left his property with a man named Posey at a place called Thompson's Ferry on the Indiana side of the river. Then he had struck up across country to find a place to settle. He had already had an idea of where he wanted to go because the widow and children of his cousin Hananiah Lincoln had settled in Spencer County, and he had heard much about its fertility and good hunting.

"And jist wait till you see the place I found! It's on a nice little stream called Pigeon Crick."

Comfortable after a good washing and change of clothing, replete with a heavy meal of corn bread, bacon, wild berries, and honey, Tom leaned back in his chair and beamed at the two children crouched beside him. "You know why they call it Pigeon Crick?"

"No. Why, Pa?"

"Because thar's times when it's filled cram full of pigeons, huge flocks of 'em. People come from all around to hunt 'em. And all about the woods are full of deer, bears, rabbits, squirrels, wild turkey, so we won't have to more'n walk out of the cabin to git all we need to eat."

Nancy bent low over her sewing, glad that Tom could not see her face. Though she had long ago resigned herself to this eventuality, now it had actually come she felt a numbed inability to respond to his exuberance. She was almost relieved when the big bone needle, honed sharp to penetrate the tough deerhide, pricked deep into her finger, stirring her senses in response to minor pain. As she sucked away the blood, its warm salt taste took away the numbness and seemed to start life flowing again in her veins. As Tom's eyes turned eagerly toward her, she was able to smile.

He continued with his story. He had selected a good lot, marked its corners with piled brush, and chopped enough trees to furnish wood for at least a small half-faced camp. Then he had gone to Vincennes, sixty miles, the county seat, and filed his claim. Never again would he get caught with a poor title. In Indiana, once his claim was paid for, his title would be from the Government of the United States, with no more lawsuits, and if they got started at once, he should get the land paid for within a year. And another piece of luck! Near the new land when he had been walking the trail he had met a big landowner named Reuben Grigsby, who had offered him a job of making brandy casks in return for the rental of eight acres of good gladly land already cleared.

"What's 'gladly' land, Pa?" demanded Abe.

The best possible, Tom told him. Hilly ground with a thick covering of rich soil. Well, to continue, he had gone back to Posey's, left the few tools he had taken with him, and come back across country on foot, not far through the woods, less than a hundred miles.

The following days were too full of activity to permit thought or emotion. Tom still had litigation pending not only on the Knob Creek farm but on the Nolin Creek property he had bought from Isaac Bush, both of them having been made defendants by Mather, who claimed that Bush and Lincoln had bought the land with a knowledge of Mather's equitable claim on the note signed by Vance, the owner before Bush. The court decided that Mather's claim was just and that Tom should recover from Bush the two hundred dollars he had paid him. This amount had not yet been paid.

On November 11 Tom went to Elizabethtown to make oath to a cross-bill against Isaac Bush, who at the same time filed a cross-bill against Vance. To Nancy's surprise he took with him two horses instead of the one he rode, making no explanation. Presently he returned, triumphant, with a wagon drawn by the two animals. It was not an imposing affair, just a simple farm cart, but Tom was as proud of it as if it had been a prairie schooner. Nancy viewed it with relief. At least she could take with her the spinning wheel and loom and perhaps the corner cupboard Tom had made for her with as fine and careful workmanship as those he had left behind in some of the homes of Elizabethtown. Tom made arches for it of hickory wood, and Nancy covered them with stout tent cloth.

This was his first trip to E-town since the court session of June, and he brought back news. "That friend of yours, Sally, her what used to be a Bush."

"Yes?" prompted Nancy eagerly, wondering why he always spoke of her so, as if she had never been his friend, as if he had forgotten he had once courted her.

"That husband of hers died, you know, that Dan'l Johnston, last July, folks said. Went suddint like. Funny we didn't hear before, but news travels slow."

"Oh!" Nancy's grief was poignant. For months her best friend had been suffering, and she had not known!

"It's no great loss, I'd say, neither to her nor her brothers. Remember how none of them would go bond for him when he got the jailer's job? And she's sure had the brunt of it stid of him, havin' to do all the cookin' and cleanin' for the jailbirds! Let's jist hope she's got a bit of her father's legacy left, but I doubt it."

Nancy opened her lips to protest, then closed them. Only a woman could understand that hard labor, poverty, even neglect were worth bearing if one loved enough. And Sally had loved Dan'l. She felt like hiding herself in the cabin and weeping.

But there was no time to weep. The days passed inexorably. A sale was planned, to dispose of most of the furniture and some of the animals. It was a big social event, with Nancy providing the dinner, assisted by some of the neighbors, Caleb Hazel's new wife, Austin Gollaher's mother, Mrs. George Redmond, and others. The chairs (with real backs) went, the puncheon table, stools and chest, the ash hopper, some of the sheep and hogs. Tom was leaving forty bushels of corn in the loft of Caleb Hazel's cabin, to remain there pending the court's decision. Much of the remainder of his bumper crop, which he had put into marketable whiskey, was now at the bottom of the Ohio River.

"We sure hate to see you folks go." George Redmond, who had been road surveyor before Tom, was only one of the neighbors who professed regret. But there was unrest, perhaps envy, in their protestations, for their land also was in jeopardy.

Now that the decision was made Tom was jubilant, and he could not wait to be gone. Nancy had hoped they might make a trip to Beechland to pay a last visit to the Berrys and Thompsons, but Tom insisted there was no time. Then there was that other who lived beyond the Beech Fork, the thought of whom would always bring the half-memory of a low crooning voice and warm encircling arms. Yes, she would have liked to see Lucy Sparrow again. But perhaps it was well that she could not. Henry Sparrow would not have been pleased to see her, and "Aunt Lucy" would be fully occupied with her eight *other* children. For Tom there was only Mordecai left in Washington County. Josiah had already moved to Harrison County, Indiana, and Cousin Hananiah was dead.

It was almost Thanksgiving before they were ready to go, the wagon packed with the little furniture that had not been sold, spinning wheel, loom, kitchen utensils, farming equipment; feather bed, "kiverlids," and clothing carefully stowed in bags to protect them from rain or snow, the precious Bible deep in the center of one of them, together with Tom's bundle of legal papers. To Nancy's joy there was room at the back of the wagon for the corner cupboard, tied on with stout deerhide thongs. It would be her job to drive the

two horses pulling the wagon, Sarah by her side, while Tom and Abe
went in front with the other two horses, herding ahead of them the
cow and her calf, a few sheep, and a small drove of hogs.

"Hogs!" one of the neighbors had scoffed. "You're takin' hogs
into a land where they say wild boars are common as rabbits in a
clover patch?"

"Not fat hogs like these," Tom retorted with good-natured stubbornness.

The time had come. Seated on the wagon, reins slack in her hands,
Nancy turned for a last look at the place which for five years had
been her paradise. No fields of waving corn now, no glory of honeysuckle and wild roses, not even the golds and scarlets and russets of
the autumn just past, only the dull browns and grays of late November not yet warmed by the pale sun. But she gazed and gazed, glad
that the blinders of her sunbonnet hid her brimming eyes from Sarah.
As so many times in her life, words from the Book sprang unbidden
to her mind.

*Therefore the Lord God sent them forth from the garden of
Eden. . . .*

"C'mon!" shouted Tom. "Sun'll soon be up. Let's git goin'!"

Nancy's hands tightened on the reins. She clucked to the horses.
The solid wooden wheels began their relentless turning. Up over Old
Muldraugh they went, the strange little procession, horses straining,
wheels grinding, hogs grunting, man and boy shouting, running,
prodding with their goads. The road, thanks to Tom's supervision,
was amazingly straight and smooth. Someone else would have to be
appointed to tend it now. Down the other side toward the little log
structure which was Little Mount Church.

"Tom!" called Nancy. She pulled up on the reins. Recognizing the
urgency in her voice, he stopped, nodding his head. "You go," he
said. "Take the children. It's good for them to remember. I'll have to
stay here with the animals."

She took the children by the hand, and together they climbed the
small knob of land to the Little Mount cemetery. "Here," she said,
and knelt beside the small plot marked by the little stone slab on
which Tom had carved the letters, "T. L. 1814." No need now to
hide her tears. This was no mere piece of ground and pile of logs
over which it was weakness for a pioneer woman to weep. This was
her very bones and flesh. She felt like Naomi, leaving her two sons in

the foreign soil of Moab. But, no, it was not Naomi she felt most like, but Ruth. For Naomi was going home. It was Ruth who was going into a strange country for the sake of one she loved. *Where thou goest I will go, and there will I be buried.*

It was time to go. She rose from her knees, took the children again by the hand, and they went down the hill.

They stopped at Hodgen's Mill, where "Missus Sarah," who had always been fond of Abe, insisted on feeding them a big meal and, to Abe's delight, read him a story from her book of *Aesop's Fables.* Then, when he had gone to the mill with his father, while Tom had a bag of corn ground, she put the book into Nancy's hands. "I want him to have it. Hide it somewhere and surprise him. I know you kin read it to him. He likes it so much, I wouldn't feel right, keepin' it." Speechless with gratitude, Nancy took the book and slipped it into the bag of "kiverlids."

They stayed overnight with Betsy and Thomas Sparrow on Nolin, and to Nancy's joy there was a reunion of all the Hanks women. Polly came with her husband, Jesse Friend, and Nannie, who had married Levi Hall.

"If you find a good place over thar in Indianny," Thomas Sparrow told Tom, "let us know. Levi and I are thinkin' we'd like to move to a place whar the land's better and no danger of bein' done out of what you thought you owned."

"Oh!" Nancy exclaimed joyfully. "If only you would come!" Suddenly she felt almost happy about this excursion into the unknown. If Aunt Betsy was there, any place in the world would seem like home. Strange, she thought, seeing the three of them together—herself, Nannie, Dennis! Though Betsy had no children of her own, she was mother to all of them, most of all to Dennis, who had known no other. She wondered, did he realize Nannie was his mother? If so, neither of them showed the slightest sign. It was far less hard leaving the following day, knowing some of them might be following the same trail later.

To make leaving even easier, Dennis had gained permission from the Sparrows to go with them. He would help them get settled in the new territory, explore its advantages, and bring back a report to his foster parents about its possibilities. His youthful strength and willingness to work would make both the journey and the settlement much easier.

In spite of Tom's eagerness to move ahead they stopped in Elizabethtown. Nancy must see Sally. She could not leave without personally sharing in her friend's grief. Tom could not enter the town with his animals. The hogs especially were a constant care, and Dennis had friends he wanted to visit. Nancy took the children and went through the familiar street to the town square. E-town was still a small settlement, boasting only a hundred and eighty inhabitants at its last census, but to her it seemed a bewildering metropolis. Her uncle Joseph Hanks was no longer there, having himself moved somewhere in Indiana. Christopher Bush had died, and she did not know where his widow was to be found. So to locate Sally she went to one of the few places she had frequented during her life there, Benjamin Helm's general store.

Abe was delighted, for he had been there occasionally with his father. Seated on a nail keg, he was soon being fed lumps of sugar by the obliging clerk and marveling silently at sight of the proprietor, J. B. Helm, who to his amazement was always wearing his Sunday clothes on weekdays!

Yes, of course, Mr. Helm could tell Nancy what had become of Sally Johnston. After Daniel's death she had moved into a small cabin owned by Samuel Haycraft. It was in an alley on the edge of town, near the mill race at Valley Creek, just off the road leading to Hodgen's Mill.

Nancy found it easily, a tiny cabin on a narrow lane. Sally was there, seated at her loom. Words were unnecessary. Arms about each other, they wept together. But Sally was not one to seek sympathy or nurse her grief. She was soon bustling about, tears resolutely banished, putting shy Sarah at ease ("You remember my Elizabeth, dear? She's nine now, jist a bit older than you!"); exclaiming over Abe ("So tall already! And only seven, like my Matilda here, yet 'most a whole head taller!"); exhibiting with pride her six-year-old John D.

She's stronger than I am, thought Nancy. She'd never be afraid, like me, of leaving everything behind, traveling into strange places. No matter what life does to her, it will never bend those straight shoulders, still those busy, capable hands, quench the courage and tranquility in those clear gray eyes. Yes, or permit untidiness in anything she touched, whether a tiny crowded cabin or her neatly combed and well-scrubbed children, or even the crisp curls of her glossy black hair!

"We like our little house," Sally said with her usual sprightly good humor. "If I git enough 'kiverlids' wove and enough orders for shirts and jeans to sell, mebbe I'll git it paid for before too long. Sam Haycraft's goin' to sell it to me for twenty-five dollars. I'm jist sorry Dan'l couldn't have seen how cosy it is, but at least he lived long enough to enjoy his son, and he did so want one!" The beautiful cherry bureau which had been her brothers' wedding gift shone with polish. It had cost forty dollars, Nancy remembered. Had she sold it, it would have paid for this humble cabin and more. Instead she chose to earn the price of it with hard labor, probably refusing the help of her six prosperous brothers. Pride? Yes. Sally had always been proud. How it must have shamed her to see her easygoing husband accept loans from them which he never repaid, until finally they had lost patience!

"Much as I miss Dan'l," continued Sally quietly, "and you know how much I loved him, I'm glad to be away from the jail. It was no place for the children, seein' folks with their hands and feet in the stocks and hearin' cries from down under in the dungeon. But it was work that Dan'l liked better than anything else he'd done, and it was a reel honor their choosin' him for such a responsible job." Head held high in proud defiance, she challenged the world to contradict her.

But it was you who did the hard work, Nancy retorted silently, cooking all the meals for the prisoners, cleaning the whole place, even the cells in the dungeon, and you'd never be satisfied unless it was all as spotless as this cabin. "Yes," she said, aloud, her eyes soft with understanding, "I know how much you loved him."

She could not stay, for Tom was waiting. My best friend, she thought as they embraced. Will I ever see her again?

So many farewells! Why did she have a premonition that for some of them it would be for the last time? They journeyed north, passing the farm which Tom had bought on Mill Creek in 1801 and recently sold. Six or seven miles beyond they stopped at the home of Tom's sister Mary and her husband, William Brumfield, where Bersheba was still living. Here again there was a happy reunion, followed by a sad farewell.

Bersheba tried hard not to show favoritism, but her preference for her husband's namesake, the second Abraham, was all too obvious. She would not let Abe out of her sight. Reluctantly he suffered her to hold him, his long spindly legs reaching to the floor, while she told him of the tall young ranger she had married six years before the Revolution, how they had followed Daniel Boone along the Wilderness Road, taken possession of 1,200 acres of virgin land, and while building his cabin his grandfather Abraham had been killed by Indians. Abe, though he knew the story by heart, was polite enough not to interrupt her. Bersheba, now seventy-four, was almost as straight of carriage and keen of eye as in the days when she had trekked with her five children over the "dark and bloody ground" to the neighborhood of her husband's cousin Hananiah, made a home for them, and managed to rear them into respectable and godly, if not (except Mordecai) distinguished citizens of the new country. She would still be living, able to tell the story to her great-great-grandchildren for twenty more years, but this was the last time Abe would ever see her.

After this the way was strange to Nancy, who felt that all the life she had known was slipping away behind her . . . as, when they forded one creek and the horses were toiling through murky water to their flanks, the corner cupboard on the rear of the wagon burst through the loosened thongs and fell back into the water. No time even to turn and watch it sinking, for she must use all her energy to urge the horses forward, gritting her teeth as they lumbered into shallow water and toiled up the farther bank. Only then could she look back. There it was, about halfway across, the fluted cornice and two six-pointed stars which Tom had carved so painstakingly just visible. Even as she watched, it sank out of sight, leaving only a few bubbles to mark its resting place.

"No good to try to save it," said Tom unhappily, knowing how much she prized it. "But it ain't as if I couldn't make you another. I will, I promise."

Yes, he might make her one. But when? It had taken years for her to get that one. Oh, he had made plenty of cupboards, but always for others because they needed the money. And with ground to clear, a cabin to be built . . .

She managed a tearful smile. "I know. It's all right. It couldn't be helped."

The next casualty was Tom's fat hogs. They were traveling an old pioneer trail leading north and went through Piney Grove, across

Otter Creek, to Big Spring, where they made camp one night. Perhaps it was a prowling wild cat or panther or even some lesser "varmint" which frightened the hogs and sent them running away into the forest. Anyway, when Tom awoke the next morning they were gone.

"Jist my luck." He made his usual complaint, preferring to blame fate rather than his own failure to build a pen of brush, also to wake at frequent intervals to check on the animals' welfare. Horses and cows could be easily tied to trees, but hogs were more elusive. Nancy regretted the loss far less than Tom. Though it meant no fresh hog meat for the winter, there were good hams stowed in the wagon, and they could make do with the game Tom claimed was so plentiful. The hogs had been a nuisance, slowing their pace and causing continual confusion. A report from a former neighbor came to Tom later that the whole pack had turned up back at the old farm on Knob Creek!

They passed through the town of Hardinsburg, where William Hardin, its founder back in 1780, had once stepped from his cabin to see an Indian pointing his gun and taunting, "Hooh, Big Bill!" While the red man had been aiming, "Big Bill" had swiftly knocked the gun from his hands and brained him. Abe and Sarah listened wide-eyed as Tom told them the story.

The children would always remember Hardinsburg for another reason. They were sitting in the wagon waiting for Tom to return with provisions when a young black woman came toward them, smiling.

"What's you name, chilluns?" she asked sociably.

"Lincoln," Abe, always the spokesman of the two, replied. She would remember it later as "Linkhorn."

"And whereabouts is you-all goin'?"

"Indianny," Abe told her.

Leaving them, she soon returned with slices of corn bread, well buttered, and two mugs of milk. Presently the young master of the house, a man named Murray, came along the road and greeted the strangers, asking the names of the children, talking with Tom when he returned and learning of his plans. Years later the little incident was to have a curious sequel.

This same man, Colonel David Murray, while sitting at his supper table, would send for Minerva, a colored servant, to come to the din-ing room, and when she came the following conversation would take place:

"Minerva, do you remember more than forty years ago that as I was entering my house in the town of Hardinsburg, I talked to a poor family in the road and you were giving milk to a little boy sitting in a wagon. I enquired their name and where they were going. To Indiana, they said."

"Yes, sir, now I think of it, I believe I do. Their name was Linkhorn."

"Yes, that is right, as I remember it. Minerva, what would you say if I told you that that little boy you fed was Abraham Lincoln, who was nominated this very day on the Republican ticket to be President of the United States?"

"Good Lawd!" Minerva would shout. But the story would not reach completion until three years later when this same colored woman would see her sons enter the Union Army to help the little boy she had once fed to become the great emancipator of her race.

But this was all in the future. Now the little boy wiped the froth of milk from his lips, crammed the last morsels of bread into his mouth with grimy hands, and politely thanked his benefactor for himself and his shy sister.

"It's right good you are to us, miss. I wisht I could do somethin' for you sometime."

On they traveled through dense forests, over rolling hills, fording streams, along a trail called the Yellow Banks Road to a small but thriving settlement named Cloverport, and there before them was a great expanse of shining water.

Abe jumped up and down in his excitement. "What is it, Pa? The ocean?"

"That's the Ohio River, son, 'most a thousand miles long. But that's nothin'. Wait till you see the Mississippi, what it flows into!"

"Are we goin' acrost it, Pa? Are we?"

"We sure are, son. And this is a good place to do it, here at Clover Crick."

Nancy gazed at the rolling stream in mingled delight and dismay. She also had never before seen a great river. Like Abe, she felt a stirring of excitement. It was beautiful, alive, a creature of steady and endless motion, not like the little temperamental creeks, now rushing madly, now slowed to a sluggish crawl. But—such a wide and frightening expanse! They must get across, but how? She echoed the boy's wonder. The crossings she had known were all by fords.

Tom left them and presently reappeared with a man named Jacob Weatherholt, who had agreed to ferry them across. The wagon, with horses and cow, was driven on a stout raft of logs, which Weatherholt and Tom propelled with poles. Nancy, Denny, and the two children were placed in a large canoe, handled by one of Mr. Weatherholt's sons. As they moved into the swirling waters Nancy held Sarah tightly with one arm, her other clutching the side of the boat, eyes fixed nervously on young Abe, who in his eager curiosity was leaning out over the water. But presently she found herself relaxing. Lifting her face to the brisk November wind, she drank deeply of its cool headiness, and when it blew back the visor of her sunbonnet, she welcomed the wider vision of the flowing water.

They camped that night on land belonging to Mr. Weatherholt, and the next day moved along an old Indian trail down the river toward Anderson's Creek, where Tom had left his goods on his previous trip.

"We're in Indianny now," he exulted. "And next month, in December, it's goin' to become the nineteenth state in the Union, yes, and it's comin' in free, not like old Kaintuck, where one man kin own another. And it's got good land laws, what's even better."

The river was alive, not only with its own flowing but with human activity. As they traveled the dozen miles down its winding length, Abe was enthralled with its pageantry—flatboats and barges, some loaded with merchandise bound for the south, corn, Bourbon, cider, apples, beef, pork, pelts, hemp, gunpowder, tobacco; others containing whole families, furniture and animals, all propelled by poles and sweeps; keelboats with partial sails; pleasure boats with gay colored awnings, driven by sets of long oars, men and women in incredible city clothes lounging on the decks. Then suddenly the boy screamed.

"Look, Pa! That boat! It's on fire!"

Tom laughed. "Naw, son, that's jist one of them newfangled steamboats, run by the stuff you see comin' out of your ma's kittles. What you see is smoke from the engine. Fust one went down the Ohio five years ago. Mebbe that's the new one called the *Washington* built jist this year. You're lucky to see one."

Their enthusiasm was contagious. Why, wondered Nancy, had she been so reluctant to take to the road again? Suppose she *had* left paradise behind. After all, according to the ancient story, wasn't it the loss of Eden which had brought mankind two of its most precious boons, the blessing of hard labor and the joy of children? And, like the storied Eve, she would have these in full measure.

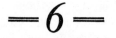

Many years later the boy Abraham, grown to fame, would confide to Henry Raymond of the New York *Times,* "Never did I pass through a harder experience than in going from Thompson's Ferry to Spencer County, Indiana."

If it was hard for a boy of seven, overly strong and adventurous, what must it have been for a woman of delicate physique and unusual sensitivity, driving a rough farm cart over sixteen miles of almost uncharted wilderness!

They had stopped at Thompson's Ferry, where Anderson's Creek flowed down to the Ohio between high banks, a bustling settlement with a big wood yard where river steamers took on fuel and a trading post where settlers could get supplies. Here Tom had sold the kegs of whiskey which he had left at Posey's, picked up the rest of his property saved from its river ducking, including his chest of tools, and they had started on the final leg of their journey.

There was a trail of sorts, blazed by a man named Jesse Hoskins, but wholly unfit for a wagon. Rocks, roots, sloughs, thickets of briars and underbrush, huge trees—hundred-foot sycamores, white oaks, hickory, ash, walnut, poplar, with branches so tightly interlaced that they turned the trail into dark tunnels—and worst of all, choking wild grapevines that took hours of cutting to penetrate! Slowly, inch by inch, yard by yard, mile by mile, Tom and Dennis hacked their way through the wilderness, felling trees, circuiting those too big to cut, clearing away underbrush of dogwood, sumac, grapevines so thick and matted that if a knife slipped from one's hands it would almost surely be lost. Tom measured one of the great trees they circuited, an oak, and they found the trunk at the height of Abe's head at least twenty-four feet around! Even Abe found an ax thrust in his hands.

Gritting her teeth to keep them from chattering, less from the December cold than from the jolting of the solid wooden wheels, Nancy forced the struggling horses through the cleared passages, the wagon grinding on stones, lurching over hummocks of stubborn yellow clay, tipping precariously on the edge of gullies.

It was even more frightening when they camped at night, for the darkness was filled with strange sounds and shapes, snapping of twigs, screaming of panthers, howling of wolves, flapping of pigeons: eyes gleaming in the glow of the fire Tom had kindled from the live coals they had brought in a kettle of ashes from Posey's.

But there was beauty in the journey. Some of the sumac was still a bright crimson. The interlacing branches of the giant trees were like the majestic arches of a great cathedral. And to her surprise Nancy found her pulses quickening with adventurous excitement. Just so her forebears must have both shivered and thrilled at the dangers and challenges of the Wilderness Road. She understood and rejoiced at the look on Tom's face as he stubbornly and with an unwonted vigor plowed his way through the almost impenetrable barriers.

"We're in free country now," he exulted, laying down his ax to wipe the sweat from his face. "Remember that, Abe. A free state, free men, free land. Freedom. It's a thing wuth workin' for in this world, and don't you forget it."

They came through at last, and there on a high knoll with forests dropping away on all sides was the spot Tom had selected for their cabin. Already he had cut trees and piled small logs for a temporary shelter. He and Dennis set to work immediately on that simple structure known to pioneers as a "half-faced camp." Choosing a spot on the southern slope of the knoll where two trees stood about fourteen feet apart, they trimmed and topped these to serve as back posts for the open-front building. Opposite these trees they drove two forked saplings deep in the ground, then laid logs one on top of the other to form the three sides, fastening them to the four posts with wooden pins. A roof was constructed of small poles interwoven with branches. Sarah and Abe were dispatched to collect brush and dry grass for the covering of thatch. When the openings between the logs had been filled with mud, it would form a tight shelter on three sides, and the fire kept burning on a hearth of tamped clay in front would provide a fair amount of heat even in the cold of winter.

"It will be fun," Nancy told the children, trying to keep all dismay out of her voice. It had been summer when she had lived in such a shelter on Knob Creek. "We'll pretend we're camping."

She tried to make the poor place homelike, as well as warm. She and the children gathered great armfuls of dry leaves to spread on the earth floor, a happy arrangement for they could be swept out when they became dirty and pulverized. They piled boughs in the corners for beds and spread skins on them for warmth under the "kiverlids." She decided to keep the feather bed safely wrapped and stored until the cabin should be built. She brought the spinning wheel and loom from the wagon, encouraged Tom to make a rough temporary table and some three-legged stools. It was hard not to mourn the loss of the beloved cupboard, especially since many of her most precious possessions, including most of the pewter plates and tableware had been stored inside it for safety.

Seldom in her ten years of marriage had she felt impatient with Tom, and almost never irritated . . . until now. They had been living in the makeshift shelter for some days when she made the discovery. Denny had been bringing water for the cooking and bathing, but there had been no time nor place for the washing of clothes. Now the need was apparent.

"Please, Tom," she said, "show us how to get to the spring. Sarah and I should be bringing the water so Dennis can help you with the clearin'. And I have to do some washin'. You should have shown us the way before this."

"I—er—me and Denny"—Tom's face wore its sheepish look—"we been tryin' to hack out a better path, but— Yes, I reckon I better show you."

He led the way down a path on the left of the half-faced camp, toward the southeast. It was narrow and winding, to avoid the numerous trees, with thick undergrowth brushing her long skirts and the ubiquitous wild grapevines pulling at her shawl. It went on and on—and on, for what seemed at least a mile. Finally they emerged into an open space, and she saw below a wide valley with cleared land and in the distance several buildings, among them a big two-storied house.

"That's Grigsby's," Tom told her. "Remember? He's the man I met on the trail when I come in here. He's a distiller as well as a farmer, and he's hired me to make him a heap of casks for his whiskey."

They descended the hill a little way to where a spring emerged into a pool of clear sparkling water. Tom took a gourd from the side, filled it to the brim, and held it out to her, eyes doglike, pleading approval. "Try it, love. You'll say it's the best water you ever tasted."

Nancy did not take it. Her hands tightened rigidly about the shawl pulled together at her throat. Under the protruding flanges of her sunbonnet her eyes blazed. "Tom Lincoln! Do you mean to tell me you picked land for our cabin with no water nearer'n a mile away? I—I—" Words choked in her throat.

He eyed her miserably, water dribbling from the gourd. It was the first time he had ever seen her really angry, and he looked as woebegone as a child caught in mischief. "It—it won't be for long, love, I promise. Thar's sure to be water somewhar near our place, and when spring comes I'll use the dowser. We'll find it."

She felt her anger slowly trickling away like the drops dripping diamond-bright from the gourd. He looked so much like Abe when his father scolded him for some childish misdemeanor! She wanted to take him in her arms and comfort him. "Here!" She reached out and took the half-emptied gourd from his unsteady hands, lifted it to her lips. "You're right. It *is* good water, good as that at Sinkin' Spring, much better than crick water." She managed a bright smile. "We'll manage."

They did, trudging the long path with their wooden buckets, plus, on washdays, an iron kettle filled with hot coals for making a fire, a bag of soiled clothes, and some of the soft soap Nancy had made. In time she came to regard Tom's lack of foresight with more amusement than irritation. How like a man, picking land nearer to a salt lick where hunting was superabundant than near a spring where his womenfolk must go to draw water! It had not been deliberate self-service, merely thoughtlessness and poor judgment, for Tom was a kindly and considerate husband and father.

The children were delighted with the situation of the spring, for it introduced them quickly to new friends, the family of their neighbor, Reuben Grigsby, father of seven sons. Sarah came back one day, eyes shining, and, seeing Nancy at the fireplace, ran toward her, bucket slopping.

"Ma, guess what! We met a boy at the spring. He's big and right strong and handsome, and his name is Aaron Grigsby. And—and he filled my bucket for me!"

Abe, following with two full buckets, looked disgusted. "Girls!" he scoffed. "Let a boy speak to 'em, and they git sweet on him! Look at her blush!"

"I ain't neither, Ma." Setting down her bucket, Sarah lifted her hands to cover her flaming cheeks. "He—he was jist nice, is all."

Startled, Nancy looked hard at her daughter. With its brightened eyes and reddened cheeks, the child's round, rather plain face seemed to blossom into beauty. Her children were growing up. Then she sighed. Already Sarah, not yet ten, was doing the work of a woman. Why should she not be developing a woman's instincts? And how old had she herself been when she had first seen Tom Lincoln? Twelve, perhaps? But in this rugged, austere country of the pioneer, children grew early to maturity. They had so little childhood! And Abe, not yet eight!

She looked then at her son, noting with suddenly alerted eyes the reed-thin body, shoulders still a little bent from the load he had been carrying, long arms beginning to develop a man's muscles, hands red and calloused, bony shins between the bottoms of his outgrown buckskin trousers and deerskin moccasins seamed and reddened with the cold, sharply angled face under the coonskin cap and black unruly fringe of hair seeming already to reveal the grim lines of hard labor. The ax that Tom had put in his hands on the inland trek had seldom been out of them since, nor would be for the foreseeable future—for the next sixteen years, as Abe himself was to record later.

Again Nancy sighed. Was life to hold nothing more for him than for his father—forests to cut, fields to plow, whiskey casks to fashion, as Tom was doing now for Reuben Grigsby, busy with his shaving-horse and drawknife, painstakingly fitting together the stout laths and binding them tightly with tapered white-oak staves? Oh—please God, no! Much as she loved and admired Tom, not just that for her son!

That night she removed from its hiding place in the feather-bed bag the copy of *Aesop's Fables* that Mrs. Sarah Hodgen had given her for Abe. A mercy she had not put it in the cupboard! Far better to lose her precious pewter tableware! And after the nightly Bible reading she produced it.

Abe's eyes were bright as the live coals embedded in the fire. "You mean—Missus Sarah *give* it to you, Ma?"

"To you," she corrected, smiling. "She knew how much you had enjoyed the stories."

She opened the book at random and began to read.

" 'A lean hungry wolf chanced one night to fall in with a plump, well-fed house dog.

" ' "How is it, my friend," said the wolf, "that you look so well? It seems that you are able to obtain a plentiful supply of food, while I strive night and day for a living and can hardly save myself from starvation."

" ' "If you would fare like me," replied the dog, "you have only to do as I do."

" ' "Indeed!" said the other. "And what is that?"

" ' "I guard the master's house at night and keep off thieves," was the reply.

" ' "If that is all, I will throw in my lot with you with all my heart; for at present I have a sorry time of it prowling around in the forest and the rain without so much as a shelter for my weary bones. To have a warm roof over my head and a stomach full of good wholesome food will, methinks, be no bad exchange." ' "

Back in the shadows Tom stirred uneasily. "Sounds like stuff and nonsense. We ain't got no time for such like. The boy's got to be at work come dawn, remember."

Nancy might not have heard. The wind was from the south, driving smoke into the camp so that her eyes ran and the tears blurred, but somehow she kept on with the fable—how the wolf spied the chain on the dog's neck, found out that he had to be tied up in the daytime, but was fed off the master's own plate and given choice morsels.

" ' "I am a great favorite and—but what is the matter? Where are you going?"

" ' "Oh, good night to you," said the wolf. "You are welcome to your dainties, but for me a dry crust with liberty is better than a king's luxury with a chain." '

"And the lesson is," Nancy finished, " 'Slavery is too high a price to pay for easy living.' "

The boy nodded. "Like us," he said. "We had it easy over in
Kaintuck, but we wanted to be free, so we come here to Indianny."

Tom rose from his stool, cleared his throat. "Come now, that's
enough. No more o' thet stuff. The good Book is one thing, and I
reckon it's right we should know what's in it. But we're pore farmers,
and we don't need nothin' more."

Obediently Nancy put the book back in its hiding place. But she
had seen the hunger and budding wisdom in the boy's eyes. She would
read to him from it again . . . and again. Yes, and she must take
time once more to teach him to read. In the past months she had
been too busy and too tired. The two terms in school had barely
taught him the alphabet. That night she dreamed she was in a vague
place filled with people. A school? A church? A camp meeting? Up
in front, so far up and so high that she could hardly see it, was a
platform, and on the platform a figure, strange yet familiar. "Abe!"
she cried, yet no sound emerged from her lips. He looked like the
boy she knew, yet he wasn't a boy but a man. He seemed to be talking, and everybody was listening, though she heard nothing. Then all
the people started to move forward, to gather about him, all but herself. No matter how hard she tried, she could not move. It was as if
there were no motion, no life, in her. Then everything faded, and she
awoke.

She was a frontierswoman, and the people of the frontier believed
in dreams, just as they believed in ghosts that haunted empty cabins
and rode on ill winds, in water wizards with magic wands, in signs
that governed the time of planting and harvest and foretold death.
She would no more have started to weave a new "kiverlid" on Friday
than Tom would have felled trees for fence rails after noon or in the
waning of the moon. A dream foretold future events. What had hers
meant? Fond mother that she was, it could have but one meaning—
that her son was intended to be more than a logger, a farmer, a carpenter. A teacher, perhaps, like Caleb Hazel? A preacher like Pastor
Elkin? Oh, she hoped it would be a preacher! After that, no matter
how much her eyes ran from the smoke, or Tom scowled and shifted
on his stool and cleared his throat and grumbled that it was bedtime,
she not only read from the Book and the fables herself but encouraged Abe to read also, helping him to stumble from written
words into sentences, first parrotlike, then with increasing fluency
and zest.

When Tom became so impatient that he objected verbally to "such fool larnin' for a farm boy," she read to him from the Discourses of Swiss Pastor Ostervald in the front of their Bible. "Many, it is true, for want of learning, may not be in a capacity to read the Scriptures, which is a great misfortune, and a shame to Christians." She looked up at him, eyes gently defiant. "Tom, I would rather Abe would be able to read the Bible than to own a farm, if he cain't have but one."

Tom was unconvinced. "He waren't talkin' to log-splitters and farmers. I reckon he had lily-white hands and shoulders stooped from sittin' at a desk. Larnin's all right for such as him, not for folks like us."

But Nancy had that sharper arrow in her quiver, and she cunningly drove it home. "Dennis can both read and write," she reminded him once more, "and surely you want our son to do as well."

It was a clinching argument, and Tom grudgingly tempered his verbal criticism. In spite of his affection for the genial and helpful Dennis, he resented any unfavorable comparisons between his own well-born offspring and one who cheerfully admitted, "I came into the world through nature's back door."

Denny was an invaluable addition to the family that winter, and he insisted on staying until the new cabin was built. Then he would return to Kentucky and persuade his foster mother and father to come here to this land of opportunity. While Tom labored on the casks for Reuben Grigsby, promised in time for the season's run on the famous Grigsby apple brandy, Dennis and Abe worked from dawn to dark at the double task of clearing land and amassing logs for the cabin—girdling the great trees to deaden them, careful to perform the task in the dark of the moon, chopping them down, piling brush around the stumps and setting them on fire, cutting logs the proper length and carting them to the spot chosen for building. At night they returned to the half-faced camp "dog-tired and hog-hungry," faces blackened by soot, hands reddened and calloused, to eat Nancy's supper of corn bread and hog meat, later to lounge in the heat and light of the fire while she and Abe read. Then, if Tom was in an expansive mood, after the children had crawled under the bearskins on their brush beds, they would listen to him spin yarns.

"Thet Reuben Grigsby," he chuckled one night after he had been visiting with some of the neighbors at the still, "he's jist like an Injun. And you know why? He almost is one. When he was four some Injuns came into his cabin near Bardstown, Kaintuck. His Pa was away, and Reuben climbed up the chimney and hid. But one of the redskins pulled him down, and he had to look while they kilt his three older brothers and sister. Then they went north, carryin' Reuben and drivin' his mother with her baby. Finally they kilt her and the baby. And when they got tired of luggin' Reuben they threw him in a river, but an old squaw swam out and rescued him. When they threw him in agin, she rescued him agin. She kep' him, nursed him when he got white swellin' in his leg, and saved it with her yarbs. That's why he limps, one leg bein' shorter. He lived with them Injuns for seven years, larnin' their ways. Watch early some mornin', and you'll see him climb on the fence, face toward the east, flap his arms, and crow like a rooster. Greetin' the dawn, I s'pose. It's a queer story. Makes you think—and remember—lots of things."

He lapsed into silence, and Nancy knew he was once more a boy of six, standing over the body of his slain father. She herself was remembering her childhood companion Sarah, who also had been saved by a kind squaw and become ardent in defense of a proud and noble people. She hoped the children were not listening. Enough that they had heard the story of their grandfather's death. Life here was hard enough without reminders of past dangers. She rose quietly and, moving back into the shadows, stood over their beds. Sarah was sleeping, but Abe's eyes were open, staring up at her. What was he thinking, feeling? Though he was of her very bones and flesh, sometimes he seemed like a stranger. The questions he asked, about things she had never even thought of!

"Whar's heaven, Ma? How do we know it's thar if we can't see it?" . . .

"Why does it say in the Book, 'Thou shalt not kill,' and then God goes and helps Joshua and them others kill all their enemies?" . . .

"Does God send people to hell, Ma, if they're wicked? But I thought you said he loves everybody!" . . .

Shrewd, serious questions for a boy of seven, for which she had no answers. But the boy could be droll and teasing too, like the time he had come when she was busy at the loom and asked innocently, "Ma, who was the father of Zebedee's children?"

She had stopped to consider, the shuttle with its dangling yarn held poised. "Why, I—reckon I don't—" Then she had seen the mis-

chievous merriment in his eyes, tumbled to the trick, and shaken the
shuttle in his face. "Oh, git along with you, you little imp!"

Now she pushed the straggling black locks back from his forehead,
patted his cheeks, smiled down at him, but he returned no answering
smile. "Go to sleep," she whispered and went back to the fire, where
Tom was piling on the fuel, in constant battle against a menace almost as deadly as the red man had once been.

For it was a winter of incredible cold and, even this far south, considerable snow. Later the year would be remembered as "eighteen
hundred and froze to death." When the wind was not blowing the little camp full of smoke, it was drawing the heat outward, leaving the
interior almost as cold as the out-of-doors. The dry grass crackled
underfoot. Ice had to be broken at the spring before drawing water.
Lips cracked. Fingers and toes, though encased in deerskin mittens
and boots, were inflamed with painful chilblains.

But the family survived, and by the first of February the weather
turned mild enough so the cabin could be started. A site had been
chosen about a half mile to the north of the half-faced camp. Though
Nancy had seen the one being built at Knob Creek, she still found
the work of construction fascinating. She and Sarah neglected housework and spent every possible moment at the building site. The hewn
logs had already been prepared and pulled to the site, about twenty
of them twenty feet long for the sides of the house, another twenty
fifteen feet, for the ends. Three or four others, each shorter than the
one below, would form the gables. Though Denny and Abe had done
much of the cutting, Tom trusted only his own skilled hands to do
the notching, so that each log would rest neatly on the one below to
form a solid wall. Four large stones were laid, one at each corner for
the foundation. Nancy was amazed at the speed with which the walls
mounted. In just a few days they stood, strong and sturdy, ready for
the smaller logs which would form the floor of the sleeping loft, the
joists of the roof, and finally the ridgepole.

Tom had gone to Grigsby's and Nancy was at the camp when Abe
had his adventure. He and Denny were working inside the new cabin,
a rifle handy in case a bear or other game came near, when they
heard a flurry of wings. Peering through a chink between the logs,
they saw a flock of wild turkeys settling on the ground outside.
Denny ran for the loaded rifle, stuck the barrel through the chink,

sighted, and pulled back the hammer. Then, grinning, he turned to Abe. "Here. You take it, boy. Git one o' them turkeys."

Obediently Abe moved forward, placed his left hand under the stock as he had seen his father do, peered through the chink bringing the muzzle into line with what might be a feathered shape, closed his eyes, and pressed the trigger. The world exploded in his ears, and the gun's recoil sent him reeling. When he picked himself up from the earth floor, there was Denny triumphantly holding a big limp shape, great wings drooping, blood dripping from a crimson projection which had once sported bright beady eyes and a proud crest.

"You done it, boy! Don't know how, but you did. Got it right in the head. Come on, let's show your ma what a hunter she's got!"

Nancy looked up to see Denny proudly sporting the trophy. "Look what your son went and done! Shot it through a crack in the cabin. Wait till Tom hears about this! I'll take it right out and dress it and we'll have it for supper."

Abe appeared presently, face deadly pale, and Nancy knew he had stopped on the way to be sick. Now he was no stranger. How often as a child she had felt the same way, pain twisting her vitals, when jubilant hunters brought home their wild birds and deer, proud wings motionless, slender leaping feet forever stilled! While Nannie had danced about excitedly, she had stood, stomach churning, bleak with suffering, hoping nobody would notice. Now she turned her back on the boy's misery, spoke brightly of the good supper in prospect, and sent him out to get more wood for the fire.

Long afterward Abe would write of the incident and add, "I have never since pulled a trigger on larger game."

Tom, inordinately proud of his son's exploit (though doubtless accidental), could not understand the boy's reluctance to accompany him on hunting expeditions. Only Abe's increasing skill with the ax and his own preference for the chase over the mundane labor of clearing land kept him from more than mild criticism.

"I declar, sometimes I think you're a queer 'un. Whoever heard tell of a boy that would ruther work than hunt!"

Both Tom and Denny were avid hunters, and without meat that winter the family would have gone hungry. But there was no lack of game. The forests were full of animals—raccoon, squirrel, possum, deer, bear, quail, wild turkeys, ducks, geese, the huge flocks of pigeons that gave the creek its name and clouded the air. Though all pioneers were huntsmen, Tom prided himself on his superior skill. As the winter progressed the walls of the half-faced camp were hung with skins, almost as profitable a commodity as Reuben Grigsby's brandy, which sold at $1.25 a gallon in Vincennes. There was a $1.50 bounty on a wolf skin. Though Tom had never shot one, there was always hope.

One day when he went out with his rifle, to Nancy's surprise, he returned almost immediately. She looked up from her work in alarm. "Why—did you forget something?"

"No," he confessed. "Bad sign, is all. Grigsby's dog crossed my path, and you know that's bad luck in the chase. Oh, I locked my little fingers together till it was out of sight, but I reckoned to be sure I'd better come home and start agin. Then the bad start wouldn't be reckoned agin me."

Nancy nodded. She wondered sometimes why a dog crossing a path could spoil one's luck hunting, or why carrying an edged tool like a hoe or ax through a house could foretell a death in the family, or the howling of a dog could mean that tomorrow you would hear of a death somewhere, but she had been brought up to believe in such signs and questioned them only briefly. The building of the new cabin also must be done in accordance with the proper signs, each feature begun in the dark or light of the moon, which made it longer to complete. If the clapboards on the roof, for instance, were not laid at the right time, they would cup and curl.

But work progressed, though slowly. Openings for the door, window, and fireplace were cut out. The cat and clay chimney was constructed. Nancy and the children helped with the chinking, Abe splitting slabs of wood and driving them between the logs, Nancy and Sarah filling the cracks with daubs of wet clay. Tom cut a hole in one corner of the low ceiling for an entrance to the loft and drove wooden spikes into the wall for a ladder, which Abe promptly christened by climbing up and down again and again, delighted with the upper room he was to share with Denny. Tom built a pole bedstead in a corner opposite the fireplace, laying slats across to support the mattress of leaves. Then at last Nancy removed the precious feather bed from its stout bag, laid it on the mattress, and covered the whole with a brightly dyed "kiverlid." When the table and stools were brought from the camp, moving was completed. She cast a regretful glance at the empty corner where the beloved cupboard should have stood.

But Tom would surely find time to build her another. And sometime, too, there would be a good puncheon floor of white oak which she could keep scrubbed and shining, and a stout wooden door instead of a bearskin hung across the opening, and perhaps—fond hope—real glass for the window. Tom had managed a good substitute until glass could be obtained, making a sash with four six-by-eight squares, then taking the skin covering of a hog's fat portion and spreading it tightly over the sash. You could see light through it, and it was almost as good as glass.

The new cabin was on a high knoll, nestled under a protecting canopy of great trees. Spring was coming. The oaks were beginning to sprout pinkish leaves. The willows had turned yellow-gold. Hickories, sycamores, oaks, poplars, were bursting into bud. And settling into her new home, the last one, she hoped, in her life of many changes, she herself was constantly bursting into song. As she traveled the path to the distant spring, spun dreams with her fine yarn, wove bright plans for the future into stout lengths of drab linseywoolsey, kept the fire glowing on the new stone hearth, measured meal from the dwindling supply and kneaded it into hoecakes, she could often be heard singing or humming snatches of a favorite hymn.

"Come, thou Fount of every blessing, Tune my heart to sing thy
     grace. . . .
  Praise the mount! I'm fixed upon it, Mount of thy redeeming love."

It was indeed to be her last home, though not in the way she had hoped.

= 7 =

Spring! Always it had been a time of joyful wonder, but this year it seemed a miracle. Incredible that out of such terrible deep cold the earth could burst into glorious rebirth! Heaven must be like this—life breaking the prison bonds of death. After this, exulted Nancy, she could never be afraid to die.

The air was filled with the rushing of wings. Passenger pigeons floated above in vast clouds, stirred the treetops like passing winds. Parakeets cried shrilly as they flew from tree to tree in bright flashes of green and yellow. The trees burst into bloom, creamy dogwood, pink crab apple, wild plum, red buds with their masses of lavender, haw trees with their white clusters. Even Kentucky had not yielded such a riot of flowers. There were wild roses, swamp lilies, honeysuckle, blue and yellow flag. Wild strawberries were so abundant that the children came home from the spring with their bare legs so crimsoned they looked as if they had waded in blood.

And at last they could be clean again! Little Pigeon Creek a mile away toward the south and west, swollen with the spring rains, though less accessible than the spring, could be visited for the much needed washing of clothes and bathing. Was it the harsh scrubbing of his deerskin trousers, Nancy wondered, or his winter's growth that so lengthened the expanse of bare shins between Abe's britches and his bare feet? A good thing his heavy winter garments could soon be exchanged for the simple knee-length shirts of summer!

No time now to spin and weave, and even household chores must be kept at a minimum. The whole family must engage in the imperative task of raising food for the coming winter. A small section of the new land had been cleared, trees girdled, cut, set fire to, smoldered into charred pieces which could be snaked away by horse and chain. Roots and sprouts must be grubbed out with ax and hoe. As they worked faces became black with soot, and the precious cleanliness must be sought again and again. Corn and beans and pumpkin seeds were planted in the light of the moon, as was proper for vegetables maturing aboveground. Potatoes and other plants maturing underground must be planted in the dark of the moon. The bulbs Nancy had brought from Kentucky were set out. Apple seedlings furnished by Reuben Grigsby gave promise of a fruit crop one day.

They were as near poverty that early spring as Nancy could remember. The corn was nearly gone. She doled it out in driblets, no more than a small hoecake for each person in a day. Though they missed Denny, who had gone back to his family in Kentucky, she was glad of one less mouth, and that an exceptionally hungry one, to feed. Until the cow "came in" with her calf, there was no milk. Hog meat and bacon, the favorite staples, had vanished with the departing pigs. The freezing winter had played terrific havoc with animals, so game was now less plentiful. At one meal the only food on the table was a dish of roasted potatoes, over which Tom pronounced his usual devout grace.

"Thank thee for these blessings, Lord. Fit us for thy humble service, we beg for Christ's sake. Amen."

Abe looked up with a gleam of mischief in his eyes. "Pa," he said, "if you ask me, these here are mighty pore blessin's."

"Mind your tongue, boy," Tom rejoined, but it was a mild rebuke, without the punishment usually following a display of impudence.

In fact, this was one of those periods that Abe was to refer to later as those "pretty pinching times." Yet there was no sadness in such hardship. They knew it was only temporary. And they would no more have thought of begging or accepting help from their neighbors than of stealing from them. Along with the compelling desire for freedom which had made them pioneers they had brought with them a fierce sense of dignity, independence, self-reliance.

Once Nancy was ashamed when a neighbor woman called at the cabin and she had nothing to offer except some slices of raw potato, but with no apparent embarrassment and no excuses she served them on one of the few pewter plates she had left.

There were neighbors, though as yet this part of southwest Indiana was sparsely settled. At the time of their settling there were nine families scattered along the area of Little Pigeon Creek. Beside the Grigsbys there were the Brooners, Peter and Nancy, with their sons Henry and Allen, who lived a mile to the southeast. Peter Brooner had the reputation of being the most skillful hunter and marksman in the region. There were the families of William Whitman and of Noah Gordon, whose farm adjoined their claim. There was William Wood, who lived a mile and a half to the north. But Nancy seldom saw them. "I'm right proud to know you," she had said to Mrs. Grigsby and other neighbor women who came to the cabin or whom she met at a "raising" or a "log-rolling." She missed the sight of travelers going by on the Old Cumberland Road, which ran by the Knob Creek cabin, and the visits of well-known neighbors and relatives, especially the monthly services at the Little Mount Church.

Though a Baptist society had been organized in 1816 by Elder Downs, brother of William Downs, who had preached the funeral sermon for little Tommy back in Kentucky, no church had yet been built, and services were held only infrequently when a traveling preacher gathered worshipers in a cabin somewhere, often many miles away. Even the people she met on such occasions remained strangers. She knew that her shyness and sensitivity set her somehow apart, that people probably considered her unfriendly, standoffish, even proud and conceited, but she never seemed able to make light conversation, indulge in gossip, discuss intimacies of home and family life with other women.

"Nat Grigsby says his mother thinks you're stuck-up," Abe told her once, " 'cause you know how to read and most women cain't, and you don't never go to her house to visit. Why don't you go, Ma?"

"I—I guess I'm jist too busy," Nancy replied, knowing it was no excuse.

"And she says you always looks sad, Ma," the boy persisted, his dark eyes probing her features. "I reckon mebbe she's right. Why are you sad, Ma?"

Why, indeed? Nancy had no answer. What did make one sad when one was happy, saddest of all, in fact, when one was happiest? Why, when you experienced the highest ecstasy of love or beauty did you feel the deepest pain? Why, when you held your newborn son in your arms, the supreme joy you had hoped and prayed for, the fulfillment of life, did you sense a bitter foretaste of death? Why did you know, when you journeyed toward new horizons, that there would always be something beyond, something you would never reach?

She smiled, dispelling all gravity from her naturally sober features, so that even her eyes seemed to change in color from grayish brown to what Denny liked to call "a bluish-green." She drew the boy toward her in a quick embrace, an unusual display of affection, for like many with deep emotions she was not a demonstrative person.

"If I look sad, son, then I reckon you do too—or will when you see more of life. For you and I are a heap alike."

That summer she lived in hope that Dennis could persuade Betsy and Thomas Sparrow to come to Indiana. She hungered for the companionship of those who loved and understood her, both friends and relatives. Though her uncle Joseph Hanks had moved to Perry County some years before, had even served on the county jury in 1815, he and his wife Mary were too far away for visiting. Tom's cousins, Austin and David Lincoln, sons of Hananiah, were only about six miles from their cabin, but six miles through pathless wilderness were no better than a hundred.

It was in October of 1817 that her hopes were fulfilled. Dennis arrived one day bringing word that his foster parents had come to Anderson's Creek by flatboat with all their possessions. They had required only a little persuading, for Thomas Sparrow was facing an ejection suit on his land at Nolin and had to move elsewhere. Tom and Denny set off immediately with horses and wagon to bring them the last sixteen miles of their journey. Nancy waited in a fever of joyful anticipation. When at last the wagon lumbered into the clearing and she ran to meet it, only the hampering folds of her long calico skirt kept her from reaching it before the children. With Betsy's arms about her—their tears of joy mingled within the confining shelter of their sunbonnets—Nancy felt the hard core of loneliness dissolve. The new cabin in the wilderness had at last become home.

She would have been glad for them to share it in spite of the overcrowding, but Thomas Sparrow insisted that the old half-faced camp would make a comfortable shelter until their own cabin could be built.

"That Darne little half-face camp!" Dennis would describe it later.

"Now," Tom told Nancy with satisfaction after the new family had been settled, "I kin go to the land office in Vincennes and git my land secure. I didn't want to leave you and the young'uns alone before."

He would travel the sixty miles each way with his neighbors, William Whitman and Noah Gordon, who also had claims to enter. He was leaving ample food for both families. He had taken a bag of the newly harvested corn to the nearest mill, Huffman's, a horse-powered affair seventeen miles away, and ground it into meal. Dennis would provide game. The children could pick nuts and berries. There was fish to be caught in the creek. And with Betsy there the time would pass quickly.

For Nancy time would never pass quickly with Tom away, especially on such a long and dangerous journey, but the worry and waiting were rewarded when he returned home triumphant.

"See!" He held out a certificate marked Receipt No. 8499. "Read it, love."

Nancy read, " 'To Thomas Lincoln of Perry County, Indiana.' "

As she continued her face lighted, for the paper credited him with the payment of $16 as "deposit on account of land for which he intends to apply." The land was described as containing two tracts of eighty acres each, the southwest quarter of Section 32, T 4 S, R 5 W.

"It's good land," he exulted, "a whole quarter section, 160 acres. I have to go again in two months and pay another $64. That'll be a quarter of the purchase price of $320."

"Oh, Tom!" Nancy was both delighted and worried. "Do you think we'll have the money?"

"No trouble." Tom was airily confident. "Grigsby wants more casks before Christmas."

Another trip to Vincennes, and he was back with a second receipt showing that he had paid the required $80. "Jist a year," he told Nancy with satisfaction, "and here we've got everything we hoped for. Title to 160 acres and a quarter of it paid for. Some land cleared and a crop raised. And a tollable decent cabin to live in." He saw Nancy's glance waver between the earth floor and the doorless opening still protected in bad weather by only a curtain of bearskins, and added in hasty, uneasy apology, "I know. Thar's lots to be done on it yet. But you know how busy I've been. And now thar's all this new land to be cleared."

The second winter in Indiana held less of discomfort and deprivation than the first. It was Betsy now who was suffering the exigencies of the little half-faced camp, and, although the weather was milder than that season of "eighteen hundred and froze to death," Nancy worried about her. During the coldest weeks she insisted that the Sparrows move to the cabin, and the little eighteen-by-twenty-foot room became almost as crowded and suffocating as the "bear's den" the irrepressible Denny likened it to. Another pole bed was erected in the opposite corner from the first, which Denny dubbed "the Sparrows' nest." Sarah slept on her usual trundle, slipped under her parents' bed in the daytime. Abe and Denny climbed each night up the creaking wooden pegs to the dark loft. Smells of frying bacon and steaming hog meat and venison mingled with those of wood smoke and rain- and sweat-soaked clothing and infrequently bathed bodies.

But for both Nancy and Abe, at least, it held times of unalloyed delight, for when Tom had been on his last trip to Vincennes he had attended a sale and seen a copy of Bunyan's *The Pilgrim's Progress*. Remembering Abe's hunger for books, he had brought it home. Abe had been so overjoyed with the gift that his eyes had sparkled. All that day he had been unable to eat and that night he could not sleep. Now in the evenings, after Bible reading and prayer, Nancy read from the old and battered copy, slowly, for it was hard seeing the words by the light of the fire, even though Abe and Denny kept it stoked until the room was hot nearly to suffocation. Sometimes for more light they burned bear's grease in the dipper-shaped metal lamp hanging from the wall, adding its rank smell to the other penetrating odors. But no one minded heat or stench. All were too engrossed in the adventures of the fabulous Christian, pursuing his troublesome journey through the Slough of Despond and the Wicket Gate, casting off his burden at the Cross, struggling up the Hill Difficulty, traversing the terrible Valley of the Shadow of Death, finding hope in the Delectable Mountains, beset by temptations, arriving at last in the heavenly City of God.

All listened with the keen interest and understanding of pioneers who themselves had known the perils of such a journey, both physical and spiritual. But Abe was entranced. He would have lain by the fire all night poring over the words and pictures if Tom had not cuffed him off to bed.

"Should have known better'n to git you a new book! We'd all go hungry if we had to depend on you to git the fields plowed and the plantin' done."

The corn crop had been meager that first year and to make sure of enough to last until next harvest Nancy once more skimped on the meal for bread, sometimes serving only fried and boiled meat, with perhaps potatoes or turnips, for days at a time. At least the men were spared the seventeen-mile trip to the nearest mill. The small amounts of corn used could be ground in the home mill Tom had made soon after their arrival, cutting off a four-foot length of big tree trunk, setting it on end, starting a fire in its top, keeping the wood around it wet so it would not burn, nursing the fire until a hole had been burned about a foot deep and clearing out the coals. Up to two quarts of corn could be put in the hole, and patient work with a stone pestle would reduce it to meal.

It was a milder winter than the first, with the three men and Abe working hard to clear more land for planting. The pounding of broadaxes, shouts of "Timber!", and the crash of great trees beat a strident accompaniment to the whirring of Nancy's spinning wheel, the clatter of her loom as she wove the thread into cloth. When spring came the cabin on its knoll was no longer imprisoned within a shroud of huge poplars, beeches, and sycamores pushing high toward an almost invisible sky. It sat in openness and sunlight, with a wider view toward far horizons.

Never had spring seemed so beautiful. Nancy drank in its fragrances, absorbed its glowing colors, vibrated to its caroling sounds with every fiber of her being, as if she might never see another. The smallest household chore became a sacrament, an affirmation of the song and Scripture she so loved. Walking with Sarah the mile to the spring and filling the buckets from its sparkling depths—*The water that I give shall be in him a well of water springing up unto everlasting life!* Spinning last summer's flax into linen thread—*A virtuous woman . . . she seeketh wool and flax and worketh willingly with her hands!* Kneading the precious meal into the few cakes of corn pone—*I am the bread of life. He that cometh to Me shall never hunger!* Planting deep in the earth some of the "yarb" seedlings Betsy had brought her from Kentucky, she sang to herself:

> *"You may bury me in the east,*
> *You may bury me in the west,*
> *And we'll all rise together in that morning."*

"We'd ought to have us a log-rollin'," Tom announced when a large area of the new land had been cleared. "Need help gittin' rid of this stuff."

Nancy was dismayed. Invite all the settlers for miles around to come to their cabin, not only friends but strangers? Feed them, when there was barely enough corn to last the family through harvest? But Tom, eager for the excitement as well as for the needed assistance, answered all her objections. There would be a dozen women to help her and Betsy. The woods were full of game. The cow had "come in" with plenty of milk. There were wild hogs to be had for the shooting. And he would build the new cupboard Mrs. Grigsby had been wanting in exchange for a bushel of corn.

The day was set. Invitations were unnecessary. The grapevine of communication was as vigorous as its namesake of tough matted undergrowth which choked the forests and interlaced the tops of the hundred-foot trees. The "raising" of a cabin or a "log-rolling," especially the latter, aroused an excess of neighborly co-operation. For all knew that the huge tree trunks, up to five feet in diameter, could not be moved by one man and his team. They came from miles around, bringing their horses, oxen, tools, wives, children, all primed for a day of grueling labor but also of riotous festivity.

Horses straining, oxen heaving and tugging almost to bursting, men grunting and sweating, handspikes prying and shoving, chains pulling, the giant trunks were pushed, rolled, dragged into great piles, and by the end of the day a fair amount of ground was cleared around the tree stumps, ready for the bull-tongue plow and grub hoe. For both dinner and supper Nancy and her helpers supplied vast quantities of food. Boiled turkeys, geese, chickens, veal, and venison were served in a variety of forms, with mountains of corn pone made from Reuben Grigsby's bushel of grain (on the promise of the cupboard yet to come), plenty of milk, and of course an abundance of the ever-present whiskey, augmented by a cask of Reuben Grigsby's brandy, which, it was claimed, was so dry it would burn like a candle.

But the climax of the day came after supper when the great piles of logs were burned. Up, up the flames mounted, reddening the sky, visible for miles around, turning the night into a blaze of glory. Abe and his friends were entranced, getting as close to the fire as possible, their small figures outlined in its glow, looking for all the world, thought Nancy with horror, like Daniel's three companions in the fiery furnace. A fiddler appeared out of nowhere, and soon the real revelry began, the "hoedown," dancing, when the sturdy pioneers, unwearied by the day's labor and encouraged by frequent visits to the sources of fresh stimulus, moved to the rollicking tunes far into the night.

Nancy did not join in the dancing, and not wholly because she was utterly weary. She stood a little apart, eyes wavering between the children, making sure they were safe, and the magic of the fire. It was beautiful and horrible, fascinating and frightening. In fact, the whole day had been a time of contradictions—pleasure, discomfort; ease, embarrassment; a glowing knowledge of Tom's approval coupled with a sense of inadequacy. She had worked side by side with the neighbor women, yet she knew they still thought her proud and aloof. Why in their presence did she freeze on the surface like the creek locked in ice? Betsy, far more a stranger to them, had been accepted, gossiping, joking, not above a bit of vulgarity, while she,

Nancy, had remained always just outside their intimate little clique of womanhood. She felt far more a part of the group when men gathered of an evening in the cabin and talked with Tom about politics and religion and slavery. Though of course she never took part in such discussions, she listened intelligently and formed her own opinions.

Tom was exultant. He now had many more acres of his new land cleared, and he set Dennis and Abe to work plowing and planting. Last season the wild hogs had been a nuisance, and he decided to protect this year's crops with a rail fence. Chopping down a sturdy oak tree, he cut it into the right lengths, made a deep cleft with his ax, and drove a sharpened oak wedge, or "glut," deep into the wood. Then, swinging his short maul, called a "froe club," with powerful strokes, he drove the glut along a widening cleft in the log until finally it split cleanly open. He proceeded to split the two halves, then the two quarters.

"Now you try it," he told Abe, who had been watching intently.

The boy began swinging the maul on another log, finding that it grew heavier and heavier as he proceeded. Sweat poured down his face, blinded his eyes, but he grimly persisted until eight good fence rails were lying on the ground, not as clean and straight as his father's, but passable.

"Not bad for a nine-year-old," approved Tom. "You'll make a rail-splitter yet. But remember," he warned, "never lay a fence-worm in the dark of the moon or the rails will sink into the ground."

That year saw new immigrants pouring into the region of Pigeon Creek. One of them was James Gentry, who had been a wealthy slaveholder back in Kentucky. Because Indiana was a free state, he had sold his slaves, though remaining pro-slavery by conviction. He bought a thousand acres of land adjoining Tom's section and moved with his wife and ten children into a big cabin about a mile and a half west of the Lincolns. Twelve-year-old Joseph Gentry soon became a good friend of Abe's and of Nat Grigsby's.

That summer of 1818 was hot. It was a stagnant heat. Heavy spring rainfalls had filled the streams, piled dead leaves into rotten masses which exuded unhealthy fumes. Though there was little rain during the summer, thick morning fogs soaked the ground. Marshes steamed. Clothes clung soggily to sweating skins. Nancy wilted in the oppressive atmosphere. Her shoulders sagged as if under an invisible burden. Usually quick of step, her feet dragged. Her natural sallowness became an unhealthy gray.

"You're workin' too hard," worried Betsy. "You're not lookin' right fit at all."

"It's nothin'," Nancy assured. "I'm jist a bit tired is all. Once the cooler air comes, I'll be same as ever."

The Sparrows were still living in the little half-faced camp. Thomas and Dennis had cleared some land and planted a small crop of corn, and they hoped to put up a cabin before winter once their claim was registered.

"Jist wait and see if he does it!" Tom Lincoln scoffed to Nancy. "If I ain't mistook, they'll still be livin' in that makeshift camp come spring."

Though a genial and well-respected person, Thomas had never been noted for promptness or love of hard labor. He had lost his land in Kentucky because of a suit brought against him and his brother-in-law, Jesse Friend, by a Mrs. Nancy Ashcraft for a "broken covenant." Thomas and Jesse had agreed to work Mrs. Ashcraft's land for one third of what could be raised, but apparently little work had been done.

Tom Lincoln was incorrect, however, in his prediction. Thomas and Elizabeth would not be living in the little camp "come spring."

The stifling summer passed, and there came welcome surcease. Nancy's eyes brightened, her shoulders straightened, and she wakened without the dread of another long day's work ahead. She loved the autumn almost as much as the spring. Eagerly she awaited the first hint of color in the forests around the cleared fields. September came, bringing days of clear coolness as refreshing as the sparkling spring water, touches of gold in the sycamores, an early hint of crimson in the maples and sumacs. But it brought also a curse far more devastating than heat. Dennis came running up from the camp one day, face pale, eyes fairly popping from his head.

"Our cow—she jist up and died! Keeled over like she been shot. Pa thinks she got the trembles!"

The "trembles"! That mysterious plague which had followed the pioneer through all his migrations, from the Carolinas to Illinois, stalking him like a hunter, hiding away for years then suddenly springing up without apparent cause, attacking milch cows first and then people, defying all known remedies, bringing severe but mercifully brief suffering before ending usually in death! The settlers called it by many names—the "trembles," the "staggers," the "bloody murrain," "swamp sickness," "puking fever"—but because it seemed to be the result of drinking the milk of infected cows, it was often called "milk-sick." No one knew what caused it, though it was suspected that the cattle were in some way responsible. Perhaps the water they drank was contaminated, or perhaps poisons in the soil evaporating in the night were sucked up by the morning dew. Or perhaps it came from some unhealthy marsh exhalation. Or it might be that the cows had eaten some poisonous plant. Not for many years, nearly a hundred of them, would it be concluded that the latter was the most probable theory, and more years before it was finally discovered that the culprit was an innocent-looking little plant known as white snakeroot, its death-dealing poison a substance called tremotol.

But to the little community along Pigeon Creek in that fall of 1818 the cause was relatively unimportant. The fact was what mattered. Cattle died in swift succession. Men and women began to exhibit symptoms—dizziness, nausea, vomiting, enlarged tongue, stomach pains, intense thirst—and, as one after the other died, panic spread through the area. Some families loaded a few possessions into carts or on horses and fled, like villagers in the Middle Ages hoping to escape the plague. Others shut themselves in their cabins in the vain belief that closed doors could shut out the angel of death.

Not so the Lincolns, especially Nancy. "I must go to them," was her first thought when she heard about more victims. And, while Tom was engaged in the new unwelcome task of making coffins, she traveled the rough paths from cabin to cabin, walking miles, pushing through the yellowing grapevines, carrying a kettle of nourishing broth and the "yarbs" she had been taught to use for fevers and other ailments. Sometimes Dennis went with her, but she insisted that Abe and Sarah remain at home. If there was risk of contagion involved, they should not share it.

There was no trained doctor nearer than thirty-five miles, but a traveling "yarb and root" doctor who came riding through bled the stricken settlers and prescribed a tea made of cornhusks and boiled roots. Nancy's own simple remedies of calomel, saleratus, honey, lobelia, and "yarb tea" probably did as much good. For the tight congestion in the bowels, which was such a painful symptom, she gave enemas of warm water, honey, and saleratus, using the usual pioneer equipment of a hog's bladder and a hollow reed. Often she grew faint from the sickening breath odors which accompanied the disease, but she shut her eyes, held her breath, and tried to imagine herself in the midst of springtime honeysuckle and roses.

"You're an angel," whispered more than one of the women who had gossiped about her "pride," her "better than thou" neighborliness.

September was more than half gone when Dennis brought word that Thomas Sparrow was showing symptoms of the disease. Nancy went to the camp immediately and in spite of her fears for her own family insisted that both he and Betsy come to the cabin. On September 21 Thomas made his will, a neighbor who knew how to write making the brief notation which he signed by making his mark, leaving all his "goods and chattels to my wife Elizabeth Sparrow. She can do as she pleases with it until her death. After that the whole property is to fall to Dennis Hanks when he comes of age." Nancy also signed as a witness, making her mark. But even before he was gone Betsy also had succumbed to the disease.

As Nancy went through the motions of nursing them, lovingly, with all the skill of which she was capable, yet knowing what the end must be, it was her body that moved. Mind and emotions were too numbed to let her think or feel. She could not even pray. The sound of Tom's hammer pounding the whittled pegs into the bored holes in two new coffins seemed to come from as far away as the big cabin James Gentry was building over to the west—or as eternity. Only when she stood on the low knoll a half mile to the south of the cabin where Dennis had dug two graves and the second pine box was being lowered into the ground did both mind and emotions leap suddenly into awareness. She saw shapes and colors with startling clarity—the heart-shaped leaves of a sycamore already turning a bright yellow, the gray scaly bark of a huge white oak, a pigeon hanging motionless in a cleft of sky, the neatly fitted cover of the box which Tom had so carefully made. This was a beautiful spot, its ground uncleared, its grove of great trees arching like a protecting canopy. Peace. Rest. Nancy almost envied Betsy lying here among the sheltering leaves as they changed color, fell gently, formed a soft red and gold and bronze and orange "kiverlid." Betsy—gone! The realization filled her suddenly with indescribable loneliness. The only mother she had really known!

But there was no time to mourn. People were still sick and dying. One was her neighbor Nancy Brooner. Tired though she was, she took the kettle of meat broth and her bag of "yarbs" and started on the mile and a half trek to Peter Brooner's cabin.

"Don't go, love," begged Tom, who was already at work with his whipsaw and planing ax, fashioning another coffin. "There ain't no call for you to kill yourself helpin' the neighbors. What did they ever do for you?"

"Let us go, too, Ma, please! Abe and I kin help."

But Nancy said no to both pleas. "Jist this once more," she told them, managing a weary smile. "She's expectin' me, and it means a lot. I won't be goin' agin, I promise."

She was glad she had come when she saw the fevered eyes light, felt the clammy hand reach out in welcome. There was little she could do, for the disease was already in its last stages, but she spooned some of the broth between the parched lips and smiled encouragingly.

"I—I'm goin' to—die—" The swollen tongue made the words barely audible.

"Tut, tut! Don't say that," comforted Nancy. "You'll soon be well and strong agin. You'll prob'ly be livin' long after I'm gone. Keep up your courage."

Perhaps when she made the prediction she was feeling the first pangs of the milk-sick, dizziness, abdominal pains, stiffness in the legs. Even before Mrs. Brooner was laid to rest in Tom's new coffin on the knoll near Betsy and Thomas Sparrow, Nancy was lying on the pole bed in the cabin corner. She did not suffer alone. It was the turn of the neighbor women now to come to her, but they could do little to help.

"You'll git better," Tom insisted, hovering over her in helpless misery.

She clasped one of his big fumbling hands and smiled up at him. "If it's God's will," she murmured, voicing the simple creed of their Primitive Baptist faith. "What is to be will be, and we can do nothing about it."

It should have been a comfort, remembering the words Ostervald had put in one of the Bible footnotes: "Nothing can hinder the execution of the designs of Providence, that whatever men do to prevent them, only serves to hasten them." But in spite of her assurance to

Tom, she inwardly rebelled. She did not want to die. What would become of Tom, of the children? Who would spin and weave their linsey-woolsey shirts, sew their deerskin trousers, wash their clothes, make the soap to do it with, knead and bake the new harvest of corn into nourishing bread? Little Sarah? She was willing and capable, but, oh, still such a child! Dear God, let her not be thrust into womanhood so soon!

She begged Tom to send Dennis and the children to the half-faced camp to stay. No one knew better than she the anguish and discomfort of watching the disease progress—the wasting of flesh, reddened eyes filled with gummy discharge, offensive odors. Let them remember her not like this, but running with them down the path to the spring, wading in the creek, spinning, kneading hoecakes, picking roses and wild honeysuckle, walking barefoot with them through the dew, scrambling on the ground for nuts, sitting by the fire and reading to them from the Book! But they refused to go. They wanted so much to help! Abe came bringing a spray of bright red maple leaves and laid it on the bed beside her.

"It's the purtiest I could find. I knowed how you liked to look at 'em."

Her heart swelled almost to bursting. Neighbor women had brought food—broth, "yarb tea," fruit juices—to tempt her appetite. Tom and Sarah and Denny had hovered about, begging to be of service but not knowing how. Yet who but Abe would remember and think to minister to her deepest need? She held the spray lovingly, fingers stroking the soft texture, eyes hungrily absorbing its beauty. What a rich glowing crimson, as if within it the slowly dying year were shedding its very life-blood! Not so delicately beautiful as the spring's honeysuckle and wild roses and lilacs and crab apple blossoms. Suddenly she felt pain more acute than that which racked her body. Never to see their brightness again? Could the beauty of paradise possibly compare with the loveliness of spring, the glories of autumn? Streets of gold! They sounded so hard and cold. Not like walking to the spring on a carpet of yellow sycamore leaves.

Time was getting short. Having seen others go, she knew the signs. It was getting hard to breathe. She could sense the coldness of her skin. Her body was racked by agonizing fits of vomiting. Before sinking into that final coma which must be such a welcome release from pain, there were things she must . . .

"Tom!" She fumbled for his hand, which seemed always within reach.

"Yes, love?"

"Please—bring the children."

They came and knelt by the bed. Her eyes, sunk deep in their sockets, were like live coals glowing in gray ashes.

"Darlings—I'm going away from you, and—I shan't be coming back. No, no!" as they began to cry, "don't weep. Jist listen. You, Sarah." She ran her fingers through the girl's long straight hair. "You're jist a child, but you got to be a woman—quick. Take care of your father and brother. And you, Abe."

"Yes, Ma?" The words were a choked mumble.

Groping, her fingers found the coarse black shock. "You—must be a—good boy." It was getting harder and harder to talk. Her swollen tongue and cracked lips almost refused to function. "Be—kind to your—father and sister. Live as—as I have taught you. Love your—Heavenly Father. And—remember"—the words were barely audible—"both of you—our—God is a—prayer-hearin' God."

Her eyes closed, leaving the drawn features empty of life. But mind and emotions raced silently on. Oh, my darlings, let life be good to you! You, Sarah, I kin see your future, a good, kind wife and mother. Mebbe that Aaron Grigsby, who likes to dip water for you at the spring. I ain't afeared for you. But, oh, Abe, my son, my son! What will become of you? Who will see that you kin read and larn things, become what's inside of you to be? I don't know what. A teacher? A preacher? It would be nice to know, to see . . . But that don't matter. I'm jist afeared your father won't help. If there kin only be someone . . . someone.

The thought came suddenly, like a bright flash of sunshine. "Tom!" The word was only a breath, but he heard it and came.

"Yes, love?"

"Sally—" She mouthed the words, not knowing whether her lips uttered them or not. "Alone—like you—please—you—loved her—once—before me—"

"Don't! I cain't bear to think of it. You're my one love."

Good. The words must have been spoken. No need to fight the agony any longer. She could slip into that blessed finality which seemed to be not so much emptiness as fullness, peace instead of painlessness, and, yes, where one could sense a distant fragrance of spring flowers.

= 8 =

It was Monday, October 5, 1818. Like most of its victims Nancy had been sick with the disease only a week. Tom could not have managed without the neighbors. He had taken almost no time to sleep except for one night, when William Wood had spelled him at the bedside. Some of the women came and prepared the body for burial, washing it, dressing it in her best Sunday calico, while Tom made the coffin.

He had used all his seasoned lumber for previous burials, but he found a new log of black cherry which could be split into boards. He knew just the right length to make them without measuring, for Nancy had been just a little shorter than himself, the top of her head coming to the middle of his forehead. While he whipsawed the log into boards Abe sat beside him whittling pegs for pinning them together, stopping frequently to rub a grimy fist across his eyes.

In spite of exhaustion Tom was glad of work for his hands to do. With his jack-plane he made the surfaces of each board smooth, as carefully and critically as if for one of his stout corner cupboards. He had been too numbed to shed tears—until now, remembering suddenly how much Nancy had wanted another cupboard, yet he had not found time to make her one. His vision became so blurred that he made an ugly nick in the smoothed wood.

He and Abe put the boards together, driving the wooden pegs tightly into the bored holes. Ready now for its burden. "Wait!" cried Abe. He scampered off, returning with a great armful of red and yellow leaves, then went again and again, until the bottom of the box was covered with a soft bed. Tom would let no one help him bring her out. She was a light burden. When he had laid her down, tenderly, smoothing the dark hair back neatly from the high, narrow brow, again Abe said, "Wait!" He ran back into the cabin and returned with a warm woolen "kiverlid." "She might be cold," he explained, tucking it about her.

Placing the box on a horse-drawn sled which Tom used for hauling wood, they started for the little knoll to the south. Neighbors went with them—Grigsbys, Gordons, Whitmans, William Wood, the Brooners who were left, even the newcomers, James Gentry and his family. It was a rough trail. Tom kept his hand on the box to steady it as the sled bumped over stones and roots and hummocks—or was it partly to maintain contact with the vanishing past as long as possible?

The knoll was beautiful in spite of the raw mounds of earth and the new gaping rectangle with dirt heaped beside it. William Roberts, a neighbor who had helped dig the grave beside those of Thomas and Elizabeth Sparrow, was waiting with others to join the little group. Autumn had provided lavish floral tributes. Crimson of maples and sumacs, golds of sycamores, bronzes of sassafras and hickories, dull reds of sweet gum, all interwove and mingled in a glorious protective canopy. The box was lowered and neighbors replaced the dirt, leaving only another raw mound of earth to be covered soon, like the others, by a luxuriant carpet of fallen leaves. There was no burial service. According to the custom of Tom's Baptist brethren, that would come later.

Standing with empty hands, fingers twisting helplessly, the sounds of thudding earth still pounding like heartbeats in his ears, Tom felt a touch on his shoulder. He looked into Peter Brooner's face, tortured like his own, and remembered that Nancy Brooner was lying under a new mound of earth.

"Now," said Peter, "you and I are brothers."

Tom nodded. They clasped each other's hands.

The little company dispersed, and the family made its way back home with the horse and empty sled. Home? Four walls as devoid of life as the box they had just left on the hill.

Always before the cabin had seemed cosy, homelike. Entering by the opening which he had long ago promised to fill with a good oak door, Tom shrank at consciousness of its stark bareness—the earth floor still uncovered with puncheon boards, the corner where the long-desired corner cupboard should be standing, the empty bed, the dying fire.

"Come," he told the others, "there's work to be done." Brusquely, to hide his emotion, he gave orders.

Denny went to the smokehouse for a side of hog meat. Abe brought wood and fed the fire, glad for the smoke that gave his eyes an excuse to smart. Sarah put the meat in the big iron pot standing with its long legs in the coals, then poured corn meal and water in the wooden mixing bowl, trying to remember just how many strokes with the paddle and kneading with the hands it took to make hoecakes thick and light. When the food was ready the four of them sat at the table.

"Fit and prepare us for humble service—" began Tom. His voice choked and he could not continue.

They ate, silently, without appetite, casting occasional involuntary glances toward the empty bed in the far corner. Sarah hung her head in mute misery, for the meat was underdone, the hoecakes flat and leathery. Afterward Abe, as he had done each night during his mother's illness, blew up the fire with the pigskin bellows and, squatting in its glowing light, opened the book they had been reading.

" 'Now at the end of this valley,' " he read slowly and laboriously, pointing out each word with a bony finger, " 'was another, called the Valley of the Shadow of Death; and—and Christian must—must needs go through it, be—because the way to the Ce—Celes—Celestial City lay through the—the midst of it. Now this valley is—is a very soli—solitary place . . .' " His voice broke.

"Enough," said Tom gruffly. "Time for you boys to git up to your loft. Time for the young'un here to git to her bed too. We've all got work to do tomorrow."

So began the year which none of the four wanted to remember.

Sarah did the best she could. She was strong and capable, and her short sturdy body was mature for an eleven-year-old. Nancy had trained her well. But now there was no mother to plan, to direct. She was no longer helper but sole housekeeper, cleaner, cook, spinner, weaver, soap maker, clothes-washer, candle-dipper, seamstress, as well as would-be mother to the boy two years her junior. She could not possibly fill all these roles with the skill and swiftness of an adult. Though the corn bread improved in time, it was never as tender and tasty as her mother's had been. She could never seem to turn it at the right time on the shovel, and as for tossing it in the air for turning the way women should be able to do, the only time she tried it had landed with a messy plop in the fire. The bacon came to the table either underdone or in hard blackened lumps. She could never seem to get the beans and turnips and meats cooked just right. Abe needed new buckskin breeches. He was growing so fast that the expanse of bare shin, reddened by the winter's cold, was steadily widening. But making new ones meant not only the preparing of skins but the slow and agonizing work of pushing the bone needle through the tough fabric, and she was too tired by the necessary chores to attempt either. And, oh, the loneliness!

"Sairy was a little gal," Dennis was to record later, "only 'leven, and she'd git so lonesome, missin' her mother, she'd set by the fire an' cry. Me'n Abe got 'er a baby coon an' a turtle, an' tried to git a fawn but we couldn't ketch any."

She lived for the brief hour at the end of day when the four of them were together in the cabin and Abe would read from the Bible as his mother had done, then perhaps from *The Pilgrim's Progress*. The Delectable Mountains, Beulah Land, The Eternal City, all lying beyond that Valley of the Shadow of Death, seemed as real and near as the wooded hill to the south where the mounds lay hidden under a blanket of leaves. There was even laughter as Abe read from *Aesop's Fables* about the foibles and dilemmas of "The Cat and the Mice" or "The Lion and the Four Bulls" or "The Ape and the Fox."

There was one ray of brightness for the children that winter after Nancy died. Andrew Crawford, a respected member of the Pigeon Creek community whose commission as Justice of the Peace that same year of 1818 rated him the title "Squire," decided to start a school. Though little knowledge or education was necessary to qualify a pioneer teacher, only the ability to read, write, and cipher to the rule of three, to wield a hickory stick and whittle pens from a bundle of quills, Squire Crawford was unusually well qualified. Though he probably did not know Latin, which would have ranked him in public estimation as a "wizard," he was versed not only in the three R's, but possessed a general knowledge and culture above most of his neighbors.

The community subscribed for the school's support.

"Please, Pa," begged Abe when a neighbor came to the cabin asking for a subscription.

Tom, noting the boy's eagerness, could not refuse. Nancy would have wanted it. He could easily spare the amount of the subscription, for there were coonskins hanging in the pole shed and hams in the smokehouse, both of which were good legal tender, far more valuable than the "wildcat" paper which was the only form of money available. "I reckon it won't do no harm," he agreed with some reluctance. "School will be over in time for plowin' and plantin'."

A schoolhouse was built on Grigsby land about a mile and a half from the cabin, a rough log house about sixteen by twenty-five feet, just high enough for a man to stand without hitting his head on the ceiling. It had one door and a window opening covered with greased paper through which the sunlight slanted dimly over the puncheon floor and split-log benches. But fortunately the pupils had little need of light, for, like all others of the time and place, it was a "blab" school, the teacher possessing the only books and the scholars repeating the lessons after him with noise and gusto.

On school days Sarah brought in the wooden tub and washed both Abe and herself until their hands and faces were as red from scrubbing as later they would be from the winter's cold. She took a fierce pride in the knowledge that they were as clean as the other children, though the dinginess and shabbiness of their clothes filled her with shame. Nancy's kettle of soap was empty, and she didn't know how to make more. Both of them needed new woolen socks and mittens. On the coldest days she roasted potatoes to keep their hands warm in their pockets, to serve later as lunch at recess. On their way to school, passing the hill with its sad little collection of mounds, she took Abe by the hand and tried to divert his attention. Already she had acquired toward him the tenderness of a mother anxious to spare him as much grief as possible. She was glad when other children joined them along the way, Grigsbys, Gentrys, Brooners, Woods, Robeys, Romines, turning their somberness into at least a semblance of jollity with races, playing hare and hounds or wet and dry stones, or, weather occasionally permitting, pelting each other with snowballs.

Squire Crawford dispensed more than the rudiments of the three R's, and the hickory stick hanging behind the desk was seldom used. Somehow he made the textbook from which he intoned come alive, and youthful tongues were soon glibly repeating one-, two-, even three-letter words from Dilworth's *Speller,* as well as tables from Pike's *Arithmetick,* to the limit of their vocal cords. But he attempted to teach his pupils manners also, new accomplishments indeed for these frontier offspring.

"You are young ladies and gentlemen," he told them firmly, "and you must learn to conduct yourselves as such."

One lesson to be learned through practice was the proper manner of introduction.

"You, Abe Lincoln," he might say, "go out of the room with your friend Nat Grigsby. Bring him back and introduce him to Miss Elizabeth Wood."

Thereupon Abe would go out, knock at the door, enter, approach the quarry with as much dignity as his partially exposed spindleshanks permitted, and say solemnly, "Miss Wood, may I present my friend Mr. Grigsby?"

"I sure am right proud to meet you, Mr. Grigsby," the recipient of the favor would try to respond without giggling.

While Abe was a most eager and attentive pupil, he was by no means the most circumspect. In fact he was more often ringleader than follower in mischief. Once he felt and deserved the full impact of the hickory stick.

Over the door of the schoolroom the squire had hung a set of buck antlers of which he was inordinately proud. To the boys they were an irresistible temptation. The long branching horns possessed all the allure of a tree ripe for climbing, though Crawford's hawk-eyed vigilance was a constant deterrent to mischief. Then one day he was called out of the building by a visitor requesting his services as justice. Instantly the room came alive. A half dozen boys, Abe included, sprang into action. Abe's long legs gave him an advantage. Leaping high, he grasped one of the protruding horns in each hand and began swinging back and forth. Sarah, eyes darting between the dangling figure and the doorway, endured agonies of suspense.

"Oh, Abe, no!" she gasped. "Git down—please!"

Suddenly there was a loud cracking sound, and Abe was hanging by one hand, a length of broken antler in the other. He dropped to his feet and stood looking at it in dismay. The other boys rushed back to their benches. "Hide it!" someone muttered. "Mebbe he won't notice." Then, "Hist! He's comin'!"

Abe looked about frantically, then laid the evidence of his guilt on the teacher's desk. Like the others, he was on his bench, head bent over his copybook, quill pen moving busily, when the squire entered.

Judgment was not long in coming. Face white with anger, he picked up the incriminating evidence.

"Who did this?" There was a long silence. Crawford took down the hickory stick from its nail on the wall and stood brandishing it. "I'll find out, you know. I ask you again, *who did this thing?*"

"I did it, sir." It was Abe's voice, quavering but clearly audible. "I—I didn't mean to. I—I was jist hangin' on it, and it broke."

"And why were you hanging on it, pray, Master Lincoln?"

"Jist—jist for fun, sir. I wouldn't have done it if I'd knowed it would break."

Crawford stood looking at the miscreant, the anger slowly fading from his face. There was a suspicious quirk to his lips. "Well, Master Lincoln"—the mildness of his voice was oddly at variance with the threat of the brandished stick—"at least you were honest enough to admit your guilt. But you have to be punished, of course. Come forward, please."

It was Sarah who winced at the sharp thwack of each blow.

"What'd you tell fur?" demanded Nat Grigsby on the way home. "We wouldn't have squealed. Mebbe he'd never ha' knowed who did it."

"I'd ha' knowed," Abe responded.

The short term was over all too soon. By the end of January most of the boys were needed at home to prepare for the spring plowing and planting, and numbers diminished so that the school was closed.

On February 10 Sarah turned twelve, and just two days later Abe became ten. Nancy's birthday had been on the fifth, and always before the week had been a time of festivity. Not this year. On the fifth, a Friday, Sarah and Abe crept out of the house before dawn, leaving the others asleep, and, climbing the little hill, pushed the dank leaves aside from the narrow mound, revealing the slab on which Tom had carefully carved the letters "N. L."

"I wisht we had some flowers to put here," said Abe wistfully, "or some bright leaves. Seems like there's nothin' we kin do for her birthday."

Sarah looked up at the overhanging trees. "Thar'll soon be blossoms," she said, shivering with the cold. "And she ain't really here, you know. I reckon mebbe she's already got to that Eternal City." In her role of big sister and comforter she spoke brightly and tried not to cry, but it was no use. They wept together. But they were young, and dawn was breaking in a rosy flush which gave promise of spring warmth to come. After leaving the knoll they started running along the rough path, faster and faster, Abe tempering his long legs to keep pace with Sarah's shorter ones, arriving at the cabin breathless and laughing, just as the sun came popping after them through the bare trees.

Tom found release from loneliness in work, but not on the cabin. Keep all his promises to Nancy now that she was no longer there to see them fulfilled? It would seem almost like disloyalty. He did cut timbers of good oak for a puncheon floor, split them and put them to dry, but when he began working lengths of seasoned cherry wood into materials for a corner cupboard, it was for Reuben Grigsby's big house, not for his own cabin. And with the wealthy James Gentry engaged in building what seemed a mansion on his thousand acres, of course carpenters were needed, and Tom was glad to hire his services, often taking Abe and Dennis with him.

But Abe, at ten, was old enough to go on expeditions alone. Previously the only mill had been near Troy, seventeen miles away, but now Noah Gordon, who lived near the new Gentry settlement, had started a horse-mill. It made life much easier. No more slow grating of the ears with the "gritter," an old piece of tin flattened out, punched full of holes, and nailed to a board! No more pounding the kernels in the wooden mortar because it was so far to go for milling! After going several times with his father or Denny, Abe often went to the new mill by himself or with one of his neighbor friends. On one occasion he was accompanied by David Turnham, son of a new settler, Thomas Turnham, who had entered Congress land across the Pigeon Creek bottoms and the deer licks, north of Tom's farm. David, though six years older than Abe, became a close companion.

That day Abe rode to the mill on his father's old gray mare, the slowest but most gentle of the family horses, the shelled corn in one of the saddlebags balanced by a load of rocks in the other. It was afternoon when they arrived, and they found a long line of customers ahead of them. The crude mill turned slowly.

"Huh!" remarked Abe. "My hound pup kin eat all the meal that thing'll grind in a day and then howl for his supper! Lucky if we git home afore dark."

They passed the time, not too impatiently, listening to the yarns spun by other waiting customers and catching up on the neighborhood gossip. It was sundown when Abe's turn came. Hitching his old mare to the sweep-pole or lever that turned the wheel, he started the wooden cog wheels turning, driving the mare round, and round, round and round. She was slow, much too slow to suit him, for David had finished his grinding and was waiting impatiently. It was getting dark, and the trail home was rough.

"Faster, faster!" he urged, pushing at the mare's flank with a stick. She obliged, but not enough to suit him. "Faster!" Finally, driven by impatience, he laid the stick on soundly, shouting, "Git up, you old hu—" But the word "hussy" was nipped in the bud, for the old mare, unused to such harsh treatment, protested with her heels, landing a smart kick on the side of Abe's head. He dropped like a stone.

Horrified, Noah Gordon stopped the mill. He ran and bent over the boy, lying bleeding and unconscious. "Run for his pap!" he ordered Dave.

Tom was fortunately working near the cabin when Dave, white-faced and winded, blurted his news. "Abe—kicked by horse—maybe dead—come quick!"

Tom had never moved faster, yet the mile-and-a-quarter trail seemed endless. Darkness had fallen, and he often stumbled over roots and stones. Mind refused to function. All his energies were expended in keeping his limbs in motion, yet they seemed as impeded as if wading through deep water. At last he reached the crowd gathered at the mill, pushed his way through, knelt beside the still figure. Then awareness rushed over him. The boy was dead, or at least dying!

"We've got a wagon ready," Noah told him, "and your horse hitched."

They put the inert form on the wagon and drove home. Tom took him in his arms and laid him on the bed where, just a few months before, another still figure had lain. Neighbors soon began to come, alerted less by word of mouth than by the frontier body's almost uncanny sensing of pain in one of its members. The same hands that had prepared the mother's form for burial now made ready to perform a similar service for the son. Though they had come as ministering angels, to Tom they seemed more like hovering vultures waiting for the feast. His comforting Calvinist faith was sorely tested. Rebellion fought with resignation. What was likely to be just *couldn't* be. Surely a just Providence could not rob him of both wife and son!

All night Abe lay unconscious, to all appearances devoid of life. The guttering candles, the solemn watchers, turned the scene into the semblance of a wake. But when the gray light of dawn crept through the open doorway—

"Look! He's comin' to!"

"Praise the Lord, he's comin' back from the dead!"

The thin body jerked, twisted. The eyes opened, then the mouth.

"You old hussy!" Abe blurted, finishing the malediction started hours before to the old mare, just as he had expected to speak it.

Years later he would try to explain the phenomenon. "Just before I struck the old mare," he would decide, "my will through the mind had set the muscles of my tongue to utter the expression, and when her heels came in contact with my head the whole thing stopped half-cocked, as it were, and was only fired off when mental energy or force returned."

Perhaps it was this second close encounter with death which made Tom more sensitive to his religious duties. As the weeks passed he worried because there had been no service held at Nancy's grave. The church at Pigeon Creek had no pastor or building as yet, and no traveling preacher had come to the community since her death. Besides, he did not want a stranger. Nancy deserved a tribute from someone who had known her.

"If only Pastor Elkin was comin' this way!" he remarked once. "He has sons here in Indianny and must come to visit them, but there ain't no way of findin' out when."

"I could write to him," suggested Abe eagerly, "not real good, but I know how to make the letters. Denny knows how, too, and he kin help me."

Tom, who could write only enough to sign his name with difficulty, looked first amazed, then skeptical, finally grudgingly approving. It was hard for him to admit that "book larnin" could be of practical use to "pore farmin' folk." "Wal, yes, you kin try, son."

Abe scouted around the neighborhood to find paper. Mrs. Grigsby gave him a piece of foolscap. Denny made him a pen from a buzzard's quill and helped him form the letters, all capitals. Neither of them knew much about spelling. Since they knew of no neighbor traveling to Kentucky, they took the letter to Troy, the nearest point on the mail route which ran from Louisville to Harmonie, taking three days for the trip. At Corydon there was a mail route to Elizabethtown.

In some way the letter reached Pastor Elkin, who, since he could not read, must have found someone to read it to him. One day about the first of June he came riding up to the cabin on his sorrel horse, big enough to have borne his two-hundred-pound weight and saddlebags over the hundred-mile journey and arrive still unwearied and skittish. The family was delighted to see him. He was a link not only with the wife and mother they had lost, but with all the religious associations of the past.

His arrival at that time was fortuitous, for according to the Primitive Baptist custom the first Sunday in June was often observed as a mass funeral for all who had died during the preceding year. Denny and Abe started out immediately to invite all the settlers in the vicinity, and word spread into the whole area for twenty miles around. When Sunday came people began pouring into the cabin clearing, some riding, two or three on a horse, some in oxcarts, their wheels huge boles of forest trees, many walking, and it was a big solemn procession which made its way along the trail and up the wooded knoll. All were mourners, whether for the dead lying beneath those mounds or for others, for few families had escaped the ravages of the milk-sick.

Pastor Elkin took his place at the foot of Nancy's grave. Tom stood at the head, with Sarah and Abe. Dennis stood by the mound of his foster parents. Peter Brooner and others went to the places where their own were buried. It was a beautiful day. Abe found himself looking up at the green interlacing branches flecked with patches of bright blue rather than down at the mound. But even that was no longer bare and brown. In fact, it was no longer a mound. Leveled by the rains and snows, it was now a bed of soft green grass dotted here and there with bright spring flowers. Most of the people were weeping, including Sarah, yes, even Pa, but somehow he didn't feel sad. It all seemed more like life than death. He slipped his hand into Sarah's.

"I reckon she ain't down thar," he whispered. "Look up instead."

Pastor Elkin began speaking in the sonorous voice whose penetrating resonance had been cultivated during whiskey bouts, rip-roaring fights, and rowdy dances before, at age twenty-two, he had been converted. He used it now with all the melodious skill he had once displayed as a rollicking fiddler.

"I came here today," he began, "because Tom Lincoln's little son, Abraham, asked me to come." Then he went on to pay tribute to Nancy, speaking of her Christian virtues, holding her up as an example of true womanhood. His eulogy was both lengthy and eloquent and audible far beyond the limits of the crowd of perhaps two hundred, for, as Dennis was to remark of Pastor Elkin later, "I have heard his words distinctly and clearly one-fourth of a mile." Afterward he spoke of Elizabeth and Thomas Sparrow, of Mrs. Brooner, and others. There were prayers and hymns, admonitions to the living as well as eulogies for the dead. It might well have been the concluding celebration of a camp meeting instead of a funeral.

Others would pay tribute to the memory of Nancy through the years in language less eloquent but as sincere and laudatory as Pastor Elkin's. One would say of her, "She was a woman of deep religious feeling, of the most exemplary character, and most tenderly and affectionately devoted to her family. Her home indicated a degree of taste and a love of beauty exceptional in the wild settlement in which she lived."

And those neighbors, many of whom stood near Tom that day on the knoll, how would they remember her? William Wood, who had watched by her bed that last week, would put some of his recollections into words. "Mrs. Lincoln was a very smart, intelligent and intellectual woman; she was naturally strong-minded; and a gentle, kind, and tender woman, a Christian of the Baptist persuasion. She was a remarkable woman truly and indeed."

But for the family who made their way back to the empty cabin no words were necessary to describe their sense of loss. It expressed itself day after day, night after night, in the dogged but purposeless activity of a lonely man; in the frustration of a twelve-year-old girl trying desperately to perform the grueling tasks of a pioneer woman; in the vain struggles of a ten-year-old boy to recapture the magic of a beloved voice as he fed wood into the fire and read familiar words aloud. Even twenty-year-old Denny found it difficult to maintain his cheerful, happy-go-lucky life style, and his spinning of humorous yarns elicited only a pretense of laughter. Up in the dark dusty loft, lying on their bed of musty leaves covered with a bearskin, he often had to wake Abe out of a terrifying nightmare.

Dreams. Tom had them too, those mysterious ventures into the unknown which the pioneer considered to be as pertinent to actual life as the signs which governed so many of his activities. Just as an owl hooting in the north could forewarn of bad weather, or a bird flying through a window could portend sorrow, so a dream could give warning or hope for the future. It was one night in November, a little over a year after Nancy's death, that Tom awoke with the memory of a dream. When he returned to sleep he dreamed it again, and so vivid were its details that in the morning they remained fresh in his mind. At breakfast, as they ate Sarah's too watery porridge, he could not keep it to himself.

"I had a dream last night," he told the family, a hint of the old brightness and humor in his eyes. "I dreamed I was walkin' along and saw a path. It led up to a house I'd never seen before. I went inside, and I could see it jist as plain, the walls, the chairs, the table, the fireplace. Thar was a woman sittin' by the fireplace, and I could see her face, features and all. And what do you s'pose she was doin'?"

"What, Pa?" "Tell us!" Perhaps it was the unusual liveliness in his voice, almost like the old flair for storytelling, that filled them with excitement.

He laughed. "Peelin' an apple," he said. Their faces fell, it was such an anticlimax.

Soon afterward he announced that he was making a trip to Elizabethtown. "On business," he explained vaguely. There had been new developments in his suit over the Nolin Creek land.

"I reckon it ain't all land business," speculated Denny slyly after he had gone. "Look how he took that best Sunday suit of hisn in his saddlebag?"

"What is he goin' for, then?" asked Abe, puzzled.

"Wait and see."

One day when Denny had gone hunting and Sarah was working in the cabin Abe climbed the knoll to his mother's grave. The great trees were almost bare, but the ground was covered with leaves, red, gold, brown, russet, yellow, bronze—beautiful. As he walked, they swirled about his ankles. Then suddenly he felt panic. Where was it? The mounds were gone. His brain whirled, then slowly steadied. There, between the two big white oaks, to which some of the red-brown leaves still clung. Frantically he began digging, pushing leaves aside, hunting. No, not here. Nearer the biggest tree. About fifteen long steps as he remembered. He began pacing, started digging again. There! His fingers scraped against a stone, and, pushing the leaves aside, he saw with relief the letters "N. L." on the little slab of red sandstone. Suppose it got lost, or got moved! Suppose when he came back someday he couldn't find the place! With his fingers he dug into the hard ground, displaced enough earth so he could thrust the stone into the hole he had made, then packed the dirt firmly around it. Good! At least as long as he lived there would be somebody who wanted to come here and remember her.

How amazed he would have been could he have looked farther ahead and seen the little knoll made into a beautiful park, with a chapel, with walks winding among the great trees, with thousands of people coming to look on the spot where he was now kneeling, reading with reverence the words on the marble monument which would take the place of the crude little slab of sandstone!

NANCY HANKS LINCOLN
Died October 5, 1818
Age 35 Years

But amazement would have turned to incredulity could he have read also the words which explained the emergence of an obscure and simple woman of the wilderness into a beloved figure of American history.

MOTHER OF PRESIDENT LINCOLN

He went down from the knoll comforted, the wind blowing dry leaves about his bare legs. It seemed also to bring a sound of singing to his ears.

"Praise the mount! I'm fixed upon it,
Mount of thy redeeming love."

PART THREE

"What did I know of Abe? What can be seen
In any child one comes to foster-mother—
Solemn and pinched, wise-eyed as any other
That has looked on death, so knows what life
    must mean.

At first I only knew the lad was quick
And warmed to love as flowers warm to sun,
That tasks to do were well and swiftly done,
That now and again wry wit would sharply flick.

But even then his face belied the laughter,
His face where torment lay as though the strain
Of something that I knew not until after
As greatness, took it out of him in pain.
More fool was I to wait so long to trace
The truth that from the start lay on his face."

"Lincoln's Foster Mother,"
Ethel Barnett de Vito

= *1* =

It was December 1, 1819. The day began like any other, except a Sunday. Nothing to show that it was to change the course of at least seven lives, shape the destiny of a nation.

She rose as usual before dawn, careful not to wake the children. But once the fire was nursed into a fresh glow, bringing the details of the tiny cabin into shadowy relief, she could not resist the temptation of bending over each child with a mother's doting pride as well as solicitude.

Elizabeth. A pretty child, dark hair a riotous mass of curls, cheeks rosy with health, a smile curving her lips as if roused by pleasant dreams. Child? Startled, Sally noted the rounding of young breasts where the thin coverlet had been thrown aside. Already at twelve Betsy was blossoming into womanhood. A disturbing, almost frightening thought for a mother wrestling alone with the struggle of keeping a family of four together! Almost with relief she turned to the trundle bed pulled into the opposite corner.

Matilda. No budding womanliness here, all child, a bundle of mischief and activity even in sleep, thin lithe body screwed into a ball, one outstretched arm ending in a tightly closed fist, pert nose twitching like a nervous rabbit's. Sally smiled indulgently. Dreaming, probably, that she was climbing a tree or riding high on her uncle Isaac's shoulders or teasing one of her timid playmates with a frog or garter snake! At sixteen Tilda would be as much of a child as she was now, at ten. Still smiling, Sally moved to the straw-filled pad where her nine-year-old son was sleeping.

John D. They had always called him that. John Daniel, Sally liked to think of him, though his name was John Davis. Somehow just using the name seemed to keep her beloved husband alive in fact as well as memory, and John D. was growing to look more and more like him.

"Spitt'n' image of his old man," her brother Christopher had once remarked with distaste. "Let's hope he ain't like him in actin' as well as looks." He had added with significant emphasis, "Or I should say *lack* of actin'!"

Perhaps it was this contempt for Daniel Johnston on the part of her brothers which now made Sally adamant in her refusal of their help, though she knew they could well afford to provide her with a much better home and pay all her bills. Brother Christopher owned at least three good lots and houses in Elizabethtown, Brother Samuel as many. Ichabod Radley, Hannah's husband, was one of the town's most respected citizens. He had been deputy sheriff as well as school-teacher. All the Bush brothers were men of means and responsibility, some of them having served the town as jailers, patrollers, and sheriffs, admired as much for their industry and integrity as for physical prowess. And in the latter respect they surpassed all rivals.

"They were stalwart men," Samuel Haycraft, the town historian, was to write of them, "men of great muscular power, there was no backout in them; never shunned a fight when they found it necessary to engage in one; and nobody ever heard one cry 'enough!'" The story of Isaac's chewing the musket ball to pieces when the bullet was being cut out of his body had long since become legend. No wonder they looked down on their sister's husband as a weakling. Even Sally's triumph in his appointment as county jailer had been sullied by their contemptuous disparagements.

"Huh! Can't even use his lily-white hands to keep the courthouse clean! And he might lame his precious back luggin' wood for all the fires! It's you what's the real jailer, sis. I b'lieve he'd let all the pris'ners out 'thout battin' an eye! And more luck to 'em. Any one's wuth a dozen of him!"

No, Sally would rather spin and weave her fingers to the bone than accept one penny from her brothers. Looking down now at her son, she noted again with both joy and misgiving his likeness to his father. The same light waving hair, finely molded features handsome almost to the point of femininity, same long lashes hiding the gaily provocative blue eyes that had once set her pulses racing—yes, and the same softly rounded chin, which bespoke weakness rather than strength

Three years now since Daniel had seen his son. But there was no time now to brood. She had already lingered too long in the past.

Swiftly she poured water into a tin basin and washed, donning the multiplicity of undergarments considered requisites even for the pioneer woman—shirt, stays, drawers, petticoats, chemise—no easy challenge to feminine modesty in a one-room cabin!—then donned over all a clean calico dress extending from throat to ankles. Closing one of the four wide drawers of her beautiful cherry bureau, her most precious possession, she let her fingers stroke the smooth polished wood in a brief caressing gesture. It was the loveliest piece of furniture in all of E-town, she was sure. Even her neighbor Mrs. Chapeze, whose house was full of fine objects, admired it and had offered to buy it. It had been a temptation, for the forty-five dollars—five more than her brothers had paid for it—would have settled all her outstanding debts, and more. Queer, to think that a bureau was worth more than her cabin and the tiny lot on the edge of town where it sat! But she had refused to sell it. For some reason it would have seemed like charity, and the Bushes had never been people to accept favors from anybody. Besides, she would not have given her brothers the satisfaction of knowing that Daniel had left her so poor she had to sell their wedding gift.

Even though it was just an ordinary day, not a Sunday or a holiday, she fastened a brooch at her throat and took time, as always, to wind each strand of glossy black hair around her fingers and to steal a quick glance at her reflection in a small mirror, another of her proud possessions, before covering all but an attractive fringe of curls with a sunbonnet. Only then did she open the door on a new day.

It had not yet dawned. Stars were still shining, but fading in the first glimmers of light. A sheen of frost lay on the brown grass, but it would be gone with the rising sun. E-town, though early to bed and early to rise, was still sleeping. Life would soon be stirring in other parts of town, but not here on Haycraft Alley. Her nearest neighbor, the Honorable Benjamin Chapeze, who lived in the big house on the adjoining lot, was a distinguished lawyer, and his wife had no need to rise early.

Sally drew a long breath of the bracing December air. Good! A day made for hard work. First the morning chores—water to be drawn from the town well, food to be cooked, the children to be washed and properly clothed and fed, the floor to be scrubbed to shining whiteness, clothes to be washed—then to the real business of the day, weaving the new crimson shawl for Mrs. Benjamin Helm, for which she had been promised three whole dollars. The money would not take care of all her bills. Fortunately she had been able to complete the payment of twenty-five dollars on the half-interest in this acre-and-a-quarter lot with its tiny cabin, according to the agreement entered into with Samuel Haycraft and his wife Peggy when on March 17 of the previous year they had conveyed to her "one undivided moiety of half part of a certain lot or piece of ground containing one and one quarter acres lying near Elizabethtown . . . it being the same lot on which Sarah Johnston holds a bond on the said Samuel Haycraft dated the 12th day of February 1817." The signed statement was safely registered in the Hardin County court records. Half of this section she had bought, the end next to the Mill Race, she had deeded to her brother-in-law Ichabod Radley, who had sold it on March of this year, 1819, to a Methodist minister, Reverend George L. Rogers, who had become her next-door neighbor.

But, though the land and cabin were fully paid for, she still owed money, a small bill at the cobbler's for the children's winter shoes, a few dollars to Jacob Bruner, the tanner, for curing the deerskins from which came the leather breeches she made to order, and small unpaid accounts at the stores. Her credit at Benjamin Helm's, accruing from her share of the sale of her father's property, had long since been exhausted. The three dollars would go toward this bill.

She sighed, and for a brief moment her shoulders drooped, not from the weight of work ahead, but from the burden of debt. Yet almost immediately they straightened. Stepping back into the cabin, she picked up two wooden buckets and went out into the lane. If she hurried, she might get to the well before other early risers and not be delayed by talkative females.

By mid-morning she and the girls had finished all the chores except the washing. It was warm for the first of December, no hint of winter yet in the air, and she set up her wooden tubs on the bench in the yard. The children helped, as with all such chores, Betsy sloshing the clothes in the rinse water, wringing them out, hanging them on strips of stout leather thongs tied together and stretched from the cabin to a hickory tree; Tilda keeping the water hot with small buckets brought from the steaming kettle on the fire; John D., when prodded to reluctant action, replenishing the fire with one or two sticks. Sally scrubbed vigorously, sleeves rolled to her elbows, hands reddened by water hotter than many women could bear, sunbonnet pushed back and dangling from its strings, letting the dampened curls run riot about her sweating face. Occasionally she leaned over, dipped her fingers into her kettle of soft soap, and slapped a small amount on the linsey-woolsey shirt, coarse-woven linen underwear, calico shift, or whatever article happened to be resting on the wooden slab with its covering of corrugated tin; yet managing somehow, whether bending over board or kettle, to keep both back and shoulders at a jauntily straight angle. So intent was she on her work that she did not notice the man passing slowly along the lane, hesitating beside the fence, moving on, then, after a little, again passing.

"Ma! Who's that man? He keeps goin' by, and lookin'."

Still scrubbing vigorously, Sally turned her head. Her hands slowed, finally remained motionless. "Why, I do b'lieve it's—!" She wiped her hands on her apron, lifted a corner of it to clear the sweat from her face, then walked to the fence where the man had stopped again, to lean on the top rail.

"Tom Lincoln! It's reely you, ain't it? I couldn't b'lieve my eyes."

"Yes, Sally, it—it's me all right."

Sally's eyes brimmed. "Oh, I've thought of you so many times, since I heard— Oh, I loved Nancy so much! Even though she was so far away, with her gone the world jist didn't seem the same. Did she go quick, Tom, 'thout too much sufferin'?"

"Yes, she—went quick all right."

Sally wiped her eyes. "And now you're back in E-town, Tom. To stay?"

"No, not to stay. I jist come"—he cleared his throat—"you might say I jist come—on business."

Sally smiled knowingly. "And I reckon I know what. You came to collect the last payment on that two hundred Isaac's been owin' you on the Nolin land. He's been talkin' about tryin' to find you."

Tom shifted his arms on the fence rail. "Yes, I done that too. I seen Isaac yesterday, and he give me the money. But that ain't"—removing his beaver hat, he turned it awkwardly in his hands—"ain't why I came."

Sally was amused. Tom had always been slow of speech, but never had she seen him so obviously at a loss for words. She regarded him with appreciative interest. Though she had always considered him more a friend of her older brothers' than of herself, she knew that only her obvious preference for the younger and handsomer Daniel Johnston had kept him from proposing marriage. Moreover, sensing her beloved Nancy's love for the awkward and slightly boorish young carpenter, loyalty to her friend would never have permitted a thought of competition. She had been young then, and his twenty-eight had seemed old to her eighteen. Now, with some thirteen years of hard experience and bitter loss behind them both, the difference in years seemed suddenly wiped out. They were just two old friends who were meeting after much suffering and loneliness.

"You're lookin' well, Tom," she said in an attempt to relieve his strange air of embarrassment. "I declar, you've turned into quite a gintleman." Her eyes danced. "Look at you! Wearin' a store-bought hat and with that wild mane of yours actually tamed to lie smooth! And even Major Helm don't look any finer when he's dressed up for church on Sunday."

Lifting nervous fingers, Tom promptly restored the carefully smoothed shock to its habitual dishevelment. "I—I come to—" Suddenly his fumbling motions ceased. His shoulders straightened. His stocky body seemed to acquire a new height and dignity. "Miz' Johnston," he said with stiff formality, "I ain't got no wife and you ain't got no husband. I came here a-purpose to marry you—that is, of course, if you're willin'."

It was Sally now who became awkward and almost speechless. "Why, I—I—you—you've took my breath away, Tom Lincoln."

"It ain't as if we was strangers," Tom continued, his voice growing firmer with every word. "I've knowed you from when you was jist a gal, and you've knowed me from a boy."

Their postures seemed suddenly to have reversed. Tom was the confident one, turned remarkably eloquent, almost glib, for one noted for slowness of speech; Sally whose usually calm features betrayed a conflict of amazement, consternation, indecision, yes, even pleasurable excitement; whose sure capable fingers moved erratically, now twisting one of her tight curls, now fumbling with the folds of her apron.

"I've got a good cabin built out thar in Indianny, and a quarter section of land, all paid fur, most, that is. I kin take good keer of you and your young'uns, Miz' Johnston."

She rallied momentarily. "Tom Lincoln! What's the matter with you? Miz' Johnston indeed! Have you forgot my name is Sally?"

"Miz' Sally then." Tom made only this slight concession to informality. Obviously he had prepared his speech, committed it to memory, and rehearsed it to the point of glibness, for now he began it all over again. "Miz' Sally, as you know, I ain't got no wife and you ain't got no husband. I come here a-purpose to marry you—that is, of course, if—"

"If I'm willing." Sally completed the words for him. She was feeling less confused. Her hands stopped fumbling, and with one of them she took firm hold of the top rail of the fence, feeling a need of steadying solidity. *If I'm willing.* A question to be faced squarely, with all her practical keenness, putting aside all the first amazement, consternation, excitement which any woman must feel at an unexpected proposal of marriage. *Was* she willing? Only once in her life had she permitted a decision, her only major one, to be governed by emotion, when she had chosen to marry against the advice of parents, brothers, friends, the man she had loved in spite of a full knowledge of his weaknesses. Fortunately this decision need involve no emotion.

"I ain't got no time to lose. I got to git back home as soon as I kin. If you're willin', let's git it done straight off."

Sally looked thoughtfully across the fence, studying the face of this man who was asking her to change the whole course of her life. She saw a round beardless face, gentle, kindly, topped by the bristling shock of heavy black hair she so well remembered. The gray eyes, set deep under heavy brows, almost on a level with her own, for she was a tall woman, looked back at her humbly, hopefully. A kind man, an honest man, she appraised silently, certainly not handsome like Daniel—no, nor so volatile or unpredictable; a man whose broad shoulders and muscular arms and rather expressionless features bespoke more physical than mental strength; the man whose square roughened hands, now resting on the fence rail, had fashioned with painstaking skill the cupboard with star-shaped ornaments which her mother had so prized.

Am I willing? Willing to entrust the rest of my life to this man who, though he once courted me long ago and was a family friend, is now an almost-stranger? Exchange my small but comfortable cabin for some pioneer hut far from relatives and friends? Leave this set-

tled town where I have spent all my thirty-one years and set out for
some unknown destination in the wilderness? No! Every instinct as
well as a goodly heritage of common sense rebelled. She had opened
her mouth for a polite but firm refusal when John D. appeared at her
side.

"Who's the man, Mama? What's he doin' here?"

"This is Mr. Lincoln, son. And this," she told Tom, "is my boy,
John D. Johnston."

Tom's somewhat expressionless features lighted. "A fine boy," he
nodded happily. "I've got a boy jist about your size, mebbe a mite
older. You'd have a right good time playin' togither, swimmin' in the
crick, gatherin' nuts an' berries, helpin' me make things out o' wood,
mebbe goin' out huntin' rabbits and squirrels. Looks like you'd be a
good hand with tools and guns and sich things." He looked at Sally,
his eyes brightly hopeful. "I reckon your young'uns need a pa, Miz'
Sally, and I know for sure my two need a ma. That's why I got to git
back soon. 'Cept for that rattle-headed Dennis Hanks, they're all
alone."

Nancy's children. Suddenly she saw them. A girl, Sarah (her
namesake?), a bit plump and stocky like her father, clear gray eyes
and a sweet smile. Twelve she would be now, the age of her own
Elizabeth. A child trying to fill the far too big shoes of a woman. A
boy with legs too long, it seemed, for his spindly body. In fact, everything about him had been long, his head, his arms, his ears, as well as
his legs. His name, too, had been long, something out of the Bible.
Jeremiah? No. Abraham. She could remember the look in his eyes,
Nancy's eyes, restless, searching. He had been seven then. What was
he like now, at ten? Still searching? And who would there be to help
him find whatever it was he was looking for?

"It was Nancy who sent me here," Tom was saying. "Not that I
didn't want to come, that is, after a while. But your name was the
last word she spoke before she died."

Sally's eyes filled. It was Nancy's face she saw now through a blur
of memory and fantasy, and with the sudden rush of affection and
loyalty she cried silently, "Oh, yes, yes, my dearest friend!" So it *was*
emotion, after all, not common sense, that governed this second
major decision of her life.

To Tom she said, "I'm willin', Tom Lincoln, but I couldn't marry you right away. There's things I must do fust, some debts I have to clear up. It will take some time of weavin' and sewin'."

"What are they?" Tom demanded. "Give me a list of 'em. I've got money. I'll pay 'em."

The whirlwind speed of ensuing developments would have distressed and flustered a woman less even-tempered and practical-minded than Sally Johnston. Tom displayed an energy and ambition foreign to his leisurely life style. Within hours he had returned bringing (thanks to the money recently collected from Isaac) receipts for all her bills and presents for the family, bright ribbons for the girls, a toy for John D., and for Sally a length of fine glossy alpaca cloth, enough for a dress.

"Prob'ly you cain't git it made for the weddin' tomorrow," he told her, "but at least you'll have it to look forrard to."

"Tomorrow?" Sally inquired calmly. After the tumult the day had already brought, nothing would surprise her.

"Yes, I already saw your next-door neighbor, Reverend Rogers, the Methodist preacher, and he kin come any time, once we git the license."

"But—my brothers—"

"I've seen them too, at least Isaac. I knowed you'd want to ask their advice, so he's goin' to bring 'em right over, your sister Hannah too. Now I'll be off to my sister Mary's up on Mill Crick. Her husband, Ralph Crume, will loan us his big wagon to take us to Indianny. I'll be back in the mornin'."

The brothers came, with Hannah. All were surprised but approving.

"You should have married him in the first place," observed Isaac.

"Yes," agreed Christopher, Jr. "He ain't so handsome, but he's wuth two of that Dan'l Johnston."

Hannah exclaimed over the alpaca. "If I work on it tonight and tomorrow mornin' you kin wear it to the weddin'. I'm jist your size, so it won't take fittin'."

The news spread quickly, and people began bringing gifts, congratulations, advice, helpful offers. Nearly everyone in the small town knew Sally and respected her. Many remembered Tom, lived in houses he had helped build, owned cupboards, clothes presses, chests he had fashioned, buried relatives in coffins of his making.

"You can't get married here," said Sally's near neighbor Mrs.

Chapeze, wife of the Honorable Benjamin, looking around the tiny cabin. "It's much too small. We'll have the ceremony in my house. I'll make all the arrangements, supper and everything."

Sally gratefully accepted. Already she had begun to pack, filling the four spacious drawers of her bureau with clothes, towels, coverlets, shawls, lengths of wool and linen she had woven, interspersing all with her best pewter plates and tableware. The feather beds, blankets, and pillows would be stowed in the cedar chest—yes, one that Tom himself had made for her mother long ago. The children were fortunately pleased and excited.

"Are we reely goin' to have a new pa, that man who give us the purty ribbons?"

"Will my new sister be jist my age, Ma, and is her name reely like yours, Sarah?"

"When we goin' to start, Ma? Will thar be wild animals, bears, lions, mebbe Injuns? I can't wait!"

The next morning Tom returned from Mill Creek with Ralph Crume's big covered wagon drawn by four horses. He had borrowed it for the journey, promising that either he or Dennis would return it. His sisters and their families would come to the wedding that afternoon by horse. His mother Bersheba was too old to make the trip, but they would see her when they stopped at the Crumes' on the way to Indiana. If they left right after the wedding, they could reach there tonight.

"You mean—you want us to leave that soon—*today?*"

"Why not? You cain't have much to do to git ready. Thar's everything waitin' for you out thar in Indianny, furniture, kittles, and all. You won't need to take much."

Sally was only mildly disconcerted. When one's whole life had been disrupted in the course of twenty-four hours, what was one surprise more or less? But, she thought with a trace of amusement, it's you, Tom, mebbe, who's goin' to be more surprised. If you think I'm goin' out thar into your wilderness leavin' my thirty years of life all behind . . . ! Fortunately, she noted, the wagon was a large one.

They went together to Samuel Haycraft's, and he issued them the license. Sally made her mark. Tom, she was happily surprised to see, was able to write his name, slowly, clumsily, but with apparent accuracy.

"Now," he said when they returned to the cabin, "we'll put what leetle stuff you need in the wagon, so we'll be all ready to leave right after."

She was right. It was he who was surprised and more than mildly disconcerted. "You mean—you want to take all—all this—them chairs, that chest, two spinnin' wheels, loom, feather beds—even that—that big bureau?"

"It's the finest thing I own," Sally told him calmly, "a present from my brothers. They paid forty dollars for it."

Tom ran appreciative fingers over the smooth polished wood. "It's a right fine piece, but—" His features were a battleground of admiration, parsimony, and just a hint of embarrassment. Perhaps he was picturing the shining treasure sitting on the earth floor of his cabin. "We—we could sell it—"

"No," said Sally firmly.

With the help of willing neighbors the furniture was loaded— bureau, chairs, chest, corner cupboard, all but the four-poster bed. "I reckon we don't need this," Tom demurred. "I got a right fine bed in the cabin, made of good hickory, stands high like this from the floor," measuring with his outstretched hand, "and stands on four posts like this, with a top bent over so." Sally agreed the bed would stay.

The day sped on. The wedding was to be in mid-afternoon, for the December sun set early. Hannah brought the new alpaca dress, just in time, for a crowd was already gathering in the big Chapeze house next door. As she slipped the lustrous fabric over the glossy curls, pulled it down over the chemise and stays and voluminous petticoats, sounds of hoofs and wheels and excited voices came from the lane outside.

"It's a perfect fit," exulted Hannah. She stood off to examine her handiwork. "Oh, if you could only see yourself, Sally! I declar, the shiny black is jist the color of your curls. And, look, I made you a little cap of the same stuff, small, so it won't hide your hair like a sunbonnet. If you only had some dainty shoes!"

"These won't show," assured Sally, lifting the wide skirt to reveal stout deerskin moccasins. "And I reckon I won't need dainty shoes whar I'm goin'."

Presently her brother Samuel came to escort her to the Chapeze house. His eyes widened at sight of her. "I hope Tom Lincoln appreciates what he's gittin'! You always was the purtiest gal in E-town,

and now half the town has come to see you married to a good man
and bid you God-speed. Ready, sis?"

Ready? Sally hesitated in an uprush of panic. For what? Only God
knew, and He wasn't about to tell.

"Yes," she said calmly. "I'm ready."

Taking Samuel's arm, she went out the door, down the path,
across Haycraft Alley. Though Benjamin Chapeze's house was just
over the Elizabethtown line and fronted on Main Street, their two
lots adjoined, and only a few rods separated their homes. The contrast between her tiny cabin and the eminent lawyer's big house of
hewn logs made her suddenly stop short and burst out laughing.

"What—!" demanded Samuel in amazement.

"Nothin' really. I jist felt all at once like Cinderella goin' to her
ball in the palace. Out of my chimney corner for an hour, then my
pumpkin shell chariot back thar in the yard ready to take me back
into it agin!"

Samuel was not amused. "Thar was never any need of you bein' in
no chimney corner. The Bushes are as good or better'n any family in
E-town, and I'll lick any man what says we ain't. You're doin' this
house a favor by bein' married in it, not t'other way round."

He was more right than he knew. Over a hundred years later, after
the house had been finally torn down to make way for a large brick
garage, its site would be appropriately noted by a bronze marker
placed conspicuously on the new building:

In a House
Which Stood Upon This Lot
Were Married on December 2, 1819
Thomas Lincoln
and
Sarah Bush Johnston
The Foster-Mother
of
Abraham Lincoln
Elizabeth Woman's Club
Feb. 12, 1927

= 2 =

Sally was torn between laughter and tears. When the wagon lumbered up the hill and into the yard before Tom Lincoln's cabin and the two children rushed out, wide-eyed, to meet them, she wanted to cry. Never had she seen such an unkempt, woebegone pair—the girl in a shift of dirty calico, hair uncombed, face streaked with soot; the boy thin and gaunt as a scarecrow, single garment of linsey-woolsey barely to his knees, pipestem legs rough and reddened, those eyes she remembered looking out from under a wild thatch of hair, restless, hopeful, but warily challenging.

"This here's your new ma, young'uns," said Tom, dismounting from his horse and helping her down from the wagon. "And look here, I've brought you two sisters and a brother."

Sally went toward them, smiling, and folded Sarah in her arms. "Remember me? You came to my house one day in E-town. Your mother was my own dear friend. I hope you and I will be friends too." Though she yearned to embrace the boy, she only held out a cordial hand. He stood ramrod straight, pride and aloofness in every line of his lank, bony body. "Of course I couldn't take the place of your mother," she said gently, "but I hope we can be friends." He seemed to be considering, his eyes probing into hers, then, nodding gravely, he extended a grimy hand.

It was in the cabin that she felt like laughing . . . yes, and crying, too. Poor gentle, undemanding Nancy! Had she actually lived for two years in this house without a floor and a decent door, and with a first-rate carpenter for a husband? And the bed! When she saw that, her reaction was all laughter. "A right fine bed," Tom had told her. Well, as he had said, it *was* made of good hickory wood, one pole thrust into the ground and connected to the two walls with a couple of crosspieces, its bottom made of clapboards. And it *did* have a top, a hickory pole that came up from behind the bed, which he had bent over and thrust through a hole in the wall! At least Nancy had had her feather bed! "A right fine bed?" Why not? One could dream as contentedly on a bed of poles as on a big four-poster, and Nancy had always been a dreamer. The cabin, Sally noted, was well built and equipped with basic necessities, a puncheon table, a few stools, a Dutch oven, a few iron pots and spoons and other kitchen tools.

"When we landed in Indiana," she was to describe her arrival long afterward with forgiving brevity, "Mr. Lincoln had erected a good log cabin, tolerably comfortable. The country was wild and desolate."

Inadequate words to depict the five days of travel preceding her arrival—the journey by raft across the half-frozen Ohio, plowing through snow, camping during sub-freezing nights, lumbering over the final sixteen miles of what Tom happily called the "new road," still head-jarring, impeded by huge trees, choked by grapevines! It had taxed all her cheerful optimism to keep the children in good spirits.

"I reckon it'll be fine weather tomorrow," she had said more than once at the end of an unusually cold or cloudy or rainy day.

There was great excitement now as Tom and Dennis unloaded the wagon, Sarah and Abe staring in amazement at the big shining bureau, the chest soon filling the space between the chimney jamb and the wall, the cupboard which Tom had once made for Sally's mother and which he now set up in an empty corner with a bit of shame-faced guilt, the bags of feather beds and pillows and blankets and coverlets, the real chairs with backs and cane seats, the pots and frying pans and kettles. Sally made sure that Abe was given a good share of the heavy loads.

"I declar, you're sure a right husky one for a ten-year-old! No wonder your mother was so proud of you."

To Sarah she said, "How wonderfully you've been takin' keer of your family! Right smart you are for a twelve-year-old. I hope you won't mind havin' another woman to help."

She must be careful, Sally told herself, not to make changes too swiftly. Her new children, yes, even her new husband, must be led, not driven. There must be no unfortunate comparison of her own neatly scrubbed and clothed offspring with the two dirty little raga-muffins who had lived for a year without a mother's care, certainly not of her own earthy efficiency with Nancy's gentle, less aggressive nature. Though she longed to plunge her foster children into tubs of hot water, scrub them with strong soap until their grimy pores were gouged clean, instead . . . "After that long trip we'll all need baths," she told her two girls, "and prob'ly your new sister would like to have one too."

Sarah was anxiously self-conscious. "I know things got turrible dirty, but—the soap all got gone, and I didn't know how to make more, and—"

"Of course," comforted Sally. "I'm glad I thought to bring along a whole kittle full. We'll make more soap together."

She soaped and scrubbed John D., to his disgust, while Abe looked on, then filled the tub again. "That's for me, I reckon." Abe grinned. "Mebbe you better do some scrubbin' on me too."

So slowly came the transformation. When Dennis returned from Kentucky, after taking back the horses and wagon to Ralph Crume and spending some time with old friends, he could hardly believe his eyes. A new door of rived oak with stout leather hinges covered the opening, its golden hues like a splash of sunshine in the seasoned logs. The walls were freshly chinked. Inside there were even more noticeable changes. Sarah's pole bed had been widened to accommodate the three girls, and both beds had not only feather beds but plump pillows and gay coverlets. The earth floor, swept clean, was covered with rugs of animal skins. New pots and kettles, scrubbed to a polish, had appeared in the fireplace area.

But he was most surprised when he climbed the peg stairs to the loft where he and Abe were accustomed to sleep. Even in its dimness he could see that the floor was swept clean. The pile of leaves and boughs and skins which had served as a bed now boasted pillows, real blankets, and coverlets. Moreover, the cracks in the roof which had let in the rain seemed to have vanished.

"I helped do it," Abe told him. "*She* came up and looked and purty quick her girl Betsy and me was doin' all this, sweepin' and luggin' up this stuff. Pa fixed the roof. I reckon we'll sleep better now."

Dennis agreed heartily. Though he soon discovered that he and Tom would find less time for hunting that winter, due to the laying of a good floor, no puncheon one but a right smooth creation made with sawed planks and planed, more work on the roof, overhauling of the fireplace, discarding the old three-legged stools and making some right proper new chairs of hickory to supplement Sally's, there were compensations. The corn bread was no longer too hard or too soggy, the venison or hog meat tough or underdone. Sleeping was much pleasanter, if not sounder, with blankets and pillows. And Dennis was discovering that working around the cabin afforded unexpected bonuses in the proximity of attractively combed and calicoed females, especially young Elizabeth Johnston, about to enter her teens and already exhibiting the physical assets of healthy maturity. And as for the presiding genius of these transformations, effecting them somehow without undue prodding, nagging, or argument, he was from the beginning her humble slave.

"You're sich a fine carpenter, Tom," she might say. "It's a pity to have jist a puncheon floor, don't you think, when you can make it out of sawed planks with your whipsaw and plane?"

Or—"Dennis, I hear thar's a place whar they're burnin' lime over near Gentry's. Do you s'pose—?" And soon the inside walls of the cabin, plus the ceiling, would be aglow with whitewash, making the place almost as light as outdoors.

Dennis resented any criticism of Sally. Once he overheard two of the neighbor women talking. "'Pon my word, Tom Lincoln's woman's body ain't cold yet, and here he's up and married agin!"

Dennis could not hold his tongue. Making his presence known, he burst into excited defense. "Ain't cold! What you mean? Nancy'd been dead more'n a year afore Tom went to git his new wife. And if anybody needed a good ma like Sally, it was his two young'uns. And she's sure bein' one. If you don't believe it, jist come and see."

The neighbors did come. They did see. Sally received all cordially, fed them corn pone, dried sugar plums, and honey cakes, or, if it was mealtime, corn bread with hog meat and venison. Noting the neat improved cabin with grudging approval, eating the well-cooked food, they were soon admitting that fourteen months were a permissible period of mourning and that Tom Lincoln had got himself a right fine wife.

Sally dutifully returned their calls, attended church when a traveling preacher came to conduct services in a cabin, but during the first few months she had little time for socializing. Merging segments of two families (three, including twenty-year-old Dennis) into one, making a neat comfortable home in an eighteen-by-twenty-foot space for eight people ranging in age from nine to forty-one, keeping all properly clothed and fed and reasonably clean against the harsh demands of winter, exacted all her abounding energy and, even more important, tact. Slowly the merging of all the diverse units into one family became visible reality. Sarah and Elizabeth, almost near enough of an age to be twins, were sisters from the beginning. John D., spoiled by all, divided his hero-worship between Tom and Denny, and ten-year-old Matilda became Abe's adoring shadow.

"My first memories," she was to recall later, "were playing, carrying water from the spring, about a mile, with Abe, who had a pet cat that always followed him."

"Ma," Sally had become to all of them . . . except Abe. Though he performed all the tasks she asked of him, not only obediently but gladly, and was volubly grateful for every small service she rendered him, there was still that look of wariness, remoteness in his eyes. While every other member of the family, including even Tom and Denny, were calling her "Ma," or, like John D., "Mama," Abe's response was invariably "Yes, ma'am," or "Thank you, ma'am," or "That's right good of you, ma'am." Strangely, it was the acceptance of this gaunt, ungainly ten-year-old that she most desired.

"He'd oughtn't to call you 'ma'am,'" Tom complained once. "I told 'em you was to be their new ma. I better remind him—"

"No," Sally interposed quickly. "Leave him be. Let him call me whatever he wants."

At least she could see that those overlong legs and bare feet were less chilled and reddened. Though she found a pair of buckskin breeches Nancy had made for him, the legs were much too short, and when he had been out in the rain and stood by the fire to dry them, one could almost see the skins shrivel and crawl up his legs. She cut down a pair of Denny's for him to wear temporarily, but immediately set to work on a pair of new ones, weaving stout linsey-woolsey cloth and sewing it into breeches, then taking lengths of tanned buckskin and foxing the legs clear to the knees. When she produced them as a surprise and Abe tried them on, finding them covering his legs to the bony ankles, he was humbly grateful.

"Oh, thanks, ma'am, thank you! It's right good of you to do all that for me."

Once Sally stood in the doorway and watched him leave the clearing and follow the path leading to the hill to the southeast. She knew where he had gone, for she herself had sought the place several times to mourn at her friend's grave. On a sudden impulse, which she instantly mistrusted as perhaps unwise, she put a shawl about her shoulders, donned her sunbonnet, and followed him.

"Whar you goin', Mama? Kin I come too?" asked the irrepressible Matilda.

"Not this time, dear."

"But—Abe went that path. I saw him. And he likes to have me with him. He says so."

"Usually, yes, but not now. I reckon he wants to be alone."

"Then why—"

But Sally was already hurrying along the path. A January thaw had softened the leaves, and he did not hear her coming. He was kneeling on the ground pushing leaves aside. She stood for a few moments looking down at him before speaking.

"I loved her too, you know, very much. She was my best friend, from when I was much younger than John D."

Unstartled, the boy looked up at her with brimming eyes. "Thanks, ma'am, for tellin' me."

"This must be a beautiful place," said Sally, "when the trees come to life." Suddenly she had an idea. "When spring comes," she suggested, "why don't we plant some flowers here, you and I, some sweet pinks or marigolds? Would you like that?"

"Oh yes, ma'am! She'd like it too, she loved flowers. Thanks, ma'am, for thinkin' of it."

They walked down the hill together, two figures very much alike in their unbending straightness, their lithe rhythm of motion. Sally had an instinctive desire to take his hand, to say, "Let's run, shall we? I'll race you to the cabin!" But she felt in him that remoteness which seemed always present. He was not really there beside her but back on the hill where his dearest memories lay buried. He did not resent her coming. He was grateful, dutiful, obedient. But he could not accept her as mother. And, oh, he needed a mother so much!

Never had the gulf between them seemed so wide and deep as on a night in January when, as usual, Sally took the Book from its place and set a candle on the table for the nightly reading. Abe and Denny shared this duty, Tom following with a short prayer. Tonight it was Abe's turn, but after he had found the place, instead of beginning to read, he brought the Book to Sally.

"You do it, ma'am, tonight, please. Ma used to read to us. It—it will seem most like she was here."

Sally took the Book with fingers turned suddenly stiff and cold. She looked down at the page, its black shapes as meaningless as hieroglyphs. She held it for what might have been a minute but seemed an eternity.

"I'm sorry," she said gently. "I—I never learned how to read. How fortunate you are to have had a mother who could!"

Abe took the Book and proceeded slowly and stumblingly with the reading, while Sally thrust her needle back and forth through the tough buckskin which would give him another pair of breeches, but her eyes blurred so the stitches were clumsy and uneven. Once more she had failed him. Not that she wanted to take Nancy's place, she could never do that. But there were hungers, needs in this awkward, fumbling ten-year-old which could not be satisfied with corn pone and bacon, no matter how well cooked, or warm shirts and breeches, no matter how well woven and sewed.

Nancy's two children had been born in February. Sally wanted to do something special for their birthdays. It was easy to plan gifts for Sarah, and on February 10, after a good dinner of corn bread, some of the sausage she had brought in a crock from Kentucky, and dried apples sweetened with wild honey, she slipped over the girl's head a new dress of flowered calico stuff she had been saving for herself. "Oh, thank you, Ma!" Eyes shining, Sarah threw her arms about Sally's neck. "You're so good to us! It's the best birthday I ever had."

But Sally had another even greater surprise. Going to a drawer of the bureau she produced a small hand mirror and held it before the girl's flushed face. "This is for you too, dear. One of my brothers gave it to me long ago."

The gift aroused great excitement, for Nancy's children had never before possessed a mirror. It went the rounds of the group, each one marveling at the self-revelation displayed. Abe stared long and incredulously at his reflected image, possibly more startled than pleased. "Land sakes!" he exclaimed. "Is that reely me?"

But for Abe's birthday two days later Sally felt unprepared, helpless. Special food, yes. A linsey-woolsey shirt bright colored with dye of roots and bark, and another new pair of breeches long enough to cover those lanky legs which seemed to grow another inch every month. But, oh, for something to help satisfy those other needs, dispel that look of sadness which seemed so unnatural in a child of ten —no, eleven, for today was his birthday! The meal was over, a sumptuous one. She had given him the new clothing and he had been duly grateful, but without the emotional joy displayed by Sarah. Then suddenly Sally remembered. Again she went to the bureau, opened a drawer, her fingers burrowing deep into its contents. There! She knew one of them must be here somewhere. There had been three of them in all.

Abe took the object she held out to him, long bony fingers closing about it caressingly, eyes brighter than she had ever seen them. "Oh! Thank you, thank you, ma'am!" It was a worn copy of Webster's *Speller,* a book popular in schools, given her by Hannah's husband, the schoolteacher, in the hope that John D. might someday find it useful. Sally had almost forgotten that there were books in her luggage. Abe could not wait to explore its contents. After the Bible reading he sat hunched up over the table, absorbing the pages until the candle guttered; then he stretched himself full length in front of the fire, poring over the words in its dim light.

"Listen to this!" he chuckled. "Lots of stuff what tells you how to behave. 'What are the ad—advantages of hu—humility? The humble man has few or no enemies. Everyone loves him and is ready to do him good.' Ha! Wonder if I'm humble. I like this one better. 'Should not beasts as well as men be treated with mercy? It is wrong to give needless pain to a beast.' Remember that, John D., when you see some of the boys catchin' turtles and settin' a fire on their backs. Look, Pa, here's one you'd like. 'Is labor a curse or a blessin'? Constant moderate labor is the greatest of blessin's.' Remember"—his eyes gleamed wickedly—"it says 'mod'rate' not 'hard.' "

"That's enough," interjected Tom. "Time for bed, all of us. We got work to do tomorrer. 'Specially you, Abe. Now you're sich a big boy, it's time you helped out by bringin' in some money. James Gentry's willin' to hire you for twenty-five cents a day to do wood choppin', and I told him you'd start tomorrer—early. Now git along to bed."

Reluctantly Abe started to obey, but Sally saw the disappointment in his eyes. Her straight back stiffened. "Tom," she said firmly, "I reckon thar's some things more important than workin' from dawn to dark and earnin' twenty-five cents a day. Not for you, mebbe, but for some folks. The rest of you kin go to bed. Abe and I are goin' to sit up awhile."

Tom's jaw dropped. It was not the first time he had sensed a certain obduracy in his new wife, an insistence on having her own way, which was not always his, but heretofore any dissension on her part had been so subtle as to seem almost like agreement. Too surprised and disconcerted to indulge in argument before the family, he departed for bed with no more audible protests than a few grunts and throat clearings. Dennis climbed up the creaking pegs to his loft. The three girls were soon asleep in their corner.

So engrossed was Abe in his new book that when the fire died down he made no move to add fuel, only slid closer so his elbows rested on the wide sandstone hearth. His lips mouthed soundlessly as his bony finger pointed out the words. Now and then he gave a soft chuckle. Rising from her seat, Sally took an armful of hickory bark and dry sassafras twigs from the wood bin and threw them on the fire. It blazed up quickly, throwing his angular features into bold relief. Keeping his finger on the page, he looked up at her with a warm, if abstracted smile.

"Thanks, Ma," he said simply.

When dawn came Tom had his way. Abe departed, the inevitable ax over his shoulder, for James Gentry's, returning at dusk to turn over the twenty-five cents for his day's work. It was the beginning of a long succession of such days when his father was to hire him out to neighboring farmers, working as hostler, plowman, wood chopper, carpenter, helping the women with their chores, carrying water, making fires, even tending babies. During that year when he had turned eleven he exhibited sudden and startling growth. Always long of body, he began to shoot up like a well-nourished sapling, a process which was to continue unabated until by his seventeenth year he would have reached six feet, four inches.

But Sally noted more than physical changes in the fast-growing eleven-year-old. He had suddenly become more thoughtful and reflective, stopping in his work, to his father's disrelish, to lean on the handles of the old shovel plow or beat the air instead of the wheat with his wooden flail, or hang negligently over the fence to talk with some passer-by. He seemed a bit shyer, too, and more timid when the neighbor women came to visit, and more sensitive to the needs of the motley household, often performing tasks before he was asked.

It seems like he grew up out of childhood, thought Sally, almost in a night.

She knew the sudden burgeoning was not easy, for Tom as well as for Abe himself. To Tom, Abe was still the child, perhaps always would be, and the emergence of an independent spirit seemed an affront to his parental prerogatives. Once Tom was telling a story of a hunting trip on which Abe and John D. had accompanied him, embroidering it slightly as interest grew more flattering. "Pa," Abe interjected after a pause, "you know that ain't jist the way it was." Tom turned and gave the boy a sharp slap, bringing tears to his eyes.

"Whar's Abe gone?" someone asked after the story, emasculated of some of its drama, came to a close. Sally knew, for she had seen him slip out, had longed to follow but had known better. It was not a time for motherly comfort. When he returned, whistling, she gave a sigh of relief.

Tom was not the only one who found the boy's increasing insistence on honesty an embarrassment.

"I know you like to go with Abe," Sally said one day to Matilda, "but he's goin' into the forest today to cut trees, and I'm afraid you might git hurt. A tree might fall on you or a branch hit you. Besides" —she well knew Tilda's yen for mischief—"you're likely to hinder Abe in his work."

Pouting, the child watched Abe grind his ax sharp, put the maul and ax over his shoulder, and start off into the forest. Usually obedient, she had no intention of following, but the temptation was too great. He was the best playmate she had ever had, and surely he could find time for one of their wild romps! When he was out of sight she ran quickly but quietly along the path to the south, down the cattle, hog, and deer tracks to the place where she knew he was cutting. When she saw him she moved even more quietly, creeping along until she was only a few feet away. Then suddenly she ran and pounced on his back like a panther, putting her knees in the small of his back and locking her hands around his neck, then with a quick motion throwing him down on his back, his face to the sun and his spine on the ground.

"S'prise!" she cried gaily.

But she was even more surprised than he, and the gay cry turned into a howl of anguish. In the fall the pole of Abe's ax had fallen on the ground, its keen edge upward. In pulling him backward Tilda fell on the sharp edge and cut herself badly.

"Oh, oh!" she moaned. "Look what you went and did!"

Seeing the blood spurting from her leg, Abe was even more frightened than she, but he acted quickly. Tearing off the tail of his long linsey-woolsey shirt, he managed to close the wound and stop the flow of blood. It was possible that by quick thinking and action he had saved her life.

When the blood had stopped flowing and the danger seemed to be past Abe took her by the shoulders and, conquering the impulse to shake her, regarded her sternly.

"Look what *I* did, you said," he whipped out angrily. "You know that waren't true, Tilda. You did it to yourself. I was jist about to begin choppin' and didn't see you."

She nodded tearfully, and relenting, he lifted the ragged end of his torn shirt and wiped her eyes. "Now—what you goin' to tell Ma?"

She sniffled. "Why, I—I'll tell her I cut myself bad on the ax, and—and that'll be the truth."

Abe became stern again. "I reckon it'd be the truth, yes, but it wouldn't be the whole truth, Tilda. If I was you I'd tell Ma the whole truth and risk what she'll do to you."

He picked the child up, her body no light load even for arms already sinewed into more than an average man's strength, and lugged her home.

Sally listened without comment to Matilda's shamefaced recital of the "whole truth," only tight lips and accusing eyes giving forewarning of the merited scolding yet to come. But now was the time for action. She removed the strip of bloody shirting, marveling at the strength and quick thinking which had torn the stout cloth, sent Abe for hot water to cleanse the wound, applied healing herbs and ointments, bandaged it with clean strips of soft linen cloth. Slowly Tilda's screams of pain abated into moans and whimpers.

"I—wasn't goin' to tell you all of it," she admitted, "not that I jumped on his back, but—Abe told me I ought to, so I did."

So, Sally discovered, there was no need of a sharp scolding after all. Abe had already taught the child a lesson far more important than obedience or caution.

But Abe's own needs, the restlessness which made him stop work to lean on the handles of his plow or lay down his ax to stare into the sky, answers to his eternal questions, she felt less able to meet. She could feed him good food, which added a bit (not enough) of substance to his gangling frame. She could quiet Tom's grumblings about the boy's laziness. She could insist that he be allowed to stretch out by the fire and read after the rest had gone to bed. But he was so different from her other four children—yes, they had now all become *hers,* her own three no dearer than Nancy's! With the girls she had no problems, except concern over the self-conscious blushes of Elizabeth, now a fast-maturing adolescent, under the daily admiring scrutiny of the fully matured Dennis Hanks. John D. was a normal, happy, often irresponsible boy who needed only loving care and discipline. But Abe . . .

"Thar's somethin' peculiar about Abe," Dennis once remarked.

"He's reachin' too fur," grumbled Tom, frowning helplessly at sight of the long figure stretched in front of the fire. "You oughtn't have give him them books. He had more'n enough to read already with the Bible and that Pilgrim's wand'rin's."

For Sally had produced another book from the drawers of her beloved bureau. To Abe's intense surprise and delight, it was *Robinson Crusoe,* which he had dreamed of finishing ever since the woman who stopped at the cabin in Kentucky had read him parts of it. Now he reveled in the exploits of the romantic castaway whose adventures seemed sometimes to parallel those of his own pioneer experience.

"Listen to this!" he exclaimed gleefully. "Crusoe made a tent out of a sail and put it in front of a cave for his first house. Sounds like our half-faced camp, don't it? He made clothes and a cap for himself out o' skins, jist like us!" Then, "Denny, Crusoe tamed a wild goat and taught a bird how to talk. S'pose we could catch a cuckoo and teach it to say reel words?" Finally, when the book was almost finished, "Pa, Crusoe jist had a big fight with a lot o' bears and over fifty wolves. Don't that beat all the huntin' yarns folks tell here in Indianny?"

Tom only grunted. Perhaps, thought Sally with indulgent amusement, some of his resentment at Abe's obsession with books was due to his own demotion as chief yarn-spinner at the family fireside! But she understood his deeper feelings of vexation. Taming the wilderness was a herculean job, demanding all the resources of physical strength available. Moreover, he himself had been inured to hard labor from the age of ten. No wonder he was baffled and disgruntled when his only son proved to be handier with a buzzard's quill pen than with a carpenter's drawknife, when he would rather sprawl under a tree with a book than go hunting!

Risking Tom's further displeasure, she produced the third book. Abe's eyes gleamed with delight. "Oooh! Thanks, Ma. *The Arabian Nights!* I've hearn tell of it."

He leafed through the pages avidly, chortling over the garish pictures, long calloused fingers eager but careful, with the delicate touch of the book lover. Soon he had the whole family, even Tom, listening to the adventures of "Sinbad the Sailor" and "Aladdin and his Wonderful Lamp," marveling at the bird so large it darkened the sun, the fish that men landed on, thinking it was an island, the serpent that could swallow an elephant, the bronze horse that could fly through the air.

Dennis was derisive as well as intrigued. "Nothin' but a lot o' yarns," he scoffed, "a pack o' lies."

"Mighty fine lies," retorted Abe.

"Huh! Fool stuff! Whoever hearn tell of a feller gittin' near some darn fool rocks what drawed all the nails out o' his boat, so he got a duckin'!"

Tom would listen with grudging interest, then, clearing his throat loudly, depart for bed with aggrieved grumblings, his male dominance sorely challenged by a quietly determined female who could dismiss his cursory, "Time for bed, everybody. Up to work at dawn," with a sweet, "Good night, Tom dear."

His patience was taxed still further when Abe snatched moments from work during the day or at mealtime to dip into the new treasure and share it with anyone willing to listen.

"Abe'd lay on his stummick by the fire," Dennis would "ricollect" later, "and read that darn book out loud to me'n Aunt Sally, an' we'd laugh when he did. I reckon Abe read that book a dozen times, an' knowed them yarns by heart."

It was on nights when he couldn't read, Sally noted, that the unrest was back in Abe's eyes, especially when neighbors came in to talk about community problems.

Plans were being made to erect a church and, since Tom was considered the best carpenter to superintend the building, meetings were often held in the Lincoln cabin. The site had been chosen, five hundred yards north of Noah Gordon's mill, between the forks of Buck

Horn Creek, about a mile from the Lincoln place. John Romine, one of the more wealthy settlers, had donated the land. Discussion not only waxed hot over plans, division of labor, the fair donations of whiskey, corn, smoked meat, wool, and linen demanded of each family, but veered into heated arguments over moot questions of religion. Jaws manipulated the syllables of long theological words with as much relish as they chomped the slices of raw turnips and apples which Sally served, washing all down with generous mugfuls of Tom's whiskey or Reuben Grigsby's brandy.

Sally kept anxious eyes on Abe during such discussions, watching his knit brows, his protruding lower lip, his fingers tying knots in his unruly hair, hoping that this time he would keep still, but that if he didn't Tom would be more patient than usual.

"Pa, what's that he said, pre—pre—"

Fortunately before Tom could deliver a stinging rebuke, Andrew Crawford, who had been his teacher, turned to the boy with a smile. "Predestination, son," he said. "It means the Almighty has got everything planned ahead of time. What's goin' to happen is goin' to happen, and it was so decided before you were born. Nothin' we do can change it."

Abe's brows screwed into deeper puzzlement. "Then I don't see—"

"Don't see what, son?"

"If that's so, what do we need a meetin' house for, anyway? If we cain't do nothin' to change things—"

Tom did act now, taking the boy by the ear and giving him a shove toward the ladder. There were murmurs of shock from the group, but Andrew Crawford only nodded his bearded head and smiled. "I see your point, son," he said genially. "But just s'pose we're *predestined* to build the church to fit in with the Almighty's plans."

After such meetings Sally worried about Abe. She lay awake listening, knowing he was not asleep. She could hear the rustling of the cornstalk mattress in the loft and the creaking of a loose floorboard as if someone was walking around, and she knew it was not the heavily sleeping Dennis. In the morning Abe would be quieter than usual, neglecting to tease the girls at the breakfast table, and Tom's impatient reprimands for his laziness could be heard more frequently. She could sense, if not understand, the convulsions of growth which were activating the mind as well as the body of this man-child, the most obedient, good-natured, loving, yet bewildering member of her new family.

"Among my earliest recollections," Abe was to record years later, "I remember how, when a mere child, I used to get irritated when anybody talked in a way that I could not understand. I can remember going to my little bedroom, after hearing the neighbors talk of an evening with my father, and spending no small part of the night trying to make out what was the exact meaning of some of their, to me, dark sayings. I could not sleep, although I tried to, when I got on such a hunt for an idea, until I had caught it; and when I thought I had got it I was not satisfied, until I had repeated it over and over again, until I had put it in language plain enough, as I thought, for anybody I knew to comprehend. This was a kind of passion with me, and it has stuck with me, for I am never easy now, when I am handling a thought, until I have bounded it south, and bounded it east and bounded it west."

No, Sally decided, she did not understand Abe. There was, as Denny said, "somethin' peculiar" about him. But what did "peculiar" mean, anyway, except "different"? And every one of her five children was different from every other. Complete understanding was not necessary for the love and concern of a parent.

It was almost with relief, however, that she faced a problem which with her feminine intuition she could understand only too well. Dennis Hanks and her daughter Elizabeth had fallen in love. The sidelong, self-conscious glances, the blushes, had been mere symptoms of a fast-developing romantic attachment. When Betsy began serving Denny his corn pone cooked by herself the way he liked it and Denny took every excuse to go with her to the spring to help carry the buckets, Sally's suspicions became certainty. But she was still unprepared when Betsy came to her in the spring of 1821, cheeks flaming, eyes downcast, hands fumbling with her apron.

"Ma—Denny and I—we—we want to git married. Do you s'pose—next time the preacher comes—?"

Nonplused, wordless, Sally looked at her daughter. Married! Someday, she had expected, in a few years, but—now! Why, the child was barely fourteen! Child? She kept looking, noting with sudden clarity the details of the slender figure, breasts gently rounded, eyes almost on a level with her own, steady but intensely eager eyes, gazing at her with a woman's full comprehension of what she was asking. Suddenly in the blushing face, the glowing eyes, the vibrantly alive body, she saw herself as she must have looked begging her parents to bless her marriage to Daniel Johnston. Fourteen—eighteen—what difference to a woman in love?

"I'll speak to Pa about it," Sally assured her with a smile.

"Married! Her and Denny!" With typical male blindness Tom had noticed nothing of the budding romance. "Why, she's only a young'un—a child!"

"She's fourteen," returned Sally, "and a woman in all but years. Girls mature early here in the wilderness. We'll have to agree, Tom."

The family, as well as the whole neighborhood, was plunged into excitement. In only two weeks the Reverend Samuel Bristow would be coming to hold a service in one of the cabins, and this time Tom requested the privilege. The cabin must be cleaned, walls and ceiling freshly whitewashed. Quantities of food must be cooked for the dinner that would follow the ceremony. Betsy must have a wedding dress. Had it been cooler weather, Sally would have cut down her own marriage gown of the glossy alpaca Tom had given her, but it was June and hot. In her clothes chest she found a length of fine soft linen she had spun and woven for one of the Elizabethtown customers who had failed to purchase it. One-time near tragedy now turned to rare good fortune! Working by the door until daylight failed, then late into the night by candlelight, she created a gown of beauty with puff sleeves, flowing skirt, high waist, tight bodice, a beautiful foil for the tenderly youthful figure.

Meanwhile Denny with Tom's help was rebuilding the old half-faced camp, while Tom constructed makeshift furniture, stools, table, clothes chest for the rude shelter. Sally provided a three-legged cooking pot, a frying pan, and some of the pewter tableware she had brought from Kentucky.

"Of course you'll come back here when the cold comes," she assured Betsy, "but you'll want a place of your own at first. It'll be some time afore you build your house."

The day came, also the preacher astride his horse, prepared on his circuit riding for a variety of auxiliary duties—christenings, weddings, trials of backsliding members, funerals. Neighbors arrived in greater numbers than usual, the prospect of a wedding stronger allure than the portrayal of eternal bliss or damnation. Fortunately it was a fair day, so the services could be held in the yard. To the impatient children, even to anxious Sally, the long sermons, both morning and afternoon, seemed interminable. But finally the moment came. Betsy emerged from the cabin, a beautiful bride in her new gown, cheeks blushing, eyes ashine, dark curls as glossily luxuriant as her mother's.

Such a child! thought Sally, a pang of anxiety mingled with her pride.

Denny appeared, stiff and red-faced in the unaccustomed confinement of new deerskin breeches, linen shirt and vest, a silk stock bought by Tom in his youthful days knotted too tightly about his muscular neck. After lengthy admonitions and a solemn ritual, accompanied by men's shufflings, women's tears, young girls' (including Tilda's) rapt envy, and young boys' (including John D.'s) snickers, Dennis Hanks and Elizabeth Johnston were pronounced man and wife.

It being Sunday, the celebration was muted. The sumptuous meal was followed by no dancing, no riotous infare. But according to custom some of the young women took Betsy away down the path to the half-faced camp, disrobed her, deposited her in the new pole bed under one of Sally's fine-woven coverlets, and later Denny's friends—Gentrys, Grigsbys, Romines, Turnhams—conducted Denny down the same path with the same climax of activity, the Sabbath only a mild deterrent to their raucous and ribald merriment.

The cabin seemed empty that night, with only two girls in the second bed and John D. gleefully exchanging his bed of straw and skins in the corner for Denny's place with Abe in the loft. Being only a .year younger than Abe, though far less mature of body, he had deeply resented his relegation to the status of childhood.

"Wal," murmured Tom, cradling Sally's head within his big muscular arm, "that was a right fine shindy. We give 'em a good send-off."

"Are you sure," whispered Sally anxiously, "you didn't mind, spendin' all that food and money for the feast and all—money you'd saved to pay on the land?"

"Mind? I should say not. Reckon our little gal desarves the best. And waren't she a purty little bride?"

"*Our* little gal." Sally breathed a sigh of contentment. At last, she felt, they had become a real family.

The sprawling little settlement in the neighborhood of Pigeon Creek was no longer a pioneer outpost. In 1821 a road was laid out between Evansville, forty miles to the southwest, and Corydon, the state capital, sixty miles to the east. It passed close to the Lincoln cabin. Poor though it was, no more than wheel tracks, it became, first a vein, then a pulsing artery in the life stream of western migration. Suddenly the world was moving past the cabin door.

It was a time of tension in the country. In Congress the question of slavery was being hotly debated. Should the Louisiana Territory, recently purchased from Spain, be slave or free, or the states formed out of it be permitted to decide the issue for themselves? A year before, in 1820, Missouri, not far to the west of Indiana, had been permitted to form a constitution without restriction as to slavery. Many passing along the road were bound for the new territory—traders, missionaries, politicians, slave drivers, pioneers looking for utopias, "nigger-ketchers" pursuing runaway slaves. Often travelers would stop at the cabin, sometimes staying overnight. Tom, always generous and hospitable, welcomed them, fed them bountifully—all but the slave hunters.

"And some of our neighbors here along Pigeon Creek," he would complain bitterly, "are catchin' runaways, chainin' 'em in their hog pens, turnin' 'em over to these 'ketchers' for the reward. Yes, and right here in Indianny, a free state, thar's folks ownin' slaves, and nobody does nothin' about it."

Abe, Sally noticed, was often far more interested in talking to the passers-by than in performing his assigned tasks, nor was Tom averse to interrupting work to pass the time of day with travelers. Hearing the clatter of wheels she went to the door one day to see an oxcart piled high with household goods approaching along the road with a man walking beside it, Tom and Abe both waiting for it by the fence.

"Howdy, stranger," greeted Tom. "You're welcome to stop and rest awhile."

"Whoa!" cried the man and, when his oxen kept ambling, hit one of them sharply on the nose with his goad stick. "Thanks, but I cain't stop. Want to make Boonville afore dark. How's the road ahead?"

"Tollable," replied Tom, raising one foot to the lower fence rail and leaning on the upper one.

Abe climbed on the fence beside his father. "What's the news, stranger?" he demanded eagerly. "What's happenin' whar you come from, out yander?"

"Hush up, boy." Sally saw Tom turn with a swift rough gesture and push his son off the fence. Abe went sprawling to the ground. But while Tom was talking with the stranger Abe went crawling along the fence-worm from angle to angle until he had reached a spot where the oxcart would soon be passing. Sally held her breath, hoping he would not be noticed, relieved when the traveler went on and Tom returned to his work. She well knew what was happening. Once more Abe had mounted the fence and was pleading with the man, "Stranger, what's the news? Please tell me!"

Fortunately Tom, back in the little lean-to which he used for a carpenter shop, was too far away to hear or notice. Sighing, Sally herself returned to her work. When Abe ran into the cabin a little later, she said in only mild reproof, "I seen you got your pa upset agin."

Abe was shamefaced but unrepentant. "I know, Ma. Pa don't think it's perlite for a young'un to talk to strangers and ask questions. But," he grinned, "I reckon I jist waren't born perlite. Thar's so many things I want to know, and how else am I goin' to git to know 'em?"

How, indeed? As so often, she felt helpless to meet the needs of this strange foster son who was fast becoming as dear as if she had given him birth. But there was one thing she could do. Taking a hunk of the corn pone she had just made, she spread it with a bit of sausage from the crock and thrust it into his hand. Already her skill as a sausage maker was praised around the neighborhood. After a hog killing she would take the best cuts of pork, pound them on a solid block of wood with a wooden mallet, add seasonings and herbs, mix, cook, then pack the savory mass into crocks and cover them with fresh lard to ripen. It was one of Abe's favorite foods. "I could smell that good sausage cooking," he was to say later, "when I was a mile away!" Now he seized the delicious morsel with a small boy's gusto and began stowing it noisily away. "Thanks, Ma."

It was the road that brought an adventure which made him seem far older than his twelve years. One day John D. came barging into the cabin bursting with excitement. "Thar's a wagon broke down a ways up the road. Pa and Abe's thar now. Pa says git ready for comp'ny."

Sally was always ready for company. The road was continually yielding its burdens, sometimes for brief refreshment, no more than a gourd of spring water, occasionally for a night or more. The pot swinging from its crane held enough hog meat for a dozen guests. Now she had only to add a couple of measures more of wheat flour and a dash more of clabber to the bread she was stirring for supper, mix it quickly to stiffen it, turn it out on her floured board, roll it thin, and cut it into biscuits with her horn ring. By the time she had stowed them in her Dutch oven, set it in the fireplace, and heaped hot ashes around it, the guests were arriving, a man and woman with their two daughters, disheveled, exhausted, but obviously of good breeding and culture. Sally greeted them with a cordiality augmented by relief. It might have been a wagonload of drunken soldiers or of rough, profane fur traders, or, worse yet, of despised slave catchers!

"We're so sorry to bother you," apologized the woman. "I promise we won't stay longer than necessary. Your good husband thinks he can get the wheel fixed so we can leave tomorrow."

They were delightful guests. After supper when the Book was produced the man offered to read from it. Then to Abe's amazed delight he went to the disabled wagon and brought back a couple of books. Heedless of thrift, Sally lighted several candles and set them on the table, and the woman read stories about the heroes of the Revolution and the founding fathers of the country. What a treat for Abe! thought Sally gratefully, wishing the family would remain with them much longer than the one night. Hunting for his face on the edge of candlelight and expecting his eyes to be riveted with ecstatic attention on the reader, she was startled by its expression. Why, he was not even looking at the woman, it seemed not even listening! His eyes were fixed on one of the girls, the golden-haired one, younger than the other and much prettier, perhaps about sixteen. Sally smiled with tender, appreciative sympathy. Here was no mystery beyond her limited, practical comprehension. She was watching the emergence of a sensitive innocent child into sudden romantic awareness. Abe, enchanted, moonstruck, was experiencing the first painful, ecstatic emotions of a male in love!

Tom repaired the broken wheel, and the visitors left the next day, profusely grateful and apologetic for having displaced the occupants of the two beds and causing so much trouble. Probably no one noticed the change in Abe except Sally, who was conscious that Tom's complaints of his son's dalliance were sharper than usual, that there were more intermissions from work to loll under a tree or lean over a fence, that the poring over a book by the fire at night was sometimes uninterrupted by the turning of a page. One day she found him sitting in the sun, back against the cabin, when she knew Tom believed him to be cutting timber. She went and sat down beside him. They were alone, for Tom was at Turnhams' building a corner cupboard and the three other children were helping Denny clear land for his new cabin.

"Sun's nice and warm," said Sally companionably. "Makes you feel good, don't it, sort of dreamy?"

He stirred, startled out of his reverie. "Uh huh, right. Sort of—dreamy."

"What you thinkin' about, son?"

"Oh—nothin', that is, nothin' much. I was jist sort of—of writin' a story—in my mind."

"Good." Sally settled back comfortably. "I like stories. Want to tell it to me?"

"Aw—" He blushed furiously. "It ain't much. Jist a yarn about a boy—and a girl."

"And the boy," asked Sally gently, "has long legs and a shock of black hair, and the girl's hair is the color of gold?"

He gulped. "You—you know—?"

"I know you've been thinkin' about her ever since she left. She was lovely. I don't wonder you remember her. But don't worry. Nobody else noticed."

"They—they'd laugh at me," choked Abe.

"I'm not laughin'. And please—tell me your story."

"You—you reely want to hear it?"

"Reely."

"Wal—" He began hesitantly, self-consciously, but, like his father, was soon caught in the fascination of storytelling. "It was sort of a—a dream. I—I thought I took Pa's horse and followed the wagon, and at last I found it, and they were s'prised to see me. I talked with the gal and persuaded her to elope with me; and that night I put her on my horse, and we started off across the prairie. After some hours we came to a camp, and when we rode up we found it was the one we had left a few hours afore, and we went in. The next night we tried agin, and the same thing happened. The horse came back to the same place. And then we decided we hadn't ought to elope. I stayed till I'd persuaded her father to give her to me. I—I guess that's the end of the story."

"It's a lovely story," said Sally, remembering the dreams she had had after her first meeting with Daniel Johnston. "And it has a happy ending."

He turned toward her eagerly. "I thought sometime I might write it, mebbe—mebbe even git it into a paper—or a book. But"—the eagerness evaporated—"naw, I guess it ain't good enough. And I couldn't, anyhow. I'll never know enough."

"Mebbe you will," comforted Sally. "Somehow I'm sure you will."

But how? And what could she do to help? Easy enough to meet the apparent needs of her four other children! Sarah—dear, industrious, dependable, kindly little Sarah—a bit stolid and slow, but so loving and lovable. She wanted nothing but to have a cabin of her own, keep it neat, and bear children, preferably, Sally suspected, to Aaron Grigsby, who, ever since meeting her at the spring, had been gazing at her with the same lovesick ardor as Abe's at memory of his golden-haired heroine. Her own Elizabeth, eyes bright with the prospect of the little cabin Denny was building for them about three quarters of a mile to the east and of the arrival of their first child. Tilda, still a happy hoyden, wanting nothing but a full stomach, time to play, and a chance to be Abe's adoring shadow whenever possible. John D. . . . Ah, John D.! Sally smiled to herself. Already he was more Tom's son than he could ever have been Daniel's. Oh, he looked like Daniel, yes, the same handsome features, blue eyes, merry smile, which still quickened her heartbeat sometimes in painful memory. Yet seeing him with Tom, one sensed that they were fundamentally akin, skillful with tools, industrious in a leisurely manner, happiest when they were off in the forest hunting game or spinning yarns in the evening by the fire.

But Abe. Troubled, she watched him grow, fed him hearty corn bread and bacon and stews with thick rich gravy which put no breadth, only length, on his lanky body, kept him clothed in constantly lengthening buckskins, endured Tom's displeasure when she insisted that he be allowed to read and scrawl words on bits of clapboard or the wooden fire shovel, even on her freshly scrubbed floor. Yet she knew it was not enough.

She was relieved when a school was opened in the Pigeon Creek community to which most of the families were subscribing. Seeing the eagerness in Abe's eyes, she determined that he should go.

"Tom, I been thinkin'," she said by way of broaching the subject. "I want our young'uns to git some schoolin'. John D. is eleven, time he learned from books, and Tilda, she's twelve. I don't want she should grow up like me, not knowin' how to read or write."

"Wal," Tom was agreeable, "I reckon we kin afford the subscription."

"It's a fur ways off," she tried to make her voice sound casual, "on Hoskins' land, more'n four miles to walk. But I reckon they'll be right safe so long as Abe goes with them."

"Abe?" Tom was startled. "You mean— But he ain't a young'un. He's twelve years old, 'most a man grown. And he's got work to do, no time for more schoolin'."

"It wouldn't be for long," she assured him, "and I reely won't feel safe about the young'uns, goin' alone."

"Wal—" Tom agreed reluctantly. "I reckon it won't do no hurt. And, as you say, it won't be for long."

The school was held in a log building on John Hoskins' farm, and the teacher was James Swaney, who at age twenty-one, having learned to read, write, and cipher to the rule of three, was considered capable of instructing others. It was not a small school, for by 1820 Little Pigeon neighborhood in the four townships of Carter, Clay, Jackson, and Pigeon, consisted of just under thirty families, with a total of over one hundred and thirty children under the age of seventeen. Of course all did not go to school, but the little log house with its one door, its greased-paper opening for a window, its benches and dunce stool and hickory stick (for discipline), was crammed full and, especially for the bigger boys on benches near the huge fireplace, heated almost to suffocation. It was not a setting conducive to the most effective teaching, and the young instructor, not much older

than some of his more obstreperous pupils, was frequently out-
"blabbed" and invariably outwitted in his attempts to impart his
meager knowledge.

"If you ask me," Tilda said once disgustedly, "we kin learn more
from Abe than from that man Swaney."

To Sally's disappointment even Abe found little in the new school
to whet his appetite for knowledge, and the four-and-a-half miles of
travel each way consumed almost as much time as was spent in the
classroom. When she inquired eagerly, "What happened today?
What did you larn?" more often than not he would shrug and reply,
"Nothin' much, nothin' I didn't know already," or launch into an
amusing story of pranks perpetrated on the unfortunate teacher.
More and more, Sally noticed, he was displaying his father's talent
for yarn-spinning.

"Blimey, you shoulda heard what happened today!" One night at
the supper table he kept them all, including Tom, convulsed with
laughter. "We ain't got no books, you know, 'cept the Bible, so we
all have to read from that. Here we was, standin' in a long line, some
big uns, some little, readin' in turn. It was that story about Dan'l and
his friends what were thrown into the fiery furnace. You know, the
fellers with the big funny names, 'member how the good Lord delivered 'em without even the smell o' fire on 'em? Wal, it come to one o'
the leetle chaps, leetle Bud, to read that verse with all the names,
Shadrach, Meshach, and Abed—Abednego. Blimey, even I can't say
'em. Wal, leetle Bud stumbled on Shadrach, floundered on Meshach,
and fell on his face over Abed—Abednego. Master Swaney give him a
sharp cuff on the side of his head, and the pore leetle feller began
wailin'. But afore the readin' come to Katy Roby at the end o' the
line, he was jist a-snifflin'. All his blunder and disgrace was forgot till
a while later he set up another wail. 'What's the matter now?' asked
Swaney. Pore leetle Bud pointed a shakin' finger at the verse that a
few shakes later was goin' to fall to him, and he quavered, 'Lookee
thar, master, thar comes them same three darn fellers agin!'"

Amid the ensuing laughter Sally glanced anxiously at Tom. Yarn-
spinning was his acknowledged talent, and she had sometimes noticed him becoming impatient when Denny usurped his special pre-
rogative. But now his face revealed only pride and satisfaction. Sally
understood and was relieved. Tom was seeing in his son and approving a likeness to himself. Physical prowess, strength in wielding the

ax, the cooper's hatchet, the froe, the carpenter's adz, yes, even expertise at yarn-spinning—these were all abilities that united them. It was the penchants they did not share, the yen for "book larnin'," the "reachin' too fur," that aroused resentment in the father.

The boy would have been most surprised of all could he have foreseen that many years later, in a great national crisis, he would be spinning the same yarn almost in the same words to illustrate his concern over the approach of three prominent statesmen who differed with him on a crucial matter of policy: "Thar comes them same three darn fellers agin!"

Whether because of the rigors of an especially hard and snowy winter or due to the frustrations of the harassed and inexperienced young educator, the school came to an abrupt end long before its short term would have expired. Abe accepted the disappointment with less regret than if the teacher had been better qualified, and whatever unhappiness he felt was fully assuaged by the gift of a book from James Swaney, who had evidently recognized the boy's unusual passion for reading. The book was Murray's *English Reader*.

"It's better than school," exulted Abe. Whenever he entered the cabin now he ran immediately to the corner cupboard where the book was kept and read from it at every possible moment. He would have taken it to the table while eating if Tom had permitted. "Bad enough you settin' up till all hours, 'thout lollin' over meals so's to be late gittin' back to work!" But if Tom happened to be away working or at the mill or hunting, Sally let him prop the book up beside his place, and often he would read aloud between mouthfuls.

It was a wonderful book, a series of prose and poetry from "the works of the most correct and elegant writers," designed to "improve youth in the art of reading; to meliorate their language and sentiments, and to inculcate some of the important principles of piety and virtue."

Many of the selections were enough to baffle and stretch the mind of a thirteen-year-old boy, to say nothing of a thirty-four-year-old unlettered woman.

"Listen to this. It's by a man named Addison on the 'plan—planetary and ter—terrestrial worlds.' The sun, which seems to perform its daily stages through the sky, is in this respect fixed and immovable; it is the great axle of heaven, about which the globe we inhabit and

other more spa—spacious orbs wheel their stated courses.' What does
that mean, Ma?"

Sally's brain whirled. The words were as incomprehensible to her
as if gabbled in a foreign language. "I—I'm sorry, but I don't know,
son."

Abe let his favorite corn pone and sausage remain untasted while
he pondered, brows furrowed. "Do you s'pose it means the sun—
reely don't move, after all, we jist think it does, and it's us that does
the movin'?" Slowly, like the day dawning, light broke over his face.
"Yah, I reckon that's jist what it means, but—whoever would ha'
thought it! Hear that, John D.?" He turned to the younger boy, who
was chomping busily. "It ain't the sun what moves up thar. It's us,
down here."

John D. was unimpressed. "You're crazy. Sun does move. I've
seen it."

Abe would find older peers than John D. equally hard to convince
of such newly gained knowledge. A half dozen years later he would
be walking with one of his school friends, Katy Roby, by the Ohio
River at sunset. "Look, Abe, the sun's goin' down," she would say.
"That ain't so, Katy," he would reply, then proceed to explain. "It
don't reely go down. It jist seems to. The earth turns from west to
east, and the turnin' of the earth carries us under. We do the sinkin'.
The sun only looks like it sinks." And Katy would scoff, "What a
fool you are, Abe!"

To Sally's surprise and joy she understood much of the poetry Abe
read, and she was even more delighted to discover that his favorites
were hers also.

"Here's one, Ma, by a man named Cowper.

'I would not enter on my list of friends,
(Though grac'd with polish'd manners and fine sense,
Yet wantin' sen—sensibi—bility,) the man
Who needlessly sets foot upon a worm.'

Ha! Bet that feller wouldn't set no fire on a turtle's back!"

"Fool stuff!" scoffed the literal-minded Tom, who happened to
overhear. "Whoever heard o' tryin' not to kill a worm! Feller
couldn't even go fishin'!"

But he grudgingly approved another reading from the same poet

Cowper, even though he had little use for poetry and did not understand all of it.

> "I would not have a slave to till my ground,
>   To carry me, to fan me while I sleep,
> To tremble when I wake, for all the wealth
> That sinews bought and sold have ever earn'd.
> No: dear as freedom is, and in my heart's
>   Just estimation, priz'd above all price;
> I had much rather be myself the slave."

Slavery! Tom Lincoln had not escaped from the problem by moving to Indiana. The "ketchers" or "patter-rollers," as they were often called, came hunting their quarries close to the cabin. One mulatto named "Yellow Joe," who had hidden in the Pigeon Creek neighborhood, was caught and held in the Perry County jail until his owners could pay the reward. The Federal Fugitive Slave Law, which declared escaped slaves the property of their masters, made capture of them and return to their owners extremely profitable. And some of Tom's neighbors were themselves slave owners.

It was a question constantly discussed, in the home, at social gatherings, and especially at church services. The Baptist preachers who came each month to Pigeon Creek were rabid abolitionists. One of the most voluble was the Reverend Adam Shoemaker, who traveled the frontier exposing the horrors of slavery so eloquently that he was dubbed the Emancipation Preacher. After one of his visits Sally was amazed and impressed to see Abe mounted on a stump in the cabin clearing, a contingent of neighborhood children gathered about in rapt absorption, while he delivered with oratorical fervor and appropriate gestures the sermon of the previous Sunday almost, she vowed, word for word.

"Slave traders, slave owners, 'patter-rollers,' stealers of free Negroes, I tell you, brethren and sistren, all are servants o' the devil, bound fur hell. Sellers of human souls they are, and the wrath of God will fall upon 'em!"

At last, after much planning, arguing, contributing of skins, corn, whiskey, and other commodities in lieu of monetary assets, the Pigeon Creek Church was to build its long-discussed meeting house.

"You should be right proud of your pa," Sally told the children.

"He's been chosen out of all the folks for miles around to see to the buildin' of the House of God."

Workers or watchers, all were participants in the project. Abe helped to fell the trees, hew the logs, and assist Tom and the neighbors with the carpentering. Sally and Tilda snatched every leisure moment to walk the mile plus to the building site and with other women of the neighborhood observe, admire, advise, serve big kettles of food to the workers. John D. became an active errand boy. Tom made a two-brick mold, with which David Turnham fashioned bricks for the chimney. John Romine and Weldon Barker operated the kiln. The work of cutting logs, hewing the timbers with the foot adz, riding the shaving-horse, was assigned to Reuben Grigsby, James Gentry, Robert Oskins, William Stark, and others. Those expert with the froe and maul split the clapboard shingles.

For the time and place it was a pretentious structure, twenty-six by thirty feet, a story and a half high, with a loft where a visiting preacher might sleep. It had two windows, each twenty by thirty-six inches, and two huge fireplaces, with a brick chimney at either end of the building. Tom worked for days fashioning a pulpit of wild cherry wood, as fine as the corner cupboards for which he was famous. He also made a walnut table which would be exhibited with pride as his handiwork a hundred years later.

To Sally's disappointment Tom was reluctant to bring his letter from the Little Mount Church in Kentucky. The church there had been part of the Separate Baptist branch, which refused to have any written creed and accepted only the Bible as its rule of faith and practice. The Little Pigeon Church belonged to the Regular Baptist branch, which had adopted a written statement of faith and government. "I don't b'lieve in tyin' myself to no creed," he averred stubbornly.

Sally herself had never become a church member but not because she was weak in religious belief. Now because of the children she felt the lack sorely. When they all went to church on a Sunday and men "saints," as the elect members liked to style themselves, went to one side and women "saints" to the other, she had a guilty feeling because she and Tom were obliged to accompany the children to the middle section of benches, reserved for nonmembers, or "sinners." But there were advantages. The services lasted nearly all day. And at least she was able to keep an eagle eye and restraining hand on Tilda and John D. and temper their fidgeting. No such trouble with Abe. He sat hunched forward, eyes on the preacher, absorbing every word and strident tone and extravagant gesture, storing them up for delivery to an attentive audience of his peers from makeshift pulpit of sawhorse or cart wheel or tree stump.

The preachers, sometimes a circuit rider, sometimes a local minister who, though serving the church regularly, carried on another occupation to supplement his stipend of corn, smoked meat, whiskey, were eloquent and devout but usually unlettered men. They were often given to strange mannerisms which would furnish the versatile Abe with exercise of his talent for mimicry that his delighted audiences would remember and report with glee fifty years later.

For instance, there was the traveling preacher who arrived in the community one Sunday morning and was invited to preach. He had a habit of rolling his eyes, of pounding the hymnbook and Bible, of indulging in pauses punctuated by groans and breathy exhalations, designed to impress, no doubt, but arousing only wonder among adults and suppressed titters among children. Accompanying these mannerisms were a loud nasal twang and singsong delivery. For years Abe would regale his friends with an accurate portrayal of this performance.

"Just like the preacher exactly," Nat Grigsby would remember. "You couldn't have told one from the other."

Sally herself had hard work restraining her reactions to another preacher's performance. He was an old man of rare piety and eloquence, a hard-shell Baptist, and was dressed in coarse linen pantaloons and shirt of the same material, the trousers having baggy legs and flaps in front, commonly called "barn doors," made to attach to the body without the aid of suspenders. A single button held his shirt in place at the collar. He arose in the pulpit and began to speak.

"I am the Christ," he announced his text, "whom I shall represent this day."

Sally felt Abe's hand pulling at her sleeve. Horrified, she saw a little blue lizard running along the floor and entering the area of the bulky pantaloons. Presently the old preacher began slapping at his legs, his motions moving higher and higher, evidently to no avail. Still he continued preaching, eloquence unabated. Unable to halt the ascending progress of the interloper, he unobtrusively loosened the button holding the waistband of his pantaloons and with a kick off came the easy fitting garment. Meanwhile the intruder had reached the region of his shirt. Next the preacher reached for his collar button, and with one sweep of his arm off came the linen shirt. Though the audience was gasping in amazement, the sermon kept on. Sally had no trouble keeping the children quiet. They were too startled and intrigued even to titter. At last an elderly sister in the "saints'" section rose and shouted, "If you represent Christ, then I'm done with the Bible."

It was an incident which the versatile Abe was to recount not only to his youthful peers but to countless other companions through years to come.

But, though Abe poked fun at the antics of preachers, even at some of the Little Pigeon "saints" who had been so derelict in duty that they had been forced to stand trial, like Brother and Sister Gibson, he never ridiculed the church itself or the religious concepts of its people. Indeed, when Sally was obliged to miss the service on a Sunday because of family sickness, he would come home and reproduce most of the service, sermons, text, hymns (though he had no voice for singing and could not carry a tune), even to the Amen. It was "better than the service itself," she often told him. And on a Sunday when there was no church service he would take down the Bible, read a verse, give out a hymn, and proceed to "preach" a fairly creditable sermon.

Not that his attempts at oratory were all Bible-oriented. He regaled the family and playmates with excerpts from the prose selections of Part One in Murray's *English Reader,* attempting to apply the author's "Principles of Good Reading": proper loudness of voice, distinctness, emphasis, tones, pauses, etc. At least once a "sermon" relic of the previous Sunday was interrupted to give vent to an impromptu lecture.

It happened on an autumn day when the weather was so fine that Sally took her small spinning wheel out-of-doors and, seated on a three-legged stool in the yard, let her eyes explore the gold and crimson splendor of the forest vistas while her fingers busily atoned for any guilt she felt for her idleness. How Nancy would have reveled in this beauty! At least she had enjoyed one such autumn paradise of splendor. In spite of her swiftly moving fingers Sally felt a rare sensation of leisure. Tom had gone hunting. Sarah, whom he had hired out to help Reuben Grigsby's wife, was gone for the day. Matilda and

John D. were in the nearby grove with Abe, detailed by his father to split rails for a new fence. She could hear the sounds of his ax and maul as he drove his iron wedge and dogwood gluts deep into the logs.

How like Tom, she thought with wry amusement, to see that everyone in the family has a job to keep them busy while he goes off hunting! But, no, that was unfair. They needed the meat he provided. And he would have been glad to take Abe with him, was annoyed, in fact, that the boy preferred splitting rails to shooting game.

The sounds of ax and maul ceased, exchanged for shouts and squeals of merriment. Not only Tilda and John D. but half the children of the neighborhood must be gathered in the grove, and Abe must be either playing a game with them or telling them a story. No, he was "preaching" again. His voice, strident and penetrating in perfect imitation of last Sunday's circuit rider, was clearly audible. She smiled to herself, glad that for once Tom was not around to order him back to work. Surprised, for he was usually one of Abe's most avid listeners, she saw John D. slip around the side of the cabin, enter, and emerge holding a gourd in both hands.

"You want something, son?" she called.

But he had already scuttled away. Presently she heard a great uproar in the grove, shouts, excited screams, shrieks of laughter. Time to investigate, she decided. There had been something suspiciously mischievous in John D.'s skulking movements. Arriving at the scene, she found a group of children, including John D., gathered about a huge land terrapin, driven into clumsy contortions by a live coal placed on its back, and frantically trying to escape its tormentors. Abe, perched on his "pulpit" of a tree stump, was vainly remonstrating, voice for once drowned out by the gleeful shouts of the boys and the girls' squeals of fascinated horror. So that was what John D. had so carefully been holding in his gourd, a live coal from the banked fire! Before Sally could intervene he had picked up the poor turtle and slammed it against a tree, bursting its shell. As it lay quivering and dying, the group's mood of hilarity suddenly muted, Abe's voice launched into the silence, this time on a new text, "Cruelty to Animals."

"We oughter be ashamed," he declaimed sternly, "doin' sich things. And you, John D. most of all, my own brother. Why, don't you know, an ant's life is jist as sweet to it as our lives are to us?"

Sally returned quietly to her spinning. No need of parental punishment for her mischievous young son! She had seen the shame on his face, the eyes near to tears. He idolized Abe, and his brother's disapproval was far more punitive than a whipping.

Little Pigeon Church provided an ever-varying source for Abe's histrionic talents. Pulpit-thumpers, wheezers, tear-jerkers, sonorous spellbinders, hell-threateners, heaven-wooers—all were grist for his fine-grinding mill of mimicry. There were Samuel Bristow, the first regular preacher at the church, who with his wife Lavina had been one of its thirteen charter members; Charles Harper, who often was selected by the church to attend association meetings; Young Lamar, who lived just a few miles south of the Lincolns, an outstanding preacher; and Adam Shoemaker, the ardent abolitionist.

Perhaps Abe would become a preacher, thought Sally hopefully. Yet sometimes she wondered what he really thought about religion. He apparently preferred reading other books than the Bible, although he could quote from it glibly. Whenever traveling preachers stopped at the cabin, he seemed always to be trying to confound them with questions, when Tom did not shush him. At camp meetings he never went forward to the mourner's bench. And he seemed perfectly contented to occupy the "sinners'" middle section of the meeting house without aspiring to the seats of the "saints."

To Sally's relief the Separate Baptist group to which Tom had belonged in Kentucky was finally united with the Regulars in a United Baptist Association. Now at last Tom could conscientiously bring his letter from the Little Mount Church to Pigeon Creek. He did so in 1823, becoming at the same time a trustee and respected leader in the church. Now Sally could join him in declaring her faith and entering the fellowship of the church "by experience."

It was on Saturday, June 7, that the church minutes recorded: "Opened a dore for the Reception of members. Received Brother Thomas Linkhon by letter." And on the following Sunday, "baptizing day," Sally stepped calmly down into the deep pool of the creek near the church to be "buried with Jesus in baptism." Often when emerging from the waters the newly designated "saints" would burst into loud shouts of triumph, amens, hallelujahs. Not Sally. As she had said long ago to Nancy when the contagious emotional frenzy of camp meeting had incited her friend to join in a display of ecstatic

ardor, "No. That ain't for you. It ain't for me neither. We keep what
we feel inside of us."

= *4* =

Birth. In a pioneer cabin it was as intimate and communal an event
as death. A family living close to a world of springing seeds, young-
bearing animals, and to each other had a first-hand knowledge of the
facts of life. And in a sixteen-by-eighteen log house there was little
privacy.

Sally insisted that Betsy come home for her first confinement, a
year after her marriage. Once more the cabin was filled as formerly,
but now it seemed bulging beyond capacity. Was it the exuberantly
paternal but restively anxious Dennis who dwarfed what had once
seemed ample space? Or were the five children suddenly turning into
adults? Why, Abe at thirteen was on a level with his father's five feet
ten!

All shared in the excitement and anticipation—yes, and in the actual event, which came suddenly and unexpectedly one night when
the family were all at home. Like most pioneer women, Sally was almost as capable a midwife as any so-called "granny-woman." Unable
to banish the males except for John D., who had fortunately gone to
bed, she put them to work bringing wood, stoking the fire, keeping
kettles filled and boiling. All shared, too, in the travail of the so-
young mother, thrust suddenly into the full comprehension of womanhood; in the relief and joy when cries of agony merged into indig-
nant squalls. Sarah and Tilda took the squirming mite, washed it in
front of the fire, and carefully dressed it in the usual soft yellow
"flannen."

"Sarah Jane," said Betsy with a smile for her mother, "after you."

Sally was disappointed. "I was hopin' you'd call her Nancy, so
there'd be another Nancy Hanks."

"Next time," assured Betsy. "Not now. This one's for you." But her next child, born a year later, would be a boy, John Talbot. It would be two years before the promised Nancy would appear.

After Betsy and Denny and the baby had gone home the cabin seemed empty, but not for long. Soon Nancy Hanks Hall (Nannie, Dennis' natural mother) came with her husband Levi and their four children from Kentucky to Pigeon Creek. Of course Sally welcomed them for her friend Nancy's sake. Again the half-faced camp was repaired and put in use until the new family could build their own cabin on land some four miles away. The young Lincolns and the Hall children were soon close friends. In fact, Sally noticed, one of the Hall boys, Squire, began early to evidence an emotion other than friendship. At public gatherings—cabin-raisings, husking bees, play parties, camp meetings—he exhibited as strong a preference for Tilda's company as did Aaron Grigsby for Sarah's.

It was soon afterward that another member of the Hanks family, John, son of William Hanks, Nancy's uncle, came to the Lincoln home to become for some years a member of the Lincoln family, later to live in other parts of the valley before moving to Illinois. Again Sally welcomed a relative of Nancy's with as much affection as if he had been her *own* first cousin. But he was an agreeable guest, a willing worker, and he gave in labor far more than he received.

Though he was seven years older than Abe, the two were so near of a size and so mentally attuned that the difference in age seemed inconsequential. One of Abe's favorite activities, however, John did not share.

"When Abe and I returned to the house from work," he remembered later, "he would go to the cupboard, snatch a piece of corn bread, take down a book, sit down in a chair, cock his legs up as high as his head, and read. He and I worked bare-footed, grubbed it, plowed, mowed, and cradled together, plowed corn, gathered it, shucked it. Abe read constantly when he had an opportunity; no newspapers then, had monthly meetings at church, sometimes at private houses. He would go out in the woods and gather hickory bark, bring it home, and keep a light by it and read by it, when no lamp was to be had—grease lamp—handle to it which stuck in the crack of the wall. Tallow was scarce."

It was in the late fall of 1823, when Abe was fourteen, that he came to Sally bursting with news. "You know what, Ma? They say

Azel Dorsey's goin' to open a school. Nat Grigsby's goin'. I sure wisht I could go."

And you shall, decided Sally silently.

She waited until Tom came in one day from hunting, looking smugly satisfied over the fat buck he had shot. "Here, Tom, rest for a while. You've had a long trampin'. And try some o' this corn bread jist out o' the oven, spread with a bit o' punkin' butter." She settled herself comfortably with her sewing. "Now—tell me about your hunt."

Chewing, he launched happily into a full account of his recent adventure, whetted to slight exaggeration by her eager interest. When he had finished, surfeited with delicious hot bread and the satisfaction of yarn-spinning, she said casually, "They say Azel Dorsey's goin' to be teachin' a school this winter. I reckon how it would be good if John D. and Tilda went. Most of the other young'uns in the neighborhood will be goin'."

Tom was in an expansive mood. "Wal, I reckon we kin spare John D. from workin', with John Hanks here. But—you're sure you kin git along without Tilda? Sarah ain't much help since she's been hirin' out to work for the Grigsbys."

"I'll git along fine." The needle hung poised, like a held breath, then resumed its even motions. Though she did not realize it, she was almost repeating Nancy's words and movements of years before. "And, Tom," she continued calmly, "I want that Abe should go too."

Tom stiffened. "Abe! You're jokin'. What would he do with more schoolin'? He knows more now than most farmers and carpenters."

"He's a right smart boy, Tom. Mebbe—who knows? He might git to be somethin' more'n a carpenter or farmer."

Tom bristled. "Why should he want to be? This is a good life, ain't it? What more could any man want? Besides"—no longer relaxed, Tom got up and walked restlessly, one big hand making a fresh riot of his black shock—"I half promised Gentry the boy could work for him this winter, doin' odd jobs, breakin' ground, splittin' rails, carpenterin'. He'll pay him twenty-five cents a day, and we need money."

"I know"—Sally's needle continued to ply firm even stitches—"and Abe's a good worker. But you know, Tom, I hear tell Azel Dorsey's a fine teacher, not only eddicated but right practical."

"Dorsey's all right," admitted Tom grudgingly. "I've knowed him for years. I reckon we're lucky to git him here to teach. They say he taught the first school in Indianny down in Rockport."

"I hear he's right good at figurin'," said Sally. "You know, Tom, it's good for a farmer or a carpenter to know how to figure right well. You don't allus find it easy to do your measurin' of boards. And," she continued with apparent casualness, "it helps if you're buyin' or sellin' land, knowin' how to set the bounds o' your fields, and how to read documents right."

Tom flushed. She had hit on a tender nerve. Not long before Tom had hired Abe to a neighbor to cut corn at ten cents a day. The neighbor had offered to buy a few acres of Tom's land at a high price. The ever-trusting Tom had allowed him to write the deed. When the neighbor had brought the document and Tom was about to sign, he had handed it to Abe. "Want to read it over, son?"

Abe had read it. "Better watch out, Pa," he had warned. "If you sign that deed, you've sold your whole farm." Tom had turned angrily to the neighbor. "Somebody's lyin'," he had snapped. "And I reckon it ain't Abe."

Abe went to Dorsey's school, in a log house near the Little Pigeon Church, about a mile and a half from the Lincoln cabin. Later Azel Dorsey was to remember this pupil of his who "was marked for the diligence and eagerness with which he pursued his studies, came to the log-cabin schoolhouse arrayed in buckskin clothes, a raccoon-skin cap, and provided with an old arithmetic which had somewhere been found for him to begin his investigation into the 'higher branches.'"

The book was a dog-eared copy of Pike's *Arithmetick,* which Tom had picked up somewhere and which Abe had tried, not too success-fully, to cipher his way through. His previous teachers had been much less qualified than Dorsey, who was able to take his pupils not only through what was known as the rule of three proportion, but even beyond. Abe now concentrated on arithmetic at home instead of reading, working problems on puncheons, clapboards, the wooden fire shovel. For a pencil he used a charred stick from the fire. For chalk he used a lump of red clay from the creek. Turkey quills made good pens for writing on paper when a bit could be secured, the ink made from blackberry briar roots. Once Sally found such a piece

with words scrawled on it. Though she could not read them, she put
the paper away carefully and later got someone to read them to her.

> Abraham Lincoln is my name,
> And with my pen I wrote the same,
> I wrote it in both haste and speed
> And left it here for fools to read.

When he came home one day with several pages of ledger paper
given him by Master Dorsey, Sally sewed them together for him into
a copybook. Abe was delighted. "Thanks, Ma, thanks!" He proceeded to cover the pages with ciphering—addition, subtraction, mul-
tiplication, table of long measures, simple and compound interest,
the single rule of three—but interspersed with such practical entries
were bits of doggerel like

> Abraham Lincoln his hand and pen,
> He will be good but God knows when.

But on the same page he wrote in a much more serious vein:
"Time what an emty vapor tis and days how swift they are swift as
an Indian arrow fly or like a shooting star the present moment Just is
here then slides away in haste that we can never say they're ours but
only say they're past."

The single error of spelling in the latter entry was an unusual slip
for Abe. Tilda and John D. were soon bringing home proud reports
of his success in the weekly spelling matches which Azel Dorsey held
each Friday. Captains were chosen in advance and it was decided by
lot which one would have the first choice. Abe was always chosen
first. From words of two syllables accented on the first syllable, like
"baker, shady, lady, tidy," the class proceeded to words accented on
the second syllable—"abase, translate, embroil," etc. Finally they arrived at the hardest of all, words of multisyllables, after which there
were few survivors.

"Abe stood up longest agin today," Tilda would report. "Everyone else went down on 'sy-sycophant,' whatever that is."

But one day she had a different report. "You know what, Ma?
Abe helped that Katy Roby win the match today! I seen him. They
was standin' on opposite sides, and Master Dorsey give out the word
'defied.' Katy began with 'd-e-f-,' then she stopped, not knowin'
whether to say 'i' or 'y.' Thar was Abe grinnin'. I seen him lift his

finger and point to his eye, and she got it right. I reckon Abe's a mite sweet on Katy Roby."

"I ain't neither." Abe looked up from his figuring by the hearth, his face red from more than the heat and light of the fire. "She's jist a good friend, is all. Anyway, she's Allen Gentry's girl."

To Sally's relief Tom began to show pride in Abe's "eddication," especially his increasing expertise in mathematics. The fact that he could correctly measure a field, a haystack, or a crib of corn impressed him mightily. Later, when Abe learned from Dorsey the simple rudiments of surveying and could determine the height of a tree on a distant hill, his respect was unbounded. No longer did he make objection when Abe lay by the fire and continued to read after the others were in bed. In fact, after the term of school with Dorsey was finished he encouraged his son to continue his study in the subject which he considered most important.

"You keep on till you know all thar is in that 'rithmetic book. Cipher it clean through."

But he still became impatient if Abe slipped a book inside his shirt when he went outside to work and if he found the boy at the end of a plowed furrow or a row of corn curled up under a tree, shoulders against the trunk, knees higher than his head, the book propped against them. "No wonder Gentrys and Grigsbys git so rich and prosp'rous. They got sons what know how to work. It ain't all luck and Providence that's agin us."

True, the Lincolns could be accounted poor by Gentry and Grigsby standards. By 1824 they were cultivating only about ten acres of corn and five of wheat. They kept some livestock, horses, sheep, cattle, but, as Tom admitted, "they didn't fetch much, cows and calves worth only about six dollars, corn only ten cents a bushel, wheat twenty-five." However, Tom was not usually one to complain, and he liked hard work no better than Abe. If his son had deserted the plow or hoe or maul for an hour of deer-stalking with his gun, he would have winked at such dereliction of duty.

Once it was the Gentrys who were to be pitied, not envied. Abe ran home from a day's work for their wealthy neighbor, panting, inarticulate, eyes wide with horror. James Gentry's oldest son, Matthew, a bright lad three years older than Abe and one of his schoolmates, had all at once, without warning, gone mad.

"He—he took a knife—tried to cut himself!" Abe finally choked out the words. "Then—he turned on his father—fought him—and—and struck at his mother. It—it was all we could do to—hold him. Then we had to—tie him!"

"Oh!" moaned Sally, her heart aching as much for Abe as for her stricken neighbors. Never had she seen him so emotionally distraught. Throwing himself into a chair, he hunched by the fireplace, shivering. Big though he had become, she put her arms about him and cradled his head against her breast. "Why!" he sobbed. "Why did it happen to him? It's worse than if he'd died."

He brooded over the tragedy for days, weeks, months. Twenty years later the memory would still haunt him when, returning to the old home, he would find his boyhood friend still alive but with reason unrestored, and would put his long grieving into words.

> Poor Matthew! I have ne'er forgot,
> When first, with maddened will,
> Yourself you maimed, your father fought,
> And mother sought to kill. . . .
>
> And when at length, tho' drear and long,
> Time soothed thy fiercer woes,
> How plaintively thy mournful song
> Upon the still night rose.
>
> I've heard it oft, as if I dreamed,
> Far distant, sweet and lone—
> The funeral dirge, it ever seemed
> Of reason dead and gone. . . .

It was James Gentry and his sons—Allen, Joseph, James, all but the unfortunate Matthew—who were to build the Little Pigeon Creek settlement into a thriving community. When William Jones opened a general store and meat market in 1823 near the junction of the Boonville-Corydon road and the Rockport-Bloomington highway, it was not long before James Gentry opened another store in competition about a hundred yards to the west across the road from his own home. Soon he began laying out lots and the settlement around the crossroads grew, becoming in time the town of Gentryville.

"William Jones is goin' to give me a job cuttin' pork," announced Abe with glee, "and renderin' lard."

"Good." Tom was delighted. "Mebbe it'll mean more money than jist splittin' rails."

"And Lord knows," grinned Sally, "you've had plenty of hog-handlin'."

It had been a new experience for her coming from E-town, where pork was a commodity purchased instead of a long evolution from squealing mite to hog jowls, hams, bacon, and huge tubfuls of lard. She had been fascinated by her first participation in a hog-killing, which was a social event as exciting as a shucking bee or barn-raising.

The hog carcass, stripped of its hair, was held by one group of neighbors head down, while others put one point of a gambrel bar through a slit in its hock, then over the string pole, and the other point through the other hock, swinging the body clear of the ground. It soon became a sport, for it took strength to hold the hog, greasy, moist, weighing some two hundred pounds. Often those with the gambrel were provokingly slow, hoping to make the holders drop their burden.

"Yes, it's a heavy hog to hold," Abe could be heard to say long afterward, faced with the burden of bringing a devastating war to an end.

Abe reveled in his new job, for it gave him a chance to talk with people, not only neighbors but travelers who brought news of distant places, politicians rooting for their candidates in the coming presidential election, fur traders, pioneers bound for the fast-developing state of Illinois, adventurers bound for even farther west. He often stayed late into the evening participating in heated discussions with his cronies, young Grigsbys, Gentrys, Crawfords, and others, all just awakening to the challenge of politics. The election of 1824 offered crucial choices. The old Federalist party had died. Jefferson's Democratic-Republican party was predominant, and it offered four major candidates, Adams, Clay, Jackson, and Crawford. Abe was all for Clay, as was his friend Nat Grigsby, but the Gentrys supported Andrew Jackson, "Old Hickory," a senator from Tennessee and military hero, and the arguments flamed hotter than the fire in William Jones's red-hot cast-iron stove.

It was Sally and Sarah who suffered the brunt of Abe's labor, for he came home with linsey-woolsey shirt and trousers stiff with grease, requiring extra buckets of hot water and huge gobs of soap. Yet he brought home much more than dirt.

"Lookee!" he exclaimed in triumph, holding up a tattered copy of an old newspaper. "Jones takes this Vincennes *Western Sun* every week, and he lets me read it!"

Tom had hard work now keeping Abe quiet when the neighbors met in the cabin of an evening, and Sally was relieved that often he did not even try. At fifteen Abe looked a man grown, taller even than his father. As at the store, discussions were largely of politics and of the coming election.

"They say Clay must be a pro-slave man," argued one of the Jackson supporters, " 'cause he comes from Kaintuck."

"Ha!" scoffed Abe. "Washington and Jefferson come from Virginny, didn't they, and that don't make 'em pro-slave. And if you ask me, that Adams don't b'lieve no how in the Rights of Man, 'cause he says no people have a right to overthrow one constitution and put up another without the consent of the guvverment. And if you ask me, Old Hickory and Calhoun and their wing are more int'rested in protectin' the South and their slaves by opposing a tariff than in helpin' out us Westerners who need it."

Tom listened to his son with amazement mingled with grudging admiration. Though he himself had strong convictions on the question of slavery and human rights, they depended on instinct rather than logic, and it was hard for him to admit that the "eddication" he had so long discounted could give a mere boy such an advantage. He's as surprised, thought Sally, as if he saw one of his young pigs grow wings and fly away.

Tom was far prouder of Abe's growing reputation in another area.

"You'd oughter see Abe in that store o' Jones's," reported John Hanks gleefully. "He has every man what comes in rockin' with laughter over his yarns. Not always fitten for women to hear, neither. I declar, I don't know whar he ever picked up sich stuff. From you, mebbe—that is, when Sally waren't listenin'."

Sally pursed her lips, trying not to smile. Men would be men, and she was well acquainted with the rough ribaldry of pioneer humor. Women had sharper ears than their husbands and fathers credited them with. She was thankful that Tom's indelicacies of speech never included profanity or, indeed, any slang other than his favorite expression of "By dear!" when he was surprised or bothered. It had not always been so. She had heard the story from Tom's own lips.

"Oh, I used to rip out an oath ev'ry time I got mad, which was right often in them days."

"And how did you stop?" Sally had asked.

"Wal, when we was livin' in Kaintuck little Sairy jist come out one day with a right bad swear word she'd heard me use, and Nancy says, 'Pa, did you hear yer little baby?' And I never swore no more, nohow."

Sally was thankful not only for Tom's comparative restraint in language but for his sense of humor, which brightened even the proneness to misfortune of which he was always cheerfully complaining. Abe certainly came by his yarn-spinning naturally, for his father was never at a loss for a story. Once Sally, half serious, half teasing, inquired of him, "Tom, you never yet told me which of your wives you liked best, Nancy or me."

"Sally," he drawled, "that reminds me of old John Hardin down in Kaintuck who had a fine-lookin' pair of horses, and a neighbor come in one day and looked at 'em and said, 'John, which one of them horses do you like the best?' And John said, 'I cain't tell. One of 'em kicks and t'other one bites, and I dunno which is wust.'"

But in the spring of 1825 there came a misfortune which even Tom was unable to minimize. With his usual optimism and good nature he had signed a note for a neighbor, and when the note came due the neighbor refused to pay.

"Jist my luck!" He made his usual complaint. "I reckon it's the hand of Providence laid on me. 'Whom the Lord loveth He chasteneth.' Seems like everything I tech either dies, or gits killed, or gits lost, includin' money. Look at Grigsby! Look at Gentry! Everything they tech brings in money. They don't git themselves in debt."

Sometimes it did seem that ill luck attended his efforts. Not long before, to save spending good grain on his horses, he had turned them out to browse. Then when he came to look for them, there was one hanging in a tree stone dead. Somehow in kicking flies its hind foot had got caught in the branches, and there it hung with "nary a smidgen of life in its body."

Ill luck mebbe sometimes, thought Sally, but not this time. And you can't blame Providence. You should have known that perticler neighbor waren't worth trustin'. And don't say, "Whom the Lord loveth . . ." If anybody's holdin' a whip to your back, Tom Lincoln, it's yourself!

She felt like accusing him aloud, but he looked so utterly woebegone, so devoid of mitigating hope, that the words died on her lips.

"Thar's a reason," she said mildly, "why Grigsby don't git himself in debt. He don't give things away like you do, and he wouldn't sign a note for a neighbor if he saw one starvin' to death. But I wouldn't have you no diff'rent for all of Grigsby's good fortune."

Though mollified, Tom still brooded. "I've got to meet that note. And 'less we kin git more money somehow, it's goin' to take everything we got."

"I kin help, Pa," offered Abe. "That new man Crawford's been wantin' to hire me. And I kin still work nights at the store."

Tom's eyes held a glint of hope. His eyes sought Sally's apologetically, before moving to his daughter. "I–I reckon I got to hire out Sairy too."

"Sure, Pa. Miz' Crawford's been sayin' she needed somebody to help her."

Tom's eyes turned back pleadingly to Sally. "If–if your ma thinks she kin git along–"

"Yes," said Sally, "Tilda and I kin git along. But it's Sairy I'm thinkin' of. It'll mean puttin' off her weddin' for mebbe another year."

Tom looked bewildered. "Weddin'? Little Sairy?"

There were hoots of laughter. "Tom," continued Sally gently, "don't tell me you haven't noticed. She and Aaron Grigsby have been sweet on each other since they met at the spring almost nine years ago, and Sairy's eighteen."

"I don't mind, Ma," said Sarah quietly. "Me and Aaron kin wait."

Josiah Crawford and his wife Elizabeth, with their five children, Abel, Samuel, Joseph, Ruth, and Mary, had moved into the community in 1824, settling on land two miles south of the Lincoln cabin. Already they had become leading citizens of the settlement. Josiah— usually called "Cy"—was what people called a "yarb-and-root" doctor, as well as being skilled at pulling teeth. His remedies were simple and often accompanied by a "heroic old-fashioned Baptist footwashing," recommended for the hour before retiring. He was once known in an emergency to call "shoemaker's wax" into service as a plaster, a remedy more difficult to remove than the disease. After an apprenticeship as dentist by primitive methods of "prying, twisting, and gouging," he managed to obtain a "twister" forceps, making the surgery less painful. Obtaining a lancet, he was later able to add the popular treatment of "bleeding" to his other accomplishments.

His wife Elizabeth was also a "doctor," serving both as midwife and general practitioner, riding on horseback all over the community and even into the wilderness with her pill bags and medical books strapped to her saddle. Sally soon became friendly with Elizabeth, finding her more congenial than any of the other neighbor women, and Elizabeth returned her devotion, remembering Sally long afterward as "a gentle, kind, smart, shrewd, social, intelligent woman, quick and strong-minded."

"Old Blue Nose," Abe called Josiah Crawford in the privacy of the cabin. Not that his employer was "old," only in his twenties, but the feature in question was long and slightly crooked, its end pimpled and blue with a network of veins. He was scrupulously fair in all his dealings, too scrupulous according to Abe, for the loss of a minute in a day's work meant a docking of so much in the twenty-five cents he paid. Of course there was no pay on the day the whole neighborhood stopped work on June 23 to attend the wedding of Agnes Gentry to Benjamin Romine, the big social event of the year, uniting two of the richest families in the community. If Sarah envied her friend the elaborate ceremony at which the Reverend Young Lamar officiated, the wedding dress which had come up the Mississippi from New Orleans, the huge dinner and infare and dancing paid for by the Gentry distilleries and cotton gin, she gave no sign. The next day both she and Abe returned to their kneading board and spinning wheel and milking stool, ax and hoe and shovel at the Crawfords'.

Josiah Crawford had many jobs for Abe, splitting rails, building a hog pen strong enough to keep out wolves and panthers, digging and lining a well. Though it was hard work with long hours, which Abe did not appreciate, he made the pen as solid as if it had been a log cabin, the well deep and neatly walled with stone.

"What I like best," he admitted, "is takin' a rest after splittin' rails, and playin' a solo on my jew's-harp."

But there were other compensations. The work demanded that both he and Sarah spend many nights at the Crawford house, and he discovered a wealth of books on their shelves. One of these was the *Kentucky Preceptor,* containing orations, speeches, and compositions to recite. He immediately began trying them out on all who would listen and memorizing them for use in the debates and exhibitions which were often held in the schoolhouse or church.

But the greatest treasure Abe brought home with him one night.

Among the books he had found a copy of David Ramsay's *Life of Washington,* and Josiah had offered to loan it to him. Abe was jubilant. Usually half starved at mealtime, tonight he had little appetite for Sally's good supper. As soon as the meal was cleared away, he was crouched on the hearth, back against the fireplace frame, lanky six-foot body doubled like a hinge rule, the book propped against his knees.

Years ago, back in his childhood, when he was first able to read, he had got hold of a small book belonging to one of his teachers, Weems's *Life of Washington,* which had captured his imagination. Sally knew what an impression the book had made on him, for she had heard him recounting some of its stories to John D., especially this very year of 1825, when news of the visit of the Marquis de Lafayette, whose steamer had come as close as the Ohio River, had been on every tongue. Over and over he would recount the incident of Washington's crossing the river at Trenton, the terrible hardships his men had endured, their fierce battle with the Hessians.

"You know, John D., it must have been somethin' right important they struggled for in them Revolution days, makin' 'em march, fight, bleed, go cold and hungry for what they called 'freedom'!"

Now Sally watched him immerse himself again in the tales of heroism, oblivious of all about him. She was glad that Tom went off to bed without any ominous clearings of his throat or rumblings about "mornin' comin' early and folks should be gittin' their proper sleep." Noticing that Abe's eyes were straining hard to see by the light of the banked fire, she set two candles on the table, even though tallow was scarce, and lighted them. "Here, Abe, sit by the table and read by these."

He did so, mumbling a hasty "Thanks, Ma," but not lifting his eyes from the page.

"Be keerful of the book, won't you, son. Remember, it ain't yours. You'll be leavin' early in the mornin', and one of Betsy's young'uns might git their hands on it."

"I'll be keerful, Ma. You know I allus am of books."

After creeping quietly into bed beside the audibly sleeping Tom, she lay and watched Abe, thinking and wondering. What was it that made this big hulking man-child different from her own son sleeping in the loft above, different even from the gentle, placid Sarah, born of the same mother and father? What fires burned within him, what drums did he hear beating as he read and read and read, head bending lower and lower as the flames in the crude lamps grew fainter? Not until they had flickered out did he finally get up, go to the little bookshelf made of two pins high in the wall with a clapboard on them, and put the book carefully on it, pushing it as far back as possible, to keep it from prying fingers. Then quietly, so as not to awake the sleepers, he tiptoed to the ladder and climbed to his bed in the loft, carefully, trying not to make the wooden footholds creak.

She slept then but was awakened by the sound of a sudden shower, wind that shook the cabin, rain that pounded against the wall beside her bed. She could even feel a touch of wetness on her face. It was time to chink the logs again. Tom had been putting it off but now that autumn was near, it could not be postponed much longer. She sighed. There were so many things that needed doing. Not until the wind had died and the rain stopped did she fall into a troubled sleep.

"*Ma!*"

Startled by the anguished urgency in the boy's voice, Sally straightened up from the fire, where she had been down on her knees stirring the breakfast porridge. "Son, what is it?"

Abe held out the book he had been reading, the *Life of Washington,* and she saw it was stained with water, the cover blotched and draggled.

"Look, Ma! I put it back on the shelf, and the rain must ha' come in through a crack in the logs, and—and jist see it! Ma, what'll I do!"

Sally took the book. It was still wet. Opening it, she regarded the discolored pages with dismay, but her response was unexcited. "It waren't your fault, son. You tried to put it away keerful. You didn't know thar was a bad crack or that it was goin' to rain so hard."

"But, Ma—what'll I *do?*"

"Go to Mr. Crawford," she said calmly, "and tell him jist what happened. Say you'll work extry to make up for it. He cain't no more than be decent."

Abe returned that night tight-lipped, brow furrowed, silent. They had agreed not to tell Tom about the mishap, but when he and John Hanks went out to the shed to feed the cattle, Sally got her chance.

"Did you tell him, Abe?"

"Oh yes, I told him!"

"What did he say?"

"Wal, fust he was madder'n an old hornet. He says the book was wuth seventy-five cents, and I gotter pay."

"Seventy-five cents!" Sally was properly dismayed.

"But when I told him I'd work it off, he sort o' sweetened up. You see, his corn is stripped to blades high as the ear, ready to have its tops cut off for winter fodder. I could cut that, he said. 'How much shall I cut?' I asked him. 'All of it,' he snaps."

John Hanks was shocked. "But—that's three or four acres! It'll take you—who knows how many days?"

Abe smiled grimly. "That's jist right. You'll see how many days. It ain't for nothin' I got these long arms and a body like a tall scarecrow. At twenty-five cents a day it oughter take three, hadn't it? Wal, you jist wait and see."

They did. At the end of two days Abe returned triumphant. "Done. Thar ain't a corn blade left on a stalk in that field. I made a clean sweep. And now the book's mine. It was wuth it."

As a result of this disaster Abe decided to build himself a little bookcase to hold his treasures. Tom encouraged any ambition at carpentering and gladly supplied his tools. Work with his father had made the boy proficient with drawing knife, plane, brace, and bit. Finding in Tom's lean-to some good walnut and poplar clapboards, he worked hard planing them to perfect smoothness and fastened them together with wooden pegs. It was an object to be proud of, and Sally was dutifully admiring, while wondering where in the overloaded cabin it could find a place. It was thirty inches high and eighteen wide and had six drawers. By crowding it between the chest and the corner cupboard, making the latter less easy of access, Sally managed to fit it into the ménage.

"Look!" Abe's fingers stroked the smooth wide walnut top. "I could use this for a desk, mebbe, to do my writin' evenin's." He looked doubtfully at Sally. "That is, if we could spare the candles."

"We'll get the candles," she assured him.

She did, even though tallow was often at a minimum. Sometimes he would write until a candle completely burned itself out. More than once, to Abe's dismay, the sputtering tallow wore little gouges in the smooth surface, blemishes which would be pointed out with wondering conjecture a century and a half later by visitors to an Indiana art museum where it was displayed.

But Abe was not one to forget what he considered unfair treatment, and "Cy" Crawford was the one who paid for his exaction of too harsh restitution. Abe had a talent for turning out doggerel rhymes, and he lampooned the man in one of them, this time not keeping his humorous caricaturing of "Old Blue Nose" within the privacy of the family. He shared his verses with some of his friends, and the "blue nose," as well as other distinguishing features of their righteous but tight-fisted neighbor became the laughingstock of the community, their fame spreading, as one report had it, "all the way to the Wabash and Ohio."

"You oughtn't to ha' done that," reproved Sally, in whose eyes Abe seldom did anything wrong.

"I know," Abe agreed sheepishly.

He had acted hastily, he admitted. And one feature of the incident made him even more regretful, he confessed to Sally. While he was pulling corn, Elizabeth Crawford, whom he greatly admired, had come out into the fields to help him pull the fodder.

"She asked me what I wanted to be when I—not when I growed up," Abe grinned wryly, "I done that already, but jist what I wanted to be."

"And what did you tell her?" Sally looked up at him eagerly, waiting with a sudden intensity of hope and trepidation to hear his answer. They were standing outside the cabin, Sally carrying a basket of wild plums she had been gathering for the making of a winter's supply of plum butter, Abe still holding the grubbing hoe from his work in the Crawford fields, his linsey-woolsey shirt, jean breeches, always too short, earth-stained. But it seemed to her they were not alone. There was another there waiting with baited breath—as if the autumn winds stirring the dead leaves on a hill not far away had summoned one of its sleeping memories into life and then subsided into anxious listening. Perhaps Abe too sensed the third presence, for he turned his eyes southward toward the tree-crested slope with its little cluster of mounds.

"I told her," he said, "that I don't allus mean to delve, grub, shuck corn, split rails, and the like. I—I mean to be somebody someday."

Sally nodded. The winds were in motion again, setting the dead leaves dancing. If Nancy could hear, she would be satisfied.

= 5 =

Winters in southern Indiana were usually mild—rain, mud, sleet, perhaps ice, very little snow. But the winter of 1825–26 was an exception. On a day in January in the late afternoon snow began to fall. It soon became a blizzard. By dusk, when she went to the door, Sally could barely see the outlines of the cattle shed and smokehouse. She was glad when Tom appeared after doing the night's chores and the door could be shut tight against the driving wind and snow. The family were all at home. Abe had split his big toe open with an ax when working in the clearing a few days before and had not gone as usual to the Turnham farm where he was presently employed at splitting rails.

"Good!" she exclaimed with satisfaction. "Here we are all safe and sound. I'm 'most glad you hurt that toe, Abe. I'd be worryin' about you gittin' home from up past the deer licks. Heaven help anybody what's out in this storm tonight! Say an extry prayer, Tom, for any pore traveler."

Tonight there was no corn meal left for hoecakes, but potatoes were roasting in the embers. Tom had sold most of last season's corn crop to finish payment on the note he had signed, and she was doling out the remainder in driblets. Someone would have to go to the mill in Gentryville soon. Meanwhile they would live on smoked meat, potatoes, and turnips, plus the savories of wild grapes, plums, berries which she and the girls had put down in crocks with maple syrup and honey. But before they sat down to eat a cry was heard from outside the cabin.

"Hel-lo! Hel—lo, thar! Hel-loo!"

Tom went to the door. As he opened it, creaking on its leather hinges, snow blew into the room. He shaded his eyes trying to see who was there. "Somebody on a horse," he spoke back. "I think it's that Wesley Hall. I seen him goin' by to the mill this mornin'." He went out into the storm, and they heard him call, "Is that you, Wesley? You git right down from thar and come in out o' the weather." A few moments later they heard him cry out, "Abe! Oh, Abe! Come out here! Come and git Wesley's grist while I put his horse in the stable. He's mighty nigh froze, I reckon."

"Let John D. go," urged Sally. "Your sore foot—in all that cold snow!"

Abe laughed. "If I walk on my heel, my foot's long enough so's to keep my toe out o' the snow, unless it's deeper'n six inches. I'll manage."

Wesley Hall, the son of Shadrach Hall, who ran a farm and tannery about four miles to the east over the Troy-Vincennes trail, was some two years younger than Abe, one of his good friends and schoolmates. They often rode to the mill at Gentryville together. Shadrach was considered one of the more prosperous settlers of the community, and both Abe and Tom had been employed at various times in his tannery, from which leather goods were shipped down the river to southern markets.

Presently Abe came in carrying a big sack of meal effortlessly under one arm, followed by a shapeless apparition in white. After shaking off the snow like a wet dog, the newcomer stood shivering by the fire. Sally brought him a chair, and soon Tom, also wet and cold, sat down beside him, slapping and rubbing his hands together.

"Wesley, you got purty cold, I reckon, didn't you?" Wesley allowed that he did and went on to explain his predicament. He had taken a big bag of corn to the mill at Gentryville to be ground, but there had been a lot of men and boys ahead of him, and when his turn came the afternoon was almost over. And grinding was slow. "You know how that is, Abe."

"Reckon I do. Horse could eat up all your grain afore you got it ground!"

By the time the miller carried out Wesley's grist and helped him mount for the homeward journey, several inches of snow had fallen. As he rode through the forest night was coming on, the snow was almost blinding him, and he was afraid he might get lost or be overcome by the cold, so he had decided to stop here for the night instead of risking the other four miles home.

"Glad you did," said Sally, "you're right welcome. And I reckon you're hungry."

"Wal," the boy grinned, "I ain't had nothin' to eat 'ceptin' some parched corn since mornin'."

"We ain't got no meal right now to bake bread, we're out jist now." Sally made the statement without apology. "But we've got some potatoes bakin', and we'll all be eatin' supper purty soon."

"Jist help yourself out o' my sack thar," Wesley told her. "I got plenty."

Sally did not hesitate to do so. Sharing food as well as lodging was an eleventh commandment in the pioneer's credo. While Sarah and Tilda mixed hoecakes Sally took a big turnip and began hollowing it out. Wesley turned in surprise at the sound of a queer grinding noise. "What's that you're doin', Miz' Lincoln?"

"Makin' a grease lamp, Wesley. Didn't you ever see one?"

"Yes, course I have, but—"

But you never saw your mother makin' one, thought Sally with indulgent amusement. She always has plenty of tallow for candles. It's only us poor folks who have to use such things.

She finished hollowing out the turnip, cut a small groove in its lip, filled it with hog's lard, laid a wick in the notch, and lit it. "Here, Abe. Go and git some bacon, please. John D.'ll hold the light for you."

Presently Abe and John D. returned with a half moon cut out of a side of bacon, and after some time the family sat down to a supper of corn cakes, baked potatoes, and fried bacon. After the dishes were cleared away, Tom said, "Now, Abe, bring out that new book and read to us."

Sally looked at him with delighted surprise. There was unmistakable pride, even a hint of boasting, in his voice. Perhaps her years of pleading, of cajoling, of conniving to win for Abe the freedom of study he so desired were ending. Tom wanted this son of a more prosperous neighbor to be properly impressed with the superior abilities of his own son, and not merely because he could throw a maul or crowbar farther than any of his peers or pick up a chicken house weighing, somebody claimed, at least six hundred pounds, and carry it off.

Obediently Abe took down a book from the shelf, one which he had recently borrowed from storekeeper Jones, stirred the fire into flame with some of the dry wood piled in a corner of the jamb, stretched out beside it, and began to read from *The Life of Dr. Benjamin Franklin.*

Wesley was later to remember climbing up the peg ladder through the scuttle hole to the loft where he was to share Abe and John D.'s bed. In fact, he would recall the "bedstid" in all its humble detail.

"It wuz a mighty sorry affair; still it answered the purpose. A hole wuz bored in the north wall and a rail-like piece wuz sloped off to fit this. The same thing wuz done in the west wall, and these two rails wuz brought together and fastened in the same way to an upright post out in the floor and then acrost these wuz laid split boards or whipped plank, or some thin slats rived out, and on these wuz a gunny sack filled with leaves gathered from the woods. On this Abe and me slept covered with bearskins."

Perhaps Wesley Hall would have slept less soundly could he have known that he would live to see his bedfellow of that snowy night in the White House.

That year of 1826 atoned for its winter severity with a mild and early spring. The hard brown earth shed its blanket of snow, and, before bursting into its annual profusion of leaves, buds, blossoms, clothed itself in deep rich mud. Horses wallowed along the road, dragging wagons sunk to their hubs. The fields were hopeless morasses. And Sally's floor . . . ! But what did that matter? And one of her joys these days was seeing small muddy footprints mingled with the big ones on the smooth scrubbed planks. Betsy had three children now and another on the way, Sarah Jane, now four, John Talbot, three, and now, to Sally's satisfaction, another Nancy Hanks, chubby and adorable at two.

One day during mud season Betsy had brought the children to the cabin on the promise that Sally would help her make a batch of soap. Since the fields were too wet to plow, Tom and John D. had gone hunting. To the children's delight Abe was at home, helping to keep the ash hopper filled with the leaching water. Wherever he went they dogged his steps, for he was a willing playmate, telling them stories, riding them piggyback, tossing them shrieking into the air and catching them, singing them songs like "The turbaned Turk that scorns the world and struts about with his whiskers curled," blissfully unconscious that he could not carry a tune.

"He's as much a child as they are," marveled Sally, watching the antics of the gawky young giant who at seventeen could get down on the floor and play "cat and mouse" with as much gusto as three-year-old John Talbot. The years of adolescence had not improved Abe's figure, only added to its incongruities. As Tom once remarked, "Abe looks like he had been chopped out with an ax and needed the jackplane to smooth him down." Today for the first time Sally was startled to see how tall he had grown. As he entered the cabin to get another kettle of hot ashes for the hopper, he almost bumped his head on the top of the doorframe, which permitted clearance of something over six feet.

"Abe!" she exclaimed jokingly. "I don't mind how much mud you carry in on the floor, for that kin be scrubbed, but jist be keerful with my whitewashed ceiling and don't git no dirt up thar!"

Sometime later, when the women were all working around the ash hopper, Abe beckoned to the children, who, exulting in bare feet after the discomfort of winter deer-hide boots, had been wading gleefully through a little pond of muddy water. When Sally re-entered the cabin she stared in amazement at tracks of small feet crossing and crisscrossing her white ceiling.

"We bin walkin' up thar, upside down!" crowed John Talbot.

"Abe held us," explained four-year-old Sarah Jane, noting Sally's dismay with some trepidation.

"You, Abe!" Sally was torn between exasperation, dismay, amusement. "What am I goin' to do with you! You desarve a good spankin'."

Then the ludicrous picture of the lanky six-footer receiving discipline across her knees assailed her, and she burst into laughter.

"Don't worry, Ma," Abe assured, his meekness belied by the twinkle in his eyes. "Jist wanted to show you folks kin walk on the ceiling same as the floor. I'll fix it good as new."

He did, walking several miles to get lime, then spending time mixing the whitewash and making the ceiling of the cabin once more white and shining.

Abe occupied a space in the family life bigger even than his awkwardly overgrown body could fill. Sally did not realize how big until he left that spring to work for James Taylor, who ran a ferry across the mouth of Anderson's Creek, where the family had landed in Indiana just ten years before. Though the cabin was still crowded with its five family members plus John Hanks when he was not away working, it seemed empty.

Even Tom, who appreciated the prospect of an extra six dollars each month, seemed bereft. "It don't seem nat'ral," he admitted, "not to have readin' of the Book at night. And them other things he reads, I kind of miss 'em."

"Do you s'pose Abe will be back for my weddin'?" inquired Sarah anxiously, for her long years of waiting since Aaron Grigsby had first looked at her with sheep's eyes at the spring were at last to be ended. "I couldn't bear it if he waren't here."

"He will be," assured Sally.

And he was, returning the first of August with his several months' earnings, which he gave to Tom in their entirety, a body sunburned and toughened by snubbing the heavy flatboat along the riverbank or propelling it across by a long sweep, a collection of new yarns, some decidedly ribald, on his tongue, and, visible perhaps only to Sally's troubled discernment, a new restlessness in his eyes.

"What's it like down thar at the ferry?" demanded John D.

It was a huge place, Abe told him, where river steamers stopped to buy or sell corn and put on fuel. Sometimes they tied up for the night and the travelers came ashore to maybe build a big fire and roast beef. There were all sorts of folks to talk to, politicians, pioneers, river pirates, slave drivers going to Kentucky. And sometimes at night you could lie on the bank and watch the big steamers go by, all lighted, and hear people singing and laughing. It was sort of mysterious and—yes, fearsome. And you wondered where they were all going and—and wished you could go there too.

"But it waren't so much fun livin' with the Taylors," he confessed. "I did everything from runnin' the hand mill to bein' maid of all work. Had to be fust one up in the mornin', tend the fire, put water to heat. And Green Taylor, who I slept with up in the loft, is a mean sort. He got mad 'cause I took a candle and read at night. But," Abe's face lighted, "they had a hist'ry of the United States and Miz' Taylor let me read it."

During these days before her wedding Sarah seemed to blossom into beauty, somber face lighting, and hazel eyes, so like her mother's, thought Sally, sparkling with rapturous excitement. The wedding dress of soft linen which together they had spun and woven and sewed gave her plump little figure, such a contrast to Abe's gangling length, a new dignity.

The wedding took place in the cabin on August 2, Charles Harper,

minister of the Little Pigeon Church, officiating. "I married these on
the same within," Harper noted in the Marriage Register of Spencer
County. It was a solemn ceremony, followed by the usual feast. Sally
was proud of the menu, which included two fat wild turkeys roasted
to a turn, a saddle of deer meat, six big vegetable pies full of turnips,
beans, and potatoes, bowls of wild honey and maple sugar, water-
melon and cherry preserves, a whole bushel of pawpaws, all washed
down with tea. Tom to her relief had decreed that there should be no
whiskey. Nor did the infare which followed include dancing, which
was prohibited by the strict discipline of the church. Abe adapted a
poem which he had found and read it with a mingling of jocularity
and sober sentiment. Titled "Adam and Eve's Wedding Song," some
of its seven stanzas were:

> *The Lord was not willing*
> *That man should be alone,*
> *But caused a sleep upon him*
> *And took from him a bone. . . .*

> *Then Adam he rejoiced*
> *To see his loving bride,*
> *A part of his own body,*
> *The product of his side.*

> *This woman was not taken*
> *From Adam's feet we see,*
> *So he must not abuse her,*
> *The meaning seems to be.*

> *This woman was not taken*
> *From Adam's head, we know,*
> *To show she must not rule him;*
> *'Tis evidently so.*

> *This woman she was taken*
> *From under Adam's arm,*
> *So she must be protected*
> *From injuries and harm.*

Was there, wondered Sally uneasily, a faintly implied warning in
Abe's choice of words, a hint that if Aaron's treatment of his bride
was in any way deficient, he would have her brother to reckon with?
Abe had always been fiercely protective of his sister, even though she

was the older by two years. Because of her slight stature and modest demeanor she had always seemed the younger of the two, yet, as Nat Grigsby was to describe her later, she was "a woman of an extraordinary mind, an intellectual and intelligent woman, though not as much as her mother." Surely, thought Sally, she would be able to hold her own in this new relationship, especially since Aaron had been her adoring shadow for ten years!

And the couple was starting life with every advantage. Tom was giving his daughter the usual dowry, "a new feather bed, with all necessary clothing, with pillows and bolster, all of decent home manufacture," and he had added a cow and calf. They would move into a new cabin only a half mile from Aaron's family, and only two miles from Tom's. Certainly Abe had nothing to worry about, though, knowing the strength of his temper when aroused and sensing a certain tension in his voice as he read the poem, she still felt uneasy.

If only Abe could be more interested in girls, thought Sally, he might be less possessively protective of his sisters. But, though he had many friends, he showed no preference for any one. There were Katy Roby, Elizabeth Wood, Hannah Gentry, Betsy Ray Grigsby, Elizabeth Ray, Elizabeth Tully. (Queer there were so many Elizabeths in the community!) Abe liked them all, played "Skip to My Loo," "Old Sister Phoebe," "Weevily Wheat," and other games at play parties, joked with them during the lunch time between church services, kissed one or the other of them when opportunity afforded, like finding a red ear at a husking bee, but, except for his dream of the "Covered Wagon Girl," he had shown no romantic tendencies. In fact, John D. was to say later, "Abe didn't take much truck with girls, he was too busy studying," and John Hanks would remember that he could never get Abe in the company of girls, that he was "not timid in this particular but did not seek such company." "Abe did not much like the girls," his friend David Turnham would comment, "at least didn't appear to."

Perhaps it was Sarah's wedding that hastened another romance to fulfillment. Sally was startled when Tilda came to her a few days later with the announcement that she and Squire Hall wanted to be married, not sometime but very soon.

"I'm seventeen," she reminded Sally calmly. "Betsy already had three babies when she was my age. It's time you woke up to the fact that I ain't your little girl any longer. I'm a woman."

Sally gazed hard at her younger daughter, as once she had looked at her older one. As before, she saw competence, certainty, the full maturity which pioneer life was bound to thrust on its womanhood. Tilda had not asked permission, she had announced her intention. She had always been independent, sure of what she wanted, yes, and honest, since the day Abe had persuaded her to tell the truth about cutting her leg on the ax.

"When did you think—" Sally asked tentatively.

"Next month mebbe," replied Tilda with the same purposeful calmness, "when Young Lamar comes to preach."

"But—so soon— How could we git ready!"

It was Sally who was the uncertain one, not Tilda. "No need to git ready, Ma, like with Sarah. And Pa won't have to give me no cow and calf. I know he ain't got it to give. We'll be livin' at first with Aunt Nannie and Uncle Levi, till we kin git our own land and cabin. I don't even need a new weddin' dress."

"My dear," slowly Sally was regaining her usual calm competence, "of course you'll have a nice weddin' dress, and a bit of a dowry too. You'll have the feather bed and pillow and bolster off your own bed for one thing. With all of you girls gone, we"—her voice broke—"we won't be needin' them any more."

So on September 14 the cabin witnessed another wedding, that of Matilda Johnston and Squire Hall, Young Lamar, who lived a few miles south of the Lincolns, officiating. Abe remained at home for the wedding. Tilda, who had been his adoring shadow through her childhood and his admiring, teasing, often quarrelsome companion in adolescence, would not have felt herself married without his presence. Sally had dreamed for a time of a possible romance between the two, but had soon become disillusioned. They were too much brother and sister for that. After the wedding was over and the crops were in, Abe returned to his work as ferryman and man of all work for James Taylor. Since John D. was able to help with the farm work, with John Hanks willing to return and assist when needed, Tom found Abe's six dollars a month more necessary to survival than his son's superior brain and brawn. And while John D. was "slower'n cold molasses," at least he did not carry a book tucked in his shirt and stretch out on his rear end to read a page or two at the end of every plowed row!

The cabin seemed incredibly huge and empty as a discarded shell.

The family of eight, which had once filled it almost to bursting, had been reduced to three. Sally could not decide which times were most lonely—the days spent performing the household tasks once shared with three daughters; the evenings when there was no longer need to brighten the fire to shine on a book, no reading except when John D. tried to stumble through a chapter of the Bible, no spinning of yarns, no stepping over a pair of long legs stretched out beside the hearth; or the nights, lying beside Tom in the dark peopled only by flickering shadows, no sound of two or three boys scuffling overhead, only the creakings and snappings and whisperings which were the unspoken language of emptiness.

Strange—it was Abe she missed most rather than the two who were of her own bone and flesh! The girls were still an extended part of her life, visiting often, asking her advice, bringing grandchildren, including Betsy's latest, darling baby Harriet. But Abe had gone into another world of activity, the first of many, she apprehended, where she could never follow. She could not explain why he had become so important to her, as much as—more than?—her own John D. It was as if her identity had somehow become merged with that of her beloved Nancy, as if somehow together they had endured the travail of bringing this strange, awkward, unpredictable, lovable, bewildering body, mind, and spirit into being.

$$= 6 =$$

It seemed the longest fall and winter Sally had ever spent. Not that it lacked activity! With the three girls gone she could have worked from dawn to dark and still not finished the necessary household tasks. And life was by no means devoid of amusements and neighborly visits. Even in winter—especially in winter when there were no crops to be sown or harvested—the Pigeon Creek community abounded in social events, and Tom was a gregarious person. Sally went with him to log-rollings, corn shuckings, hog-killings, sugar-boilings, weddings, and he accompanied her to spinning parties and quilting bees, where his temperate habits excluded him from the men's chief diversion of drinking but permitted a full play of his yen for discussing politics and yarn-spinning.

And of course there was always church. In winter services were usually held in cabins rather than in the church building. Families thought nothing of traveling eight or ten miles. Sally would don her best dress of linsey-woolsey—it had taken four yards, a yard wide, to make it, short-waisted with narrow skirt—cover her black curls with her "cornfield bonnet," scoop-shaped, flaring in front and long though narrow behind, bundle up in a shawl, and ride horseback, while Tom walked along beside her, also in Sunday best, buckskin breeches, shirt, and linsey-woolsey coat, which Sally had made in the new fashionable style, short-waisted like her dress, its "claw-hammer" tail split to the waist.

When they arrived at the house where the service was to be held, they would find whiskey, sugar, glasses, a pitcher of water set out, a basket of apples or turnips for refreshment, with now and then hoe-cakes with honey or maple syrup. All would eat, gossip, socialize, until the preacher was ready to begin, when, as one attendant was to remember later, "he would take his stand, draw his coat, open his shirt collar, read his text, and preach and pound till the sweat rolled from his face in great drops."

For Sally such gatherings were oases in the long winter-desert of loneliness, often bringing reunion with not only friends but family, Dennis and Betsy with their four children, Sarah and Aaron, Nannie and Levi Hall with Squire and Tilda, John Hanks, who was still living in the community—all but Abe. Others, it seemed, missed him as much as she did.

"Don't seem the same 'thout Abe. Nobody to preach us the sermon after we've done forgot it."

"Old Tom kin sure spin a yarn right good, but he don't hold a candle to Abe."

"Like to know what old Abe thinks about this tariff business. West wants it high so's to sell grain and wool. South don't. Who's to say what's best for us?"

"Story folks is tellin' down around Troy about Abe. Seems he went to a cornhuskin' and got a red ear, and what did he do? Went and kissed the girl that Green Taylor thought was his. Next day they got into a fight, and Taylor hit Abe with an ear o' corn. They say Abe'll have the scar long as he lives!"

Abe came home in the spring, and suddenly the cabin seemed full again to overflowing. Surely he had grown another inch! Sally regarded him anxiously, looking for signs of the reported fight, then laughed at herself. Already at eighteen Abe's face so resembled the seamed bark of a rugged oak that one more mark would scarcely show. Yet—was there a faint scar over his right eye?

It's like that fairy story he read us of the sleeping princess, she thought. Everything was asleep. Then it came alive.

It wasn't all Abe's return, of course. It was partly the coming of spring. The dogwood and apple trees were in bloom. The willows were turning from gold to green. The oaks and maples were budding. The flowers she had planted—poppies, marigolds, touch-me-nots, sword lilies, hollyhocks—were all bursting out of the ground, some of the early ones blossoming. But it was Abe who brightened the cabin at night for reading, who brought color into its dullness. Like the time he and John D. came in from plowing, laughing "fit to kill."

"Ma, you should ha' seen us. John D. was holdin' the plow, and I was drivin' the old nag. You know how lazy he is, like pullin' teeth to git him from one end of the row to the other. Wal, he went rushin' acrost the field so even I with my long legs could hardly keep up. When we come to the end o' the furrow I found an enormous chin fly fastened on him, and I knocked it off. 'Why'd you do that?' asks John D. ' 'Cause I don't want the pore old nag to git bitten,' I tell him. 'But that's all what made him go!' says John D. And by gum, he was right! If I could ha' caught that old chin fly, I reckon I'd ha' put it back."

Long afterward, in a dark moment of the nation's history, Abe would tell the same story, applying it to a troublesome cabinet member stirred to unusual activity by an itching for his own job. "Now if that man has a presidential chin fly biting him, I'm not going to knock it off, if it will only make his department go!"

Now that Abe was eighteen, he was subject to militia duty, and he had to have a rifle before muster day. He and Harry Brooner decided to buy one together. They traveled sixty miles to Vincennes, purchased one for fifteen dollars, and returned in time for the mustering

out in May. But Abe brought back from Vincennes more than the
rifle.

"You know what?" he demanded of his father indignantly. "They
atcherly got Negro slaves workin' there. I saw 'em haulin' wagons in
the streets, bein' whipped along jist as if they was horses! Don't they
know the Indiana constitution forbids ownin' slaves? Why don't
somebody do somethin' about it?"

"Who?" retorted Tom bitterly. "Don't you know some o' the very
ones what oughter be doin' the enforcin' are the ones what are
keepin' slaves?"

Abe went for Training Day to a hill about a mile southeast of the
cabin. Nat Grigsby and others of his young friends were involved.
From now on he would be subject to call at any time to join troops
going into western and northern Indiana to quell any Indian uprising.
Though the campaigns of Andrew Jackson—"Sharp Knife," he was
called as well as "Old Hickory"—had decimated many Indian tribes
and driven others beyond the Mississippi, many still clung stubbornly
to their lands assigned to them forever by white men's treaties, and
even in Indiana there were still fears of such uprisings.

But nature was soon to arouse fears more devastating than a nebulous attack by marauders. A woman who lived on Pigeon Creek, a
mile southwest of the cabin, foretold its coming. Not exactly a witch
or a necromancer, merely with gifts which earned her the title of
"Miracle Woman," she fed on the pervasive pioneer beliefs in magic,
omens, mad-stones, and other superstitions. "Thar's goin' to be a
turrible storm," she predicted, "worse'n we've ever seen," and she
even foretold the day. That morning she told some people passing
her cabin, "It's comin' before nightfall, a turrible hurricane."

"How can you tell?" they asked skeptically, for it was a fine clear
morning.

"I seen two little haystacks made of fog down thar in the middle
of the meadow."

It came, a storm so violent that 1827 would be remembered long
as "the year of the hurricane." That night wind howled like a ban-
shee and shook the cabin until it seemed it must be torn from its
foundations, as indeed some stouter houses were. Tall trees crashed,
their deep-bedded roots ripped up like frail stems. Rain pounded,
penetrating even the most freshly caulked cracks. There was no
sleeping. Abe and John D. came down from the loft, and the four of

them huddled together, listening, waiting, wondering. When Abe prepared to go out to the cattle shed to see how the cows and horses
were faring, the door was almost ripped off its hinges.

"No use," Tom told him with cheerful resignation. "It's the
workin's of Providence. It'd be jist my luck to lose all the stock."

In the morning they looked out on devastation. But the cabin had
not been in the actual path of the hurricane, which had cut such a
wide swath through the Buck Horn Valley that a half century later
its path would still be visible. Though the cattle shed had been blown
down, the animals proved to be unharmed. While Tom attended to
them, Abe traveled about the neighborhood checking on damages.
Fortunately the storm had despoiled mostly forest land. However,
some hewn-log houses had been blown down, many animals killed,
but there had been no human casualties. Sally learned with relief that
Betsy's and Sarah's homes had not been touched, though the brunt of
the hurricane had barely missed the latter's tiny cabin. Tom's
gloomy forecast of ill luck had this time proved unfounded. All the
family and most of the neighbors had escaped with only minor
damage.

"It jist waren't to be," he explained his good fortune cheerfully.

But belief in the supernatural power of the "Miracle Woman," in
fact in all signs, dreams, omens, was strengthened. Even Abe, who
was inclined to scoff at many current superstitions, was impressed.
And he would never rid himself entirely of the sense of fatalism
which pervaded this world of his youth. "I can't help feeling this
way," he would confess later when accused of being superstitious.
"My father was like this before me."

For once fortune seemed to be smiling on Tom. His land holdings,
though shrunken, had become more secure. A government act permitted any settler to relinquish parts of his land to the government
and receive credit on payment for the remainder. In April Tom had
gone with two of his neighbors to Vincennes and relinquished half of
his quarter section, applying his credit to the remaining eighty acres.
He had been able to complete payment for the half-quarter section
by applying it to another relinquishment to which he had received
title. On June 6 of that year, 1827, he received a patent signed by
President Adams for the west half of the quarter section.

"Now," Sally told herself with relief, "Abe won't need to go so far away to work. We can get along with less than that six dollars a month."

But she was doomed to disappointment. It was Abe himself who suggested going back to Anderson Creek.

"I been thinkin'," he said after the plowing and planting were finished. "If I should build a little flatboat down thar, I could take stuff down river to N'Orleans. You'd oughter see all the boats what go by, loaded with tobacco, pork, corn, beeswax, skins, what have you."

"I know," said Tom. "I've seen 'em." In fact, he could hear himself making the same speech to Nancy years before. "Thar's money to be got down thar, all right."

"We might have extra ourselves to take down at end of summer," Abe continued eagerly, "so if you'll let me build the boat—" Sure of his father's enthusiastic permission, he looked hopefully at Sally.

Heart sinking, she made all the objections she could think of. "It's too dangerous, son. All those rocks and shoals, and—and pirates!" Unwittingly she also was echoing words Nancy had once spoken.

"Nonsense, Ma. I'm strong. I kin look after myself. Besides, Pa needs the money."

It was two against one, three, for the sparkle of adventure was in John D.'s eyes also. Sally packed Abe's summer clothes in a stout knapsack, linen breeches, shirts, a linsey-woolsey jacket for cold mornings, a pair of deerskin shoes for good measure, though of course he would go barefoot most of the time. The shoes were no great addition for river running, for, as one pioneer put it, a wet moccasin was no more than "a decent way of goin' barefoot." Tom gave him tools for building his flatboat, and they saw him off.

Sally wondered and worried about him all summer. But she had other concerns. Sarah was having a difficult pregnancy. Betsy, with four children five years old and under, was taxed physically and mentally beyond her strength. Sally trekked the two and more miles to their cabins every day or two. John D., cocky in his young manhood, taxed Tom's patience with his independence and often became involved in fights with his peers. Only Matilda, gay, impetuous, easygoing Tilda, happy with her marriage to Squire Hall and their tiny new cabin, offered no worries.

Abe returned in the late summer, taller if possible, tanned face a little more like a weathered oak bole, and—could it be?—even greater length and strength in the arms that wrapped her in a stifling bear hug.

"You're thin," she chided when she had got her breath. "I reckon that Taylor woman ain't fed you right well."

He had built his flatboat but had decided it was not big enough to carry a load of produce to New Orleans, so he had hired it out to James Taylor for trips across the Anderson River and along the Ohio as far as Troy. But it had brought him one adventure which he related with gusto to the assembled family, including Dennis, Levi Hall, and his sons.

"Wal, thar I was, standin' on the bank of the Ohio River lookin' at my new flatboat and wonderin' whether I could make it stronger or improve it in any partic'lar, when two men come down to the shore in carriages with a heap o' trunks. Thar was a big steamer hove to out in the middle o' the river waitin' for passengers to come so it could git goin'. Wal, thar was lots o' boats thar on the shore beside mine, but they come up to me and says, 'Who owns this boat?' 'I do,' I says. Then one of them says, 'Will you take us and our trunks out to that steamer?' 'Sure will,' says I, thinkin' to myself, Mebbe they'll give me two or three bits. Wal, I lifted the trunks onto my flatboat, and the two men sat on the trunks, and I sculled 'em out to the steamer."

"And did they pay?" demanded John D.

"Jist wait," drawled Abe. "Wal, I lifted up their heavy trunks and put 'em on deck. The steamer was jist about to put on steam agin, when I called out that they had forgotten to pay me. Then what do you s'pose?" He paused, whetting their appetites for the climax. "Each of 'em took from his pocket a piece o' money and threw it down on the floor o' my boat." Putting his hand in the pocket of his linen breeches, Abe drew out a coin and held it up. As it caught the gleam of the fire and shone, there were gasps of amazement. "That's right. They give me two whole silver half-dollars. I could hardly believe it, me, a pore boy, earnin' a dollar in less'n a day and that by honest work! I—I tell you"—his eyes shone as brightly as the coin—"the whole world looked diff'rent, bigger somehow and—and fairer. It seemed as if thar was nothin' a pusson couldn't do if they wanted to bad enough."

"Whar's the other one?" asked John D., his eyes both curious and covetous.

"Wal"—Abe laughed shamefacedly—"I hate to tell you. I was lookin' at them coins, thinkin' of all the things I could do with 'em, and one of 'em slipped through my fingers and rolled off into the Ohio River. Gone forever. Good thing mebbe." He looked significantly at John D. "Danger sometimes of a feller gittin' too cocky."

There had been another unpleasant sequel to the incident. Abe did not divulge the facts immediately, but in coming days the story emerged. Abe had been charged with a penal offense, arrested, and brought to court.

Taylor's ferry operated on the Anderson River within the state of Indiana. Across the Ohio on the Kentucky side were a family of Dills who were licensed to run a ferry across the Ohio. They had arranged a bell on each side of the river so travelers could alert them. One day Abe heard this bell ringing on his side of the river. No Dills appeared. Time passed. The bell kept ringing. Travelers must be impatiently waiting. He got on his flatboat and sculled it across. No sooner had he arrived than John and Lin Dill rushed out of the bushes, seized him, and tried to duck him in the river, but they were no match for their rawboned, muscular opponent. After a few well-directed blows with his fist, Abe demanded an explanation.

"You been takin' away our customers," accused John, "runnin' your own ferry acrost the river. We're the only persons with license to do that. You'll either take a thrashin', or we'll haul you into court."

Abe chose to be hauled. "Take me to court, and I'll beat you," he vowed.

They marched him up the bank, through cornfields and orchards, past some slave quarters to the big house of Squire Samuel Pate, Justice of the Peace. At the request of the Dill brothers, the plaintiffs, the squire held court. A curious crowd of neighbors, Negro slaves, and the squire's family soon gathered. John Dill made his complaint. Abe had taken passengers from the Indiana side and delivered them aboard a steamer which had stopped midstream, violating the rights of the Dills, who had an exclusive license to transport across the river.

It seemed a clear case. An Act of Congress had given Kentucky jurisdiction of the Ohio River to the high water mark on the Indiana side. The squire was about to render a decision for the plaintiffs when he noticed his ward, Caroline Meeker, a pretty, brown-eyed, curly-haired girl, looking intently at Abe. He also looked, noting the awkward figure in linsey-woolsey shirt, homemade breeches dyed with walnut bark, big hands folded around a coonskin cap. Caroline did not like the Dills, and the squire shared her distaste. Would the defendant care to speak? he inquired. The defendant would.

"I'd jist like to ask a question," said Abe, rising to his full height.

"Very well," said the squire, "but I don't see what question it could be. The facts are beyond dispute."

"Do the rights of John Dill, under his license," asked Abe, "forbid any other pusson operatin' a ferry from the Indiana bank to the middle of the river?" He continued. "I didn't go acrost like they said. These men came to the bank to catch a passin' steamer. It couldn't land because o' low water but stopped in the middle. John Dill's boat was on t'other side o' the river, and he waren't in sight. The men needed somebody to take 'em or they'd miss the boat. I took 'em. And I didn't take 'em acrost the river, I set 'em only halfway. Does Dill's license say nobody kin help a stranger to git on his boat when the boat's thar and thar's no other way?"

Squire Pate dismissed the case. But that was not the end of the story.

"He asked me to stop awhile," Abe told Sally, "and we sat on the porch. He told me it was a good law point I raised, and everybody, farmers, ferrymen, and such, should know somethin' about law. He invited me to come back and go to magistrate's court and listen to what goes on."

Sally was even more interested in the fact that his subsequent sallies during the summer to the Kentucky side of the river had involved not only sessions in the courtroom but prolonged visits with the squire's attractive niece, Caroline Meeker. It was time Abe, at eighteen, began to show more romantic interest in girls, and this one sounded worthy of even her fastidious approval.

She was glad, however, when he did not return to the ferry work that fall but chose to hire out to David Turnham, William Wood, storekeeper Jones, and others, even though the cabin saw him but little. At least she could stoke his lean body with a good hot breakfast, pack him a big lunch, see that he had clean clothes, wait up for him at night and make sure he was fed when he came in late, which he often did.

She sensed a change in Abe. He had suddenly become independent. One small sign was his failure to turn over the silver half-dollar to his father when he relinquished the rest of his summer's pay.

"The first dollar I ever reely earned," he commented with satisfaction.

A second sign was a disregard of his father's attempts to govern his activities. Though he dutifully turned over to Tom each day's pay, whether money, farm produce, or store merchandise, he arranged for his own employment, left when he pleased, returned home when he pleased.

"Fool boy," Tom might fume. "I told Reuben Grigsby he'd help make brandy casks today, but off he's gone agin this mornin' to work for David Turnham."

"He ain't a boy any longer, Tom," Sally would remind him mildly. "He's eighteen. We're lucky he ain't gone off and left us altogether. At least he comes back home nights."

"Nights yes, but what time!" With Tom it was another grievance. "What's he doin' all that extry time he spends at Turnhams'? You cain't cut cordwood or split rails by candlelight!"

Abe made no secret of what he was doing, not only evenings but every minute he could spare from work. David Turnham, who had been sworn in as constable, had obtained a copy of *The Revised Laws of Indiana*. Since David was loath to have the book leave his house, Abe was devouring its 438 pages in great hungry gulps on the premises.

"You'd oughter see, Pa"—he had to share his excitement—"what wonderful stuff they've got in that book. It's a grand state we got here in Indianny. You should read our constitution! It tells all about how the printin' press shall be free, and anybody kin examine what the legislature and all the rest of gov'ment has done. And it says how slavery is a tyranny, how nobody kin hold 'any part of the human creation in slavery.' You'd like that. But it ain't so good sayin' if children are bound out and run away and ketched they kin be thrown into jail and returned jist like slaves. I'm sure glad you didn't bind me out when you hired me to sich folks as Crawford!"

Tom was mollified and allowed it was a good thing for Abe to read such a book, provided it didn't take him away from proper work. He was also pleased when David Turnham made Abe a constable's deputy, for he himself had served as constable back in Kentucky. But he looked with disfavor on Abe's frequent trips to Boonville fifteen miles away and to Rockport, the county seat, when courts were in session, partly because they deprived the family of his working days' pay, but also because they took him beyond the familiar realities of life as he knew it, into activities unrelated to land, tools, cupboards, corn, horses, hunting. And when Abe came to him one day with what seemed a startling suggestion, he was horrified.

"Pa, I been thinkin'. Mebbe I could be a lawyer. Thar's a judge down in Rockport, his name's John Pitcher, he's a sheriff too. I asked him if he'd let me study law with him in his office, and he didn't say I couldn't. Do you s'pose I could?"

Tom gaped. "You mean—not work any more? Of all fool ideas! Why—how would we git along without the money you earn us? We—we're pore folks! And sich things ain't for us. We're farmers, carpenters. You're aimin' too far agin."

"Lots o' pore folks have gone places and done things, Pa, bigger even than law. Look at Ben Franklin. His pa was jist a tallow maker and soap boiler."

"You ain't no Ben Franklin," retorted Tom. "You're jist Abe Lincoln."

Abe yielded, but Sally knew he had not given up the idea. She could tell by the outthrust angle of his lower lip, which indicated stubbornness as well as intense concentration. Compliance meant no agreement but acknowledgment that his father did indeed need the money or commodities his work produced.

"Don't worry, son," Sally comforted at the first opportunity. "Your time will come. I reckon sometimes it don't hurt us none to wait."

He sighed, then gave her a shamefaced grin. "Mebbe Pa's right. Mebbe I was reachin' too far. Judge Pitcher told me I'd better give up the idea. I could tell by the way he looked at me he thought I didn't have what it takes. And no wonder. I sure ain't much to look at."

"Nonsense!" Sally contradicted him fiercely. "Don't never let anybody tell you you cain't do a thing or that you ain't as good as anybody else. Ain't that what the constitution you read about meant when it says the good God created all of us equal?"

He patted her cheek. "Mebbe I won't never amount to much," he said, "but if I do I'll tell the world I owe it all to my angel mother."

Which one, Sally wanted to ask him, little realizing that generations to come would be asking the same question when he was to make the same statement. But the words died long before they reached her lips. For what did it matter? She and Nancy, had they not long since become one in their shared motherhood? It was like growing a flower—no, one could never compare Abe with a flower!—more like raising a tree. Who could tell which gave more to its growth—the one who planted, watered, protected it as a tender shoot, or the one who nourished, trimmed, pruned, tried to shape it into a thing of usefulness if not—she smiled wryly—of beauty? Which—or neither? For the secret of growth was in the plant itself. As the good Book said, it was one who planted, another who watered, but God gave the increase.

$$=7=$$

Hoping Tom was asleep, Sally tiptoed to the door and opened it. A gust of wind and shower of rain almost threw her off balance and took her breath away. She closed it hastily.

"Won't bring him home any sooner watchin' for him," said Tom from the bed. "You know how he is when he's workin' at Jones's store. Men and boys hang around as long as Bill Jones keeps the fire goin'. And Abe'll stay as long as thar's somebody to spin yarns to or argue politics. He'll be home when he gits ready and no sooner."

Tom's feelings about these extracurricular activities of his unmanageable son were ambivalent. While he begrudged time spent in unremunerative pursuits like reading, public speaking in the lyceum which had been started in Gentryville, jaunts to law courts, he took pride in the fact that Abe with his yarns and antics attracted so many customers to William Jones's store that the ambitious James Gentry had felt forced to open another store close by in competition.

"The snow's changed to rain," Sally said, still shivering. "It's a turrible night to be out. I hope he kin find his way home."

Tom snorted amusement. "Him! Git lost! He knows these woods like an Injun. He could find his way home if there waren't a right good road between here and Gentryville." Dismissing all worries, including the storm which lashed the cabin on this twentieth day of January, he turned to the wall and went peacefully and audibly to sleep.

Abe arrived in time, thoroughly soaked, still aglow from the evening of stimulating argument, hungry for the hot lunch she always had waiting for him. Ruefully he pointed at the widened expanse of bony shin below his buckskin breeches, already shrinking visibly from the morass of slush and water he had waded through. She brought him clean dry clothes and turned her back while he dried himself and changed by the fire. Sally was relieved, but her worry that stormy night had not all been for Abe. Only when he was ready to climb the ladder to the loft did she voice her even deeper concern. They spoke in whispers in order not to waken Tom and John D.

"I couldn't git to see Sairy today the way I've been doin' every day. She's not s'posed to be due for another week yet, but she ain't been feelin' too good. I wisht you'd check on her tomorrow mornin', son, before you go to work."

Abe's rugged face softened with the protective tenderness he always manifested toward his "little sister." "I will, Ma. I'll go fust thing in the mornin', early. Don't you worry. I'll make sure she's all right."

But neither promise was to be kept. Soon after daybreak Abe had gone to the smokehouse for a slab of bacon to fry for breakfast. An exclamation from Tom drew Sally to the door. Aaron, Sarah's husband, and his young brother Redmond were saying something to Abe, who, looking suddenly as if they had struck him, sank down slowly on the sill of the smokehouse, his face buried in his hands. The two Grigsbys then turned slowly toward the cabin. Heedless of the cold slush Sally ran out into the yard. "What is it? What's happened?"

"It's Sairy," blurted Aaron. "She's dead—and our baby too."

"Oh—dear God, no!" Sally felt the coldness creep up from her feet through her body. Even her lips felt stiff. But no time to think of self! Which one needed her most—Abe, crouched by the smokehouse openly weeping, the first tears she had ever seen him shed, or Tom, standing in the cabin door, face working, big calloused hands fumbling with the folds of his shirt? Tom, of course, to whom Sarah, gentle, trusting, quietly courageous like her mother, must have been a constant comforting reminder of a happier past. It was like losing Nancy all over again. Without hesitation she went to him, put her strong arms about him. "There, there, love, I know. I understand. We'll jist have to bear this together."

Aaron, stricken with grief, managed to give the sorry details. Sarah had begun labor last night, during the storm, ahead of time. He had run to his parents' house a half mile away for help. His father Reuben had yoked oxen to a big sled, driven to the cabin, wrapped Sarah in bear- and deerskins, laid her on straw in the sled box, and they had driven her as carefully as possible over the rough snowy ground to the Grigsby house. Aaron's mother had done the best she could, but Sairy had just kept getting worse.

"Doctor?" inquired Abe, the eyes which had so recently shed tears now hard and bright with suspicion. "Thar was no doctor called?"

Oh yes, a doctor had been called. Dr. Moore, who had been in Rockport, had moved to Illinois, but someone had gone for another doctor, who had arrived so drunk that they had had to put him to bed, even though Sarah was getting worse and worse. Mrs. Josiah Crawford had come and used all her midwifery skills, but to no avail. Finally, about midnight, William Barker, Mrs. Grigsby's brother, had gone west to Warrick County for Dr. Davis. The Pigeon Creek was so high that they had lost much time getting back, and then it had been too late. The child, a boy, had been stillborn, and Sarah—

Abe was not satisfied. "Why weren't we called?" he demanded. "The storm, you say? You travel through floods to the next county to git a doctor, but you can't come two miles to git her own blood kin?"

There seemed to be no answers to his questions. Abe was further disturbed, as was Tom, because, instead of laying Sarah beside Nancy on the hill, as they wished, the Grigsbys had neighbors dig a grave some fifty feet east of the Pigeon Creek meeting house, where they buried her and the stillborn son in the same coffin. It was one of the first graves in the new cemetery.

In the weeks that followed Abe continued to brood. In spite of Sally's assurances that everything possible had been done to save her, he insisted that Sarah had died because of neglect. And indeed, William Barker had said frankly, "They let her lay too long." Though Abe maintained his friendship with Nat and the other younger Grigsbys, he nursed a smoldering animosity toward the older brothers, Aaron, Reuben, Jr., Charles, Redmond.

"Abe's no fun any more," complained John D. "He don't tell yarns, and he allus looks like a thundercloud."

Yet his mood was one of melancholy rather than anger. He read just as avidly, but if he shared passages from books with the family they were usually sad and introspective, often poetry, like the one which even in happier times would always be one of his favorites.

> 'Tis the wink of an eye, 'tis the draught of a breath,
> From the blossoms of health, to the paleness of death,
> From the gilded saloon, to the bier and the shroud,
> Oh, why should the spirit of mortal be proud!

Sally was almost glad when Abe came back from his work in Gentryville with the news that James Gentry had asked him to go with his son Allen to New Orleans with a flatboat of produce. Not that she had fewer qualms over the dangers of such a trip, but anything which brought that look of zestful adventure back to his eyes was cause for thanksgiving. He would be bowman, oarsman, a job well suited to his long arms and excessive strength, with wages of eight dollars a month. They wouldn't be going right away. First they must build the flatboat for Gentry's load of meat, potatoes, kraut, hay, corn. At least, thought Sally, she need not begin to worry yet.

Abe returned home occasionally while building the flatboat at the steamboat landing and wood yard below Rockport. He was full of pleasurable excitement. Living with Daniel Grass, who had been a justice of the peace, a county judge, and state senator, he had access to a wonderful library and after supper was done he could build up the fire, get a book, stretch out on the floor, and read until midnight.

"Miz' Grass says I'm like to bake the top of my head or else wear myself out for lack o' sleep," he chuckled.

Sally regarded him with solicitous affection, noting the lively luxuriance of the unruly shock of hair, the restless vitality in every feature. "If you'd been goin' to do that," she quipped, "you'd ha' done it long ago."

The voyage was postponed longer because Allen Gentry and his new wife, who had been Katy Roby, were expecting their first child, due in December, and he wanted to wait until it had safely arrived. It came December 28, a boy, and immediately they began loading the flatboat. Abe had to drive Gentry's hogs through the woods the fourteen miles from Gentryville to the landing and slaughter them, a job he disliked intensely. He returned home briefly for his little homemade trunk, carefully packed by Sally, and with a sinking heart she saw him off, its hefty bulk balanced jauntily on his shoulders. Twelve hundred miles and more of river turbulence in winter, with risks of snow, ice, hurricanes, to say nothing of the usual hazards of shoals, snags, whirlpools, river pirates!

The winter seemed long. With every blizzard or windy blast that shook the cabin Sally pictured the frail craft being buffeted, swirling about, swamped, perhaps already lying at the bottom of the treacherous giant waterway. Tom also was following his son's progress, but more with excitement than anxiety, reliving his own adventure for the eager John D.

"He should be out o' the Ohio and into the old Mississip' by now. Oh, the sights he'll be seein', you wouldn't believe the huge steamboats, big as tall houses, towns bigger'n you kin imagine, wild turkeys on the shores so thick you kin shoot 'em right from the boat, and when you git to N'Orleans! Narrow streets, funny houses all colored, with iron railin's, a big cathedral, and people in queer clothes talkin' in all kinds of funny languages!"

John D. was entranced. "When Abe goes agin, mebbe I kin go too!"

Spring came, and one day in mid-March there was Abe, trunk on his shoulder, buckskin breeches shrunk halfway to his knees from many wettings, linsey-woolsey shirt torn and bereft of buttons, wearied but unquelled by his eighteen-mile trek across country from a steamboat, eyes still alight with adventurous excitement but deep with some new inscrutable gravity.

Mingled with her relief Sally felt a strange sense of loss. He's gone away from us, she thought, much farther than twelve hundred miles, and not only into manhood but into a new world. He'll never be the same again.

It was she who noticed the white streak creasing his tanned forehead. "Somethin' happened to you," she said anxiously. "How come you got that scar?"

"Oh, that! Jist a little trouble we run into. It's the other fellers got the real scars."

He told them the story, attempting to belittle its horrors. They had tied up to the shore to trade at a sugar plantation between Natchez and New Orleans and had lain down to sleep. Abe had heard a noise. "Who's thar?" he had shouted. Springing to his feet, he had discovered a band of black pirates trying to steal their cargo. Rushing toward them with a hand spike he had knocked one into the water. Two more, who attempted to leap on board, were also pushed off. When the others turned to flee, Abe and Allen had jumped ashore and chased them but in vain. Yes, they had got hurt some, a few scars like this one, but it had really been nothing to worry about, Abe hastened to assure them, noting the horrified look on Sally's face. And they hadn't stayed around to tempt the pirates to return. Cutting loose, they had floated down the river and tied up again, being sure one of them kept awake watching for further trouble.

"Tell about N'Orleans," begged John D. excitedly. "I reckon it was right wonderful."

Oh yes, New Orleans was a wonderful place, warm like spring even in winter, big stores, strange rich foods, houses like palaces, theaters, docks with ships from all over the world. They had been to see a play with a real fine actor named Junius Booth, one of that poet Shakespeare's about a king, *Richard the Third*. But—Abe's face darkened and, getting up, he moved restlessly, his head, Sally noted, almost touching the low ceiling—there were things not so fine too, slaves being lashed through the streets dragging loaded carts, markets where they were being sold.

"It made me hot all over," Abe muttered between clenched teeth. "I wanted to take my fists and hit somebody, but it wouldn't ha' done no good. I—I jist wisht thar was somethin' a pusson could do to stop such things."

But the river life had fascinated him. As weeks went by his restlessness became more evident. "I'd like to be a river pilot," he confessed to Tom and Sally. "It's an exciting life and profitable too. You git to meet all kinds of people, no end to the things you kin learn."

Sally sighed. Of course. He was like a pastured colt smelling the lures of the open range. Twenty years old. Had there been reluctance in his dutiful handing over to Tom all the money earned on his journey? But—a river pilot! She could almost sense an uneasy stirring at the mound up on the hill. This an end to Nancy's fond dreams for her son? Something wonderful! *Mebbe a teacher—or even a preacher!*

"I'm goin' to see Uncle Wood," Abe told her one day. "He's a big man and knows a lot of people. Mebbe he'll recommend me for a job on some steamer plyin' up and down the river, like the one Allen and I come back up on." William Wood, who lived a mile and a half north of the cabin, was one of Abe's most admired friends, so close that he had long dubbed him "Uncle."

Sally waited in trepidation. His face when he returned was noncommittal. "Wal, son, what did he say?"

"He says no," returned Abe, pushing out his lower lip in disgust. "I ain't of age. I told him all I wanted was a chance, but he wouldn't. He reckons I oughter stay and help Pa leastways till I'm twenty-one."

Sally, commiserating, breathed a sigh of relief. Almost another year of respite. Many things could happen before then. It was just as well that she did not know then how many.

To Tom's satisfaction Abe exhibited a sudden capacity for industry of the sort approved by his father, who frequently complained that when his son had farm work to do, he had to "pull the old sow to the trough." Soon after their conversation, William Wood saw Abe furiously whipsawing lumber and was told that he and Tom were planning to build a new house. It was to be of hewed logs, one story with a porch in front and would have two rooms, an east one and a west one, the building fronting south with a fine chimney at the east end. It would stand on the Gentryville road leading to Hoffman's mill. There was a fine knoll there, heavily timbered with hickory and white oak.

But Abe's activity was equally furious in other pursuits. Was it an incident that happened one rainy night on the road which drove him into a frenzy of writing? John D., returning from Gentryville after an evening at the store with Abe and David Turnham, was consumed with wonder and disgust.

"That Abe! You know what he went and did? We was comin' home and saw this man lyin' in a mud puddle. Drunk. Abe went and shook him, but he wouldn't budge. 'Sarves him right,' we said. 'None of our business.' But would Abe let him be? No. They must save him. 'All right,' says Dave, 'you kin make a fool of yourself, but I'm not.' So we come on and left him. Last we saw, Abe had the man flung over his shoulder and was carryin' him to Dennis' cabin. No knowin' when he'll be home."

Not that night. Abe appeared early in the morning, having worked over the drunkard with Dennis, rubbing him down, warming him by the fire, making sure he had suffered no ill effects. It was soon after this that he tried his hand at writing a poem for which he became quite famous in the community. It was titled "John Anderson's Lamentation."

> O sinners! poor sinners! take warning by me;
> The fruits of transgressing behold now and see; . . .
> Much intoxication my ruin has been;
> And my dear companions have barbarously slain,
> In yonder cold graveyard her body doth lie
> Whilst I am condemned, and shortly must die.

Sally was no literary critic, she could not even read, but she knew what she liked, and she preferred the article which Abe wrote on the subject, inspired by one of the papers William Wood subscribed to, one on politics, the other on temperance. So did "Uncle Wood." So impressed was he with Abe's temperance article that he sent it to Aaron Farmer, a Baptist preacher he knew, who sent it to an editor in Ohio, and it was published. Having been ardently engrossed in the election of 1828, when he had been a firm supporter of Andrew Jackson, who had championed the policies of his idol Henry Clay, Abe now tried his hand at a political paper, which he also showed to William Wood. The foremost lawyer of Spencer County, Judge John Pitcher, chanced to pass, read it, and was impressed. "It can't be beat!" he said. This also was published in a small paper.

"Look, Ma!" Abe exhibited the printed sheet and pointed to his name in triumph. "That's me. Want to hear some of what I said?" She listened obediently, humbly, while he read, declaiming as if to one of his lyceum audiences.

" 'The American government is the best form of government for an intelligent people. It ought to be kept sound and preserved forever, that general education should be fostered and carried on all over the country; that the Constitution should be held sacred, the Union perpetuated, and the laws revered, respected, and enforced.' "

Sally's eyes filled. The words, unintelligible on the printed page,

were shining clear. "It's good, son," she said. "You don't have to explain it to me so I can understand, the way you do so many things
you read. I'm right proud of you."

She was not so proud of another piece of writing he produced. At
last, in that year of 1829, there came the opportunity he coveted of
getting his revenge on the older Grigsby sons. It happened in April
not long after his return from New Orleans. Two of the Grigsby men,
Reuben, Jr., and Charles, were being married to Elizabeth Ray and
Matilda Hawkins. It was a double wedding, a splendid affair, with a
long procession of guests on horseback, a huge dinner, and afterward
the usual infare lasting far into the night. There was no riotous dancing and rowdiness, however, only innocent kissing games like "Old
Sister Phoebe," "Thus the Farmer Sows His Seed," and "Skip to My
Loo." The Grigsbys were strict Baptists. The Lincolns had not been
invited, possibly because of Abe's known displeasure over what he
considered negligence in his sister's death. The slight did nothing to
soften his antagonism.

After the infare there was of course the usual ritual of putting the
brides to bed, blowing out the candles, and escorting the grooms to
their respective destinations. However, as was rumored later, mischief had been planned. It had been arranged that the couples should
be put to bed, yes, but in the wrong beds! Soon there erupted
screams and much confusion. Doubtless the men knew the voices of
their respective brides, or vice versa. Candles were lighted and the
joke explained to everybody's satisfaction. But the rumor gave Abe
just the opportunity he needed. He wrote a satire called "The Chronicles of Reuben." Watching him at work, his lower lip stuck out ag-
gressively, Sally became suspicious, but when he began reading it to
her, she was agreeably surprised, for it sounded exactly like Holy
Scripture.

"'Now there was a man whose name was Reuben, and the same
was very great in substance; in horses and cattle and swine, and a
very great household. It came to pass when the sons of Reuben grew
up that they were desirous of taking to themselves wives, and being
too well known as to honor, in their own country, they took a journey into a far country and there procured for themselves wives.'"

It sounds like Isaac and Rebekah, thought Sally, her suspicions
allayed.

"'And it came to pass that when they were about to make the return home, that they sent a messenger before them to bear the tidings to their parents; so they inquired of the messengers when their sons and their wives would come. So, they made a great feast and called all their kinsmen and neighbors in, and made great preparations; so, when the time drew near, they sent out two men to meet the grooms and their wives with a treat to welcome them and accompany them; so, when they came near to the house of Reuben, their father, the messengers came on before them and gave a shout, and the whole multitude ran out with shouts of joy, and music playing on all kinds of instruments of music, some playing on harps, and some on viols, and some blowing on rams' horns, some casting dust and ashes toward Heaven; and amongst the rest Josiah blowing his bugle, making sound so great that it made the neighboring hills and valleys echo with the resounding acclamation; so when they had played and harped, sounded, till the grooms and brides approached the gate, the father Reuben met them and welcomed them in to his house, and the wedding dinner being now ready, they were all invited to sit down to dinner.'"

"I declar," exclaimed Sally admiringly, "it sounds jist like a psalm! I reckon David himself couldn't do better!" But as the reading progressed admiration receded into doubt, doubt into consternation.

"'And when they had made an end of feasting and rejoicing, the multitude dispersed, each to his own home; the family then took seats with their waiters to converse awhile, at which time the preparations were being made in an upper chamber for the brides to be first conveyed to their beds, by the waiters, placing one in a bed at the right hand of the stairs and the other on the left. The waiters came down and Nancy the mother inquired of the waiters which of the brides was placed on the right hand and they told her. So she gave directions to the waiters of the bridegrooms, and they took the bridegrooms and placed them in the wrong beds, and came downstairs; but the mother being fearful that there might be a mistake, inquired again of the waiters and learning the fact, took the light and sprang upstairs, and running to one of the beds exclaimed: "Reuben, you are in bed with Charlie's wife!" The young men, both being alarmed, sprang out of bed and ran with such violence against each other that they came very near knocking each other down, which

gave evidence to those below that the mistake was certain. They all
came down and had a conversation . . .'"

"Abe!" interrupted Sally in shocked amazement. "That don't
sound like you. It ain't nice. You can't let folks read sich a mean
piece o' writin'!"

But Abe could and did. He had nursed his grievance too long to
let the opportunity pass. He made several copies of his masterpiece
and distributed them in strategic places. The Grigsbys were outraged.
Though they hid the copy they got hold of, to be found when their
house was torn down many years later, there were others. The young
bride of Reuben Grigsby, Jr., insisted tearfully that there was no
truth in the story, that "Lincoln just wrote it for mischief," but the
damage had been done. Even Nat, Abe's loyal friend, said that it had
hurt the family. But Abe showed no concern or remorse . . . then.
He firmly believed that the Grigsbys had caused the death of his beloved sister.

The Grigsbys could not accept the indignity without some retaliation. It came in an argument between Abe and William Grigsby, fifth
of Reuben's seven sons, over the ownership of a little dog. Each
claimed a neighbor had given him the dog.

"I'll fight you for it!" challenged Bill Grigsby, though both knew it
was not the dog they were fighting over.

Abe looked down at the smaller youth and shook his head. "I
know you're a good fighter, Bill, but you and I both know you're no
match for me. I ain't goin' to fight you."

John D. stepped forward eagerly. "Let me do it, Abe. Let's see if I
cain't lick him!"

The argument, which had taken place near Gentryville, had drawn
spectators. Soon the fight assumed all the proportions of a fist duel,
with seconds appointed by each side, Aaron Standage and James
Taylor for John D., William Whitten and William Bolen for Bill
Grigsby. Soon it was apparent that John D. was no match for his opponent. Abe, harried by guilt, could not intervene, for there was a
code for fist fighting. No one could step inside the ring. Only when
one of the seconds violated the code did Abe move in. Bursting inside, he seized Bill and threw him off. "Now!" he faced the crowd.
"I'm the big buck of the lick. If anyone doubts it, come on and whet
your horns."

No one came. Abe's strength was too well known to provoke any challengers.

News of the fight reached Sally before its participants. Wordlessly, lips tight, she applied first aid to John D.'s swollen, battered flesh while Abe stood by, sheepish, shifting awkwardly from one big foot to the other. Only when John D. was well anointed and bandaged did she calmly but scathingly vent her disapproval.

"You'd ought to be ashamed, both of you, but you, Abe, more than John D. It's time you grew up and acted like the big hulk of man you look like. You'd oughter make peace with your neighbors."

Abe did. He began with a simple little act of neighborliness. It was the habit of the community to take their tools to Reuben Grigsby's to be sharpened on his good grindstone. One day while Betsy, the new wife of Reuben, Jr., was turning it, Abe offered to help her. They worked with increasing co-operation together. "It's all over," Nat was to comment finally with relief about the feud.

Toward the end of that summer of 1829 the milk-sick struck again. Throughout the Buck Horn Valley there was panic, especially among those who remembered 1818. Dennis was one of them. His good-natured face, round and placid, acquired new lines.

"This country ain't for me," he said to Tom. "It was all right when it was jist me, but now I got a wife and four young'uns. I been talkin' to Squire Hall, and he feels the same way."

Was it coincidence that John Hanks, who had moved to Illinois the year before, began sending alluring accounts of the fertility of the new country? "There's sod out here," he wrote, "that's never had a plow stuck in it. All it needs is the turning."

Even though the milk-sick passed this time without leaving any casualties in the family, the seeds of unrest had been planted. Dennis made a trip to visit John on his new farm in Macon County, Illinois, to assay the prospects for himself, and he returned enthusiastic. He had soon persuaded his half-brother Squire Hall to join him in plans for moving in the spring.

Sally heard the news with a conflict of emotions. See her two daughters, her grandchildren, probably her beloved Abe as soon as he turned twenty-one, move into a new world, leaving her behind? Yet here was home. The new house, finer than any she had lived in since her marriage, was nearing completion. Never to live in it? Was it coincidence again that in September she and Tom had made a trip

to Elizabethtown and sold the small lot and cabin where she had
lived, receiving $123 for it, a very good price for the property she
had bought long ago for $25?

"We'll do what you say," Tom told her as the weeks went by and
they had made no decision. "I'm willin' to go or stay. But—it'd be
mighty lonesome without 'em."

Had the issue ever been doubtful? What was life in a new cabin,
no matter how big and fine, with no young feet to track mud on its
smooth plank floors? What were lands, even though struggled for and
sweated over and finally paid for, if the fruits they yielded could not
be shared with loved ones? It was decided. On November 26, 1829,
Tom gave a bond for his eighty-acre tract to Charles Grigsby, and on
February 20, 1830, Tom and Sally signed a warranty deed to Charles,
selling the west half of the southwest quarter of Section thirty-two
in Township four south, Range five west, containing that same eighty
acres, for $125, Tom signing his name and Sally making her mark.

There were other sales. As David Turnham reported later, "I
bought the hogs and corn of Thomas Lincoln when he was leaving
for Illinois; bought about a hundred hogs and four or five hundred
bushels of corn, paid 10 cents per bushel for the corn, hogs lumped."
They would not be leaving as poor people. In cash they would take
with them about $500.

It was like cutting off all one's moorings and moving out into the
unknown. In December the Little Pigeon Church granted "Brother
Tho. Lincoln and wife a letter of Dismission." But to Sally's grief the
latter action had an unfortunate sequel. In January "Sister Nancy
Grigsby informed the church that she was not satisfied with Bro. and
Sister Lincoln," and the action was recalled until the church should
be satisfied. The previous year there had been a heated battle among
the members between the doctrine of predestination and that of the
Arminian or free-will conviction. Perhaps there was a mistaken idea
that Tom might harbor some of these latter views. (Because of Abe's
probing questions? He had written a poem about one of the church
trials which he called "The Neighborhood Broil.") But at the next
meeting Tom was able to convince the body of his creedal loyalty,
and the matter was settled. Indeed, in February, when "Sister
Grigsby laid in a charge against Sister Elizabeth Crawford for "false-
hood," Tom was one of the committee of five men to "settle the
above case," so the Lincoln name must have been completely

cleared. "Sister Grigsby" apparently was prone to insinuations of unacceptable conduct.

Winter a slow time of year? Never had a winter moved so fast! It rushed along like Little Pigeon Creek swollen by the January snows and rains. January . . . February . . . "We oughter leave," said Tom, "by the first of March. Must git a crop in thar before summer." The days raced past, each with too few hours for all the tasks of preparation—constructing wagons, getting animals to pull them, spinning, weaving, sewing, deciding what to take and what to leave, visiting neighbors, receiving neighbors. Strange! When she had married Tom, it had taken just one day to end one life and start another.

Sally had no fear of change. She had always taken life as it came, approaching the future with confidence, leaving the past without regrets. The return to E-town, the sight of the places she had lived with Daniel, even the meetings with her brothers, had aroused no feelings of nostalgia. It was like a garment she had worn long ago, outgrown, and discarded. Just so she would discard the outworn clothing of the last ten years. She would be taking with her everything that really mattered, her children, a few possessions that were especially dear, like the bureau, the cupboard Tom had made her, the Book, the spinning wheel and loom, memories.

The last Sunday came, the day before they were to leave. They attended services in the church, said their good-bys to friends, visited the grave in the new little cemetery, returned to the cabin. The three wagons were waiting, ready for an early start tomorrow, one at each of the three family cabins. For the first time in months, it seemed, Sally's hands were idle. Nothing left to do. Tom and John D. had gone to Dennis' house to check on last-minute preparations. Abe was away somewhere. Now . . . the time had come for one final tryst.

It would soon be dark, but the path was well traveled and she knew its every twist and turn. It led to the top of the wooded hill with its little cluster of what had once been fresh mounds. The one she sought was just here, midway between the two big trees. Someone had recently been here, she noted without surprise. The earth had been brushed clean and smooth, the simple marker with its initials "N. L." cleared of concealing dead leaves and grass. She stood looking down at it.

Nancy, dear—she felt rather than spoke the words—this ain't good-by, 'cause you ain't really here. But wherever you are you must know

I've tried to do my best. Mebbe I've failed sometimes. We lost Sairy. But she was a right good woman and you'd ha' been proud of her. And Abe, your little Abe, your big wonderful, funny, lovable, unpredictable Abe! I ain't done for him what you could have. I ain't smart with books and sich things like you was. But I've loved him—yes, as much as you could have, I think. He's a man now, jist turned twenty-one, and he'll be leavin' us soon. We've done all we could for him, you and me. Now we kin jist hope . . .

Startled, she became suddenly conscious of a tall figure moving out of the shadows by one of the big trees. "Oh—Abe, it's you! I'm sorry. I wouldn't ha' come if I'd knowed you was here. You'll want to be alone. I'll be goin'—"

He stood beside her. "No, Mother, don't go." She was surprised. It was the first time he had called her that, not "Ma." "You belong here, with me. As you said that first time you found me here, you loved her too."

They stood for a long time without speaking. "I hate to leave her here," he burst out suddenly, "nobody to keep the leaves off or bring any flowers or—or nothin'!"

"There'll be flowers," she said quietly. "The ones we planted will soon be comin' up and bloomin'. And the blossoms will be fallin' all about from the trees come every spring. And you ain't leavin' her, son. You're takin' her with you. All her fine mind and love o' things beautiful and never bein' quite satisfied, allus lookin' for somethin' more—they're all a part of you, son—yes, and her dreams, too, that you'd be somethin' big and wonderful, somethin' more'n jist a farmer or carpenter or rail-splitter or"—she hesitated, wondering if she dared —"or even a river pilot."

"Yes," he said. "I know."

They stood awhile longer while the shadows deepened.

"Wal, your pa'll be wonderin' whar I am. I better be goin'."

"Yes, Mother. I'll go with you."

They went down the hill together.

PART FOUR

"All that I am, or hope to be, I owe to my angel mother."

Abraham Lincoln

"Once when Lincoln referred to the fact that he owed much to his mother, I asked, 'Which mother?', to which Lincoln replied, 'Don't ask me that question, for I mean both, as it was Mother all my life, except that desolate period between the time Mother died and Father brought Mother into the home again. Both were the same mother. Hence I simply say, 'Mother.'"

Governor William Pickering

= 1 =

Unlike Nancy when leaving one home, one state, one life for another, Sally did not look back. Her shoulders under their swathings of neat calico and linsey-woolsey shawl were ramrod straight. Her bright dry eyes, framed by the crisp black curls and calico sunbonnet, looked straight ahead. But Abe, beside her on the seat of the wagon, pulled up on the reins and peered around its canopy for a last lingering look at cabin, woods, fields, the shell of youthful memories he was leaving behind. For he was his mother's son, the hard realities of life always glimpsed through a softening glow of sentiment, moments of most satisfying fulfillment always clouded with a hint of melancholy. Was he perhaps even then experiencing the emotions which many years later, on his first return to the scene, would find expression in an attempt at poetry?

> My childhood home I see again,
>   And gladden with the view;
> And still as mem'ries crowd my brain,
>   There's sadness in it too—
>
> O memory! thou mid-way world
>   'Twixt Earth and Paradise;
> Where things decayed, and loved ones lost
>   In dreamy shadows rise—
>
> And freed from all that's gross or vile,
>   Seem hallowed, pure, and bright,
> Like scenes in some enchanted isle,
>   All bathed in liquid light— . . .

> Now twenty years had passed away
> Since here I bid farewell
> To woods and fields, and scenes of play
> And schoolmates loved so well— . . .
>
> The very spot where grew the bread
> That formed my bones, I see.
> How strange, old field, on thee to tread,
> And feel I'm part of thee!

"Come on, boy!" cried Tom, riding up beside the motionless wagon. "What you waitin' for?"

"Nothin', Pa." Abe snapped the reins. "We're comin'."

Half the neighborhood had gathered to see them off—Grigsbys, Romines, Brooners, Turnhams, Gentrys, and many others. Some of the boys insisted on accompanying them for several miles on their journey. It was an impressive cavalcade. The three covered wagons, each of the first two drawn by two pairs of oxen, the third, Tom's, by two spans of horses, were enough to arouse envy in young spirits tired of the grueling struggle with inferior soil and eager for adventure. Abe was especially proud of Tom's wagon, which he had helped build, fashioning the solid wheels out of boles of gum trees, fastening on the iron rims, rounding off the hickory pegs, putting cleats under the floor to hold it firm.

Dennis, who had gone to spy out the "Promised Land," bringing back glowing reports of its "flowing with milk and honey," was in his element.

"If you could jist see it, you'd all be comin' with us. Prairies far as you kin see, rich, never been teched by a plow, windin' rivers and cricks, groves o' oaks, maples, elms, bigger'n you've ever seen. John Hanks'll have a quarter section all ready for us, logs cut for a cabin. We'll have a big crop by fall, not like the skimpin' ones we all got last year. You know what 'Illinois' means? It's 'the land with plenty to eat'!"

There were thirteen in the party of pioneers, ranging in age from Tom, fifty-two, to John Johnston Hall, eleven months; three families: the Lincolns, Tom, Sally, Abe, and John D. Johnston; the Hankses, Dennis, Betsy, and their four children; the Halls, Squire, Matilda, and their small son.

Of course there was a stop in Gentryville, where more neighbors

assembled to bid the travelers God-speed. Abe had business at
Jones's store, where he had worked so long and spent so many provocative evenings.

"I've saved a little money," he told Sally. "I thought mebbe I
could buy some things and sell 'em on the way. You know what
women like, Ma. Please—come with me and choose."

Sally agreed. Together, and with the help of William Jones, they
picked out many small items which she was sure would appeal to
women in cabins along the way—needles, pins, thread, buttons, some
kitchenware, a few bolts of cloth. To her surprise Abe had saved
thirty dollars out of his earnings. So—already he was asserting the independence of a young man come of age less than a month ago! He
was no longer turning over every cent of his earnings to his father,
and right it was that he should not. At her urging he also included in
his stock one large item, a set of knives and forks. She could see the
eyes of some beauty-starved pioneer wife lighting at sight of them.

"The friends I left that parting day—"

Abe's poem years later would revive the emotions felt now when
his companions of the last fourteen years, especially Nat Grigsby and
Joe Gentry, turned back after accompanying the party for a "sabbath
day's journey." The gala excitement of departure was over. The caravan settled down now to slow grueling travel, which was to become
increasingly difficult and monotonous during the hours, days, weeks
that followed. The ground, frozen during the night and early morning, began to thaw. The solid wooden wheels sank in mud to the
hubs. Both oxen and horses strained as the wagons groaned for a
foothold. Often the men had to put their shoulders to the wagons to
force them through the mire. It was possible to make barely two
miles an hour. Streams, even Pigeon Creek, were so swollen that in
fording them there was danger of being swept away. Since the wheels
of the wagon were low, Sally was obliged to leave it when they
crossed Pigeon Creek and was taken across on one of the horses.
They stopped to camp that night on the farm of a fellow Baptist
whom Tom knew, making a fire to cook their supper, sleeping in the
wagons.

They journeyed north and westward, often leaving the mired road
for higher ridges with no marked trails, leading directly through the
forests, necessitating the cutting of trees. Travel was easier early in

the morning, but as the day advanced the way would become miry, and the loads would jolt and roll, horses floundering, oxen straining and unable to move even with the encouragement of goads and sharp yells. Sometimes it was necessary to unharness and use all eight pairs of oxen to draw a single wagon through a deep slough. Weather added to the discomfort. In addition to mud there were snow, sleet, rain, and chilling winds. Each morning there was a thin coating of ice on the streams, and the oxen would break through each time they came to a ford. Yet all the time they were going north so there was less likelihood of a warm spell which might make the ground too muddy for even difficult travel.

Never had Sally's endowments of good nature and calm competence been more sorely needed. She directed camping arrangements and the cooking of meals, sometimes in the rain over sluggish fires. She nursed sniffling and squalling children, gave common-sense advice when the men were uncertain about a stream-crossing, held the squirming year-old John Johnston Hall during jouncing miles so Matilda could get rest, and, as she had done on a similar trek ten years before, ended the worst days with bright predictions of better to come.

"I reckon it'll be a fine day tomorrow."

But it was Abe who kept the spirits of the travelers from being mired along with the wheels. He joked, told stories, carried the children on his shoulders, sang songs atrociously off-key, once cheerfully waded an icy stream to prevent what the children would have regarded as near tragedy.

He had brought along his little pet dog, Honey. There had usually been a "Honey" since the first one had followed him and Austin Gollaher on Kentucky jaunts. They came to a long corduroy bridge laid over a wide swamp. Water with a thin sheet of ice covered the logs. Wooden posts marked the path of the bridge. The first two wagons had crossed successfully. Abe was driving the wagon pulled by oxen. Though he coaxed and threatened, the beasts would not venture on the ice. Finally he was obliged to use force, swinging his long lash across their backs. Gingerly they moved across. All had reached the other side when they heard a despairing howl. There on the opposite side was Honey. Soon the children were howling in sympathy. Abe pulled off his shoes, rolled up his breeches, and, disregarding the women's protests, waded into the icy water, crossed the bridge, took the frightened animal in his arms, and waded back again.

"You'll catch your death!" worried Sally, but Abe only grinned. The delight of the children and the dog's frantic leaps of joy had repaid him for all risk and discomfort.

At every lone cabin or little settlement he would stop to display his wares and usually returned exultant, for he was making money.

At the end of the first week the caravan pulled into Vincennes on the Wabash River, the last town before crossing into Illinois. They spent Saturday and Sunday there, all enjoying the welcome respite in their own way. Tom found a blacksmith to reset the iron tires on his wagon. The women used the facilities of an inn to wash, rest, scrub the children and their clothes. Dennis, Squire, and John D. roamed the wide streets of this biggest and most progressive metropolis of Indiana. Abe to his delight discovered the office where his beloved *Western Sun* was printed, made the acquaintance of its editor, Elihu Stout, and watched him setting type. He emerged with a new proud possession, a copy of a newspaper some three weeks old.

Though Monday dawned cold and blustery Tom had the wagons on the road again early, moving toward the ferry. With the river in flood as well as icy, crossing was rough and treacherous, but at last the wagons, all three of them, were safely on the other side. Now began the longest and most monotonous trek of the journey, one hundred and twenty miles and more north along the Wabash, then northwestward over the virgin prairie. But Tom, riding along beside the wagons, was exuberant. In spite of the long sojourn ahead in the wilderness, he had already sighted the Promised Land.

"Thar! We're here, folks, in the land o' plenty. Illinois—'land whar nobody goes hungry' or, as some folks calls it, 'land o' full-grown men.' " Stopping beside his own wagon, where Sally was driving the two spans of horses while Abe sat beside her hunched over his newspaper, he exclaimed impatiently, "By dear! Take your nose out o' thet thar paper, boy, and watch for somethin' wuth seein', land what's never been teched by a plow, fit to grow corn higher'n a man kin reach!"

"Yes, Pa, I see it." But Abe did not lift his face and Tom, disgusted, rode on to Dennis' wagon in search of more sympathetic eyes and ears.

"Listen to this, Ma!" Abe could have been back at the old farm for all the attention he paid the new landscape. "Thet printer couldn't have give me a more wonderful paper. It tells all about thet big fight they been havin' in the Senate, you know, in Washington. Thar's a man named Hayne what's been sayin' those slave states down south have a right to decide things for theirselves, not the Union government, things like the tariff, mebbe even git out of the Union if they cain't git what they want. They say it's the states what are the supreme authority, not the Union government. Thar's another feller, Dan'l Webster, that's jist made a speech. Listen to what he said, jist last January, in a debate they had. 'It is, sir, the people's government, made for the people, made by the people, and answerable to the people,' and hear this, Ma." Abe's voice rose to such heights of resonance that Dennis, driving the wagon ahead, peered around the canopy in alarm. "'Liberty and Union,' says this man Webster, 'now and forever, one and inseparable!' I reckon that's the most pow'ful speech what was ever made."

Sally scarcely heard the words, and if she had they would have had little meaning. Washington was far away. It required all her energy at the moment to keep the jolting wagon in the rough wheel tracks. She was glad when Abe finally put aside his paper and resumed his stronger, steadier hold on the reins. Now she could look about on this new world of her future. Promised Land! Nothing but another wilderness like the one they had already passed through. More days of wallowing through mud or turning aside to break a track through forests, fording swollen streams, camping at night in wild land or perhaps outside a tiny settlement. One of them she and the older children would always remember, for it was called Palestine, at least a suggestion of some distant Canaan! In the settlement they found a large crowd assembled about the land office. "Shows you we ain't the only pioneers lookin' for good land," exulted Tom. "Good thing we're goin' on further west!"

More days, nights, and other settlements, at last one called Darwin, where they left the river trail and struck off northwestward. So this was prairie, brown withered grass as far as one could see, bleak, dismal. Tom's boyish exuberance subsided into a dogged but persistent optimism. It took all of Sally's pretended cheerfulness and Abe's infectious humor to keep spirits from foundering in as deep sloughs as the wagons. That they were able to do so Dennis would testify nearly sixty years later when asked to detail his memories of the long trek.

"It tuk us two weeks to git thar, raftin' across the Wabash, cuttin' our way through the woods, fordin' rivers, pryin' wagons out o' sloughs with fence rails, an' makin' camp. Abe cracked a joke ev'ry time he cracked a whip, an' he found a way out o' ev'ry tight place while the rest of us was standin' round scratchin' our fool heads. I reckon Abe and Aunty Sairy run that movin', an' a good thing they did, or it'd been run into a swamp and sucked under."

But there was no need for a pretense of cheerfulness once they entered what was later that year to become Coles County and crossed the Embarrass River at Parker's Ford, near which they camped the night of March 10. They were only a few miles now from the farm where Sally's sister Hannah and her husband Ichabod Radley had moved from Elizabethtown in 1828, and Tom had promised her that they would stop there. They did, arriving that very day of March 11.

It was a joyful reunion, for the two sisters had not seen each other since Sally's wedding day. "But we ain't stayin' long," Tom insisted, "jist overnight. Time's gittin' short. We got to git our cabin built and a crop in."

"If you'd got here earlier," Hannah told them after serving the thirteen travelers a bountiful supper in her one-room cabin, "some of you could have gone over to my daughter Hannah Sawyer's jist two miles north and one mile over west. She's got a four-room house and could put you up more comfortable. Her husband John, you know, was the first settler here in Paradise settlement, come here afore we did, in October of '26. But I reckon you've traveled far enough today and would all rather jist set awhile and visit and then bunk any place, even if it's on the floor. You're all welcome to stay."

They all did. The prospect of goading tired oxen even a few miles farther in the chill March darkness appealed to none of them. Ichabod Radley, with his two sons John and Isaac, went to the Sawyers', leaving the loft for the men of the party. Sally shared the one bed with Hannah, and to the others, after some hundred and fifty miles of jouncing roads and ten nights in a rough wagon, straw-filled mats and blankets on a floor near a warm fire seemed unbelievable luxury.

"I do wisht you wouldn't go on," said Hannah wistfully the next morning. "Thar's good land right here in Paradise."

Paradise! Another word for heaven, better even than the Promised

Land, especially with loved ones nearby! Sally looked hopefully at Tom, but he shook his head. No, John Hanks already had good land picked out for them. It was best they should move on, and right now before the day got gone any further.

They stopped briefly at the Sawyers', where Hannah's sons, John and Isaac, declared they would accompany them on horseback as guides on the rest of their journey. In spite of Dennis' somewhat truculent assurance that, having been there before, he was a perfectly capable guide, they insisted. And when they entered the level, almost trackless "grand prairie" to the north and west, even Dennis was glad of more experienced guidance.

Three days more at about fifteen miles a day, and they were in the bustling town of Decatur, county seat of Macon County, founded just a year before by one of its first settlers, Stephen Decatur. In spite of Tom's impatience that they move on, Abe insisted on getting down from the wagon to get a better view of the new courthouse, a two-story building of hewn logs still almost as unweathered as when shaped by the broadax just a few months before, in 1829. He gazed at it fascinated, oblivious of Tom's nervous jitterings and reminders that "time's a-movin' and we've still got a heap of a way to go." While he stood staring, two men, distinguished in tall hats and black swallowtails, emerged from the door.

"Lawyers!" Sally heard Abe mutter.

As if in the presence of royalty he snatched off his coonskin cap and stood holding it, humility and reverence but also a kind of helpless appeal in the gesture. They passed the raw young giant in shrunken buckskins and homespun with only hasty, contemptuous glances in his direction. As Abe hoisted himself back into the wagon, Sally was startled by the look of grim frustration in his eyes. Her heart ached for him.

If they could only have looked ahead a quarter of a century, seen two other men, also distinguished in tall hats and black swallowtails, emerge from the same door! One of the two, very tall and angular, would walk out a few feet in front of the building, shift his position two or three times, and say to his companion, "Here is the exact spot where I stood by our wagon when we moved from Indiana twenty-six years ago; this isn't six feet from the exact spot!"

And if they could have looked still further ahead they would have

seen the same crude building, carefully preserved, bearing a bronze
tablet with the words:

IN THIS MACON COUNTY'S
FIRST COURT HOUSE
BUILT IN 1829
ABRAHAM LINCOLN
PRACTISED LAW WHILE ON
THE EIGHTH JUDICIAL DISTRICT

THIS TABLET PLACED BY THE LINCOLN
MEMORIAL COMMITTEE OF THE
ASSOCIATION OF COMMERCE, DECATUR

Sally reached out and patted one of the bony knees. "You know,
son," she said, "it takes more'n high hats and fine clothes to make
men what reely count for somethin'. And who knows? You may be
doin' somethin' jist as important and helpful to folks as them two
someday."

He looked down at her, smiled, clucked at his team, and they followed the two ox-drawn wagons out of the town and westward.

$= 2 =$

The caravan proceeded some seven miles west and two miles south
of Decatur to John Hanks's cabin, arriving on March 14, just two
weeks after leaving Pigeon Creek. John and his wife Susan welcomed
them heartily, absorbing the extra thirteen people—fifteen until the
two young Radleys left for home—into their household with good-natured ease. The men soon left to examine the site which John had
picked for Tom. It was about six miles away down the Sangamon
River, a fine location on a bluff overlooking the river at the juncture
of timber and prairie lands, with plenty of water nearby. As promised, John had cut logs for the cabin, and they were well seasoned,

ready for the broadax, handsaw, and drawknife. Tom, Dennis, Abe, and Squire started work immediately. While one felled trees, another hewed timbers for the cabin, and the other two cleared the ground of its accumulated growth of underbrush. After building the cabin they erected a stable and small smokehouse. With many hands working, completion took only a few days.

When Sally saw her new home she could scarcely believe her eyes. It was by far the best cabin she had ever lived in, as good as or better than the unfinished one left behind in Indiana. The logs were carefully hewn, put together with real nails instead of wooden pegs. The door and floor were of puncheon. The gable ends had been boarded with planks rived out of oak timber. There was a good roomy loft and, of course, a huge fireplace. Even after all her furniture plus the thirteen members of the three families had moved in it did not seem overcrowded.

"Now," said Tom hopefully, "if we kin jist git a crop in afore summer . . ."

They did. Ten acres of the unbroken fertile land were soon plowed and corn planted. Abe and John Hanks started splitting rails to fence it in.

"Ef I had a dollar for every fence rail I've split," Abe joked once between powerful blows with his maul, "I'd be rich enough to buy up this whole state. But these rails are sure special, made out o' the best black walnut you could find!"

They were indeed special, at least two of them destined to shape the future not only of the young rail-splitter but of a nation, for, as one historian was to write, they would "electrify a state convention and kindle throughout the country a contagious and passionate enthusiasm which would reach to endless generations."

Though she had dreaded the prospect, now that he was of age and had got the family settled, Sally fully expected Abe to leave home in pursuit of that dream of which he had caught restless glimpses. Was she relieved or troubled when he showed no inclination to do so? He went away, yes, but only to hire himself out to their new neighbors for work such as he had done in Indiana—rail-splitting, plowing, land clearing, wood chopping, carpentering. He seemed contented enough. If he returned at night he would play with the children, tell them stories, spin yarns with Tom and Dennis, then climb to the loft without stretching out by the fire to read. But—she did not want him to be contented. Shrewdly she sensed that without the driving restlessness, the constant "reachin' too fur" which Tom distrusted, the dream would soon fade and something, she did not know what, but something of great importance would be irreparably lost. True, he exhibited a new insistent independence. Instead of turning over all his earnings to his father, he paid his board, and, to Sally's consternation, he no longer permitted her to supply his clothing needs.

"You've got enough to do," he said when his shrunken buckskin breeches revealed not only bony shanks but bare knobby knees, "with a houseful of eight grownups and five young'uns to manage 'thout sewin' for a big lout like me. I guess I kin git my own britches." And he did, bargaining with a neighbor, Nancy Miller, to split 400 rails for every yard of brown jeans, dyed with white walnut, which she would supply. In her wood lot, about three miles from the home cabin, he split 1,400 rails in all, and she made him the trousers.

He soon acquired a reputation for strength in the neighborhood. "Strong as an ox," one employer approved, but other comments of his associates were not so complimentary. "Abe was the roughest-looking fellow I ever saw," George Close, a fellow worker, was heard to remark, "he was so tall, awkward, and wrinkled."

But Close became more favorably impressed with another of Abe's unusual features. He was present with John Hanks and Abe when the latter made the first political speech of his life. It was an election year. A man by the name of Ewing, later to become acting Governor of Illinois and a United States senator, and John F. Posey were running for the House of Representatives. They came to Decatur looking for votes. At a meeting in the square where there were several speakers Abe and his two companions were in the crowd of listeners. John Posey made a speech which all three boys considered extremely bad.

"Abe," said John Hanks, who had heard his cousin hold forth from wagon wheel and tree stump in Indiana, "you could make a right better speech than that feller. Why don't you git up thar and try it?"

"Yeah," agreed George Close, who had already sampled Abe's talents for mimicry and satire, "git up thar and show him what he looks and sounds like. Abuse him right plenty. I dare you to."

Abe demurred. "Aw, I couldn't. I don't know these folks. They'd jist laugh at me!"

But John had already seized one of the speakers' boxes, pushed Abe forward, and urged him to mount it. The sight of the towering figure in rough country garb, such a contrast to his dapper predecessor, attracted the attention of the crowd and reduced it to silence. Always ready for amusement it prepared to be entertained. Someone guffawed. "Hush up, you," yelled another. "Let the bumpkin speak."

"Friends, neighbors, fellow citizens . . ." Obviously nervous, Abe began, his voice rather high and squeaky but becoming louder and more confident as he proceeded. "What we jist heard reminds me of a story. Have you heard about the steamboat captain who ran short o' fuel on the river and steered to a woodpile along shore? 'Is that your wood?' he asked the man standin' by it. 'Sure is,' said the man. 'Want to sell it?' 'Sure do.' 'Will you accept wildcat currency?' 'Sure will.' 'How will you take it?' asked the captain. 'Cord for cord,' says the man."

After the laughter had subsided Abe became suddenly serious. "Wal, folks, we want to be keerful that what we git from the folks we elect ain't wildcat currency. It takes a heap of a lot of it to be wuth much. Now I've got some ideas what might be wuth a lot to all of us livin' here on the Sangamon."

"You should ha' heard him," John Hanks told the family delightedly when he and Abe returned to the cabin that night. "They laughed at first, but before he got through they waren't laughin'. He told 'em all about the Sangamon River, how it could be made navigable and bring commerce clear up here from the Illinois and Mississippi. They was all ears, even Posey. He came up to Abe afterwards and talked with him. Abe, tell 'em what he said."

"Oh, not much," Abe modestly disclaimed. "He jist asked me whar I'd larned so much, and I told him by readin'. And he told me to keep on, to persevere."

That night, to Sally's relief and satisfaction, he built up the fire after the others had gone to bed, stretched out in front of it, and read.

Tom was delighted with the reputation his son was acquiring in the area, not, however, for his talents in speechmaking. "Folks say he's the best rail-splitter in all Macon County," Tom boasted to Sally. "Since Major Warnick hired him thar's no end to the jobs he kin git."

Major Warnick, the county sheriff, owned a big three-gabled house across the Sangamon River, its log construction dating before the organization of Macon County. His hiring of Abe to split a thousand rails for fencing was indeed a recognition of his superior skill. Abe shared the assignment with John D., who like himself was now capable of a man's job. Abe did not return home as often as formerly while working for Major Warnick, and when he did come at night it was often late. Gleefully John D. explained the reason. Abe, he was sure, had fallen in love with Polly Warnick, oldest of the major's six daughters. After work he was hanging around with the family in the Warnick living room discussing politics and books with the major but really "takin' ev'ry chance he kin git to moon over pretty Polly and mebbe help her pass the honey cakes."

At last, thought Sally. And she began asking eager questions of John D. Oh yes, he answered, Polly was really pretty. And she seemed to know a right lot of things, as if she had read books. And, yes, of course the Warnicks were a very respectable family, a big farm, fine house, money, well "eddicated" and all.

"But if you ask me," John D. concluded, "Abe ain't got a chanct. Polly's got half the young hopefuls in the county hangin' round. Besides, I reckon her pa'd never go for her marryin' a poor no-count. He likes Abe for rail-splittin', even for arguin' with, but not for a son-in-law."

He was right. Before the summer was over Polly Warnick was married to Joseph Stevens, whose property, social position, and substantial financial prospects made him a desirable suitor. When Abe next appeared Sally regarded him anxiously for signs of grief over thwarted hopes. "I'm sorry, son," she commiserated. "I know you must feel bad losin' her."

He grinned, wryly. "Wal, Ma, you cain't reely blame her. She knew what she was doin'. Thar waren't much choice between what she got and a poor hulk like me."

"Don't talk that way about yourself," chided Sally. "I reckon someday she'll find out what she missed."

She was more right than she knew. Not only Polly Warnick but several other young women, including Miss Jemima Hill and a Miss Green, would be proud to confess that they had received romantic attention from the rejected suitor. Indeed, as one researcher years later would remark, "If all the different visitors who boasted that

Abe Lincoln courted their grandmothers stated the truth, he must have been the busiest of philanderers."

Illini, the Indians had called this country of theirs, "land of full-grown men," tall men like this rawboned young immigrant whose six-foot-four bulk was slowly shaping its contours with ax and maul and hammer; of tall prairie grass growing six or eight feet high in soil so tough that no plow could cut it; of tall trees which must be felled to make way for the white man's conquest; of tall corn.

"Never seen sich a crop!" exulted Tom as his first planting matured. "Look at them stalks, higher'n even Abe kin reach! And them ears, long as your forearm and so full they're 'most bustin' open!"

It did seem like a Promised Land. There were not only rich soils, fine logs for the cutting, but plenty of game, wild hogs, deer, turkeys, and a myriad of bees for the making of honey. And it was a paradise as yet almost untouched. There were few settlers. Even Decatur, the only town, had only one building of any size beside the courthouse, and that was Uncle Jimmy Renshaw's general store. Though Tom occupied his land only under squatter's claim, prospects for security were rosy. Dennis and Squire had also taken up claims and were building themselves small cabins.

But like many Edens, in this there were lurking serpents. That fall the first one reared its head. A severe epidemic swept through the area. Members of all three families were afflicted with frightful fevers, chills, and ague, the bane of the prairie country in those years, the result of undrained lowlands, fogs sometimes so thick it was like plowing through a dense obstacle merely to reach the outbuildings. Tom, now over fifty, proved especially vulnerable. James Renshaw's store in Decatur entered charges in his name for large quantities of "barks," the prevailing remedy for ague, Peruvian bark to be mixed with whiskey. Though there were no deaths in the three families, all were left perilously weak and an easy prey to lesser ailments.

"So we left milk-sick which mightn't ever have come agin for *this!*" complained Dennis bitterly. "If you ask me, we jist jumped out o' the fryin' pan into the fire!"

Then came winter. Unfortunately it was the worst one in the known history of Illinois, called forever after the "winter of the deep snow." The first blizzard began four days after Christmas, burying the area under two and a half feet. The storm came with such suddenness that people on the roads had difficulty reaching home. Some made their way only by hanging to the tails of their steers. Others were found weeks later in drifts, their flesh gnawed by wolves. Then came cold rain, freezing as it fell, making a thick crust of ice, to be covered by another deep fall of snow.

For two months the country lay under about four feet of hard-packed snow and ice. It was like being buried in a white tomb. It was difficult to get out even to have corn ground at the mill, and what travel was possible was endangered by wolves, able to travel far better than men and heavier beasts on the crust. Cattle and horses perished. The crop of winter wheat was killed. Many families, provisions exhausted, were half starving. Temperatures fell to twelve below zero, remaining there for weeks. Though game was unbelievably plentiful, the starved deer whose slender hoofs pierced the crust being so vulnerable that they could be killed in herds, hunters were equally vulnerable, and few ventured out.

Abe and John D., with their youthful strength, helped the families survive, especially Abe, who made frequent trips carrying provisions from cabin to cabin, some of them twenty or thirty miles apart. But when the snow began to melt there was a long period when Abe was unable to help. While on an errand for Warnick, piloting his canoe across the ice-clogged river, his craft had overturned and before he could reach the Warnicks' house his feet had frozen. For four weeks Mrs. Warnick had tenderly nursed him while Abe, utilizing the leisure time, had thoroughly devoured and digested his employer's copy of the Illinois *Statutes*.

On hearing of the accident Sally was far more concerned over the danger to Abe's feet than over the lack of his assistance. She begrudged that Warnick woman the privilege of nursing him, even while blessing her for it. Heaven knew she had had plenty of nursing to do herself in the last months! And of course it was time she came to accept the fact that this son who had become as dear to her as her own would soon be completely independent of her care. Still, she dreaded the inevitable day of separation. It came sooner than she had expected but accompanied by another upheaval of such change that it became only one more element in the shock of adjustment.

The snows finally melted, flooding the prairies, choking the river below the cabin to roaring overflow, draining away some of the good soil carefully cleared for next season's plowing. They seemed also to have drained away much of Tom's zest and ambition.

"This country ain't for us," he announced with finality. "If this here's the Promised Land, then give me the wilderness. We're goin' back whar we come from, to old Indianny."

Sally was dismayed. True, the new land had been harsh and unkind, and they had all suffered intensely, but she was not one to retreat. "They say it's never been like this before," she comforted. "Snow don't usually come higher'n a man's knees, not to his waist, and it don't last so long. Next winter'll be better."

But Tom was determined and to her disappointment Dennis agreed. He did not, however, want to return to Indiana. That land around Paradise had looked good to him, and he would like being near the Radleys and Sawyers, who had urged them to settle in the neighborhood. Tom finally agreed, though reluctantly. They would try Coles County, but if he didn't like it there, he would keep on going back where they had come from.

Abe returned from Warnicks', his oversized feet, Sally noted with relief, almost restored to normal. But he would not be going with them on their next journey. Denton Offutt, a trader on the Sangamon, had offered him and John Hanks fifty cents a day apiece to take a boatload of produce to New Orleans.

John D.'s face lighted. "Oh, Abe," he blurted eagerly, "kin I go too?"

"I reckon so," agreed Abe, "that is, if Ma and Pa say so. We'll need another hand on the flatboat, and I reckon Offutt'd pay you the fifty cents too."

John D. turned pleadingly to Tom and Sally. He was still under age. "You said mebbe I could go next time Abe went. Kin I, Ma, Pa? Kin you git along without me?"

"Sure," agreed Tom quickly. "It's time you started earnin' good pay."

"Ma?"

Sally drew a deep breath. No! Not yet! Not her baby! Bad enough for Abe to be subjected again to all the perils and temptations. Her— baby? For a third time she looked hard at one of her offspring, surprised that she had to look up so far to see his face. Of course. John D. was twenty, a man. And he was taller than Tom, broader of shoulder.

"I'll take good keer of him, Ma," interposed Abe, "bring him home safe and sound." He grinned. "Yes, and I'll see that we're both unsoiled by all the sin and sich in N'Orleans."

She saw them leave one day in March, to travel in a canoe down the Sangamon, still swollen by the spring freshets, to the meeting place with Denton Offutt a few miles from Springfield. She and Tom stood on the high bluff above the river and watched them launch the canoe, paddle out into the swirling eddies, steady it into even motion. The frail craft on the rushing, tortuous stream seemed somehow symbolic of the uncertainty not only of the adventure on which they were embarking but of life itself. Where was it taking them, these two sons she loved so deeply, one the child of her body, the other in some strange way the offspring of all her inmost yearnings? Would she ever see them again?

As if to answer her question Tom took her hand and drew her away. "Come, love. Don't watch 'em out of sight. Don't never do that less'n you want never to see 'em agin. They say it's bad luck."

Gratefully Sally clung to his strong gnarled hand as they went back to their lonely cabin.

$$= 3 =$$

Not until May, when the snow had all melted and the ground had dried sufficiently for travel, was it possible to leave on the return journey. Once more the wagons were loaded, the members of the three families assembled (eleven now instead of thirteen, with Abe and John D. away), and the caravan set off on its long trek. Back to Indiana? Yes, said Tom, who had reconsidered his decision to stay in Illinois. He had had enough of this "Promised Land." The fever and ague, the terrible winter, had sapped not only energy but hope and ambition. He wanted the comfort of a familiar land and clime, even if less productive. No, said Dennis and Squire, remembering the tall corn which had burst from the virgin soil. As they followed the trail through the great prairie, already the tough spring grass was shoulder high, a rippling blue-green sea with its acres and acres of blooming iris.

"Beautiful," thought Sally when she took a moment to lift her eyes from the rough narrow trail over which the two spans of horses dragged the jolting wagon.

It took three days as before, traveling about fifteen miles a day, allowing time for meals, setting up and taking down camp, watering and feeding the stock, to reach the Sawyers' farm in Coles County. Tom and Sally went on another two miles to the Radleys', where they received a warm welcome, lavish hospitality, and shrewd advice.

"Nonsense!" scoffed Hannah. "Back to Indianny when thar's good land right here jist waitin' to be taken?"

"No money to pay either, at least not at first," urged Ichabod Radley. "It's all government land waitin' to be settled. I'm still occupyin' this land here by squatters' rights. In fact, there've been no land entries here in the Paradise area until March of this year. We can find you a good piece to start on, and you can enter it later."

Tom was not hard to persuade. In his weakened condition he was already fatigued by the forty-five-mile journey, and the prospect of another hundred and fifty miles of camping, river crossings, creek fordings, to say nothing of the uncertainty of a location on arrival, loomed like an insuperable mountain. When John Sawyer proved equally persuasive with Dennis and Squire, the decision was made.

With Ichabod's help Tom settled on a forty-acre tract of public land in what was known as the Buck Grove neighborhood near Wabash Point about two miles northeast of the Radleys, so named because, as John Johnston Hall was to explain later, "men found two big bucks what had been fightin' with their horns locked together and they had died that way." While a cabin was being built there Sally stayed with Hannah, the other two families remaining at the Sawyers' larger house. Tom had plenty of help building the cabin. In addition to Dennis and Squire, he was assisted by John and Charles Sawyer and a neighbor, Elisha Linder, who, like Charles, had settled in this Wabash Point area in 1827, a year later than John Sawyer.

Though hastily built, it was a comfortable cabin, solid on its four great cornerstones, its round logs a good four inches in diameter. It had not one but two rooms, its door facing north. Sally took possession of it with her usual cheerful competence, undisturbed by the necessity of sharing it, at least for the present, with five other adults and five children. In fact, her greatest regret was the absence of the other two members of family who, for all she knew, might be roaming the streets of a sinful city or lying in the depths of the terrifying Father of Waters.

When Abe and John D. finally appeared one day in June her satisfaction was complete. To her the story of their adventurous three months was unimportant. They were safe. Her household was once more intact. While the rest of the family clustered about the newcomers, listening, demanding, absorbing every exciting detail, she bustled about providing more substantial welcome—for Abe his favorite fresh corn bread with sausage, for John D. a vegetable pie filled with turnips, beans, and potatoes. It was John D., flushed with the intoxication of his first real adventure, who burst into an excited account of their journey, and Abe, amused and indulgent, yielded to him.

"You tell 'em, John D.," he urged, mouth stuffed with corn bread and sausage. "But don't do no embroiderin' now, don't make us out heroes. Tell it jist like it was."

John D. began, elation only slightly quelled. They had gone down the Sangamon in their canoe, the three of them, a wild journey, with whirlpools sucking them in and waves 'most high as the bluffs so they like to have drowned—here a warning glance from Abe—well, they'd really had an easy trip, landing at a place called Judy's Ferry. Leaving their canoe in charge of a Mr. Mann, they had walked to Springfield, about five miles, and found this man Offutt. He'd been at a tavern having a gay old time. From there they'd gone to Spring Creek with Offutt, five miles north, where the flatboat was to be. No boat. So Abe had gone back to Judy's Ferry, got the canoe, and floated it down to the mouth of Spring Creek, where they'd cut timbers to make a boat. Then they'd rafted the logs down to Sangamontown, where they'd made a shanty which they'd lived in while building the boat. It had taken four weeks, a heap of hard work—here a sheepish sidelong glance at Abe—that is, for Abe and John Hanks. Abe had been full of jokes and fun, kept them all amused, made a hit with all the other workers. They'd all sit on a log at noon and he'd tell yarns. They called it "Abe's log." When he'd reach the point of a good story, they'd whoop and roll off.

They'd built a big boat eighty feet long, eighteen wide. They'd loaded it with barrel pork, corn, live hogs, and started off. Offutt had gone with them. Everything had gone well until they got to a place called New Salem, where a man named Rutledge had a mill dam. There the boat had got stuck on the dam, for a night and part of a day.

"You should ha' seen Abe!" John D. was now sure of himself. "Thar was the whole town come to look, wond'rin how we was goin' to git off. Wal, it was Abe found us a way. He borrowed us another boat, unloaded some of our stuff on it, rolled the barrels forrard, then bored a hole in the end of our boat what was over the dam, tilted it up so the water run out, and over she went! Folks 'most shook the mill to pieces with their cheerin'—that is, they made a right lot o' noise. Abe was a reel hero."

"Aw, it was nothin'," interposed Abe. "Anybody could ha' done it. Jist took a little common sense."

The story continued. On down the river, purchase of more hogs, tried to drive them, couldn't, ran them back in their pen, caught them. Abe held the head of the hogs, John Hanks their tails, while Offutt sewed up their eyes. Carried them about a mile to the river. Abe cut their eyes open. Lots of excitement and fun!

Sally winced. How Abe must have hated such a cruel act, however necessary! She looked from his face, tight-lipped and frowning, to John D.'s, alight with gleeful excitement, and suddenly she remembered the bleeding, quivering turtle.

"What a ride!" exulted John D. "We lived right thar on the boat, kept our victuals and slept at one end, went down by a kind of ladder through a scatter hole. We used plank and cloth as sails, went rushin' by all them cities, folks came out and laughed at us. And then— N'Orleans! Thar it was we saw Negroes chained, bein' whipped, draggin' carts through the streets like oxen. Yes, and we saw an auction whar they was sellin' 'em. Thar was a gal, reel purty, up on the block. Men was comin' up and pinchin' her, lookin' at her teeth, makin' her prance up and down, seein' how strong she was. Yes," he grinned, "and I reckon they had some other idees too."

Abe suddenly got up from his chair and walked to the fireplace where Sally was bending over a steaming kettle. Looking up, she saw his face, crimsoned by the light of the fire, gaunt features set in grim, harsh lines. His big hands were clenched.

"It was awful," she heard him mutter. "I'd seen it afore, but never like that. If—if I ever git a chanct to hit that thing, I swar to God I'm agoin' to hit it hard."

The three of them and Offutt had gone to St. Louis on a steamboat, where Offutt had left them. Then, after walking to Edwardsville, twenty-five miles north of St. Louis, John Hanks had gone on to Springfield, leaving Abe and John D. to come east to Coles County, a good hundred-mile trek.

"Abe's lucky." John D. sounded envious. "Denton liked him so well he's givin' him a job over thar in New Salem whar he made himself sich a hero. Goin' to pay Abe fifteen dollars a month to run a store for him. But if you ask me, old Abe's got another reason for wantin' to go back thar." John D. chuckled. "Thar's a gal, purtiest thing you ever saw, gold hair like ripe wheat with the sun shinin' on it, what you could see under her slatted sunbonnet, blue eyes. We seen her when we went in the tavern run by the man what owns the mill, name of Rutledge. You'd oughter seen the way old Abe looked at her!"

Abe swung about, cheeks redder than the fire could have made them. "Fool talk, John D." Though his voice was carefully controlled, his eyes were blazing. "You know I was jist bein' perlite to that Ann Rutledge. Stick to the truth, why don't you?"

John D. grinned. "Oh, ho! So you found out her name!"

"Wal—I jist heard somebody mention it. Anyways, you don't think a purty gal like that would pay any attention to the likes of me."

John D.'s grin widened. "Reckon you're right. You sure waren't much to look at, leastways thar on the flatboat when she stood on the bank watchin', rolled up jean trousers, homespun hickory shirt, buckeye chip hat."

Abe returned the grin, but there was no humor in his eyes. "You know, John D., if you'd paid more attention to business and less to watchin' other people work, Denton Offutt might've given you a job too."

Sally's heart sank. Not one disappointment but two. Abe was not staying. And John D. . . . She gave him a long slow look. Never had he looked more like Daniel. Not only the same handsome features, curling hair, dancing blue eyes, but—yes, the same insouciant, devil-may-care smile and jaunty lift of head and shoulders. *Spitt'n image of his old man.* Her brother's words came back to her. *Let's hope he ain't like him in actin' as well as looks, or, I should say lack of actin'.* As soon as she had opportunity she anxiously questioned Abe. Had John D. shirked his share of the labor on their trip? Had he taken pay without doing his job proper?

"Wal," Abe hesitated, "you know John D. He never did like work too well. But then," his eyes twinkled, "neither did I. Remember how Miz' Crawford told somebody I was never one to work like killin' snakes?"

Abe stayed at the new home less than a month, just long enough to help with the building of Dennis' cabin on public land near the Lincolns and to gain a reputation as the strong man of Coles County. It happened at the "house-raisin'." Like all such events, it was a social festival and attracted a conglomerate of visitors, strangers as well as neighbors, from the whole Wabash Point area. Sally and Betsy, as well as all the other women of the families, Halls, Radleys, Sawyers, were present, serving the usual enormous dinner.

The walls of the new cabin were up and it was time for the crowning act, the laying of the ridgepole. Abe stood on the plate at one gable end while Dennis stood waiting to put the heavy pole in place at the other. It took two men to lift it from the ground and hoist one end of it to Abe, who pulled it easily to the top of the plate, then, lifting it to his shoulders, slid it slowly across the open space to Dennis. It was a feat of unusual strength, and when the big log was in place the watching crowd burst into cheers. Among them was a burly young giant who, when Abe jumped to the ground, swaggered toward him, arms akimbo.

"So you're Abe Lincoln," he greeted insolently. "I've heard about you."

"Have you?" returned Abe pleasantly. "I hope it's good, what you've heard."

"I've heard 'bout how strong you are and how some folks think you could lick anybody around here."

Abe looked the other up and down. Their eyes were on a level, which meant he was the same height, six feet four, but the newcomer's shoulders were broader and his arms were almost the thickness of the log Abe had just lifted. "You seem to know my name," he said, "but I haven't the pleasure—"

"I'm Dan'l Needham. You mean you've never heard tell o' me?"

"I'm afraid not. You see, I'm new in these parts."

"Wal, I'm s'posed to be the champeen wrestler in Coles County. Ain't many around your size, and I seen you lift that big log like it was a cedar sapling. Mebbe you think you could lick me?"

"Mebbe," returned Abe. "But I ain't got no hankerin' to lick anybody."

"Huh! Scairt mebbe? 'Fraid you might git licked?"

"No. I ain't scairt."

"Then s'pose we try a hug."

Abe looked around. The confrontation had drawn a crowd. He was surrounded by faces, composite, individual . . . Sally's, anxious, troubled; John D.'s, hopeful, expectant (it was probably John D. who had boasted of his physical prowess); Tom's, proud, a bit smug with belief in his son's superiority; others curious, speculative, appraising, ready to register either admiration or contempt. "Rassle 'im, Abe!" someone shouted. He turned back to his burly challenger.

"Sure," he said calmly. "I don't enjoy a fight, but I'm willin'. No doubt you kin throw me easy enough. You're in practice. But jist name the time and place."

"Now," snapped the champion. "Here. I'll wager I kin throw you three times out o' four."

It was a wrestling match that became legend in Coles County. The two were well matched in height and strength, and it was an exhibition to be long remembered, though no one, least of all the contestants, could have guessed how long. Arms locked bodies in a viselike grip, strained, pushed, twisted, grappled, while minutes passed and the crowd waited, breathless and silent. Then with a sudden swift motion Abe lifted his opponent and flung him to the ground. The crowd cheered, not only Abe's relatives but strangers who had grown tired of the champion's bullying manner. But immediately he was up again, face like a thundercloud, lunging forward. Again they grappled long and hard. Again Abe threw him, and the crowd erupted into even louder cheers. Once more Needham was on his feet, fists clenched, face murderous in its fury.

Oh dear! thought Sally, anxiety turned to apprehension. She had wanted Abe to win, of course. Now she was sorry he had, for he had made an enemy.

"All right. You've thrown me twice, Lincoln," snarled the former champion, "but I swear you cain't whip me."

"I don't want to whip you whether I kin or not," said Abe equably, "and I don't want to git whipped neither."

"Wal, I dare you to whip me. Throwin' a man's one thing, but thrashing him's another."

As Needham came toward him brandishing his fists, Abe stood his ground but made no move forward. "I've no special desire to do either," he countered, "but if you ain't satisfied and have to be convinced through a thrashing, I'll do that too, but for your sake, not mine." His antagonist hesitated, obviously confronted with an unfamiliar situation. "You're still champeen o' Coles County, Needham," Abe continued, smiling. "I'm jist a visitor, goin' away right soon. Why don't we jist call it quits, shake hands, and be friends?"

He did come forward then, holding out his hand. For a moment the other stood gaping, anger slowly evaporating. Then, grinning sheepishly, he thrust out a beefy hand.

"He's made a friend," marveled Sally, "instead of an enemy."

Abe departed for New Salem in July. "I may be back," he told the family cheerfully. "Bad penny, you know. I'm goin' to help Offutt build his store, then clerk in it. Mebbe it'll be a success, mebbe not."

But Sally knew he would not be back, at least to stay. She packed extra clothing for him, bombarded him with motherly advice more appropriate for a boy of eleven than for a man of twenty-two, and saw him off down the path leading to the road west, careful not to watch him travel out of sight. Anyway, she could not have seen him even had she kept looking, her eyes were too blurred with tears. She would not have kept him, nor would she have wanted the pain of his leaving to be any less. It was part of the bitter-sweetness of being a mother. Had Mary felt like this, she wondered, seeing her Son leave the Nazareth carpenter shop for the long road leading into uncertainty? Sacrilege even to think it? No, decided Sally. There was something of divinity in all motherhood.

The cabin was full of life and activity, yet without Abe it seemed empty. Even Tilda's two-year-old John Johnston Hall noticed the incompleteness. "Unc' Abe, whar he gone? Want Unc' Abe, tell John story." Life went on as usual, almost, but it lacked that extra ingredient which made it zestful and exciting. It was like bread without salt.

Letters came sometimes, and either Dennis or John D. read them to the family at night around the fire, but their laborious, mechanical rendition did not sound like Abe, and Sally took them to Ichabod, the schoolteacher, who could make them sound almost like Abe speaking. It had been election day when he arrived in New Salem, and they had needed a clerk. Someone had asked him if he could write. "Oh, I guess I kin make a few rabbit tracks." So that first day he had sat with his goose quill and registered ballots, writing down each voter's choice of a candidate when his name was bawled out.

Abe and Offutt had finished the log store by September, and he was selling all sorts of merchandise: salt, sugar, tea, whiskey, tobacco, hardware, dishes, calico, bonnets, shoes. But Offutt was a hustler, a schemer, especially when inspired by corn juice. He envisioned a huge flatboat running up and down the Sangamon the year round, with rollers for shoals and runners for ice, and with Abe as its captain. Meanwhile Abe was tending store, not too expertly. One time he had found he had charged a woman six and a quarter cents more than he should have. That night he had had to walk several miles into the country to give her the four-penny piece which made up what he owed her.

Unfortunately he had been forced into another fight. There was a rough gang outside of town called the Clary Boys; they ran a saloon and were noted for rowdiness. They had a champion, Jack Armstrong, who put up a bet with Offutt that Abe couldn't throw him. It was a real shindy. Folks had come from miles around, and bets had run high. Armstrong was strong as a bull. Abe had held him off, worn him down, kept his temper until his opponent had fouled by stamping on his right foot with his boot. Abe had seen red, lifted Armstrong up by the throat and shaken him, then flung him to the ground. Funny! Now Jack and his cronies were some of his best friends. Though he didn't drink whiskey or gamble, they had accepted him. He visited in their homes, judged their horse races, settled their disputes.

Sally listened eagerly, hopefully, but often with disappointment. A fighter, a storekeeper, a river pilot? Was this all his future was to be? "Mebbe I failed him somehow," she confessed to that ever-recurring vision of a dreaming Nancy. "If you'd only lived, he might've kept lookin' higher an' further." As each letter came her ears strained for some signs that their hopes were still alive.

They came. There was a man in New Salem named Mentor Graham, a schoolteacher, who was helping him with studying. Abe had got a new book called *Kirkham's Grammar,* borrowed it from a neighbor named John Vance who lived six miles away. He could study it while working, prop it up on a counter, lay his head on a stack of calico prints, and read. It was hard work, but he was learning, felt he had mastered it in just three weeks. Mentor Graham had another pupil, name of Ann Rutledge. Abe lived at the tavern her father owned, and sometimes they studied grammar together. . . . There was a debating society in New Salem, and Abe was a member. When he had got up to make a speech, he could see folks smiling, expecting to hear a funny yarn, but he guessed he had surprised them. Maybe they were finding out he had more in his head than fun and jokes.

Then in the spring of 1832 Ichabod Radley came to the Lincoln cabin carrying a copy of the *Sangamo Journal* for March 9.

"Listen to this, folks! Our Abe's runnin' for the state assembly. Here in this newspaper he's announced his platform, internal improvements, better educational facilities, a law to limit interest rates. He's sure the Sangamon River can be made more navigable by cutting a deeper, straighter channel, much cheaper than railroads. It will make the state more prosperous. And here's something new. He says he's for women's suffrage, that means women being able to vote!"

"Abe—the assembly!" Tom was skeptical. "He's reachin' too fur agin. He'll never make it."

"Don't be so sure," said Ichabod. "That boy of yours may be smarter than you think. And he sure chose a right popular plank for his platform. Everybody's talking about that little steamer, the *Talisman,* that's lying up at Beardstown, waiting to try its luck on the Sangamon soon's the ice goes out."

Abe was involved in this adventure, as one of his letters related. He and several other men went down the river and cleared the channel of snags and limbs, then spent four days breaking an ice jam at the river's mouth, after which the little steamer chugged triumphantly up to within seven miles of Springfield. Abe's dream of cheap navigation seemed about to be fulfilled. But the river level fell swiftly, and the boat had to start downstream. Abe was put in charge as pilot. At New Salem part of the dam had to be torn down so she could pass. But the steamer reached Beardstown safely. It had been an exciting adventure and had earned Abe forty dollars.

River pilot again! thought Sally, her hopes ebbing. She was even more disturbed when the next letter came. Offutt's store had failed to yield sufficient profits to its ambitious owner, who had decided to speculate in seed corn and cottonseed. With his job about to "wink out" Abe was enlisting in the new Indian war threatened by the encroachment into Illinois of Chief Black Hawk.

News of the danger was just reaching Coles County. Though much of northern Illinois was still unsettled and roamed by marauding Indians, for years there had been no hint of any uprising. Now suddenly panic spread across the state. In 1804 the Sauks and Foxes had sold their land in the northwest of Illinois to the government, but with the provision that they could hunt and raise corn there until it was surveyed and sold to settlers. Envious of the land where the Indians returned to visit their ancient village and burial place, the settlers—squatters—had finally succeeded in evading the terms of the treaty and getting the desired land surveyed. The two tribes had been forced to sign another treaty yielding all the lands east of the Mississippi. But Black Hawk, Chief of the Sauks, believing like all Indians that land could not be sold, that it was a gift from the Great Spirit for his children to live on and cultivate but only for their subsistence, had brooded over the wrong done to his people. Forced to leave their growing crops in the Illinois country in 1831 and faced by famine conditions in the new area, on April 6, 1832, he crossed the river with five hundred braves, their squaws and children, bearing a flag of truce, and marched thirty-five miles north to the land near Rock River where he had been born and which was held sacred by the tribe.

"We come to plant corn," was his explanation to the settlers. But they did not believe him. Panic spread. Many fled to the forts. General Atkinson at Fort Armstrong applied to the government for reinforcements. A member of the undisciplined militia shot down one of the Indians bearing a flag of truce, and war erupted. Hence the summons which had caused Abe's enlistment.

"I'm goin' too," announced John D., eyes aglow. "If Abe kin fight, so kin I."

The other men of the family regarded him with the envy of responsible husbands and fathers for an unattached male—Dennis with his new cabin, land, and four children, Squire with his small son and wife Tilda soon to give birth to another child. Even Tom, struggling with diminished strength to break new land, looked regretful. "Don't blame you, son. Effen I was young and strong like you, I'd go too."

Perhaps he was remembering the small boy of six standing over the slain body of his father.

Sally's heart sank, but she did not protest. John D. had been restless since Abe left, like a boat without a rudder. He had gone from one job to another, showing little interest or, she suspected, diligence in any of them. In December he had sued George Hanson, a neighbor, for $12, pay claimed for breaking seven acres of wheat land. Though he had been awarded $7.92½, the defendant had refused to pay it and was bringing a countersuit this April to prove no doubt that the work had not been done properly. Perhaps even a dangerous war, with Abe for a steadying influence, was better than this negligent drifting.

But the weeks that followed were sheer torture. Their only surcease from depression was the arrival of another Nancy, little Nancy Ann Hall, with Sally the capable midwife. With a young mother to nurse, an active three-year-old, and a squalling newborn baby to liven the cabin, four other grandchildren frequently running in and out, there was little time to worry about a war being waged in a wilderness more than two hundred miles to the north.

And then suddenly one day in mid-July it was over. "We're here, Ma." There was John D. in the door, and Abe was just behind him. They looked disheveled, bedraggled, dirty, unshaven, deathly tired. And of course hungry. The necessity of ministering to their physical needs overcame the urge to display maudlin emotion. She hugged them both, filled kettles of water for hot baths, rummaged in the chest for clean clothes, mixed corn meal for hoecakes, all with as steady hands and dry eyes as if Abe had not been away for a year and both of them had not just weathered the peril of scalping knives. Otherwise she would surely have cried and made a fool of herself.

The two seemed reluctant to talk about the war, though the family was all eager with questions. Oh yes, it had been exciting enough, conceded John D., that is, if you could call getting mired down in swamps, crawling knee-deep through mud, sleeping in leaky tents when the spring rain was pouring down, exciting. And Abe had been made a captain, he told them proudly, elected over another man from New Salem named Kilpatrick.

"Fine captain I was," interposed Abe wryly. "You oughter seen me. Once I was marchin' with a front of over twenty men acrost a field when we came to a gate. I couldn't remember for the life of me the right word to get the company endwise, so we could git through, so as we came near I shouted, 'This company is dismissed for two minutes, when it will fall in agin on t'other side o' the gate.' Yes, and one night my men stole a quart of liquor, and were too drunk the next mornin' to fall in. For their disobedience I had to wear a wooden sword for two days."

"But they sure learnt to obey," insisted John D. in stout defense. "A poor Indian took refuge in the camp one day, and the men wanted to kill him, even though he had a safe-conduct from the General. Abe stood up mad as a cornered bull and dared anyone to lay a hand on him. And believe me, nobody did!"

Black Hawk had been conquered all right. It was Abe who answered the question, lips grim and eyes bleak under their heavy brows. They had pursued him as he fled westward with his band, all practically starving. There had been a battle at a place called Bad Axe River, no, not a battle, a massacre. Old men, women, and children had been slain, even though they had pled for mercy and raised flags of truce. Poor old Black Hawk had been captured and carted away, probably to be put on exhibit like a captured lion in a cage.

"And all he wanted," Abe concluded bitterly, "was to git back some of the land that rightfully belonged to him."

Oh yes, he admitted, the Indians had done their share of the killing. At Kellogg's Grove he had helped bury five of General Stillman's men just killed in a sharp battle.

"I kin still see 'em," he remembered moodily, "the red light of the mornin' sun streamin' on 'em as they lay heads toward us on the ground. And every man had a round red spot on top of his head, about as big as a dollar, where the redskins had taken his scalp. It was frightful, but grotesque; and the red sunlight seemed to paint everything all over. I remember one man had on buckskin trousers—like these."

To Sally's disappointment Abe was not staying. He must return to New Salem immediately to wage his campaign for the legislature. Election day was only a little over two weeks away, and he must get around the country, talk to farmers, visit country stores to hobnob with loungers, perhaps make some informal speeches. She regarded with dismay his old calico shirt, battered straw hat, and the six inches of blue socks between his heavy brogans and the legs of his buckskin trousers. "You can't go like that, son, meetin' people! What'll they think of you? Wait till I kin make you some new shirts and pants."

He smiled down at her. "Reckon they'll jist have to take me as I am, Ma. Anyways, nothin' I'd wear could make me look handsome."

This time she did not even go to the door to see him off. She was afraid she might be tempted to watch him out of sight.

It was two years before Abe returned to Coles County, and in all that time Sally could never quite accustom herself to his absence. Sometimes in an evening she found herself lifting her long skirt to avoid stepping on a pair of legs stretched out in front of the fire. When a hog was killed she might set aside extra meat for the sausage he liked so much. She would think, "I must tell Abe about the new preacher we had Sunday. It'll make him chuckle." And once without thinking she even lighted a candle and placed it on his desk so it would be ready for him to write and read by.

News came of him. He might send a message by a traveler going through, and occasionally there would be a letter. He had not been elected to the assembly, almost, it seemed, to Tom's satisfaction. "Didn't reckon he would. Sich things ain't for the likes of us." But Abe was not discouraged, for in his New Salem precinct he had received 277 of the 300 votes. He had met many people, learned how to speak better, and of course he would try again. . . . He was hunting for work, thought he might take up blacksmithing. One of his friends, Jack Kelso, lived at the smithy and he had a lot of books Abe liked to read, knew Shakespeare and Burns. . . . No, not blacksmithing. He was buying a store with a man named William Berry.

"Buyin' a store!" Tom was dumbfounded. "How'd he ever git the money to do that!"

Ichabod Radley consulted the letter. "Evidently he didn't. It seems they signed a lot of notes. They bought out another store too, signed a note for that for $600, plus a horse, saddle, and bridle."

"Oh—by dear!" exclaimed Tom in exasperation. "Signin' notes! He'd oughter know better after what he saw happen to me."

"A storekeeper!" thought Sally in dismay. "Sellin' bacon, muslin, calico, and sich, and of course whiskey, all stores sell whiskey. Jist that for Abe? Oh, it ain't what Nancy would have wanted!"

Tom's fears were well founded. Judging by Abe's future letters, the store was not prospering. His partner Berry was a disappointment, depleting the barrels of whiskey before they could be sold.

Tom shook his head disgustedly. "Don't sound good. One podner a drunk, t'other with his nose forever in a book, prob'ly po'try."

Abe's nose was in books, yes, as subsequent letters showed, but not poetry. In the fall of 1833 he began to study surveying and was appointed deputy by John Calhoun, the county surveyor. In six weeks he had mastered the subject. Too poor at first to buy tools, he used a long straight grapevine until he had earned enough to acquire compass, flagstaff, and chain. Immigrants were pouring into Illinois, wagon roads being opened through woods and prairies, and surveyors were in demand. He had had to go further into debt for fifty dollars to buy a horse, but the pay was three dollars a day, the most that he had ever earned. And he had also been appointed postmaster of New Salem.

"Not much of a job," he confessed. "Carry the letters mostly in my hat and keep them there till I can deliver. But a good chance to read all the printed matter. Got a pair of buckskins for one surveying job, and Hannah Armstrong, Jack's mother, foxed them on my pants so the briars won't wear them. Ma'll be glad of that."

Sally was glad, though she begrudged other women the privilege of clothing her two sons. At least John D. showed no inclination to move away. The war seemed to have cured him of the yen for adventure, and since his return he had worked fairly steadily. On receiving his army pay in 1833 he bought forty acres of public land in the same survey township as Tom's cabin, paying fifty dollars. Sight of the new tract, better than the land where he had settled as a squatter, aroused Tom's never wholly submerged roving instincts.

"S'pose I buy it from you," he suggested to John D. "We kin build us a cabin and all move thar."

John D. was agreeable. He was looking with romantic interest at Mary Barker, an attractive young neighbor just turning eighteen, and cash in hand was an inducement. So on March 14, 1834, he sold his property to his stepfather for seventy-five dollars, making a very good profit. Thanks to the usual cabin-raising, the new home was soon erected. Cheerfully resigned to change, Sally saw her household effects once more loaded into the wagon, by now much the worse for wear, and carted two miles southeast into what was known as the Muddy Point neighborhood. And with equal equanimity on October 16, 1834, the day of his wedding, she welcomed into her home Mary, John D.'s bride. At least the new move did not take her into loneliness. All her immediate family, Hannah, Betsy, Tilda, with their children, were on their own farms nearby—all except Abe.

It was Ichabod Radley with his *Sangamo Journal* who revealed the latest and most astounding news of Abe. "This time he made it, got elected to the Illinois Legislative Assembly!"

Tom was almost speechless. "My Abe—in the legislature!" But incredulity changed swiftly to pride and satisfaction. "I allus knowed he had it in him, reckoned he'd go fur."

Sally smiled knowingly. Mingled with her triumph was a hint of sadness. He's goin' so fur, she thought, that he'll never come back to us.

She was wrong. That November she heard a shout from John D. She went out, and there was Abe riding into the clearing on a sorry-looking nag. Or—was it Abe? He looked so different when he dismounted that she had to look twice to make sure. But the strength of his long arms gathering her into a smothering hug was as familiar as the brown, lined face and shock of black hair.

"I—I almost didn't know you," she gasped when he finally released her. "You—look so—different."

"It's the clothes." He grinned apologetically. "Some of my friends thought I ought not to go to the legislature lookin' the way I usually do, so I got me a tailor to make me this outfit."

He had gone to Coleman Smoot, a wealthy farmer, he told them later, and said, "Smoot, did you vote for me?" "I sure did." "Then that makes you responsible. How about loaning me two hundred dollars to buy some clothes so I can make a decent appearance at the legislature?" "I'll do just that," Smoot had replied. So here Abe was, dressed in the sixty-dollar suit he had purchased with some of the money.

Sally looked him up and down from head to foot appraising the new suit of butternut jeans, tailored in the latest style, noting also the too short sleeves, yes, and the couple of inches of woolen socks between trouser legs and buckskin shoes. Even the best tailor would distrust his measurements of those arms and legs!

He had soon exchanged the new suit for his usual buckskin and homespun and spent the few days of his visit helping Dennis and John D. split rails to fence in the new property, rails that a quarter-century later would be ferreted out and carted away by trophy hunters. But evenings were spent in the cabin in political discussion with relatives and neighbors. Abe was a member of the Whig party, supporters of Henry Clay and his policies of using the national government to develop the country's resources through conservative banking, internal improvements, and a protective tariff for infant industries, the group taking its name from the eighteenth-century party which had opposed the British king. Since most of the relatives and neighbors were Jacksonian Democrats, arguments often became heated.

"You and your Whiggery!" scoffed Ichabod Radley good-naturedly.

"You and your 'King Andrew the First'!" retorted Abe, knowing that Ichabod, who subscribed to a newspaper, was familiar with the cartoons being circulated depicting the autocratic President Jackson.

"How'd you do it, son?" Tom probed. "Make speeches? You allus did have a gift of gab, took it from me, I reckon."

"Well"—Abe lounged deeper in his chair, haunches balanced on its edge, bare feet thrust toward the fire—"I did some electioneerin', you might say. Rode up and down the county, speakin' any place I could find folks, in public squares, schoolhouses, at house-raisin's, log-rollin's. Did a mite of wrestlin', weight-liftin', helped farmers cut their grain. Met some mighty fine people. That was the best part. It was one of them, another candidate named John Stuart, got me to studyin' law. That's what I'm doin' now. Mean to get admitted to the bar. He lets me borrow books from his office in Springfield. It's twenty-two miles away, but it's worth the time walkin'. Gives me a chance to read along the way. In fact, the first book I borrowed I got forty pages read on the way home."

Tom gulped. "You mean—you think you kin git to be a *lawyer?*"
Abe chuckled. "You sound like one o' my friends that I've done
some farm work for over to New Salem. I was sittin' like this bare-
footed on a woodpile readin' one o' these books when he came along
and asked me what I was readin'. 'I'm not readin','' I told him, 'I'm
studyin'.' 'Studyin' what?' he wanted to know. 'Law, sir,' I told him.
He looked at me for a while with mouth wide open, then blurted out,
'Great God Almighty!'"

Sally could not restrain her curiosity about another of Abe's possible involvements. "You still livin' at that tavern," she ventured to
ask once, keeping a keen eye on his face, "the one whar that purty
gal is, let's see, what was her name, Ann?"

His face showed her what she wanted to know. It lighted like a
sunburst. "Ann Rutledge." He repeated the words with the reverent
intonation of a priest saying a "Hail, Mary." Then he sobered. "No,
I'm not livin' there. James Rutledge lost both his mill and tavern this
fall. It's sad because he was one of the most prosperous men in New
Salem, one of its founders. No, I—I don't see Ann much any more.
She used to come every day to the post office lookin' for a letter from
a man she was engaged to, a man called McNeil, though that wasn't
his real name. He was really McNamar. Came to New Salem and
bought up lots of property, smart man he was. No wonder Ann loved
him."

Abe went on talking, walking restlessly, as he had once walked in
the loft, trying to explain a mystery to his satisfaction. "But he was a
queer fellow, said he took a different name so his parents wouldn't
know where he was. He wanted to earn ten thousand dollars, then go
back East and bring them back to enjoy his prosperity. Well, he did
go back, left three years ago, and all this time she's been waitin' for a
letter."

And you've been lovin' her, thought Sally. Aloud she said,
"Mebbe now she knows it ain't likely to come."

"Yes, she's about given up hope." Abe sounded more cheerful.
"We've done lots of things together, studied with Mentor Graham,
gone to cornhuskings, picnics, horseback riding. And we'd sit and
talk by the fire evenings in the tavern. She wants to go to college in
Jacksonville, where her brother went." Abe's speech, somewhat less
careless since his exposure to *Kirkham's Grammar*, reverted to its
former colloquial forms. "She ain't jist purty, Ma, she's beautiful. I

sure wisht you could see her, hair like autumn leaves, blue eyes, fresh as a flower. Yes, and a right fine mind, too. She learnt that grammar quick as I did. When we got through studyin' it, I bought the book and gave it to her, wrote her name in front of it."

At last, thought Sally happily, Abe's really in love and with a real fine girl. It just has to come out right. No girl with any sense could choose that other scamp, or anybody else for that matter, instead of Abe!

He donned his new suit again and left for Vandalia, the state capital, in time for the opening of the legislature on December 1. It wasn't just the bareness of trees, the frozen ground, the coming of the winter's cold which made life at Muddy Point seem suddenly dull and empty.

Many months passed before they saw Abe again, and his letters were infrequent. When one occasionally appeared Sally listened anxiously, hopefully, for some word of the girl he loved, but none came. *Ann.* She repeated the name often to herself. Beautiful, reminding one of things soft and fragrant and gentle, yet gay and full of laughter, perhaps because it sounded so much like *Nancy.*

And then suddenly in the fall of 1835 he was there. No sixty-dollar suit this time, only buckskins and linsey-woolsey shirt and jacket, all the worse for wear and hanging on his bony frame like garments on a scarecrow, for never had he looked so thin and gaunt. But it was when she saw his face that Sally's heart smote her. There had often been a sadness about his features, but this was more than melancholy. It was the face of a man who had been to the depths of grief and bitterness and come out drained of all hope and courage and laughter, almost of the will to live.

"You're lookin' peaked, son," Tom commented anxiously. "Look as if you'd been through a grist mill or else pounded in a mortar."

"You might say that." Abe's grin was wry and humorless. It had been a bad year for him, he explained. The assembly had gone well, and he had earned enough to pay his debt to Smoot. But the store had failed. His partner, William Berry, had died, leaving him with an appalling debt of about eleven hundred dollars.

"Eleven hundred!" Tom gasped. "It sounds like—like—"

"Like the 'national debt,'" Abe agreed. "Guess that's what I'll have to call it." The few groceries left had been seized by creditors. The people who had bought the store had cleared out without paying. The creditors had been kind, all but one. A man named Peter van Bergen had sued him for a note of $379.82 issued in 1833. He had seized Abe's horse, saddle, bridle, and surveying instruments, but a friend, Uncle Jimmy Short, had bid them in for $120 and restored them to Abe, giving him time to repay. Of course he would pay all his debts to the last cent even if it took him the rest of his life, which it probably would.

"I told the creditors," he concluded, "that if they'd let me alone, I'd give them all I could earn over my bare living, as fast as I could earn it."

"By dear!" Tom clucked in sympathy. "More Lincoln luck. But whom the Lord loveth . . . No wonder you look like somethin' the dog drug in."

But debts, Sally suspected, had not brought that look of hopelessness to his eyes. He had suffered some deep soul distress. Would he tell her? She must not question, just wait patiently. She was alone in the cabin, busy at the loom, when the light from the door cast a long shadow. She did not turn, but her hand lay poised on the shuttle.

"Ann died," said Abe with bleak quietness.

"Oh—my dear boy!"

Sitting on the floor beside her, long arms around his scissored legs, he talked, more to himself than to her, giving vent to long suppressed emotion. Ann had finally given up looking for the letter. Her family had been hard up, after losing both mill and inn, and had gone to live on a farm in the country. She had worked for a while for James Short, a near neighbor, and Abe had talked with her there when visiting Uncle Jimmy. He had finally told her he loved her, and—yes, she had promised to marry him. She would go to Jacksonville and spend the winter in the academy, and he would keep on studying law, and when he was admitted to the bar they would be married. But— Abe's voice broke; then, after a moment's silence he continued quietly without apparent emotion. The spring and summer, as Sally knew, had been hot and wet, with an outbreak of sickness, chills and fever. Ann, one of the victims, had asked to see him, and he had gone. They had spent an hour together. She had died on August 25. He could hardly remember what had happened since. He supposed he had attended to his postmaster's job and surveying. He had been sick, perhaps with the same fever, and his friend Bowling Green had taken him to his home under the brow of a big bluff half a mile north of New Salem, where he and his wife Nancy had nursed him with the help of Dr. John Allen, who had cared for Ann.

Sally longed to comfort him, but he was as remote and lonely in his suffering as on the day she had followed him up the hill and found him pushing back the dead leaves from the mound of earth.

"I found a poem once," he said. "I wrote it in the copybook you made me. Remember? I've been saying it over and over these days." He repeated the words, but in such a low voice that she had to strain her ears to hear.

"Oh! why should the spirit of mortal be proud?
Like a swift-fleeing meteor, a fast-flying cloud,
A flash of the lightning, a break of the wave,
He passeth from life to his rest in the grave."

She reached out her hand and laid it on the wild mop of black hair, smoothing it into a semblance of order. "I know, son," she said gently. "You and me, we love harder than most folks, I reckon, and suffer more when we lose. But I guess it's wuth it."

He looked up at her gratefully, as long ago he had looked up from the mound. "Thanks, Ma."

She found the worries of motherhood heavier than usual that winter, with Abe away somewhere unhappy, and John D. . . . Which was harder to bear, she wondered, knowing that a son was suffering or that one was involved in unseemly, if not criminal behavior? In November, John D. and Squire Hall, summoned to court as witnesses in a trial, were arrested for "assaulting an officer in attempting to execute process" and for "gaming." Bail for each was set at a hundred dollars on the first charge and at fifty dollars on the second. Tom managed to raise bail for John D. by borrowing money on his land. The case dragged on until April, when John D. was acquitted and Squire was found guilty. But still it was not settled. Sentence was not imposed until the next October, when Squire received a sentence of a five-dollar fine and twenty-four hours in the county jail. Both were found not guilty on the gaming charge. Because of Tilda, Sally endured as much worry and shame over Squire as over John D.

Tom also had his troubles. In March 1835 he and Dennis and John D. and Squire signed a one-year lease on a saw and grist mill for which they agreed to pay $220.12½ at the end of a year. The proj-

ect did not succeed, and when the year ended a balance of
$134.87½ was still due. The owners brought suit and demanded
damages of the full amount of the original agreement. There followed long and bitter litigation, but in October 1836 the four of
them confessed a judgment against them for $138.67. Tom's only
satisfaction in the sorry outcome of the venture came when the clerk
drawing up the confession had left a space and had already entered
the word "his" preparatory to writing "his mark," and he was able to
say with dignity, "No, I kin write my own name." And he did,
laboriously but legibly—"Thom. Lincoln."

Sally's worry over Abe was somewhat allayed when one of his
New Salem friends, William Greene, stopped at the cabin on a trip to
Kentucky to deliver a letter and of course bring news of Abe. He was
running again for the legislature, making a name for himself with his
speeches.

Greene chuckled. "You should have heard Abe at one of them
meetings. Thar was another candidate, George Forquer, a big orator,
got up to talk after Abe got through. Began by sayin' that this young
man would have to be taken down, and he was sorry the job fell to
him. Slashed out with a lot of ridicule and gaff. Abe stood near him,
arms folded, not interruptin', but after he got through Abe started.
Forquer had been a Whig like Abe but had changed his politics so's
to be appointed Registrar of the Land Office. The day before Abe had
gone past Forquer's house and seen on its roof the only lightnin' rod
in the town or county. Wal, you should have heard Abe! He got up
with his arms folded and begun in that drawlin' voice of his, 'The
gentleman commenced his speech,' he said, 'by sayin' that this young
man would have to be taken down. I'm not so young in years as I am
in the tricks and trade of a politician. But live long or die young, I'd
rather die now than, like this gentleman, change my politics and at
the same time get an office worth $3,000 a year, and then have to
erect a lightnin' rod over my house to protect a guilty conscience
from an offended God.'" Greene chortled with glee. "Wal, you
should have seen that crowd! Abe's friends carried him out of the
courthouse on their shoulders."

Tom was torn between pride and lifelong prejudice. "Wal I s'pose
all that readin' and eddication's got him whar he is, ef that's whar he
wants to be. Me, I hain't got no eddication, but I git along better'n ef
I had. Take bookkeepin'. Why, I'm a good enough bookkeeper for

what I need. Look up at that rafter thar. That's three straight lines made with a firebrand. Ef I sell a peck of meal I draw a black line acrost, and when they pay I take the dishcloth and jist rub it out. And that's most as good as yer eddication."

Sally listened hopefully for some indication that Abe had recovered from his deep despondency. It came. "We've got a new young woman in town, name of Mary Owens, come from Kentucky to visit her sister, Mrs. Able. She's a stunner, dark curly hair, blue eyes, a little too stout, but handsome. All the men are at her feet, includin' Abe. And is Mrs. Able a matchmaker! When she went to visit her folks in Kentucky, she told Abe that she'd bring Mary back with her if he'd agree to marry her. Abe had met Mary three years before and admired her. Abe laughed at the jest and jokingly agreed. But she did bring Mary back with her, and who knows? Mebbe it won't be a joke, after all!"

Abe was too busy to come home that year but news came of him. He was admitted to the Illinois bar in September. At the assembly that winter he was one of the "Long Nine," all Whigs and averaging six feet in height and over two hundred pounds in weight, hence their nickname. He was leading the fight to move the capital from Vandalia to Springfield, advocating raising vast sums for railroads, canals, river improvements, funded, like his own sorry experience in the world of finance, on credit and destined, because of the Panic of 1837, for the same unhappy outcome. And he was arousing shocked opposition by refusing to vote for resolutions disapproving the formation of abolition societies.

"He found just one man to agree with him, a Dan Stone, and they signed a protest," explained Ichabod. "While they believe Congress has no power under the Constitution to interfere with slavery in states where it's permitted, and they don't think abolition societies help, they include in their resolution their belief that the institution of slavery is founded on both injustice and bad policy. Took a lot of courage." Ichabod shook his head doubtfully. "It may hurt him. People are rioting against abolitionists, raiding their printing offices. Abe had better be careful what he says and does if he wants to get ahead in politics."

"Abe'll never be keerful what he says and does," said Sally firmly, "if he knows a thing is right."

Changes! Sometimes they were as abrupt and devastating as the drop in temperature at noon on December 20, 1836, forty degrees almost instantly, bringing a roaring murderous wind and freezing the falling rain suddenly into icicles. The clothes of a man walking or working were frozen solid, and geese and chickens walking on the wet ground were held fast by their feet. It was told afterward that a herd of a thousand hogs being driven to St. Louis banded together for warmth, those inside smothering and those outside freezing, where they all remained in a solid mass for weeks. The winter that followed, as bitter and disastrous as the one of 1830, would be remembered as "the winter of the sudden change."

Tom decided to move again in the spring. "Alexander Montgomery's offered me $140 for this farm," he announced to Sally. "That's 'most twice what I paid for it. It'll pay for that eighty acres I bought last January for $100 and git me clear o' that mill lease judgment. But Montgomery wants to move right in."

Sally gasped. "But—whar'll we go, Tom? Thar's no cabin on that eighty acres."

Tom had an answer to that. There was a small shelter on the land he had bought earlier about a half mile south of their Muddy Point farm. They could live there during the summer while he and John D. cleared land on the new property over to the east. John D. was planning to buy another tract adjoining his, and they would decide later where it was best to build the cabin for both their families.

Sally sighed, but she made no protest. By accepting Tom Lincoln and leaving for the unknown within twenty-four hours she had attuned herself to the idea of sudden change. In May they moved to the little shack a half mile to the south on an eighty-acre section of land which Tom had bought in 1834 on credit, giving a mortgage to the School Commissioner of Coles County. Sally went to see the new

land Tom had bought the preceding January on a public land entry
and found it good, an open stretch of ground sloping gradually to a
tree-bordered stream on the east, located in a section called Goosenest Prairie and only eight miles from Charleston. But somehow the
new cabin did not get built that summer. Clearing land and planting a
few crops had exhausted all the energy which Tom, never strong since
his bout with ague, and John D., never prone to hard labor, seemed
able to expend.

"We cain't live here for the winter, Tom," Sally objected. "It ain't
much better'n a half-faced camp."

The problem was solved when in August John D. purchased on
credit forty acres of land south of Tom's section, with a makeshift
cabin on it built by a squatter a few years before. They moved there
immediately and with her gentle prodding of Tom and sharper prodding of John D. in improving roof, beams, door, chimney, fireplace,
plus much scrubbing, crack chinking, whitewashing by herself, Sally
turned the sixteen-by-eighteen-foot shelter into a place of tolerable
comfort. They could build a new cabin on his own property, Tom
promised, a real house, better than she had ever lived in.

There were other changes that year, the birth of Elizabeth Jane to
Matilda and of Thomas Lincoln Davis to John D.'s Mary, who had
been viewing the fertility of her husband's sisters with mounting de-
spair. She need not have worried, for in the next ten years she would
produce five more sons and one daughter!

Poor Tom! He was always in trouble, it seemed, over money.
"You're goin' to have a reel bedstid," he insisted to Sally when they
moved into this, their fourth shelter in Illinois, "not one of them pole
things." So the end of the year found him sued for a debt of $9.00
for a bedstead. A summons was served on him to appear in January,
when he was fined for $10.25, including costs.

The next time Tom was involved in one of these minor lawsuits,
which seemed to be indigenous to the area and times, he enjoyed unexpected legal defense. Once more it was John D.'s propensity for
getting into debt and Tom's good nature which got him into this further trouble. The two of them had signed a note in April 1839 for
$26.82½ bearing 12 per cent interest, due on December 25. Judg-
ment was made against them for $30.77 and costs. Tom appealed to
the Circuit Court in March 1840, but the case was not due to come
up until the court session in the fall.

"Abe's comin' to Charleston," reported John D. excitedly one day in September. "He's been goin' all over the state makin' speeches, arguin' with that man Stephen Douglas. They had a big meetin' in Springfield with twenty thousand people! Took fourteen teams to haul the delegation from Chicago, and they was three weeks on the way. They brung one oxcart holdin' a log cabin drawn by thirty yokes of oxen, for old Tippecanoe Harrison. Abe made a speech. Imagine, our Abe!"

Tom shook his head doubtfully. "He'll git in trouble if he goes tootin' about Harrison around here. Most folks in these parts is Jackson Democrats. And I reckon he cain't hold his own agin that Douglas. He'll jist make a fool of hisself."

Sally had little interest in or knowledge of politics, and the words bandied among men who met evenings in the cabin—state bank, internal improvements, tariff, stable currency—might have been Greek for all she understood them. She knew vaguely that Abe was something called a Whig and that he supported the policies of Henry Clay, and that General William Henry Harrison, running against the incumbent President Martin Van Buren, was the candidate he was backing in the coming election, also that Abe was one of the men called "electors" for Harrison. All that seemed important to her was the fact that Abe was coming. It had been nearly three years since she had seen him, and the news coming from him had been sparse and conflicting. He was a full-fledged lawyer now, living in Springfield. It had seemed once that he was going to marry that Mary Owens, and she had been glad, for it had meant that he had recovered from his despondency over the death of his beloved Ann. But apparently nothing had come of the romance. The letters he had written recently had spoken of a Mary Todd, a Kentucky woman who was visiting her sister in Springfield.

"Huh!" Dennis had snorted after reading one of Abe's infrequent letters. "Sounds as if he's aimin' purty high. This Mary Todd's sister is the wife of one of the big men in Illinois, Ninian Edwards, whose father was governor, and he's attorney general. And these Todds are a high and mighty family over in Kaintuck. Judgin' by that party Abe tells about, that co—cotillion, he seems to be runnin' in purty high sassiety. Mebbe he'll git too big to bother with us no more."

Sally did not accompany the men to Charleston in late September when Abe made his speech at the big noisy political rally. She did not want to go. If Abe was going to be worsted in argument, "make a fool of hisself," as Tom feared, she did not want to hear it. And if, as Dennis feared, he was "gittin' too big" to bother with the family, then she didn't want to bother him, either. If he was still the Abe she knew, he would come to them.

Tom returned, amazed, bewildered, jubilant. His son—*his son!*—had taken that big crowd of people, half the population of Coles County, by storm, twisted it around that long bony finger of his like it had been a piece of grapevine. He'd told a funny story that had made the feller on the other side look sillier'n a wet hen. Yes, and he'd picked his arguments off like they'd been pin-feathers off the same hen. He knew his facts too, must have studied every public document since Van Buren got to be President, and used words Tom had never heard of like he'd been born knowing them. He couldn't believe his eyes and ears.

Sally nodded, eyes bright with satisfaction. She was not surprised. But her most urgent question had not been answered. "Is he comin' home?" she demanded.

Tom wasn't sure. He had hardly had a chance to talk with Abe, he had been surrounded by so many important people. And he was traveling all over making these speeches. Perhaps he wouldn't have time.

He came, looking and acting much as he always had once he had exchanged the sixty-dollar suit, now the worse for wear, for homespun jeans and linsey-woolsey. To Sally's relief there was a gaiety about him which bespoke, if not exuberance, at least contentment. With his long gaunt face, deep-lined and sallow, there was always a hint of melancholy in his looks, but Sally, who probably knew and understood him better than anyone else in the world, judged only by his eyes. Deep-set, lustrous, they revealed his emotions as clearly as a forest pool reflected the moods of its surroundings, dark and fathomless when encompassed by shadows, glowing bright in sunlight. Now the shadows caused by Ann Rutledge had gone, or at least retreated into the depths. If this Mary had brought the new look to his eyes, then Sally blessed her. But perhaps it was not Mary. Perhaps it was just the stimulus of this exciting political tournament. Which? Before he left she determined to find out.

Men gathered once more in the evening to discuss politics, and Abe shared his views with family and neighbors as zestfully as with Springfield's uproarious mob of twenty thousand. But he enlivened talk of banking, tariff, internal improvements, and other sober issues with lighter details of the campaign.

"The Democrats accuse us Whigs of being stylish and rich," he chuckled, balancing his buttocks on the edge of one chair while resting the heels of his bare feet on the back of another. "They call us 'rag-barons.' Well, I was debating with a Democrat named Taylor, 'ruffled shirt Taylor' they call him, but he was dressed plain and sober at this country meeting, and was he lighting into us Whigs for being such fops in dress and manners! Well, I knew how he was usually dressed, so while he was talking I slipped up, caught his coat, which was buttoned up close, and tore it open. Ha! There for all to see was a ruffled shirt, a gorgeous velvet vest, and a big gold chain dangling at least a dozen rings and seals. Well, when my turn came, that was all I needed. There was I in my buckskin pants and coarse linen shirt. 'Behold,' I say, 'the hard-fisted Democrat. And here, gentlemen,'" springing from his chair Abe laid his hand over his heart and bowed, "'here at your service is your aristocrat, your rag-baron with his lily white hands. While Colonel Taylor was riding in fine carriages, wearing ruffled shirts, kid gloves, massive gold watch chains with large gold seals, I was a poor boy, hired on a flatboat at six dollars a month, and had only one pair of breeches to my back, and they buckskin. Now if you know the nature of buckskin, when wet and dried by the sun it will shrink, and my breeches kept shrinking until they left several inches of my legs bare; and while I was growing taller they were becoming shorter, and so much tighter that they left a blue streak around my legs that can be seen to this day. If you call that aristocracy, I plead guilty to the charge.' Well, Colonel Taylor couldn't call us 'rag-barons' after that!"

Abe frolicked with John D.'s three-year-old Thomas and his namesake, two-year-old Abraham Lincoln Barker Johnston, and rocked baby Marietta to sleep. He approved Tom's exchange of the eighty acres he had entered on public land in 1837 and on which he had never got around to building the promised cabin, for a better section of land to the west of John D.'s.

"You showed good judgment. That upland prairie land could never be drained properly. Your new eighty is well drained and much easier to farm."

But he was not as lenient in his judgment of his brother's activity or lack of it. "You were going to build a new cabin," he told John D.

with more sternness than usual. "You promised Ma you would, and here you've been living three years in this makeshift overcrowded shack, adding another to its occupants every year. Seven people in a room sixteen by eighteen is too much. It's hard on Ma. Come on. We're going to cut logs up on the new eighty for a new cabin, a good big one, and I'll expect it to be built before I come again."

John D., whose chief faults were indolence and procrastination, readily agreed, and they began cutting. Though Abe was scheduled to appear at a law case in Tremont in late September, he sent word to have the case postponed, which meant that he was still in Coles County when Tom and John D.'s appeal would come to trial at the Circuit Court on September 30.

"S'pose I handle the case for you, Pa," he suggested. "You claim you paid that bill. Maybe I can prove it." At the doubtful, wary expression on his father's face Abe laughed heartily. "I reckon you still can't quite swallow the idea that I'm a real, honest to goodness lawyer, can you, Pa?"

Tom echoed the laughter, but weakly. "Wal—"

"Or maybe, like lots of folks, you think lawyers ain't to be trusted," Abe chortled. "Reminds me of a story I heard. A minister and a lawyer were riding together. Says the minister to the lawyer, 'Sir, do you ever make mistakes in pleading?' 'I do,' says the lawyer. 'And what do you do with mistakes?' asks the minister. 'Why, sir, if large ones come, I mend them; if small ones, I let them go. And pray, sir, do you ever make mistakes in preaching?' 'Yes, sir, I have.' 'And what do you do with mistakes?' 'Well, sir,' replies the preacher, 'I dispose of them the same way you do. Not long since I meant to say that the devil was the father of liars, but I made a mistake and said the father of *lawyers*. The mistake was so small that I let it go.'"

Sally's knitting needles flew faster, and she smiled contentedly. There hadn't been so much laughter in the house during the three years of Abe's absence.

Abe handled the court case. Digging into the county files he found that Tom had indeed paid the note in question, as evidenced by a receipt signed and dated in May 1839, and the previous decision was reversed. Having been saved the payment of $30.77 and costs, Tom discovered to his surprise that his son had not only become a "real lawyer" but his legal acumen surpassed that of others whose efforts had usually cost rather than saved him money.

Sally was not one to pry, and fortunately Abe answered her questions without her asking. "I know you're curious, Ma," he grinned, "you being a woman." Yes, he told her, he was still keeping company with this Mary Todd he had written about. Many much more important and—he smiled wryly—handsomer men had been courting her, including the Honorable Stephen Douglas, and he couldn't understand why she should prefer him, but she seemed to.

"And why not?" Sally spoke stoutly in defense. "I cain't see why any woman wouldn't pick you stid o' that Douglas folks talk so much about."

Abe laughed and patted her shoulder. "Well, about all I've got that he hasn't is a foot or so extry in height. But they don't call him 'Little Giant' for nothing. If what Mary wants is somebody who's going places, she ought to choose him, not me."

Sally's eyes sharpened. "Is that all she wants, Abe, jist somebody what's goin' places?"

"Can't be," he replied soberly, "if what she wants is me." His face clouded. "But sometimes I wonder if I'm the right man for her, me with my homely face and awkward scarecrow body and her with those blue eyes and rosy cheeks and feet that were born dancin', me pore and with no more'n a year of schoolin', her rich and educated in a fashionable French boardin' school and used to havin' her own way. It's like matin' a crow with a hummingbird, or maybe a barnyard rooster with a peacock. No wonder we don't always see eye to eye."

"It'll be all right if you jist love each other enough," Sally assured, but her shrewd eyes regarded him doubtfully. "Jist be sartin sure, son. It's your whole life."

Neither of them could have guessed that three months later on the day in Abe's life that would be referred to as "that fatal January 1, 1841" a romantic impasse between the two lovers—quarrel, doubt, disillusionment?—would jeopardize their relationship and plunge Abe into the deepest melancholia of his life, perilously close to imbalance, from which only the tender ministry of friends, especially of his associate, Joshua Speed, would rescue him.

Though the cabin could not seem exactly empty when Abe left this time, with two men, two women, one of them again pregnant, two small children, and a squalling baby filling its sixteen-by-eighteen foot space, it was a fullness without zest or flavor.

Yet Abe had left some of his energizing vitality behind, for John
D. and Tom continued hewing timbers for the new cabin on Tom's
lot, and soon there was a house-raising. It was decided, as Abe had
suggested, not to make it a larger cabin but to move their present
shelter to the new one, joining the two together. It was a gala event
for the Goosenest neighborhood, and people came from as far as
Charleston to see the building hoisted on the log rollers, ox-drawn
across the fields, and set down beside the new structure.

It was by far the most comfortable, even luxurious home Sally had
ever had. A house of hewn logs, with two whole rooms, a warm
chimney in the center between them, a passageway on its south side,
a closet on its north, a loft over each room, the one on the new part
reached by a ladder hinged to the ceiling beams so it could be kept
out of the way in daytime!

No more crowding of four adults and three children into cramped
sleeping-eating-cooking-living quarters! Precious privacy in the room
where she and Tom slept in a real bedstead! A new kitchen with everything much handier, iron hooks for pots and kettles, dough tray
and dye pot and candle mold convenient to reach, plenty of room for
Tom's reap hook and meat saw in one corner. This was her eighth
move since marrying Tom twenty-one years ago. Her last? I hope,
she thought, that I'll live here for the rest of my life.

In December 1840 Tom purchased from John D. for fifty dollars
the forty acres on which they had lived for the past three years. Always unhappy, in spite of his yen for wandering, unless he had roots
in the soil, he wanted to be able to call the whole one hundred
twenty acres his own. Besides, John D.'s struggles with finances put
ownership of the land in constant jeopardy. Yet purchase of the land
did not end Tom's troubles. His good nature and family loyalty led
him to sign another note for John D., and by the fall of 1841 it
looked as if he might lose not only the east forty he had just bought
but also the land on which the new cabin was built.

When Abe visited Charleston in October 1841 for cases in the Circuit Court and came out to the farm, Tom blurted out his troubles.
Abe listened gravely. Before he left he took Tom and Sally to the
courthouse in Charleston and made legal purchase of the "east forty"
for two hundred dollars, the agreement giving Thomas and Sarah
Lincoln "use and entire control" of the property "during both and
each of their natural lives." It further stipulated that he would sell

the land to his stepbrother John D. for two hundred dollars, the price he had paid, within one year after the deaths of Tom and Sally, without interest except "after the death of the survivor as aforesaid."

"It's not to be thought of as mine," he told them firmly. "It's yours, to use just as you want to. But nobody—and *nothing*"—he paused significantly—"no note you sign out of the goodness of your heart—can take it away from you."

Sally felt stricken, but whether because of the sacrifice of one son or the failings of the other she could not have told. "You—you're sure you can spare it, son?"

He grinned. "I know. You're thinking of that 'national debt.' It's gettin' paid. Shouldn't take more'n another seven years, good biblical number, like Jacob serving for Rachel. Yes, Ma, I can spare it. The law business is beginning to pay. And, remember, I'll always be part of the family."

Sally was still troubled. "John D.—you know he means well—"

"I know." Abe smiled, his eyes lighting with affection. "There's not a kinder or honester person in Coles County—or all Illinois. He's my brother and your son—and we both love him."

If Abe had been plunged in melancholy during recent months, he did not show it. A summer visit to his friend Joshua Speed's home in Louisville, especially the comfort of Speed's warmhearted Christian mother, had restored his emotional stability. No one could have guessed that a few months before he had written his law partner, John T. Stuart, "I am now the most miserable man living. If what I feel were equally distributed to the whole human family, there would not be one cheerful face on earth. I must die or be better, it seemed to me." He had evidently recovered from the severing of his tie with Mary Todd.

Sally was both relieved and regretful. She wanted Abe to be happy, and he had obviously loved Mary. But there had been something about the attachment which disturbed her. A crow mated to a hummingbird? Or a barnyard rooster to a peacock?

Though Abe was in Charleston in May 1842, pleading or defending cases in the Circuit Court, and visited the farm briefly, he gave no hint of a continuing romance with Mary Todd, but somehow Sally sensed that he had not fully recovered from his emotional involvement. "You ain't happy," she ventured to accuse him. "Are you still thinkin' about that—that pretty bright hummingbird?"

Abe, sitting moodily in front of the fire, looked up at her, startled. "I–I guess maybe I am, Ma. I don't like to think I may have made anybody unhappy."

"Mebbe it's both of you that's unhappy." Sally nodded with astute understanding.

All that summer and fall she waited, wondering, expectant, yet somehow fearing. The few letters Abe wrote contained no mention of Mary Todd or of any other woman, though they made reference to the gay social life in the burgeoning young city of Springfield. Abe had changed law partners. He was now associated with Judge Stephen T. Logan, a prominent attorney, who was campaigning for Congress, so Abe was exceptionally busy. Then came disturbing news. Abe had become involved in a duel with a man named Shields, who had become incensed over a newspaper article humorously ridiculing his position as one of the Democrats in power who were refusing to accept bank notes on the discredited state bank in payment of taxes, and though the article had been signed "Aunt Rebecca," Shields had accused Abe of authorship. Remembering the "Chronicles of Reuben," Sally's heart sank. But the crisis passed, a seriocomedy, and Sally, who had pictured Abe either shot or arrested as a murderer, breathed a sigh of relief. She could not know that this unfortunate episode, of which Abe would always be ashamed, would be the catalyst bringing him and Mary Todd back together.

The news came in November, not in the form of an invitation, merely an announcement, and that as brief as Abe's conclusion to another letter he wrote to a fellow lawyer.

"Nothing new here, except my marrying, which to me is a matter of profound wonder."

"What's that?" demanded Tom, gazing stupefied at Dennis, who was reading them the letter Abe wrote his family. "Abe says—he's *married?*"

Dennis was just as bewildered. "That's what he says. But he don't say who to."

He didn't need to, thought Sally. Somehow, since that last time he had talked she had known it was inevitable.

It was Ichabod Radley, reader of the *Sangamo Journal,* who gave them the details. Abraham Lincoln and Mary Todd were married on a Friday evening, November 4, with rain pouring outside, in the parlor of the luxurious home of her sister, wife of the Honorable Attorney General Ninian W. Edwards, son of a former governor of the state. The bride, long a belle of Springfield, a grandniece of a former governor of Kentucky, was fashionably attired in a gown of changeable silk, shot with blue and flame color, with flowers and an ostrich plume in her hair. A sumptuous wedding feast was served. The Reverend Mr. Dresser, pastor of the Episcopal Church, was the officiating clergyman. The newspaper account did not report that because the wedding had been planned only in the preceding twenty-four hours, the icing was still warm on the wedding cake.

"I wisht he'd have invited us," mourned Betsy, a desire echoed by Matilda. "Seems as if he should have, his own sisters! And not askin' even his mother and father!"

As it happened only one of Abe's relatives had been invited, John Hanks, who was still living near Decatur. "I hope you will come over"—Abe had sent him a hasty note—"be sure to be on deck by early candle light."

Sally smiled to herself, picturing how they all would have looked in that "luxurious house" and at that "sumptuous feast," she in her best but faded old alpaca and poke bonnet, Tom in his homespun trousers and linsey-woolsey shirt and jacket, a couple of barnyard fowls in a garden of peacocks! No, she would much prefer to meet Abe's new wife when he should bring her here to his home. Immediately she began to prepare for their coming, scrubbing, whitewashing, weaving new curtains for the windows, polishing all the pans and kettles until they shone. Would he bring her soon, or wait until his usual time of coming to court in May?

Winter passed. Spring came. And then suddenly there was Abe, alone. Her joy at seeing him was clouded with disappointment. "I thought—but prob'ly you couldn't bring her, it's sich a long trip, around the circuit—"

Abe hesitated. He looked embarrassed. "I knew you'd want to see her, Ma, and I'd like to have brought her, but—well, the fact is, we're having a little one in August."

Sally brightened. Of course. No need for him to be embarrassed or sorry. A woman six months along shouldn't be traveling. Another grandchild! She was getting used to their coming now, Tilda's Sarah Louisa and John D.'s Squire just two years ago, and John D.'s Richard this year—but Abe's! She could hardly wait. Now she would be able to welcome both his wife and his son at the same time!

A blessing she could not know that she would never look on the faces of his wife and children!

$$= 6 =$$

Ten years of time. How should you measure their passing? By days, weeks, months, winters merging into springs? By the numbers of white hairs in the sleek black curls framing your sunbonnet and the slow sagging of a man's shoulders? By births and deaths? By weddings of grandchildren whom a few days ago, it seemed, you were rocking to sleep? By the high moments when a tall lanky figure came ambling up the path from the road shouting, "Here I am, Ma," and the embrace of his long arms nearly crushed your bones and drove the breath from your body?

It was the custom for lawyers to be assigned to the different circuits in Illinois, and though Abe was officially associated with the Eighth Circuit, which included the neighboring county of Shelby, he often had cases in Coles. Sessions were held twice each year, in the spring and fall, so during the 1840s and well into the '50s there were few years when he did not come to Charleston at least once. Though it was more convenient for him to stop with Dennis, who since 1834 had had a home in Charleston, he never left without visiting the farm. Sometimes he would walk the eight miles, sometimes borrow Dennis' horse and wagon and drive, later come with his own horse, Belle, and buggy, with which for years he drove about the circuit.

Whenever he came Sally usually managed to be at the door waiting for him. If she did not hear the sound of hoofbeats or the children's excited shouts announcing "Uncle Abe," some sixth sense would apprise her of his nearness—or perhaps when she knew he was in Charleston she ran to the door so many times to look down the path that he could not have taken her unawares. Never did he come empty-handed. The floor of his buggy would always be piled with

groceries—sacks of sugar and flour, corn meal, beans, candy for the
children, sometimes a bit of calico or alpaca for a new dress for
Sally. And invariably he would press money into her hand, in spite of
her protests.

"You do too much for us, son. That wife o' yours, she's used to
havin' nice things, and I know they cost you plenty. The calico'll be
right handy, but the alpaca! For an old lady like me it's jist folderol.
Don't keep spoilin' us."

Births. Seldom was there a time when there was not a baby for
Sally to hold or rock. John D.'s Mary produced one regularly—
Thomas, Abraham, Marietta, Squire, Richard, Dennis, Daniel—and,
since Mary's strength, never robust, was weakened by constant child-
bearing, Sally was more mother than grandmother to the seven.
Betsy's eight, except Charles and Theophilus, were all either married
adults or adolescents during the forties, but of Matilda's eight, Sarah,
Joseph, Amanda, and Harriet were still candidates for a doting
grandmother's arms. Strange, then, that with twenty-three grandchildren always near enough to love, those arms should sometimes
feel empty!

Robert, born in 1843. She tried to picture him. Was he like Abe,
with long arms and legs, unruly black hair, deep-set eyes that looked
able to see right through you, big ears sticking out at an angle, as if
cocked for listening?

He'll be one today . . . two . . . three . . . she would think when
August came around each year. The same age as John D.'s Richard
here. And she would give Richard an extra hug and piece of corn
pone spread with maple sugar for Abe's Robert, named after his Virginia grandfather, who was president of a bank, owner of mills and
factories, and very rich.

Of course Abe never said that his wife wanted nothing to do with
his poor country relations. He didn't need to. Sally understood when
Abe once brought her picture, a daguerreotype. She looked a long
time at the straight proud figure in bouffant skirts, billows of lace
over the bare shoulders, bracelets on the white plump arms, a heavy
necklace about her neck, and a chaplet of flowers crowning her head.

"She's beautiful, Abe," she said at last. "Jist the sort of wife a
man like you should have, one what's goin' fur. She'll help you go
places. I—I jist hope she'll make you happy."

The family, too, understood, and long afterward Matilda's son

John Hall would put it into words. "When we ast him why he didn't bring his wife up to see us he said, 'She is very busy and couldn't come.' But we knowed better than that. You see, he was too proud to bring her, 'cause he knowed nothin' would suit her, nohow. Of course she hadn't been raised the way we wus, and wus different styled from us, and we heard too that she wus as proud as spades. No, and he never brought nary of the children, either."

Sally could learn little about his new son from Abe, whose descriptions were often more humorous than enlightening. After one of his visits to Charleston Dennis had a story to tell.

"Thar was Abe leanin' against the side of the courthouse down in town," he related, chuckling, "lookin' as if he'd lost his last friend. 'What troubles ye, Abe?' I asked him. Wal, he jist looked at me with one of those pecoolar expressions of his and said he was worryin' about his little baby boy. 'What's the matter with him?' I asks. 'Nothin' new,' he sez, 'but I was wonderin' what I should do if he grew up with one leg short and the other leg long. Mary is low, and I'm tall, you know, and that's the long and short of it.' "

It was from one of Denny's children that Sally learned more about Abe's family than he ever told her. Harriet at eighteen was beautiful, intelligent, high-spirited, and ambitious. Though she had suitors among the Charleston swains, especially Augustus Chapman, in business with good prospects, she was not ready to marry young as her two older sisters had done. She had exhausted all the educational opportunities for young women in Charleston, but she wished for more. Her mental acuteness had appealed to Abe, and they had had a special relationship. When he came to court in October 1844 he made a suggestion.

"How would you like to go back with me and go to school for a year or so? There's a good academy in Springfield."

"Oh—could I?" Her face lighted, then darkened. "But—are you sure Mrs. Lincoln wouldn't mind?"

"It was she who suggested it. She's heard a lot about you. You can be good company for her while I'm away on circuit, and maybe help some with the young'un."

"If you ask me," Betsy told Sally testily, "it ain't a companion she's after but a nursemaid."

After the adjournment of court Abe drove off to Springfield with Harriet beside him in the buggy drawn by Belle, his bay mare. She wrote back gaily that they had stayed overnight at a real hotel, for the trip had taken two days. Her letters during the following months were brief and noncommittal. She came back with Abe in May 1846, two months after Edward, Abe's second son, was born."

The family could not wait to bombard her with questions. "What's she like?" . . . "Is she as handsome as her picture?" . . . "What kind of house have they?" . . . "Do you like her?" . . . "Is she a good mother?" . . . "Is Springfield bigger than Charleston?" . . . "Did you have to work hard?"

What was Mrs. Lincoln like? Perhaps it was significant that in her whole report Harriet referred to her as "Mrs. Lincoln," not "Aunt Mary." Well, she was handsome all right, if fine clothes and a pretty face with red lips and flashing eyes and an alluring smile could make a woman handsome, though she was a trifle too plump and not just because little Eddie had been on the way. She gave lots of parties and big dinners with sometimes a hundred people. . . . Yes, she was a good mother, though she thought everything Robert did was just right, and if anybody corrected him it had to be Uncle Abe. She liked to show him off and dress him like a little gentleman, all in velvet and ruffles. . . . Their house? Harriet looked around the humble cabin, finding nothing with which to make comparison. Well—Mrs. Lincoln thought it was too small and wished it had two floors instead of one and a half. It had a kitchen, living room, and two bedrooms on the first floor and two low ones under the roof. The furniture was —she looked around again, shaking her head—luxurious. In the back yard was a privy, a woodshed, and a stable for the horse. They had a cow, which grazed on the common or along the sides of the streets. Uncle Abe curried and fed the horse, milked the cow, brought in wood. . . . Springfield? Well, it wasn't such a wonderful town. The streets were full of mud, hogs wallowed in front of the houses. Refuse was all over the streets. It was not much bigger or better than Charleston. . . . Did she have to work hard? Harriet gave a faint smile. Well—at first she got the idea that Mrs. Lincoln had wanted her for a nursemaid, but Uncle Abe had put his foot down, told his wife they had brought her there for an education. Of course she had helped with the housework and baby tending, even though there was a servant. Mrs. Lincoln never seemed able to keep her servants very long. . . . Did she like her? Well—Harriet considered—Mrs. Lincoln was kind and most of the time good-natured, though she did have a temper. Yes, Harriet decided, on the whole she guessed she liked her. And it was obvious that, in spite of the fact that they often quarreled, Uncle Abe loved her and—she worshiped the ground he walked on.

Sally breathed a sigh of relief. The question she was most anxious to ask was answered. If two people just loved enough . . .

Evidently Harriet had satisfied her yen for adventure and further education, for the following year she married Augustus T. Chapman, and they settled in a home in Charleston.

That summer of 1846 brought an unexpected blessing. Abe appeared one day in July. "I've got to think something out," he told Sally and Tom. "There's something I've got to study." This time he had walked all the way from Springfield, about a hundred miles, and Sally was alarmed, he looked so tired. "I'll just lay around and think for a couple of days," he said. He stayed for two weeks rather than two days, as one of the Hall boys was to remember, "just a-layin' around and a-thinkin'." It was like old times, thought Sally happily, cooking his favorite foods and running to the door every few minutes just to look at him, reveling in the sight of his long body humped against a tree or of his jackknifed legs reared up out of the grass. After two weeks he said, "Well, I've done enough studying and I reckon I'd better go back to Mary."

She never found out what his problem had been and probably could not have understood it if she had. That was the summer he was campaigning for Congress, his party having nominated him by acclamation in May. The war with Mexico had just been declared. Was he struggling with his growing conviction that the war was both unnecessary and unjust, perhaps already formulating what would later become his "Spot Resolutions," demanding of the President whether the "spot" claimed as the site of Mexican aggression was really on American soil? Or was he probing his soul for an answer to his opponent in the political race, the fiery circuit rider, Peter Cartwright, who was accusing him of unorthodox beliefs? At least it was soon after this that he published one of the few statements he would make about his personal religious belief.

"That I am not a member of any Christian church, is true; but I have never denied the truth of the Scriptures; and I have never spoken with intentional disrespect of religion in general, or of any denomination of Christians in particular. . . ."

In fact, his religious views, as his law partner William Herndon was to express it later, "could be summed up in these two propositions: the Fatherhood of God and the brotherhood of man. He fully believed in a superintending and overruling Providence that guides and controls the operations of the world but maintained that law and order, and not their violation or suspension, are the appointed means by which this Providence is exercised."

Was it some of these problems he was pondering during those two weeks of "a-layin' around and a-thinkin'"? No one ever knew. To Sally all that mattered was his being there, and she treasured every moment.

Tom was amazed that his son would even think of running for Congress, especially against such a popular and powerful opponent as Peter Cartwright. "He's reachin' too fur agin. 'Course he'll never make it."

But he did, winning by a majority of 1,511 in the district, to Tom's amazement, chagrin, and, yes, pride. Sally shared only the pride. She had known he could do it. Tom was less proud of having a congressman son in Washington than having a lawyer son in Charleston. Protesting the injustice of a war in Mexico or introducing a bill to end slavery in the District of Columbia seemed far less impressive than making a family named True pay damages to Henry Eccles for destruction of buildings on his property, or clearing Wesley Gillinwater from a charge by William Frost that he had called Frost a thief, or winning a slander suit for Thomas McKibben against Jonathan Hart on the claim that Hart had called McKibben a horse thief. In the latter suit Abe had had his fee of thirty-five dollars assigned to his father, as he did for many of his suits pleaded in Coles County.

Tom, always in need of having his ego bolstered, derived satisfaction from having neighbors and acquaintances look at him with respect, even a bit of awe, as the father of such an important son. And when such a local personage as Orlando Ficklin, legislator, congressman, lawyer, or Usher Linder, who had been attorney general of Illinois, both of whom were associated with Abe on the circuit, stopped him on the streets of Charleston, doffed their tall hats, and inquired solicitously after the family of their friend Mr. Lincoln, usually sharing with him some droll story or exploit of Abe's, his stooped shoulders assumed an almost jaunty straightness.

Linder told him about the time when, making a public speech in

Springfield, he had been grossly insulted and threatened by some ruffian in the gallery, and Abe and his friend Edward Baker had insisted on escorting him to his hotel, one on each side of him, to protect him if anybody tried to attack him.

"You know what your son said to me? He said my quarrel was his quarrel and that of the great Whig party, and my speech had been the greatest one made by any of us, and they wanted to honor, love, and defend me. That was no ordinary compliment coming from your son, for he's no flatterer. It was one of the proudest moments of my life."

Abe only occasionally shared one of his circuit experiences with the family and usually then only one he could tell with a chuckle.

"Did I tell you about the case tried before a justice of the peace in a little old schoolhouse where I had to stoop to get in the door, and the seats were so low I had to double my legs like a jackknife? Horribly uncomfortable, nigh unbearable. No loss without some gain! I says to the judge, 'Your Honor, with your permission I'll sit up nearer to the gentlemen of the jury, for it hurts my legs less to rub my calves against the bench than it does to skin my shins!' So there I was, up next to the jury, where I always like to be."

Or—"One night Judge Treat, with me and three other lawyers, were staying at a farmhouse east of here and were all put in two connecting rooms to sleep. In one of them was a fire which cast fitful flashes of light, sort of ghostly. Judge Treat was cold in the room with no fire, and getting up in his long nightgown to visit the fireplace, he woke up General Linder, who's a mite superstitious. Thinkin' he was seein' a ghost, Linder put up the most terrible shriek, which I vow chilled my blood to the end of its capillaries. No one could imagine what an awful terror that voice conveyed!"

He never boasted of his successes. If he told them of a law case, it was either one he had failed to win or which afforded opportunity for one of his humorous yarns, like the case of the stolen hens.

"Did I ever tell you about the case I tried over in another county where the defendant was accused of stealing hens? Well, there was not the slightest doubt he was guilty as a fox caught in a chicken coop. Of course he got convicted. After the court was adjourned, as I was ridin' to the next town, one of the jurors came cantering up behind me. 'You did right well,' he complimented me, 'the way you handled that prosecution.' I thanked him, trying my hardest to look modest. Then he went on, 'Why, when I was young and my back was strong, and the country was new, I didn't mind takin' off a sheep now and then what didn't belong to me. But stealin' hens! Oh, Jerusalem!' "

But there was one case right there in Charleston about which Abe did no joking. Never had Sally seen him so torn between duty and conscience. It came up in Circuit Court in October 1847, and it involved the freedom of a black woman, Jane Bryant, and her four children. It was Illinois law that once a black had established permanent residence in the state he became free.

Robert Matson of Kentucky owned farm land in Coles County and was in the habit of bringing in slaves each spring to work it and taking them back in the fall. His foreman, Anthony Bryant, having become a permanent resident, was free. That spring Matson had brought Bryant's wife Jane with their four children to work the farm, but before he could return them in the fall Bryant had taken them to the homes of two Coles County abolitionists, Rutherford and Ashmore, for protection, to prevent their being returned to Kentucky. Matson filed a claim, and they were lodged in the Coles County jail. Matson swore they were his slaves, that under the law they must be kept, advertised, and their labor sold to pay for their keep. The sheriff filed a claim against Matson for $107.30 for "keeping and dieting five Negroes" at 37 cents each a day. Ficklin, representing Ashmore, filed for their release through habeas corpus. Then Matson sued both Rutherford and Ashmore for taking his slaves from him.

Abe was in Charleston that October for the Circuit Court. Usher Linder, representing Matson, asked him to help him in the suit, and Abe, without knowing what was involved, agreed. Dr. Rutherford, who was also his friend, came to beg his services.

"I found him at the tavern," Rutherford was to recount later, "sitting on the verandah, chair tilted back, against one of the wooden pillars entertaining the bystanders and loungers with one of his stories. Before he could start another I called him aside. "

When Rutherford made his request, Abe looked troubled. Since he had already counseled with his friend Linder, he felt he was under professional obligation not to represent the other side of the case. Rutherford went away, hurt and irritated. Though Abe secured a possible release from Linder, he found Rutherford had employed another lawyer and he felt bound to fulfill his agreement with Linder.

Before the case came up on October 16 he spent some time at the farm, moody and preoccupied.

"I don't like it," worried Tom, "I thought you didn't b'lieve in folks havin' slaves, yet here you are helpin' this man from Kaintuck take away this Bryant's wife and young'uns."

"I know," returned Abe, his face seeming even more gaunt and hollow-cheeked than usual. "And I don't like slavery any better than you. But I'm a lawyer, Pa, and it's my duty to uphold the law, just as it's my duty, if I don't like the way it's written, to try and change it. Slavery's recognized by the Constitution, and a slave owner has his rights, even in a free state."

Sally's heart ached for him. He's tryin' to decide what's right and wrong, she told herself, and it ain't easy. But once he gits his mind made up, I reckon there'll be no stoppin' him.

Abe argued the case for Matson in a courthouse crammed to the doors with a curious and emotional crowd, including his father. He began by admitting that if the Negroes had been permanently located by their master in Illinois, such action made them free. Then with cold, unemotional logic he presented the facts, that apparently Matson had publicly declared that he was not placing them there for permanent settlement and that he had made no counter statement. It was considered by many present that it was a weak presentation, eloquent and technically flawless, but fatal to his client's case. The decision was in favor of the Negroes, and Jane Bryant and her children were free.

Abe returned to the farm before leaving for Springfield, soon to depart with his family to Washington for his first term in Congress. He's glad he lost the case, thought Sally, noting the relaxed lines of his face and his lighthearted gaiety as he romped with the children.

The following year Tom and John D. were again in financial trouble. It was over a debt of seven years' standing when Tom had mortgaged his farm for fifty dollars. He thought he had paid it long ago but could find no receipt.

"We've got to write to Abe," he told John D. in December 1848. "You sit down and write. I'll tell you what to say."

Obediently John D. wrote.

"Dear Son I will in form you I and the old womman is in the best of health at this time and soe is all of the relations at present. I be-lieve I injoy as good health at this time as I have for many years and

I hope these few lines will find you enjoying the same state of health. I was gratly in hopes that you would have come a past heer on your way to Washington as I wished to see you, but as you faild to come a past, I am compeled to make a request by letter to you for the Lone of Twenty dollars, which sum I am compeled to razes, or my Land will be sold I have beged time Till I could wright to you to send me that a mount of money by Letter Send it to me if you can, for neither I nor Johnston can razes it for we have nothing that will bring money."

The letter went on to tell about the debt which he thought he had paid. As for the lawyers' bills which Abe had given him for some of his work in Coles County to collect for his own use . . .

"Yes, what about them?" demanded Sally, interrupting Tom's dictation with shocked disapproval. "Why can't you git the money for them and use it to pay our debts? Abe's done enough for us already. You shouldn't be beggin' him for money."

Tom fidgeted uneasily. Well, he *had* tried to collect on the notes. In fact, the one on Robert Mattison he had tried to sell for fifteen dollars cash and couldn't, people knowin' Mattison wasn't one to pay. So James Miller had offered John D. twenty dollars in goods at his store in exchange for the note, and Tom had been advised to take it.

Sally's lips set tightly, but there was more of pained resignation in her eyes than anger. So that was how John D. had got that new suit of store clothes he had been wearing to the play parties and cornhuskings! She should have known that he had not earned the money for it by hard work. If only Tom would not spoil him!

"Don't worry, Ma." John D. laid down his quill, came to her side, and looked down at her, smiling, blue eyes mischievously alight and lips quirked in the expression that reminded her so poignantly of Daniel. "We ain't askin' for much. And old Abe kin afford it. Why, he's bein' paid eight whole dollars a day for jist sittin' over thar in Washington and tellin' us what to do. He's a rich man!"

Sally shook her head helplessly. It was only this year, she knew, that Abe had finally, after long struggle, succeeded in paying off his "national debt." "But—" she began.

He chucked her under the chin, exactly as Daniel had done when he wanted to forestall criticism, and looked down at her with the same guileless charm. "Come on, Ma. Don't look so glum. Old Abe's family, ain't he? It ain't like we was askin' help from strangers."

She did smile, sighing at the same time. She would have been still more disturbed had she known that John D. added a letter of his own to the one he wrote for Tom, asking for eighty dollars for himself. The reply came as soon as the slow mails permitted, with an enclosure of twenty dollars and a letter. John D. read aloud the words intended for his father but not the letter to himself, which commenced at the bottom of the page.

"Dear Johnston: I do not think it best to comply with your request now. At various times when I have helped you a little, you have said to me, 'We can get along very well now,' but in a very short time I find you in the same difficulty again. Now this can only happen by some defect in your *conduct*. What that defect is, I think I know. You are not *lazy,* and still you *are* an *idler.* . . .

"You are now in need of some money; and what I propose is, that you should go to work 'tooth and nails' for somebody who will give you money for it. Let father and the boys take charge of your things at home—prepare for a crop, and make a crop; and you to go to work for the best money wages, or in discharge of any debt you owe, that you can get. And to secure you a fair reward for your labor, I now promise you, that for every dollar you will, between this and the first of next May, get for your own labor, either in money, or as your own indebtedness, I will then give you another dollar. . . .

"You say you would almost give your place in Heaven for $70 or $80. Then you value your place in Heaven very cheaply for I am sure with the offer I make you get the seventy or eighty dollars for four or five months work. You say if I will furnish you the money you will deed me the land, and, if you don't pay the money back, you will deliver possession. Nonsense! If you can't now live *with* the land, how will you then live without it? You have always been kind to me, and I do not mean to be unkind to you. On the contrary, if you will but follow my advice, you will find it worth more than eighty times eighty dollars to you. Affectionately your brother, A. Lincoln."

Sally never knew that John D. had asked Abe for money. As with every letter written to his father by Abe, she took this one from John D. and placed it carefully with others in a drawer of her bureau. Before putting it away, she smoothed it out and looked yearningly at

the unintelligible black markings on the sheets. If only . . . Had she
but known it, there were blessings sometimes in being unable to read.

$$= 7 =$$

It was just before dawn, Friday, May 25, 1849. Sally went to the
bucket of water, wrung out a cloth and, returning to the bed, laid it
on Tom's burning forehead, as she had been doing over and over
through the night. He stared up at her, eyes wide and empty. "Abe—
where is he? I want to see Abe—my son."

"Yes, love, yes. We'll try to git him. Lie back now, or you'll git to
strainin' for breath agin."

She went into the adjoining room and wakened John D. He struggled up out of a deep sleep and started up in alarm. "Pa—?"

"He's no better. You must go git the doctor agin. And he keeps
askin' for Abe. I want you should write him."

John D. dressed quickly, saddled his horse, and rode off through
the gray dawn to Charleston. After summoning the doctor, he went
to Harriet's house, asked for a quill and paper, and wrote to Abe.

"Dear Brother: I hast to inform you That father is yet a live &
that is all & he craves to See you all the time & he wonts you to
Come if you ar able to git hure, for you are his only Chil that is of
his own flush & blood & it is nothing more than natere for him to
crave to See you, he says he has all most Despared of Seeing you, &
he wonts you to prepare to meet him in the unknown world, or in
heven, for he thinks that ower Savour Savour has a crown of glory,
prepared for *him* I wright this with a bursting hart, I Came to town
for the Docttor, & I won you to make an effort Come, if you are able
to get hure, & he wonts me to tell your wife that he Loves hure &
want hur to prepare to meet him at ower Savours feet, we are all
well, your Brother in hast J. D. Johnston."

John D. persuaded Harriet's husband to write also. Tom had been severely ill for four days, Gus Chapman stated in his letter, with lesion of the heart, and was very anxious to see Abe. "I am told that His Cries for you for the last few days are truly Heart-Rendering." He added, "If you are fearfull of leaving your family on account of the Children & can bring them With you we would be very Glad for you to bring them, the Health of our place is excellent & Harriet & I would be very glad to Have you bring them as we are very comfortably fixed & will do all we can to render your stay agreeable. Yours in great Haste, A. H. Chapman."

Three days later Chapman wrote Abe again, telling him that his father was out of danger and was not afflicted with the disease of the heart as Dr. Allison had supposed but that his illness had resulted from an unusual amount of matter confined to his lungs. He hoped Abe would receive this before he left and was sorry if his last letter had caused him to leave any important business.

But Abe had already left for Coles County before the second letter arrived. Sally's joy over his coming was mingled with contrition. "If I'd ha' known," she apologized, "I wouldn't have had John D. write. You're so turrible busy. But your pa was so sick—"

"Of course." Abe patted her cheek reassuringly. "You know I'd want to be here."

When he had driven up with his own horse and buggy, probably having stopped at the Chapmans', Sally had been hopeful. "I—I don't s'pose you brung your wife or any of the young'uns? Harriet said Gus invited them."

"No." His eyes evaded hers. "It—it was hard right now for Mary to get away. Little Eddie hasn't been well. You know he's always been ailing."

"Oh, poor lamb!" Sally was instantly concerned. Though she had never seen them, Abe's two boys were as genuine objects of her love as her other more than twenty grandchildren. "His Robert Todd would be just your age," she would think, putting a slab of hoecake into Richard's grubby hands. Or, rocking four-year-old Dennis Friend to sleep, she would close her eyes and imagine she was holding little Eddie. Since the death of John D.'s Daniel just the year before, a weak mite that had lived less than a year, her capacity for vicarious motherhood had become inexhaustible.

"And your poor Mary!" she added now. "Of course she couldn't think of comin'. No good mother would. I hope you'll tell her how much we think of her and love her."

Again Abe patted her cheek. "I'll tell her," he said gently. "And she *is* a good mother, just as you have always been, Ma. And nobody knows that better than me."

Considering that Tom's recent cries for his son had been "Heart-Rendering," his reception of him now was strangely cool. Abe had come from the Chapmans' in haste without changing into more informal clothes, and Tom looked with disfavor on his conventional lawyer's garb, impressive in spite of its undeniable shabbiness—tall hat made shapeless from serving as a depository for papers, ill-fitting swallowtail coat, "high-water" pantaloons, and good leather, though unblacked, boots.

"You'd better git out o' them fancy togs," he said sourly, "and git out thar in the field hoein' corn. John D. says the crop ain't doin' so well, and I ain't been able to work much. That is, ef you ain't got so hifalutin' you're too proud to handle a hoe."

"No, Tom, no!" Sally intervened, shocked and distressed. "Abe's jist come, wantin' to see you because you was so sick. He ain't here to work. The farmin's John D.'s job. Abe's got more important things to do—"

Abe had flushed, a hot retort obviously on his lips. All the old conflict which had once tainted the father-son relationship seemed suddenly to have reared its head. Sally held her breath, crying silently, *Try to understand him, Abe. He's been sick. He don't mean it. He's really turrible proud of you. It's jist that you live in sich diff'rent worlds.*

Abe laughed good-naturedly. Straddling his long legs across a chair, he dangled his arms over its back. "You ain't the only one, Pa, what think I ain't got too much to be proud of. Listen to this." As sometimes in telling a story, he lapsed into the more careless speech of his pre-*Kirkham Grammar* days. "It was last year. I was goin' to Washington, on the stage from the tavern in Springfield, and thar was a man from old Kaintuck in my carriage. Guess he must ha' thought I looked like somebody with my long sad face, and he got friendly. Offered me a chaw of tobacky. 'No, sir, thank you,' says I. 'I never chew.' Purty soon he pulls from his pocket a leather-covered case and offers me a see-gar. 'No, thank ye, sir,' I says. 'I never smoke.' On we go, and as we near the station whar the horses are to be changed, he takes out a flask, pours a cup o' brandy, and holds it out. 'Wal, stranger,' he says, 'mebbe you'll take a little of this fine French brandy.' 'No, thank you,' says I, 'I never drink.' When we change stages he looks at me hard, shakin' his head as if I was some queer animal in a zoo and says, 'See here, stranger, you're a strange feller. I may never see you agin, and I don't want to offend you, but I want to say this: my experience has taught me that a man who has no vices has damned few virtues. Good day.' "

Tom laughed, and to Sally's relief the moment of tension passed. Bless you, son, she thought in silent gratitude. If there was further antagonism during his brief visit, it stayed beneath the surface. Though to come to Coles County Abe had postponed a trip to Washington to advance his candidacy for appointment as Commissioner of the General Land Office, he seemed in no hurry to leave. He regaled the family with details of his last year in Congress, his repeated failure to get a bill passed emancipating slaves in the District of Columbia; his trip through New England making speeches for Zachary Taylor, whom he had helped nominate as the Whig candidate for President.

"Imagine me, the country bloke with hayseed in my hair, goin' to Massachusetts, the most cultured state in the Union—yes, and to a grand dinner at the house of Levi Lincoln, a former governor! He said we might be related. Suppose we are, Pa?"

Tom shook his head. So far as he knew his family tree had put down its humble roots back in some obscure boondocks of Virginia, though he had heard rumors some of them might have been once in Pennsylvania. As a matter of fact, though Abe would never know it for a certainty, he and Levi Lincoln were related, both being descendants of Samuel Lincoln, who had migrated to Massachusetts from the west of England in the mid-1600s.

As always, Abe took time to romp with John D.'s children, paying special attention to the oldest, Tom, now twelve, who had been a cripple from birth. He kept them spellbound with descriptions of Niagara, which he had visited the previous fall on his way home from Washington.

"Imagine, its plunging, its roaring, its foaming, its mists, and when the sun shines, always rainbows! Think of it, young'uns. When Columbus discovered this continent, when Christ died on the cross, when Moses led Israel through the Red Sea—even when the first man came from the hand of his Maker—even then Niagara was roaring. The Mammoth and Mastodon, now so long dead, have gazed on Niagara. In that long, long time, never still for a single moment, never dried, never frozen, never slept, never rested. Imagine it, young'uns!"

He's a poet, thought Sally, looking at him in wonder, like that Shakespeare he used to read to me.

Then, though further postponement of his Washington trip might jeopardize his coveted appointment, Abe stayed just long enough to goad the reluctant John D. into hoeing and weeding the neglected corn by setting him an example.

"He might ha' stayed to finish it," complained Tom. "It ain't right, leavin' me and John D. with all that work to do."

Strange, thought Sally for the hundredth time, that Tom could be so sternly critical of his own son yet so unfortunately lenient with hers! Yet perhaps not so strange. Tom had never understood Abe. How could a plover be expected to understand an eagle that had somehow got hatched from its nest? John D. was another plover, though even Tom sometimes criticized the gaudy plumage of his stepson, which had won him the reputation of being the Beau Brummel of Goosenest Prairie, sporting the finest clothes to be had, whether they were paid for or not.

True, John D. was not always in favor with Tom. There was the time John D. had gone off on one of Tom's good horses and been away for some days, returning with a pair of young steers for which he had swapped the valuable horse. Arriving at night after the family had gone to bed, he had tied the yoked steers to a young sapling, and when Tom had gone out in the morning he had found them tangled in their ropes, stone dead.

"Got some beef, Granddaddy?" one of John D.'s sons had asked soberly.

"Yes," Tom had replied. "Beef to my sorrer."

Yet even such flagrant breaches of responsibility had not weakened the bond between them. And the delight Tom took in John D.'s children had undoubtedly strengthened the affection he felt for their father. As they had come year by year he had rocked their cradles, tossed them in his strong arms, been able to stop their crying as even their mother Mary could not do by singing to them his favorite song, "He-oh-a-nay, he-oh-a-nay, whoop!" "It's what the Injuns sing to their papooses," he had told them gaily, and never had it failed to turn tears into laughter. Tom had never been the same since the death of little Daniel. Nor had Sally herself. Another Daniel! She had suffered the loss of the first, it seemed, all over again, holding the small lifeless body in her arms.

John D. was restless. He had never liked farming, and the following winter he heard of an opportunity to increase his scanty income in a job offering the least possible exertion, carrying mail from Greenup in Cumberland County to Charleston, a distance of twenty-two miles.

"I'll write to Abe," he announced with enthusiasm. "Get him to back me for the job. He's a big man. They'll listen to him."

Abe's return letter was dated February 23, 1850. "Dear Brother," he wrote, "Your letter about a mail contract was received yesterday. I have made out a bid for you at $120, guaranteed it myself, got our P M here to certify it, and send it on. As you make no mention of it," the letter concluded, "I suppose you had not learned that we lost our little boy. He was sick fifty-two days and died the morning of the first day of this month. He was not our *first,* but our second child. We miss him very much. Your Brother in haste, A. Lincoln."

Abe's beloved Eddie, dead! Sally's grief eclipsed all her joy in John D.'s good fortune. Though they had never held the little four-year-old, her arms felt as empty as when they had laid the body of baby Daniel in the tiny coffin Tom had made. Here Abe and his Mary had been grieving over their loss for almost a month, and she had not known! It was as if somehow she had failed them.

But there was little time for grieving. With John D. away on his mail route much of the time Tom and the older boys must put in the crops. Tom had never recovered completely from his sickness. The oldest boy Thomas was poor help because of his crippled body, and the next two, Abraham and Squire, had inherited some of the carefree ways of their father. Sally often went into the fields to hoe and weed. John D.'s wife Mary had become a helpless invalid since the birth of her last child, and Sally was burdened with the whole care of the household. The only oasis in the desert of that long hot summer was Abe's brief visit on his round of the Eighth Circuit. He had not secured the Land Office appointment, due probably to his unpopular condemnation of the Mexican War, and was now devoting himself, with his new partner, William Herndon, to his law practice.

Sally regarded him anxiously, but, except for deeper grooves in his lined face and its habitual look of sadness, he seemed to have left grief behind him. Mary was pregnant again, he told her, and they were both looking forward to another "young'un" to take little Eddie's place. In fact, because of a lawsuit in which he had just participated the mood in the cabin was one of hilarity rather than sadness. Its details would soon be bruited with glee all over Coles County and in coming years over an ever-widening area as "The Hog-Killing Case."

A poor man in the county had been indicted for hog stealing. "Are you guilty or not guilty?" asked the court. "Not guilty." "Who is your attorney?" "I ain't got one, and I'm too poor to hire one." "In that case," said the court, "I will appoint one. Have you any preference among the members of the bar?" "I'll take that long tall one sittin' thar," he said. So Abe was appointed to defend him. Taking the man into a back room, he asked what were the facts of the case.

The man said, "Ain't got no facts. We'll jist jump in and fight 'em on gen'ral principles and you'll clear me as I know you kin." "No facts!" exclaimed Abe. "Here are a half dozen witnesses swearin' you stole those hogs. How is it you can tell me nothing? It's curious, mysterious." "It may be curous, mysterious to you," said the defendant, "but it ain't to me. It's clear as gunshot."

Abe scratched his head, saw something queer in the case but didn't know what. They went back into court and pleaded, "Not guilty." All the witnesses swore the man had stolen the hogs and sold them to various persons. It seemed a plain case of hog stealing. When the prosecutor finished, the defendant leaned toward Abe and whispered, "Itch in, go it on gen'ral principles, with a whoop and a yell, and I'll be cleared, you bet!" Abe was more and more puzzled. He got up and made an eloquent speech, appealing to the jury's sympathy but presenting no evidence, then asked the court to instruct the jury that if after all the evidence they had any doubt of the defendant's guilt, they would find him not guilty. The jury went out, returned. "Have you found the verdict?" They answered, "We have." All was suspense. The clerk read aloud, "We find the defendant not guilty." The prosecuting attorney sprang to his feet and demanded a new trial, which was denied.

Abe was even more mystified. It had been a plain case of hog stealing. He took the man out of the courthouse and walked away with him where no one could hear. "Now tell me the facts," he said.

"Come, let's have no fooling now." "Well, Lincoln, my good feller, I'll tell you. I did steal them hogs and more even than they said, lots more, and I sold 'em to my neighbors, the jurors. They knew that if I was convicted they'd have to pay for them hogs to the folks they reely belonged to. Now do you see why I knowed I'd be cleared?"

"Reminds me of another hog story," Abe drawled after the laughter over this one had subsided. "A man over country raised a porker so huge that strangers went out of their way to see it. One of them came one day and inquired about the animal. 'Wal, yes,' said the farmer, 'I got sich a critter, a mighty big one, but I guess I'll have to charge you about a shillin' for lookin' at him.' The stranger gazed at the man, pulled out a shilling, handed it to him, and started off. 'Whar you goin'?' asked the farmer. 'Don't you want to see the hog?' 'No,' said the stranger, 'I've seen as big a hog as I want to see.' "

It was well that Abe had brought laughter into the cabin for a few brief hours that summer of 1850, for in months to come there would be many tears. That fall and winter would be an even more dreary desert, with no oases. On September 1 Sally closed Mary Johnston's tired eyes and, with the help of Tilda and other women neighbors, prepared her wasted body for one of Tom's sturdy cherry coffins. The tears she shed were of relief as well as sorrow, that the months of suffering were ended. She had loved Mary deeply, gladly undertaken the responsibilities the weaker woman had been unable to bear. Now she cheerfully assumed the continued management of the household, including John D.'s six children, ranging in age from Thomas, age thirteen, to Dennis, five.

It was John D., volatile, emotional, who mourned most deeply. For a time he seemed lost, at loose ends. He had long since forfeited his mail carrier route because of failure to keep his appointments and, with the crops in, there was little to occupy him except hunting, visiting the neighbors, and hanging about haunts of doubtful repute in nearby towns. Sally worried about him constantly. She was relieved when suddenly the handsome features sprang into fresh alertness and the blue eyes, so like Daniel's, radiated the old sparkle, though the source of this awakened excitement became the cause of greater worry.

"Missouri!" He spoke the word with awed exhilaration, as before him men had mouthed "Kaintuck," "Indianny," "Illinois," "Utopia," "The Promised Land." "It's the place we oughter be goin', Pa. People have been pourin' in ever since it became a state. Climate better'n here, winters not so cold. Folks say they grow corn ninety bushels to the acre!"

"Slaves," commented Tom. "State was let in to have slaves if they wanted under that Missouri Compromise thing." But there was a gleam of interest in his eyes.

Sally's heart sank. She had seen that gleam before. Impossible that at age seventy-two, after a severe sickness from which he had never fully recovered, he should even toy with the idea of further pioneering! But as the days passed and the nebulous fantasies became actual planning, she listened to the excited conversation with mounting dismay. John D. would go on a scouting trip to Missouri and look into prospects. It would be easy enough to sell the farm, all except the part Abe had bought for Tom, which was always called the "Abraham forty." John Hall, oldest son of Squire and Tilda, who lived on adjoining land, was planning to be married and had his eye on it.

The prospect of fresh adventure seemed to have given Tom a new lease on life. He set about repairing the old wagon, which had already endured three long treks. He swapped one of his good horses for two sturdy oxen better suited to the drawing of a pioneer wagon. And, strangely enough, he also began working to improve his present property, displaying more energy than he had been able to summon in years. One day a neighbor who was passing saw him grubbing up some hazelnut bushes.

"Why, Grandpap," he said in surprise, "I thought you was thinkin' of sellin' your farm."

"So I am," Tom returned with a grin, "but I ain't goin' to let my farm know it, not yet."

Sally remained silent. Even after John D. made his scouting trip to Missouri and returned with tales of a land flowing golden with wheat and cotton, if not with milk and honey, she remained calm on the surface, like the nearby stream, hiding its turbulence under a coating of ice. They would wait until spring to leave, John D. decided, as pioneers usually did, arriving in time to put in a crop before summer. Sally thought of finding someone to write to Abe but decided against it. A letter told of the arrival of his third son, Willie, in December, and she knew he had enough responsibilities of his own. Only to Tilda did she reveal her profound anxiety.

"Your pa's so excited and happy I cain't bear to spoil it. It'd be like prickin' a lovely rainbow bubble. And he seems almost hisself agin."

"But you cain't move agin," moaned Tilda. "It ain't right, at your age." She smiled. "Not that you look much older than you did when we was young'uns!"

It was true. At sixty-two Sally was still straight as an Indian, cheeks smooth, black hair, though threaded with gray, crisply curled in the frame of her sunbonnet.

"It ain't me I'm worried about," said Sally. "I could stand movin', startin' all over agin. It's Pa. He seems all young and strong agin, but it's like a fever. It ain't nat'ral. Anyway, thar's time yet. Nothin's reely decided, and mebbe somethin' will happen."

Something did. Tom's new-found strength suddenly ebbed, like the pricked bubble. He became seriously ill. Alarmed, John D. wrote two letters to Abe, urging him to come, but received no answer. After a visit to the farm Harriet wrote him, and on January 12, 1851, Abe sent John D. a reply.

"Dear Brother: On the day before yesterday I received a letter from Harriet. She says she has just returned from your house; and that Father is very low, and will hardly recover. . . . I received both your letters, and although I have not answered them, it is not because I have forgotten them, or been uninterested about them, but because it appeared to me I could write nothing which would do any good. You already know that I desire that neither Father or Mother shall be in want of any comfort either in health or sickness while they live; and I feel sure you have not failed to use my name, if necessary, to procure a doctor, and any thing else for Father in his present sickness. My business is such that I could hardly leave home now, if it were not, as it is, that my own wife is sick-abed. (It is a case of baby-sickness, and I suppose is not dangerous.) I sincerely hope Father may yet recover his health; but at all events tell him to call upon, and confide in, our great, and good, and merciful Maker, who will not turn away from him in any extremity. He notes the fall of a sparrow, and numbers the hairs of our heads; and He will not forget the dying man, who puts his trust in Him. Say to him that if we could meet now, it is doubtful whether it would not be more painful than pleasant; but that if it be his lot to go now, he will soon have a joyous meeting with many loved ones gone before; and where the rest of us, through the help of God, hope ere-long to join them.

Write me again when you receive this. Affectionately, A. Lincoln."

Sally understood. Of course Abe could not come. She was not alone during these agonizing days. Tilda and Betsy came to help with the nursing. Neighbors were kind. One of them, Mrs. Jane Fury, came often and read the Bible to Tom, a service which Sally, with all her love and solicitude, was unable to render.

At last, on January 17, 1851, it was over.

"The end came real suddenlike," she was to tell Abe later. "He'd had smotherin' spells like the one he had when you were here the last time, and then he seemed to get better. Then reel early one mornin' when it was just startin' to git light, he said to me, 'Sarah, I'm goin'.' And that was all. He was gone, that very minute."

A few days after his seventy-third birthday Tom Lincoln was laid in the last coffin he had made (he had always kept one on hand for emergencies) and buried in the Shiloh cemetery a mile and a half west of the cabin. Thomas Goodman of Charleston, minister of the Shiloh church as well as of others in the area, preached the funeral sermon. Since there was no Baptist church in the vicinity, Tom and Sally had faithfully attended services conducted by pastor Goodman in a church belonging to the Disciples of Christ. The funeral was held in the cabin, with the preacher standing in the open doorway, women and children inside the house, while men of the family and other neighbors stood outside. They need not have stood very near to participate for, as one neighbor child who lived half a mile away, related long afterward, she had heard it plainly, preacher Goodman being "a great man to 'holler.'"

Pastor Goodman was sincere in his eulogy, for many years later he would remember, "In his case I could not say aught but good. He was a consistent member through life of the Church of my choice—the Christian Church or the Church of Christ—and was as far as I know—and I was a very intimate friend—illiterate, yet always truthful, conscientious, and religious."

Some were critical because Abe had not come to the funeral. Not Sally. "He would ha' come if he could," she defended him stoutly. "He loved his father. But a sick wife and a new baby—he did right to stay right whar he was most needed."

Only to herself did she confess a hurt and disappointment. Had the gulf between them, growing wider through the years, been even deeper than she had thought? Had Tom's badgering finally aroused resentment rather than understanding? No. Abe was too big and generous for that. No matter how wide or deep a gulf, love was always able to cross it. And there had been love between Abe and his father.

$$=8=$$

A new year, a new decade, a new life. At first there was little change. The cabin must be cleaned, John D.'s family fed, spinning, weaving, sewing, soap making, washing, and other chores to be performed. At least, there was no more talk of Missouri. Hopefully, Sally planted flower seeds in front of the cabin, sweet pinks, marigolds, larkspur, bachelor's-buttons.

Abe came to Goosenest Prairie shortly after his father's death. He was comforting, loving, reassuring. "This will be your home, Mother, as long as you live, or as long as you wish. I promise."

He had inherited the eighty-acre farm from his father, but he had no desire to profit from it. He agreed to sell the eighty acres, with the cabin, to John D. for one dollar, reserving the "right of dower of Sarah Lincoln, widow of the late Thomas Lincoln, deceased." It was understood that John D. would give his mother a home there as long as she lived. The "Abraham forty" he would keep in his own name for Sally's protection. While there, Abe asked for the family Bible and entered additional notations about the births, marriages, and deaths of his father and mother.

After the barrenness of winter, the long months of grief and loneliness, spring came as always with its renewal of life. The cold winds riffling the dead prairie grass turned warm. And as the seeds she had planted sprang into green shoots Sally regained her usual equanimity and courage. Even without Tom life would go on much as it always had in the cabin.

She was mistaken. One day soon after Abe left, when John D. had been away for some days, his absence unexplained, he came riding

into the yard. "It's Pa, Grandmarm," announced young Dennis excitedly, "and he's got a woman with him."

Sally ran to the door. Betsy? Tilda? No, he was coming up the
path leading a stranger by the hand. Not a woman exactly, a young
girl, slender, pretty, eyes bold yet a little frightened. There was
conflict also in John D.'s expression—bravado, embarrassment, apology, a bit of sheepishness.

"This is Nancy Jane Williams, Ma, that is, she was Williams. Now
she's Johnston. She and me was married jist now. She's my new
wife."

Sally remained silent for a full minute. Words sprang to her lips.
*Married! No—you couldn't! Why, it's only six months since Mary—!
And—this slip of a girl? Why, she can't be more'n sixteen, and you're
forty-one! Oh, my son, what have you done!*

But she did not speak them. It was the frightened, not the bold
look in the girl's eyes which stifled them. She reached out her arms.
"My dear, I'm so sorry we didn't know. John D. should have told us.
We'd have given you a better welcome. You say your name is—
Nancy?" She choked a little on the word. "It's a beautiful name. I've
always loved it. Come in, my dear. And, children"—she turned to the
surrounding faces, a mixture of curiosity, wonder, disbelief, hostility
—"say hello to—to your new mother."

It was Betsy, Tilda, and Harriet who voiced the emotions Sally
had felt but not expressed.

"Shameful! Why, she's jist a chit of a thing!"

"Sixteen, not much older'n John D.'s Thomas. He must have been
out of his mind."

"You can't stay there, Mother. Come to us." Both Betsy and Tilda
were urgent.

"No, we want you, Grandmarm." This from Harriet. "We have
lots of room. And you'll be right in town, near the church, near Aunt
Betsy. Please come to us."

Sally refused all their offers. She agreed that John D. and his new
wife should be left alone, at least for a while. Her niece Hannah Sawyer had been wanting her to come for a visit, and she would go
there for a few weeks, or perhaps months. She did so, but before the
end of summer John D. came to Wabash Point, urging her to come
home. The family was at loose ends, the children unruly, Nancy unable to manage. Gratefully, for she had been homesick, Sally returned

with him, assumed management of the household to the inept Nancy's relief, and tried to restore order to the totally disorganized family.

But once more, to her dismay, the restlessness was in John D.'s eyes. He talked again of the alluring prospects in Missouri, and once she overheard him talking with her grandson John Hall about a possible sale of the land. The farm, all except the "Abraham forty," was now his, the deed having been enclosed in a letter from Abe the last of August. John D. had read her the letter.

"Inclosed is the deed for the land. We are all well, and have nothing in the way of news. We have had no cholera here for about two weeks. Give my love to all, and especially to Mother."

Bless you, Abe! With every such indication of his affection her heart swelled with thankfulness. Since Tom's death he had regularly sent her ten dollars every month. Since John D.'s work was, as usual, spasmodic, the money had been spent on necessities for the family.

Abe was in Charleston the first of November for the Eighth Circuit court, but to her disappointment he was unable to visit Goosenest Prairie, law cases having consumed all his time before the court moved on to Shelbyville. Soon after a letter came to John D. which he did not read aloud in its entirety. But from his dour expression she could almost guess what was in it.

"Dear Brother: When I came into Charleston day before yesterday I learned that you are anxious to sell the land where you live and move to Missouri. I cannot but think such a notion is utterly foolish. What can you do in Missouri better than here? Is the land any richer? . . . You have raised no crop this year, and what you really want is to sell the land, get the money and spend it. . . . Now I feel it my duty to have no hand in such foolery. I feel that it is so even on your account; and particularly on *Mother's* account. The Eastern Forty acres I intend to keep for Mother while she lives. If you *will not cultivate it,* it will rent for enough to support her. Her dower in the other two forties she can let you have, and no thanks to me.

"Now do not misunderstand this letter. I do not write it in any unkindness. I write it in order, if possible, to get you to *face* the truth. Your thousand pretenses for not getting along better are all nonsense. *Go to work* is the only cure for your case."

John D. read her the postscript of the letter. "A word for Mother. Chapman tells me he wants you to go and live with him. If I were you I would try it awhile. If you get tired of it (as I think you will not) you can return to your own home. Chapman feels very kindly to you, and I have no doubt he will make your situation very pleasant."

John D. sold the farm to his cousin John Hall for two hundred and fifty dollars. He wanted also to sell Abe's forty acres, putting the money at interest for Sally. To this plan Abe acquiesced, provided the land could be sold for three hundred dollars. But before he made a deed he insisted that the money must be secured beyond all doubt, so that it could be put at interest for her at 10 per cent. John D., who had hoped to get a hundred dollars out of the sale for himself, putting only two hundred at interest for Sally, was thwarted in this proposal by another sharp letter from Abe.

No! "She had a right of Dower (that is, the use of one-third for life) in the other two forties, but it seems she has already let you take that, hook and line. She now has the use of the whole of the east forty as long as she lives; but you propose to sell it for three hundred dollars, take one hundred away with you, and leave her two hundred at 8 percent, making her the *enormous* sum of 16 dollars a year. Now if you are satisfied with treating her in that way, I am not. . . ."

John D. left with Nancy and his younger children in February 1852, not for Missouri but for Arkansas, buying a farm on the White River near where Nancy's father and mother now lived. Sally's grandson John Hall moved into the cabin with his young wife, Elizabeth Jane, and he invited Sally to live there with them. Except for brief visits with her daughters and with the Chapmans in Springfield, she was to remain there for the rest of her life.

She was not unhappy. Tilda's son was kind, his wife easygoing and good-natured. Both were young and as the babies came Sally felt herself needed. She was surrounded by the familiar, her bureau, the corner cupboard Tom had fashioned with such painstaking care, Abe's old desk-bookcase, the bed she and Tom had shared, her spinning wheel and loom, even the iron andirons, grindstone, soap kettle, cooking pots, and all the other utensils they had brought from Indiana, for the Halls, newly married, had few possessions. She had enough income from rent of the "Abraham forty" and the money Abe insisted on sending to feel independent. Tilda, since Squire's death in 1851, was lonely, and Sally spent much time with her on the neighboring farm, both as companion and as helper in caring for the younger of her eight children.

Yet life was a monotone, without the vibrant color of the years when she and Tom had loved, raised children, scrimped, built cabins, yes, even climbed mountains, forded streams, braved wild animals, wrested new land from the wilderness. Perhaps it was better so, that as one grew older life should be reduced to duns and grays.

There were black stains among the dull hues, as when John D., after returning from an unsatisfactory few months in Arkansas to settle near Mattoon, died on April 1, 1854. Poor John D., she mourned as they laid him to rest in the little cemetery. So handsome, debonair, jaunty, lovable, yet so gaily irresponsible, leaving behind him a young wife, seven children including a baby, another John D., some unpaid notes to Charleston merchants, and personal property appraised at $55.90. The two oldest boys, Thomas and Abraham, were already becoming involved in minor misdemeanors in and about Charleston.

In 1851 John D. had suggested to Abe that his namesake Abraham live in his Springfield home and attend school, but Abe, passing the decision to his wife, had refused. Mary Lincoln had been wise, thought Sally. The thirteen-year-old boy about whom she knew nothing, except that his father was a shiftless ne'er-do-well, would have been a poor influence for her own Robert, age eight, and William, eleven months.

"Stuck-up old high and mighty!" John D. had fumed. "Don't want to dirty her fine house with us poor relations." But Sally had not agreed. She had much more sympathy for Mary Lincoln than the rest of the family.

There were flashes of bright color amid the duns and grays, for twice each year Abe came to Charleston and almost always visited the cabin. Sally counted the months, weeks, days between his visits. When each spring and fall the Circuit Court came to Charleston it was a gala occasion. Women and children piled into wagons and flocked with their men to town, camping out for the three or four days of court, buying provisions for the next six months, listening to political speeches, watching wrestling matches, attending magic lantern shows. Not Sally. She remained in the cabin, making ready, watching. She made up the bunk bed in the southwest corner of the new room with her best sheets and coverlet, for since Abe had become a famous lawyer the family had decided he should sleep no longer in the loft. She cooked all the food he liked best and which could be made ahead of time, leaving his favorite corn cakes to be made fresh. But much of the time she just watched, waited.

"Grandmarm used to stand and look down the road out of that air winder," John Hall would remember, pointing to the south side of the west room, "and watch and watch fur Uncle Abe, and when she'd see him comin' she'd put her hands together and drop down on her knees and say, 'Thar comes my boy, my boy.' Grandmarm was allers the first to see him comin' down the road or across the medder and she'd jest stand still and cry and cry and say, 'Thar comes my boy Abe.' Oh, it was joyful to see those two meet. Wal, he never did stop comin' nohow, and after he got to be a big man and wore a high hat he come jest the same, and it was never mentioned between Uncle Abe and grandmarm that it was strange and wonderful that he should be so great and honored a man for she never thought that nothin', no' how, was too great for him and often said, 'Thar's no stoppin' for Abe,' and one time when she said so to Uncle Dennis Hanks he says, says he, 'Why, I larned Abe to write with a feather pen made from a buzzard's wing and that's what made him so smart.' But grandmarm 'ud jist smile, quiet like and say, ' 'Twas in the boy else it'd never come out in the man.' "

To Sally he was always just "her Abe." One day she met the lawyer Usher Linder on a street in Charleston. "That stepson of yours, Mrs. Lincoln," he said, "I wonder if you know what a famous lawyer he's getting to be. People talk about him all over the Eighth Circuit, want him to represent them. For one thing, he's honest, which is more'n can be said for a lot of us. Like that 'dirty hands case,' as they call it. Abe brought suit for a client to collect some money he said was owing him. At the trial the defendant produced a receipt for the bill in full. Abe left the courtroom. The judge called for him. They found him washing his hands in the tavern. 'Tell the judge I can't come,' said old Abe. 'My hands are dirty and I came over to clean them.' "

Linden chuckled. "And, say, did you know he had a town named after him? It was over in Logan County. He was attorney to promoting the town. 'What name will you give it?' he asked his clients when writing the paper. 'Lincoln,' suggested somebody. 'You'd better not do that,' says old Abe, 'for I never knew anything named Lincoln that amounted to much.' But they named it after him just the same."

"It sounds like my Abe," said Sally, pleased but unsurprised.

Nor would she have been surprised to learn that more than a hundred years later twenty-six states out of the nation's fifty would have towns of the same name, most of them derived from the same source.

Abe always came, sometimes in his buggy drawn by "Old Buck," lolling back against the seat, long legs over the dashboard, reading some book, which in those years of the mid-fifties was likely to be Euclid, the first six books of which he was bent on mastering. He would alight from the buggy shouting, "Hallo thar! Ain't you all glad to see me?" give Sally a bear hug, toss his silk plug hat, its lining bulging with papers, on a chair, put down his threadbare carpet bag containing an extra shirt, underwear, a homemade yellow flannel nightgown, hold out his arms to one of John's young'uns, and be ready for romping, devouring huge quantities of Sally's corn cakes as fast as she could make them.

Sometimes he would come walking from Charleston. Once Sarah Louisa, Tilda's daughter, had found him striding along the road and persuaded him to stroll through the woods with her so she could hear the latest news. Sally, standing at the gate holding a bunch of hollyhocks and "bouncing betties" that she had been picking in the front yard, saw them coming, the tall, ungainly figure wearing his stovepipe hat, in his hand an old black canvas satchel, beside him a young girl trying hard to keep up with him.

"Well," said Sarah Louisa, laughing, "I'd heard tell about how Uncle Abe was allus so kind to dumb critters, but till now I never knew how much! You should ha' seen him. On the way we run across a couple of big black snakes a-hangin' from a pawpaw tree. I said, 'Uncle Abe, come quick and kill them black varmints!' But what did he do? Jist turned around and seed them two, a-hangin' from a branch a-gettin' warm in the sun, and he walked off and wouldn't touch 'em. He says to me, 'No, no, their lives are just as sweet to them as ours are to us.' What do you think of that!"

"Sounds like him," said Sally, remembering the turtle.

For Abe the visits were welcome respites during his four hundred or so wearisome miles on the circuit, plagued by bumpy roads, black dust, insect pests, swarms of flies in the tall prairie grass, mosquitoes from still undrained pools. For the assembled family they were respites from farm drudgery, glimpses of a fascinating outer world, and always, when Abe was present, laughter.

"Did I ever tell you about the man I met in the stagecoach who gave me a present? No? Wal, this stranger says to me, 'Excuse me, sir, but I have an article in my possession which belongs to you.' 'How's that?' says I. He took a nice-lookin' jackknife out of his pocket. 'This knife,' he says, 'was placed in my hands some years ago, with the injunction that I was to keep it until I found a man uglier than myself. I have carried it all these years. Now let me say, sir, that I think you are fairly entitled to the property.' "

All laughed heartily, no one harder than Abe himself—all, that is, but Sally. The idea that anyone could call him ugly! Homely, perhaps, if you could call a rugged oak bole homely, but—ugly!

It was after 1854 that the conversations around the fire turned soberly to politics. After his failure to secure the land office appointment, Abe had devoted himself chiefly to his law work. Now something had happened to arouse his profound concern, and he was plunged again into political action. Though Sally listened intently, she understood only vaguely what the men were discussing. It was something called the Kansas-Nebraska Bill, opening the possibility of slavery into the vast areas across the Mississippi River. The new act passed by Congress, sponsored by Illinois Senator Stephen A. Douglas, and signed into law by President Franklin Pierce, gave the people of Nebraska the right to admit or exclude slavery as they chose, thus virtually repealing the Missouri Compromise of 1820, which had prohibited slavery above the thirty-six degree thirty minute latitude.

"And just four years ago," Abe said bitterly, "Douglas said the Missouri Compromise was akin to the Constitution and 'canonized in the heart of the American people as a sacred thing, which no ruthless hand would ever be reckless enough to disturb'! No wonder he says this new law of his will raise 'one heck of a storm'!"

It did, for the issue of the extension of slavery aroused seething dissension, and Abe as a leader of the Whig party was thrust into its vortex. Men from Charleston attending the state fair in Springfield in October brought back exciting news of debates in which Abe had responded in heated language to a fiery speech by Stephen A. Douglas. Sally was visiting the Chapmans later in October when Augustus brought home a copy of the Springfield paper telling of a debate held between Abe and Douglas in Peoria.

"Listen to this. Here's what Uncle Abe says in reply to Douglas' argument that every new grouping has the right to decide for itself whether it shall be free or slave.

" 'The doctrine of self-government is right, absolutely and eternally right, but it has no justification as here attempted. Or perhaps I should rather say that whether it has such just application depends upon whether a Negro is not, or is, a man. If he is not a man, in that case he who is a man may as a matter of self-government do just what he pleases with him. But if the Negro is a man, is it not to that extent a total destruction of self-government to say that he too shall not govern himself? When the white man governs himself, that is self-government; but when he governs himself and also governs another man, that is more than self-government. It is despotism. . . .

" 'Little by little, but steadily as man's march to the grave, we have been giving up the old for the new faith. Near eighty years ago we began by declaring that all men are created equal; but now from that beginning we have run down to the other declaration that for some men to enslave others is a "sacred right of self-government." These principles cannot stand together. They are as opposite as God and mammon.' "

Augustus looked about him in amazement. "Can you imagine Uncle Abe being able to talk like that?"

"Yes," said Sally, who had listened to a boy reading from Shakespeare and Franklin and Jefferson as he lay by the fire. "Yes, I kin imagine it right well."

Dissension over the question of slavery ripped the old political system apart, as those opposed to its extension—anti-Nebraska Whigs and Democrats, as well as Free-Soilers—gathered to form a new party known as "Republicans." By 1856 Abe had become a leader in this new party in Illinois, and as he rode about on trains, in buggies, in stagecoaches, making speeches, sometimes two in one day, his law practice suffered and to Sally's disappointment he often did not appear in Charleston on the circuit. Still he took time to rescue one of John D.'s sons from at least two serious predicaments.

In the summer of 1856 Thomas Johnston stole a watch from an old man named Green at Champaign, some fifty miles north of Charleston, and was put in jail in neighboring Urbana. He asked that his trial be delayed until his uncle could come to defend him. Soon after Abe and his lawyer friend Henry C. Whitney came to Urbana for a political meeting.

"There's a boy in the jail I want to see," Abe told Whitney, "the son of my stepbrother, whom I loved very much." He knew that Tom was also under a charge of stealing at Charleston.

Abe visited the jail and promised to help his nephew. "But it's the last time," he warned. "If you continue your thieving, I'll do nothing more for you."

After he had visited the jail, Whitney remembered, he had never seen Abe look more sad. He visited the Greens, and they agreed not to press the case, so Tom went free. Abe gave him some money, stern advice, and sent him home. For the case against Tom in Charleston, resulting in a fine of one dollar and costs and a sentence of one hour in jail, Abe arranged for the payment of the fine and costs.

Bless him, thought Sally, who had shed many tears over the sins of her wayward grandsons, for Abraham also had been in trouble with the law, having been indicted at least once for gambling. Yet even Abe's obvious love and concern could not compensate for his long absences.

The new Republican party of Illinois, meeting at their state convention in Springfield in June 1858, decided that it was going to give their state senator Douglas a "run for his life." By unanimous vote it passed a resolution: "Abraham Lincoln is the first and only choice of the Republicans of Illinois for the U. S. Senate." The campaign was on, an extravaganza of parades, brass bands, flags, rockets, red fire, massed throngs, and a series of scheduled addresses by the opposing candidates, acquiring such fame that they would be known for generations to come as the "Lincoln-Douglas debates." Chicago, Ottawa, Freeport, Jonesboro . . . From one center to another the candidates and their supporters traveled by train, stage, boat, buggy, speaking to tens of thousands of people, the battle between the "Little Giant" and his long-legged, long-armed opponent drawing headlines in papers all over the country, favorable or unfavorable, depending on the political affiliation.

The Philadelphia *Press,* speaking of Lincoln: "Poor fellow! he was writhing in the powerful grasp of an intellectual giant. His speech amounted to nothing. . . ."

The New York *Evening Post:* "In repose, I must confess that Long Abe's appearance is not comely. But stir him up and the fire of genius plays on every feature. Listening to him, calmly and unprejudiced, I was convinced that he has no superior as a stump speaker. . . ."

The Missouri *Republican:* "The joint discussion between the Tall Sucker and the Little Giant came off according to programme." Twelve thousand people had heard it.

"They're coming to Charleston!" Augustus Chapman drove to Goosenest Prairie with his horse and buggy to take Sally to town for the big event. "You must stay at our house if you want to see Uncle Abe. He'll have no time to come here. And, I'm telling you, you'll be amazed at the rumpus he's rousing!"

As they drove into town Sally *was* amazed. Crowds were already gathering, filling the two hotels. Banners hung from buildings. At the fairground where the debate was to be held benches were being set up, a platform being erected. It was like a big camp meeting.

"They're doin' all this for—for Abe?" Sally marveled.

"Not all," said Gus grimly. "Remember, Stephen Douglas is a hero here in Illinois. There are probably more Democrats here in Coles County than Whigs—or, as the party calls itself now, Republicans."

The Chapman house, even with its three good-sized rooms, all on one floor, was bulging with guests, as were most of the homes in Charleston, for people were pouring in from all over the county. They came in loaded wagons from Dog Town, Greasy Creek, Paradise, Muddy Point, Farmington, Goosenest Prairie. The Radleys were there, the Sawyers, Maltilda, now married to Reuben Moore of Farmington, some staying with Harriet and her husband, others with Dennis and Betsy.

It was Saturday, September 18, 1858, the most important day in the history of Charleston. Douglas and Lincoln had arrived in Mattoon the night before, Douglas in his special train car, Abe managing through his friend Whitney to get a chance to rest in an unoccupied space in an apartment car. Huge parades escorted the parties from Mattoon, though Douglas did not ride in his, preferring to come by train, his "Douglas Special," with baggage car, several coaches, and a flat car equipped with a brass cannon to announce his arrival.

Sally, wedged into the waiting crowd along the path where the Republican parade would pass, could not believe her eyes. There was a huge float drawn by eight horses, decorated with white muslin and silk and wild flowers, carrying thirty-two girls in white dresses and green velvet caps, each representing a state of the Union. Harriet, by her side, read her the words on the huge sign it bore: "Westward the Star of Empire Takes Its Way, Our Girls Link-on to Lincoln. Their Mothers Were for Clay." Another girl, riding a white horse, bore a banner that said, "I Will Be Free." The float was supposed to represent the Ship of State.

Sally watched, bewildered, eyes blinded by the bright sun and resplendent colors, ears pounding with the din of numerous brass bands and fife and drum corps, mind trying vainly to absorb the words on signs and banners read for her benefit.

"Edgar County Good for 500 Majority for the Little Giant!"

"This Government Made for White Men—Douglas for Life!"

"Abe the Giant Killer!"

"Support Abraham Lincoln, the Defender of Henry Clay!"

There was a giant banner eighty feet long hanging from the courthouse to a building on the west side of the square. Though it said, "Coles County 400 Majority for Lincoln," Sally's eyes saw only its picture of Abe looking like a boy again and standing in a wagon driving an ox team. She knew without being able to read the words that it was "Old Abe Thirty Years Ago."

But—where was *he?* Color, noise, splendor, excitement—they had only one meaning. Abe. She was going to see him.

"Look! There he is!" Harriet pressed her arm excitedly. "There's Uncle Abe!"

Yes, there he was, riding in a carriage, drawn by a span of cream-colored horses. Sally scanned his face anxiously. He looked tired and even thinner and more gaunt than usual, as if he hadn't been eating enough. What a pity he wouldn't have time to come to the cabin so she could feed him good hot corn bread spread with sausage meat!

"Wave to him!" urged Harriet. "Let him know you're here!"

"No, no," said Sally. "He's busy. He ain't got no time for us."

But the carriage had stopped. The tall figure leaped out of it, and suddenly she felt herself enfolded in the long familiar arms, half suffocating in their embrace.

"Thanks for comin', Ma," he said, giving her a hearty kiss. "I'm right glad you're here. Jist your bein' here helps a lot." Then he was back in the carriage and moving on.

That afternoon Sally sat with other members of the family on one of the rough backless benches in the fairground. She felt lost in the huge crowd, bigger even than the largest camp meeting she had ever attended. "There must be twelve thousand here," exulted Dennis. "Imagine! All comin' to hear Abe!"

"*And* Stephen Douglas," reminded Augustus grimly.

They had been lucky to get seats, for most of the crowd had to stand. Doubtless Abe himself had arranged for them to be seated, not in the front row, as Mrs. Stephen Douglas was placed, but at least not far from the big eighteen-by-thirty-foot platform.

"I hear tell Douglas got mad comin' from his hotel," chuckled Dennis. "When his carriage come along in the parade thar on the line o' march was a little banner showin' old Abe holdin' a club and jist about to slay the 'Little Giant.' Stuck his big gray hat out o' the carriage and said he'd git out o' the procession ef he couldn't be treated with respect!"

When Sally saw the "Little Giant" her heart sank. Though short of stature he was faultlessly dressed, confident in mien, towering over the crowd in spirit if not in body. While Abe . . . Oh, dear, she thought, his collar's all wilted, and his clothes . . . Even to her loving eyes and in much finer garb than he had ever worn in the old days, he seemed rough and uncouth beside this dapper, self-assured man of the world.

She was not the only one who thought so. Lew Wallace, later noted as the author of *Ben Hur,* was in the audience and afterward recalled that when Lincoln rose to speak, except for his "benignant eyes, a more unattractive man I had never seen thus the center of regard by so many people." Though his voice was clear without being strong and he seemed "easy and perfectly self-possessed," Wallace, a Douglas supporter, still felt like laughing. Until after ten minutes he was listening breathlessly, wondering if Douglas could possibly counter such effective arguments.

Abe spoke for an hour, then Douglas followed. Their arguments were much the same as in previous and following speeches. Douglas defended his "squatters' rights" policy. "Let each state mind its own business and let its neighbors alone! . . . If we stand by that principle then Mr. Lincoln will find that this republic can exist forever divided into free and slave states. . . . We can go on as we have done, increasing in wealth, in population, in power, and in all the elements of greatness, until we shall be the admiration and terror of the world."

Abe countered with his own position which, while not abolitionist, was antislavery. "You say slavery is wrong; but don't you constantly argue that this is not the right place to oppose it? You say it must not be opposed in the free states, because slavery is not here; it must not be opposed in the slave states, because it is there; it must not be opposed in politics, because that will make a fuss; it must not be opposed in the pulpit, because it is not religion. Then where is the place to oppose it?" Referring to the Supreme Court decision that slaves, since they were property, could not be voted out of new territories, Abe reverted to his usual humor. "I say, Douglas's Supreme Court cooperating with him, has *squatted* his 'Squatter Sovereignty' out. His argument is as thin as soup made by boiling the shadow of a pigeon that has starved to death."

Then he was all seriousness again, shaking his long finger, his voice whipping over the crowd like a lash. "Slavery! That is the real issue. That is the issue that will continue in this country when these poor tongues of Judge Douglas and myself shall be silent. It is the eternal struggle between these two principles—right and wrong—throughout the world. They are the two principles that have stood face to face from the beginning of time and will continue to struggle."

Sally did not follow the arguments. She knew only that Abe, *her* Abe, was keeping these thousands of people as spellbound as when he had stood on a stump and shamed the children for putting a live coal on the back of a turtle. Applause and cheering were quickly silenced so no one would fail to hear the speeches. Even those sitting on the east and south fences of the fairground did not lose a word. After the debate, when Lincoln and Douglas left the platform side by side, there were more parades. Mrs. Douglas in a stylish lavender-checked silk dress and a flamboyant bonnet was much in evidence. But not Mrs. Lincoln. Sally had hoped she might at last get a glimpse of Abe's wife, but Mary Lincoln had not come.

She saw Abe again that day, for he came to the Chapmans' house for supper before going to the huge political rallies, the Democrats in the courthouse, the Republicans in the public square. There were receptions and parties long after midnight. And, since his next appointment was in Sullivan on Monday, he was able to spend Sunday with his relatives. It was a quiet day, a lull after a torrential storm. That night, with Dennis and Betsy, Tilda, Harriet, and some of the grandchildren gathered around the candlelit room, Abe, jackknifed into a chair, feet propped against the wall higher than his head, spun yarns and joked.

Sally felt a strange sense of unreality. It could have been almost any evening in the past—yet none of them.

Abe had to leave early in the morning, by four o'clock, to get to Sullivan in time for his two o'clock meeting. John Will, who had brought him from Mattoon, was taking him in the same carriage. Sally got up in time to see him off. He tried to press fifty dollars into her hand, but she shook her head.

"No, Abe. Thank you, but I don't need it. Buy somethin' for your wife or that little new son of yours you love so much, named after my Thomas, the one you call Tad because—"

Abe laughed. "You remember? Because he had such a big head and tiny body when he was born he reminded me of a tadpole."

Once more he was the stranger of yesterday, tall silk hat, stiff pleated shirt, bow tie, frock coat, dignified and impressive in spite of their ill fit. She watched him go down the path to the waiting carriage, enter it, heard the driver "cluck, cluck" to the horses, saw them start along the street. Then quickly she turned back into the house, careful as always not to watch him out of sight.

$$= 9 =$$

Abe did not win the senate seat which he had struggled for. Although the Republican legislative candidates polled four thousand more votes in the November election than their opponents, the outdated apportionment law favoring the Democratic southern districts of the state assured Douglas' re-election by the state legislature. The vote there was fifty-four for Douglas and forty-six for Lincoln.

Sally sensed how deeply Abe must be disappointed. So keen was her sympathy with his moods and objectives that she could have understood his feelings as he walked home on election night. "The path had been worn pig-backed and was slippery," he would record later. "My foot slipped from under me, knocking the other out of the way; but I recovered and said to myself, 'It's a slip and not a fall.'"

Yet somehow she was infinitely relieved that he was not to become further embroiled in the frightening dissension which seemed to be sweeping not only the state but the country. Even a woman, and an illiterate one, could sense the undercurrents of violence which were stirring. Abe was fearless and outspoken on this explosive question of slavery. There had been catcalls and hoots of derision amid the applause during his speech in Charleston. Though it had been twenty years ago, she still remembered her horror when Elijah Lovejoy, a Presbyterian minister who edited an Abolitionist newspaper, had been murdered down in Alton, Illinois, after his printing presses, three of them in turn, had been seized and thrown into the river. And, though Abe claimed not to be an Abolitionist, his denunciations of slavery and virulent opposition to its extension in the territories had won him political enemies.

At least, thought Sally with relief, he's here in Springfield, not in that hotbed of Washington!

She had other worries as a mother. Tilda had not been happy in her marriage to Reuben Moore, and when the latter died in June 1859 she was left destitute. Before his death they had agreed to a separation and signed a contract which would give her six hundred dollars as her share of their jointly owned property. But Moore had destroyed this contract and in his will cut her off from any part of his estate. She appealed by letter to Abe to help her win the case, an application for her dower rights against the children of Reuben Moore. Though Abe was unable to come when the case was tried in October 1859, he requested Usher Linder to act in her behalf. Tilda won her suit, receiving as part of her dower rights the Moore house in Farmington, later known as Campbell, the nearest settlement to the Lincoln cabin. Through all the months of her worry and destitution Sally agonized with Tilda, comforted, advised. Tilda had had one son by Reuben, little Giles, who, together with the Moore children, was a defendant in the suit.

Though Sally's permanent home remained in the old cabin now owned by her grandson John Hall, she paid long visits to the Hankses and Chapmans in Charleston and to Tilda in Farmington. In December 1859 she was seventy-one years old, still Indian-straight, keen of mind and energetic, but suffering from occasional crippling bouts with rheumatism. However, she permitted no physical disability to prevent her sharing of labor in every household.

"How I wish ye could have seen and knowed grandmarm," John Hall was to tell an interviewer long afterward. "Jist after my third child wus born she got crippled, but she couldn't lay still in bed nohow. So she got my woman to tie a string to the cradle, and there she would lay and rock the baby."

Twenty-four living grandchildren and now constant additions in another generation, so many that she could hardly remember all their names! Yet still her arms felt an emptiness for never having held those other three, Robert, so old now that he was somewhere in school in the East, Willie, who must be almost ten, little Tad—no, not *little* any more, for he had been born back in 1853, and here it was now, 1860.

Abe had not come to Charleston since the great debates, but news came of him through Augustus Chapman's newspapers, Charleston lawyers who had met him on the circuit in other counties, occasional letters, the political gossip which could travel the hundred miles from Springfield to Charleston even faster than the big modern steam train, which, leaving Springfield about ten in the morning, arrived at Charleston a little after six in the evening, with only two changes, plus frequent stops to "wood up" for fuel.

Abe was speaking in Wisconsin at a state fair, in Ohio, at Columbus and Cincinnati. He was making speeches for the new Republican party in Kansas, which would soon come into the Union as a free state. He was trying to quell the incendiary furor over John Brown's attempt to instigate a slave revolt and his tragic end, praising the old man's courage while condemning his lawlessness; assuring northern critics that responsible Republicans repudiated such violence; assuring frightened Southerners that the North offered no objection to Brown's punishment, but warning that if they should attempt to destroy the Union "it will be our duty to deal with you as old John Brown has been dealt with."

In February 1860 he was in New York giving a speech to fifteen hundred people at Cooper Union, the largest assemblage, it was noted, "of the intellect and culture of the city." At New Haven, Connecticut, he was conducted to his lodgings by a brass band after an impressive speech. He was making a triumphant tour of the East.

Echoes of his speeches were heard even in such remote hamlets as Goosenest Prairie.

"Even though much provoked, let us do nothing through passion and ill temper." . . .

"Neither let us be slandered from our duty by false accusations against us, nor frightened from it by menaces of destruction to the Government nor of dungeons to ourselves." . . .

"Let us have faith that right makes might, and in that faith let us, to the end, dare to do our duty as we understand it." . . .

And then . . . "You won't believe this," said Dennis one day to Sally, "but they're sayin' "—he gulped—"they're sayin' Abe—*our Abe* —might git to be President of these United States!" He was obviously as amazed as if one of his farm horses had been entered in the Kentucky Derby.

Sally caught her breath, not in amazement, in distress. It had been frightening enough picturing him as a senator in that faraway Washington with the country torn by dissension. But—*President!* "Heaven forbid!" she murmured.

"It won't need to," Dennis quipped with irreverent levity. "Abe ain't no more likely to be President than I am to be Prince o' Whales. Mebbe he's got to be somebody here in Illinois but this is a big country."

Augustus Chapman, a loyal supporter of the new party and much more knowledgeable about politics than Dennis, also was skeptical of the rumor. "Even the Illinois Republicans aren't all behind Uncle Abe. A lot of those that used to be Whigs here in the north of the state think this Senator Seward's the right man, brilliant, well known all over the country, and Edward Bates is right popular in the south. Side of those two a raw westerner hasn't much chance."

But as spring came to Illinois the idea gained momentum like the swollen streams rushing headlong to the Father of Waters. The state Republican convention held in Decatur in May resulted in a resolution that "Abraham Lincoln is the choice of the Republican Party of Illinois for the Presidency." It was John Hanks, visiting Coles County soon after, who gave the family an account of his part in one of the convention's most dramatic acts. He had been walking along a street in Decatur one day when Dick Ogilvie, one of Abe's supporters, had come along and accosted him. Though he knew John had always been a Democrat, Ogilvie knew also that he was a relative of Abe's.

"Didn't you split rails with Abe Lincoln down on the Sangamon when he and his father moved to Illinois?" he had demanded.

"Sure I did," John had replied.

"S'pose any of those rails are still there in the fences?"

"Sure. Plenty of 'em."

They had gone down to the old place and found the fences. John had taken his knife and dug into one of the rails. Black walnut, and the stumps were still there to show where they came from.

"So we took two o' them rails," continued John, "to the makeshift buildin' whar the convention was bein' held. Someone had announced that an old Democrat had a contribution to make, and ev'rybody got up, cranin' their necks. So in I come, with them two rails on my shoulders with a banner what said:

ABRAHAM LINCOLN
THE RAIL CANDIDATE FOR PRESIDENT IN 1860
TWO RAILS FROM A LOT OF 3,000 MADE IN 1830
BY JOHN HANKS
AND ABE LINCOLN, WHOSE FATHER WAS THE FIRST
PIONEER OF MACON COUNTY

"Course that last waren't reely so," admitted John. "Tom waren't the fust. Fact is, I was here before him. But no harm to do a little fibbin' in a good cause. Wal, that thar convention went wild. Made so much to-do some o' the makeshift roof come down on their heads. When it got cleared up old Abe got up slow like, pointed at the rails, and drawled somethin' like, 'Wal, I cain't say whether I made them thar rails or not, but I sure have mauled some better ones.' No more danger of a divided delegation! Who knows? If old Abe gits to be President, mebbe it was old John Hanks what got him thar."

The swelling tide rushed on. When in June the Republican National Convention met in Chicago, a city already rivaling its industrial sisters in the East, the "rail-splitter from Illinois" was from the beginning one of the foremost candidates. Seward, Lincoln, Cameron, Chase, Bates. Soon the balloting narrowed down to two, Seward and Lincoln. Ballot after ballot as tension rose. Seward 173½, Lincoln 102 . . . Seward 184, Lincoln 181 . . . Lincoln 231½, needing 233 for the nomination. Then the Ohio delegation shifted four of its votes to Lincoln. Others followed. By acclamation the vote was made unanimous.

Wild yells, banners tossed, cannons blasted, the bells of the city clanged. Telegraph wires hummed, sending the news across the country, even into the small town of Charleston in Coles County, that a son of the West, a tall gaunt awkward giant of a man with big calloused hands and scraggy face, born in a log cabin, raised to hard labor, a humble country lawyer, a "rail-splitter," "diamond in the rough," "Honest Abe," had been nominated for the highest office in the land.

"Wal, Ma, how does it feel? Mother of a mebbe President?" . . . "Ain't it excitin', Grandmarm? Imagine! Uncle Abe!" . . . "We're so happy for you, Mrs. Lincoln. It must make you very proud." . . . "Tell us, would you ever have thought when he was growing up . . . ?" But the reactions were not always complimentary. In some faces she saw simple curiosity, envy, in others outright hostility. For political cleavages were deep. On the street, in church, even at neighborhood gatherings Sally encountered tightened lips, averted faces.

Yes, of course she was proud. And, yes, she had known Abe was special all the time he was growing up. Quietly she lived through the next months, waiting, listening. The Democrats had split into three factions, Douglas for the Northerners, Breckinridge for the South, Bell for a new Constitutional Union Party. If the Republicans won, a half dozen southern states threatened, they would secede from the Union.

"It won't be easy for Uncle Abe if he's elected," worried Augustus Chapman. "I reckon he'll have a powerful lot of trouble."

"Then mebbe it's jist as well he cain't win," said Dennis cheerfully. "No chanct at all with that Douglas runnin'."

Sally hoped he was right. She didn't want Abe to be President. She wanted him to be safe and happy in Springfield, traveling twice a year on the Eighth Circuit, not in that Washington sitting on the edge of a boiling cauldron. She kept having dreams, and she had grown up in a world which believed in dreams. Hadn't Tom dreamed of seeing her in her cabin before coming to marry her? She dreamed about Abe, and always he seemed to be heading toward some unknown tragedy—riding on his horse toward an abyss and vanishing, piloting his flatboat toward churning rapids, digging a deep well with the earth falling in . . .

Yet slowly her Calvinist heritage brought calmness of a sort, resignation, even acceptance, and she stopped dreaming. What was to be would be. Not that things were settled by blind fate, though in her pioneer world there was a strong belief in fatalism. No. Had she known better how to express it, she might have called it Destiny. There was something Abe had read to her out of that man Shakespeare. She tried hard to remember it. "There's a–a Divinity that–shapes–" Yes, that was it. "There's a Divinity that shapes our ends."

She was staying with Betsy on Election Day, a cold bleak November day with a hint of storm in the air. Like most of the town men Dennis went to the railroad station to learn the returns as they came in on the telegraph. She and Betsy did not go out. They kept their hands busy knitting socks, talking about unimportant things, and waiting. It was late that night when they heard bells ringing, shouting outside, and Dennis came bursting into the house.

"He's won! Our Abe's on top! Didn't I tell you he would?" He picked Sally up in his strong arms and spun her around. "How does it feel, Sally Lincoln, to be mother of the President of these United States?"

The vote had been decisive. Though his three opponents polled almost a million more votes than Abe, in the electoral college he would have 180 votes, Breckinridge 72, Bell 39, and Douglas only 12. His own Sangamon County had not voted for him, but he had carried all the northern states except New Jersey, not one in the South.

Though she was in the habit of spending the cold months in town, Sally insisted on going back to the farm that winter. She wanted to be among old, familiar things, away from the curiosity, the sudden almost obsequious respect, the envy, the frequent hostility that the townspeople accorded her, yes, and as far as possible from the news of an exploding, disrupting country.

Yet it reached her just the same. John Hall brought it from his trips to Charleston, Tilda from nearby Farmington. Neighbors, more attentive than usual, were anxious to share news, gossip, speculation, as well as food and drink, with the family which had suddenly sprung into incredible prominence.

In December South Carolina seceded from the Union. Between

January 9 and 11 Mississippi, Florida, and Alabama followed; on January 19, Georgia; in February, Louisiana and Texas. Revolt was sweeping the South. Federal forts and arsenals were being taken over. The lame-duck Congress was desperately trying to keep the Union together. The future President, waiting in Springfield, was being tormented by visitors, office-seekers, politicians, many urging him to compromise his position on the extension of slavery. By January, Washington, surrounded by slave territory, was tense. There were rumors of a plot to seize the city, threats of secessionist intentions to prevent the new President's inauguration, if necessary by assassination.

I know now, thought Sally, how Mary must have felt when she knew her son was going to Jerusalem. Sacrilege, such a thought? Again she asked the question, and again she answered it. No. All mothers became one in suffering.

Would she see Abe again before— Asking herself the question, she stopped, then finished firmly—before he went to Washington? No, of course not. He was too busy with important affairs to take time for a visit to his family. They couldn't expect it. Still, from force of habit, every time she heard the sound of a horse or wagon wheels or even a voice outside, she could not help running to the door.

"I know," said Elizabeth sympathetically. "You're hoping he might come."

The last week in January there was trouble with the chimney in the old cabin, and John and Elizabeth insisted that Sally go to Tilda's house in nearby Farmington until it could be fixed. She was there on the first day of February when Andrew Allison, a neighbor who lived a mile or so northwest of town, rode up to the house on his sweating horse, so full of excitement that he could scarcely speak.

"Miz' Moore! Miz' Lincoln! Guess who's comin'! I jist passed him ridin' in a buggy down the road, wheeled my horse round and rode fast as I could to git here fust! It's *him*—the President!"

Sally was in the door waiting when the buggy drove up. She saw three men in it, Gus Chapman driving, John Hanks, and— But it couldn't be Abe! Even when he alighted, came running up the path, gathered her into his long arms in the familiar hug, she could not make him seem real.

"You—you've got a beard!" she gasped. "I 'most didn't know you."

He laughed. "Right, Ma. You know who made me grow that? A little girl by the name of Grace Bedell. She wrote me that she thought I'd look better with a beard. I wrote her back that I didn't have a daughter but if I had and she'd asked me to grow a beard, I would. Then, too, some of my friends thought it would make me look more dignified. Does it, do you think?"

She regarded him fondly. "You look all right to me, son, beard or no beard. But—I reckon it does make you seem different—or mebbe it's because you've got to be somebody so—so important."

"I'm just the same old Abe, Ma. Nothin's changed me."

Oh, but you are changed, she thought, her eyes hungrily absorbing his features. The lines are longer, deeper. And your eyes, there's a sadness that wasn't there before. You look as if you've got a terrible load on your shoulders.

Aloud she said happily, "You've really come. I didn't think we'd see you again before—before you went to Washington."

"Ma! Did you really think I'd go without coming to say good-by?"

There was time before dinner, he decided, to go and visit his father's grave at Shiloh cemetery about a mile to the west, going by way of the cabin at Goosenest Prairie. While he and Gus Chapman were away on this trip and Sally and Tilda bustled about getting a festive dinner, John Hanks related some of the events of the previous day. They had arrived in Charleston a little after six in the evening. Abe had stopped last night at the Marshalls' big house on Washington Street. People had found out he was there, and hundreds had come to see him. The town's brass band had serenaded him, but Abe had refused to make a speech, telling one of his funny stories instead. The next morning he had gone to Dennis' house for breakfast, and more crowds had come. Abe was going to stay at the Chapmans' that night before leaving for Springfield in the morning.

Village neighbors had heard about Abe's coming, passed the word around, and insisted on helping with the meal. Chickens were killed and hastily prepared, pies were baked, chimneys began pouring forth smoke as the women of Farmington assisted in preparing dinner for the President-elect of the United States. It was the most exciting event that had ever occurred in the little town. School was dismissed, and the pupils with their teacher, Mr. Osborne, joined the crowd outside the Moore house gathered to greet the famous guest and shake his hand. Abe, always at home with children, shook their hands, joked. When one of them, little Emma Allison, who had recently injured her right hand in a sorghum mill accident, held out her left hand, he stooped and kissed her. "I'd rather be in your places than mine," he told them soberly. After he had gone in the house the children one by one put their feet in the overshoes he had left outside the door, so they could say afterward they had stood in the shoes of the President.

Tilda had set tables made of planks and sawhorses reaching from living room to kitchen. Sarah Louisa Hall, Tilda's daughter, was there, with her new husband Merrill Fox, also Tilda's sons, John Johnston and Joseph. Many of the neighbors who had helped with the dinner stayed. The festivities lasted until mid-afternoon. Sitting in her rocking chair, Abe standing beside her, one big hand rocking it gently while he rested the elbow of the other arm on the mantelpiece, Sally wished the afternoon would never end. Though she was going back with him to the Chapmans' to spend the night, she wanted every moment to last.

"Mr. Lincoln was simplicity itself," schoolteacher Osborne was to remember. "He seemed to enjoy it so much that his face was continually lit up with a sunny smile. All were at their ease."

"You're luckier than I was," said David Dryden when his son-in-law Osborne introduced him. "I got beaten for circuit clerk in Clark County."

"So?" said Abe, smiling. "Then just pick up your flint and try again. And I'm not so sure it was such good luck my winning, after all. Only God knows, and right now He's not saying."

Abe had brought Sally a new black dress and a fur cape as presents, and he insisted on her wearing the cape when they drove to Charleston. John Hanks and Gus rode back in another wagon, so for the few miles she had Abe all to herself. He told her of his trip to the cemetery, how he had cleared the ground about Tom's grave, cut the letters T. L. on a walnut board which he had taken with him, and placed it on the grave. He would send money, he promised, for a monument as soon as Gus Chapman told him what the cost would be.

The eight-mile ride was all too short. They talked of former days, reminisced, laughed, sat for long moments in silence. It was like reliving more than forty years in less than two hours. Or like what they said about a man drowning. . . . No, not that. She must not think of death, not yet. This was life, the best she had ever known.

That evening at Chapmans' another crowd soon gathered, and after supper Abe went to the Town Hall where a big reception had been arranged, people coming to greet him regardless of party politics. There were men there who remembered him as the stalwart young ox driver who had come with his family to Illinois. One man brought a horse which Abe in the days of his law practice had recovered for him in a replevin suit. Another remembered the details of his famous wrestling match with Daniel Needham. Of course they expected to hear a speech.

"You, my friends, are anxious to hear from me, what I think of the outlook for the future, but I am equally anxious with you, to see what lies before us, and you will therefore have to excuse me from saying more, but if it will be any gratification to you, I shall be glad to take each one of you by the hand." And he did so, yielding to the expressed desire of some of the bolder women that they might say they had kissed the cheek of the President of the United States.

Once more he had to leave by four in the morning to catch the train. Again Sally got up to bid him good-by. "I—I'm afraid I'll never see you again," she said brokenly when his arms went about her. "There are people who hate you, who—who want to kill you."

"No, no," he reassured her. "They won't do that. Trust in the Lord and all will be well. And—whatever happens, we will see each other again."

"God bless you and keep you, my good son," she sobbed. His own voice was too choked to answer.

Sally's eyes followed him as he went out into the dark where the buggy was waiting, climbed inside, and started away. This time she watched him out of sight.

Strange, that one could live life so normally in one small home when beyond its boundaries the world was being riven into fragments! that winters could merge into springs as usual, land give forth corn and wheat and roses when earth out beyond had become battlefields sown with flesh and blood! that one's hands could spin and weave and bake bread and scrub things clean when others were brandishing guns and swords!

But it was only in body that Sally performed the motions of normal living. In mind she was far away from whatever home she happened to be living in, with the sons-in-law and grandsons and other men of Coles County who were marching away in blue and fighting under incredible odds to drive back, maim, kill other men in gray; with the mothers and wives and sisters who were seeing men in both colors march away; especially with the grim, harassed, tortured, but intrepidly laughter-rousing man in far-off Washington who was commander-in-chief, shaper of a nation's destiny, beloved leader, butt of hatred and criticism in the war-torn country.

"As if it waren't enough his havin' this gol-durned war on his shoulders," Dennis grumbled to Sally. "Half the folks who ever shook his hand here in Coles County are pesterin' him for a job!"

Including, he might have added, his own son-in-law Augustus Chapman, who was anxious to be appointed postmaster of Charleston. Not securing the appointment, six months later, in 1861, Gus entered the Army as a major, was promoted to lieutenant-colonel in 1863, and served with distinction throughout the war.

And Dennis himself, though possibly without his consent, was not entirely free from the taint of seeking patronage, for somewhat later Betsy, Sally's daughter, wrote to Abe asking that Dennis be appointed postmaster. This also was not done, for, as Henry Whitney commented, "Lincoln regarded his obligation to duty as stronger than that to friendship."

Much later Dennis denied his responsibility in the seeking after patronage.

"As for myself," he wrote Abe's law partner Herndon, "I did not ask Abe rite out for an office only this I would like to have the post office in Charleston. This was my wife that asked him. He told hir that much was understood as much as to say I would git it. I did not care much about it."

Nothing for himself perhaps, yet Dennis was not above asking favors for his family. "Remember my Boys if you can," he wrote Abe in the spring of 1864. "I don't ask anything."

Nor were his sons-in-law hesitant about asking their powerful relative for favors. Allison Poorman, husband of Amanda, wrote Lincoln begging "for a permit to trade within the lines of the Western Army in all kinds of Merchandise, Liquors excepted." If Lincoln would grant this favor, it "will not soon be forgotten." And William Shriver, husband of Mary, another son-in-law of Dennis, requested a permit to trade "in Cotton and Hides for shipment North" within the lines of the Cumberland, Mississippi, and Arkansas.

Abe helpfully endorsed these applications and sent them on to the proper department. "The writer of the within is a family connection of mine, and a worthy man; and I shall be obliged if he be allowed what he requests, so far as the rules and exigencies of the public service will permit."

Sally resented all attempts to capitalize on intimate relationships. She wished fiercely that there were some way to protect him from all such unnecessary burdens, even the writing of occasional letters to members of the family, though she treasured every word and asked that each letter be read to her over and over.

She mourned the death of twelve-year-old Willie, who had fallen sick with a fever in February 1862 and lay dying upstairs while Abe welcomed guests in the East Room of the White House with, as one woman commented, "a sadder face than I have rarely seen." She agonized with the father who, lifting the cover from the face of his child, had murmured, "It is hard, hard, hard to have him die!" and with the mother so stricken with grief that never again would she enter the room where her son had died.

Even though she had never met Mary Todd Lincoln, Sally felt

during these tragic years a peculiar affinity with this woman who when Washington was in danger of falling refused to leave the side of her husband; who, though a Southerner and accused by some Northerners of being a traitor, stood staunchly in support of the Union cause; who could participate in the rejoicing of a nation over victories at Baton Rouge and Vicksburg, even though in the former battle her brother Alexander had lost his life and in the latter her brother David had been shot; who, though three of her brothers had died in the Confederate Army, had not permitted herself to shed a tear, in public at least, over any one of them. Silently Sally mourned with her.

Though the men of the family talked glibly of battles being fought in places with strange names—Bull Run, Antietam, Fredericksburg, Gettysburg, Chattanooga—Sally paid little heed to the details. Except that victory or defeat meant for Abe success or failure, she had little interest in their results. Of course she wanted the Union preserved, but largely because that was Abe's obsessive goal. Each day she waited in trepidation, fearing news of loss more tragic than defeat in battle. Each night she went to her bed with a prayer of thanksgiving.

"He's still safe, still alive!"

Only when the news came of his signing of the Emancipation Proclamation did she voice exultation. "He's done it! Didn't he say if he ever got a chance to hit it, he'd hit it hard? He's done freed the slaves!"

"Not yet, Grandmarm, that is, not all of 'em," corrected John Hall. "Thet thar proclamation jist frees slaves in the seceded states and not all of *them*. An' we got to win the war afore any of 'em'll be free. And even then it's got to be passed by Congress."

"It's a start," said Sally confidently. "We kin trust our Abe. He'll do it."

Her greatest bitterness during the war came from the factions right there in Coles County, even in Charleston, who expressed vocal antagonism to Abe, his policies, and the war itself, those who believed in compromise with the secessionists. By the fall of 1862 these dissenters were dubbed "Copperheads," a name adopted because of their fancied resemblance to the deadly snake which struck without warning. Once she herself to her utter dismay became the target of their attempts to discredit Abe and his party.

She was staying in Charleston with Betsy at the time. Going shopping one day she took into a store a small piece of calico to match with goods of the same pattern which she had bought previously. Someone saw her putting the sample in her pocket and leaving without making payment. She was taken to the county jail. Shocked, the local judge and clerk sent immediately for Judge Joseph Cannon, who had recently had Coles County added to his judicial circuit. Coming to Charleston, he consulted with the disturbed local judge. Though Mrs. Lincoln had admitted to having the cloth in her possession, they did not believe she could be a thief. In fact, they thought she was more likely the victim of a conspiracy, another episode in the Copperhead war.

Sally, detained in the jail, had never been more frightened, not for herself. But suppose the news got to Washington that the mother of the President was a thief! He would be disgraced! She had been too conscientious to deny the accusation, which was that she had been seen putting the cloth in her pocket and leaving without paying for it. Then there came a very kind-looking man, and in response to his questioning she blurted out the whole story. To her infinite relief he believed her.

"If we should prosecute Mrs. Lincoln," Judge Cannon told the local officials, "we would be joining in a conspiracy to injure the President." The complainants were summoned, and the judge expressed his disgust at their conduct and warned them that if they gave publicity to the affair the consequences would be most unpleasant. Fortunately they kept silent. Yet Sally would never recover from the hurt and indignity.

Once the Copperhead opposition exploded into open warfare. It was in March 1864.

"Abe," wrote Dennis Hanks to his cousin, "we had a horible time a Munday of court it broke up got in to a fuss by a drunkin Soldier I never saw such a time Thare was 8 or 10 killed in the fight one you no Doct York of paris Edgar County young E. winkler was wounded. . . ."

It was called the "Charleston Riot," a fight occurring between some soldiers on leave and some local "Copperheads," in which six soldiers and three civilians were killed and four soldiers and eight civilians wounded. It was the last day of furlough for men of the 54th Illinois Volunteer Infantry, and they were in town for a final celebration before rejoining their regiment. The "riot" was the blood-iest affair of its kind in the North during the war.

Twenty-nine persons were arrested by the military for partici-pation in the fight. Fifteen of them were sent to Fort Delaware in the East. Responsible people in Coles County, including Marshall and Ficklin, wrote Abe seeking release for the prisoners, some of whom were apparently innocent of the charge. At least, let them be handed over for trial by the civil rather than the military authorities.

"Most of them," wrote Marshall, "are poor miserable devils that can do little good or harm in any way. The leaders and indeed most of the actors in the affair here have so far escaped arrest."

But the President was under terrific pressure, by the military, who wanted revenge for their slain soldiers, by the election campaign marked by bitter opposition even from members of his own party, by the tense war situation. His action was delayed. Even a visit to Washington by Attorney Ficklin failed to secure the prisoners' release.

"I bet ten agin one I could git them boys off," boasted Dennis, "even if them smart lawyers cain't."

So confident were his boasts that finally friends of the prisoners raised twelve hundred dollars to send Dennis to Washington. In May he started off. Sally, staying in town with Betsy in their little second-floor apartment, watched from the window as a cheering crowd gath-ered about him in the square, ready to accompany him to the station. Neither she nor Betsy was able to join them. Now seventy-six, Sally to her disgust was becoming so crippled with rheumatism that she felt herself a burden to others, and Betsy had been ailing for some time.

"Denny'll be seein' Abe," rejoiced Sally. "He'll be able to tell us all about him."

"He sartin sure will," rejoined Betsy wryly, "with a speech a mile long."

Sally wondered how, with such an agonizing load on his shoulders, Abe could find time to concern himself with her needs. Only the pre-vious month he had sent Dennis fifty dollars for her use.

"Dere Abe," Dennis had written back, "I Received your Letter Check for $50.00 I shoed it to mother She crid like a child Abe She is mity childish heep of truble to us Betsy is very feble and has to wait on hir which ort to have some person to wait on hir we are getting old we have a great many to wait on of our connections they will cum to see us while we live. . . ."

Dennis returned and, as Betsy had predicted, immediately launched into a "speech a mile long." Yus, he'd been thar and seen him, and he was the same old Abe, lookin' fair to middlin', a mite thinner mebbe, cheeks more holler, eyes sad like a hound-dog till he started yarn-spinnin', then they lit up like a prairie fire.

"Thinner," worried Sally, "cheeks more hollow, eyes sad. Oh, my poor Abe!"

"Feller what stood at the door says thar's jist a sartin way to git in, but anyhow the President was busy. Then I says, if you'll jist show me the hole whar the President goes in, I'll git to see him. 'What's your name?' asks he. 'Hanks,' says I. 'I'm an American citizen, and I want to see Abe Lincoln.' 'That man talks like the President,' another one says. I waited a minute and nobody done nothin', so I jist speaks up agin and says I, 'Ef you'll take me up to his bedroom I'll have no trouble in gettin' in.' A feller took me up to a door to whar that Seward feller was a settin', and I looked through a bunch of men and saw Uncle Abe by a stove playin' with his little boy and handin' him some lemonade or somethin' and laughin' and talkin'. 'Abe,' I calls out in a loud voice, 'what you doin' thar?' Abe knowed my voice and says, 'Dennis, is that you?' He then invited me in and asked Mr. Seward and them other fellers to step out, 'fur,' says he, 'I want to see this man privately.' So they all goes out but me and Uncle Abe. He then asks me, 'How is mother gettin' along and all the rest of the family?' "

There was much more to the monologue. Dennis had told his business, and Abe, he remembered, had sort of agreed to free the prisoners. Though the order of their release would not come until the following November, Dennis would always believe that it was his visit which had persuaded the President to act. But he brought back a souvenir of the trip far more precious to him than a promise.

"Look!" Gleefully he pulled from his pocket a heavy, old-fashioned coin-silver watch with a steel chain. "Thar was Abe with this big watch an' a chain spread over his wescoat. I plagued him about bein' so fine, and he says, 'Denny, I bet you'd carry a watch like this if you had one, you old coon.' So he takes it right off and gives it to me. Says he kin git himself another right handy."

It became his most precious possession. Thirty-five years later, a very old man, Dennis would waken with a frightened cry, like a child out of a nightmare. "Whar's my watch? Whar's my watch?"

"Here, Father," his daughter Sarah Jane Dowling would comfort him, "here's your watch. Uncle Abe gave him that watch," she would explain to the woman who had come to interview the dead President's cousin, "and he gets to dreaming that someone is trying to rob him of it."

"It's beautiful," Sally told him now, remembering that it had once belonged to Tom. "I'm so glad you have it, Denny."

It was fortunate that she could not know the ill feeling between members of her family of which she was at least partly the cause. Soon after his return from Washington, with Betsy's illness growing steadily worse, Dennis wrote to John Hall.

"John I want you to cum and take grand Mother and keep hir until I see that your ant lives or not. . . . The time has cum that youall cant trot a round and she doo the worke for all. . . . Now John I have bin to see old Abe and now I say to you that that forty acres of land was left for your Grand mother's support and if you don't tend to it I will tend to it for you . . . but if you will rather pay the back rent rather than keep hir you must do it shore. . . ."

John Hall came and took Sally to the old home. The following December Betsy died, after a long sickness. While grieving for her daughter, Sally was thankful for her release from suffering. Only two of her children were left now, Matilda and Abe.

She would have been even more distressed had she known of the letters Harriet and John Hall were sending Abe in this crucial time of his presidency, each accusing the other of mistreating her.

"I was down to see Grand Ma Lincoln," wrote Harriet in January 1865. "She seems to be failing fast and is grieving herself to death about Mother. She is so destitute of every comfort. . . . I for one will do as I have always done my part in her behalf and now want you to assist me by giving my Husband a situation so that he can support his family and take good care of her as long as she lives if we should be spared that long. You can do this and not discomode yourself in the least and I think that Augustus deserves your favor. He has always been a strong Union man and spent both time and money in your election has now been in the Army for 3 years and 3 months and would remain longer if the family was better situated. . . ."

In his turn John Hall was writing similar accusations. "Private.

Dear Uncle, This leaves us all well but Grand Mother. She is quite puny. I write to inform you that Grand Mother has not and does not receive one cent of the money you send her Dennis and Chapman keep all the money you send her. She now needs clothing and shoes, they have the money in their Pockett. . . . I and my Mother are now taking care of her and have for the past four years. If you wish her to have anything send it by check here to the Bank of Charleston. . . ."

Sally felt no destitution. She was back in her own home, John and Elizabeth were kind to her, and the terrible war was drawing to a close. Her Abe had been elected for a second term. He had done all he set out to do, saved the Union, freed the slaves. And it was a morning in April, spring was coming. Already the warm winds were blowing over the prairies. The new sun was turning the morning dew into diamonds. The perennials she had planted by the cabin long ago were bursting into new life.

She was feeling almost young and spry again, had put on her apron and was helping Elizabeth cook corn bread for breakfast ("You kin make it so much better, Grandmarm, the children love your pone!") when the news came. They tried to break it to her gently, but there was little of gentleness to be found in the sharp deadly report of a gun. It sounded as sudden and loud and final in an Illinois cabin as in a theater in far-off Washington.

Sally groped for the folds of her apron and put it over her face. "Oh, my boy Abe, my boy!" she murmured. "They've killed you, I knowed they would, I knowed they would."

After some time she went to the door and looked out. It was still a morning in April. Dew was still on the grass, tears now instead of diamonds. The red and gold tulips were swaying in the warm wind. And away over the hills to the east the sky was very blue, a few white clouds floating in its depths like outspread wings. She stood looking at them a long time.

He's all yours now, Nancy dear, she thought. But thank you for sharing him with me a bit of a while.

Then she went back into the cabin and continued to make her corn cakes, putting the meal and water in the wooden bowl, kneading them into a soft dough, spreading the cakes in her iron pan and standing it by the fireplace, turning them at just the right time so they came out plump and nicely browned, just the way Abe had liked

them. She had never been able to keep him filled up. Now there were
other children to feed.

Life went on. Springs kept coming, four of them in all, the years
bringing only a few events worth recounting. One day she got a letter
just before Christmas in 1867, two years after Abe's death.

"Mrs. Sally Lincoln, My Dear Madam: In memory of the dearly
loved one, who always remembered you with so much affection, will
you not do me the favor of accepting these few trifles? God has been
very merciful to you, in prolonging your life and I trust your health
also has been preserved— In my great agony of mind I cannot trust
myself to write about, what so entirely fills my thoughts, my darling
husband; knowing how well you loved him also, is a grateful satisfaction to me. Believe me, dear Madam if I can ever be of any service to you, in *any respect,* I am entirely at your service . . . I will be
pleased to learn whether this package was received by you— Perhaps
you know that our youngest boy, is named for your husband,
Thomas Lincoln, this child, the idol of his father—I am blessed in
both my sons, they are very good and noble. The eldest is growing
very much like his own dear father. I am a deeply afflicted woman
and hope you will pray for me—I am, my dear Madam, affectionately
yours, Mary Lincoln."

The package came. Among other small articles it contained a bolt
of cloth, serviceable material, enough for the making of a dress. Sally
fingered it thoughtfully, shaking her head. If only once she had come
herself or let her children come! Now, poor woman, she was trying
to atone with a piece of cloth. A few days later another letter came
containing express receipts for the shipment mentioned "also ten dollars which please accept for the making of the dress. . . ." Mrs. Lincoln requested an answer certifying that the box and money had been
received.

"It will make you a nice new dress," Sally told Elizabeth Hall
cheerfully. "I sartin sure don't need it."

During these last four years Sally had her picture taken. A photog-
rapher from Charleston came and requested the honor of preserving
the likeness of the stepmother of the martyred President. She regarded the result with both humor and distaste. Even her mirror was
not so brutally revealing. Must she be remembered so—no more
black crisp curls peeping out from under her bonnet, smooth cheeks
sunken, eyes which had once been keen and sparkling staring with

apparent sadness out of their deep sockets, only the strong dark brows and a hint of a smile on the firm lips giving a suggestion of the vigor and energy which had once possessed the lithe, Indian-straight body? But, then, no one would want to remember her.

Once a man came to see her. His name was William Herndon, Abe's law partner, and he was writing a book about Abe. She showed him the old Bible with Abe's name in it, the bureau she had brought from Indiana, some of the books Abe had read, the pins stuck in the wall leading up to the loft where he had sometimes slept. She told him some of the things she remembered, how Abe had read everything he could find, how when he came across a passage that struck him he would write it down on boards if he had no paper, how he had ciphered on pieces of wood and when they got too black, he would shave them off with a drawing knife and go on again; how when folks had come to the house he would listen, then after they had gone have to understand everything, even to the smallest thing, repeating it over and over until it was fixed in his mind, then never losing it; how he would hear sermons and come home, take the children out, get on a stump or log, and preach them almost word for word.

"Abe was a good boy, and I can say what scarcely one woman, a mother, can say in a thousand and it is this: Abe never gave me a cross word or look and never refused in fact, or even in appearance, to do anything I requested him. I never gave him a cross word in all my life. He was kind to everybody and to everything and always accommodated others if he could, would do so willingly if he could. His mind and mine, what little I had, seemed to run together, more in the same channel. . . .

"He was dutiful to me always. He loved me truly, I think. I had a son John who was raised with Abe. Both were good boys, but I must say, both now being dead, that Abe was the best boy I ever saw or ever expect to see. I wish I had died when my husband did. I did not want Abe to run for President, did not want him elected, was afraid somehow or other, felt it in my heart that something would happen to him, and when he came down to see me after he was elected President, I felt that something would befall Abe and that I should see him no more. Abe and his father are in heaven, I have no doubt, and I want to go to them, go where they are. God bless Abraham."

So William Herndon recorded his interview with Sally Lincoln, putting her colloquial speech into slightly more conventional language. When he began questioning her, he noted, "she awoke as it were a new being, her eyes were clear and calm; her flesh is white and pure, not coarse or material; is tall, has large bluish gray eyes; ate dinner with her, sat on my west side, left arm, ate a good hearty dinner, she did.

"When I was about to leave, she arose, took me by the hand, wept, and bade me good-by, saying, 'I shall never see you again, and if you see Mrs. Abraham Lincoln and family, tell them I sent them my best and tenderest love. Good-by, my good son's friend, farewell.'"

Sally Lincoln died April 10, 1869, just four years after her stepson Abe. She was eighty-one years old. The fourteen-year-old girl who helped "lay her away" remembered later that the pillow of excelsior placed under her head in the coffin had no pillow slip, so a neighbor furnished a big white handkerchief to put under her head. They had put on her the black woolen dress which Abe had brought her on his last visit in 1861.

"She would have wanted that," said Elizabeth Hall, carefully smoothing the folds of the soft fabric.

She would have been glad too that the funeral was held right there in the old cabin where she had lived so many years, the family seated all about her inside, the neighbors and others outside, while the pastor, the Reverend Aaron Lovins, stood in the doorway. A member of the Disciples of Christ, he had been preaching at the schoolhouse a mile and a half south of the cabin, where Sally and the Halls had been attending services. She would have been surprised to know that her funeral was the "most largely attended of any one that ever died in the locality."

She was buried beside Tom in Shiloh cemetery, where Abe had placed the crude marker on his last trip, intending to supply a more durable monument. Not until 1880 would either of the graves be suitably marked, when a stone bearing only the name of Thomas Lincoln would be erected. As the years passed souvenir hunters chipped bits from this stone until it became unsightly. Finally, in 1923 another monument was erected, this time paying tribute also to the woman who, though not giving him birth, had done more than any other person to shape the life of the country's best beloved and most noted President and through him the destiny of the nation. It read:

> LINCOLN
> THOMAS AND SARAH BUSH LINCOLN
> 1778–1851   1788–1869
> FATHER AND STEPMOTHER
> OF OUR MARTYRED PRESIDENT
> THEIR HUMBLE BUT WORTHY HOME
> GAVE TO THE WORLD
> ABRAHAM LINCOLN

Author's Notes

Though I have called this a biographical novel because of its imaginative elements—dramatization of incidents, dialogue, character interpretation—I have tried to be meticulously true to facts as far as careful research has enabled me to discover them.

The intimate relationship between Nancy and Sally, though purely imaginary, is entirely possible. Thomas Lincoln is credited with having courted Sally before marrying Nancy, and, given their proximity, they were doubtless acquainted, if not intimate.

I must express appreciation to the University of Maine Library, which put all its facilities at my disposal, especially to the staff of its Inter-library Department, who secured rare books, magazine articles, and other archives for me from all over the country.

Though footnotes or specific reference to sources are not essential to a novel, I would like to make the following comments about resource materials relating to the four sections.

PART ONE: "Who was she?" Anyone attempting to write about Nancy Hanks, whether historian, biographer, or novelist, must ask this question. During the last hundred years she has been accorded at least a half dozen sets of parents.

According to Lincoln's biographer and law partner, William Herndon, Lincoln testified to his mother's background as follows: "Lincoln and I had a case in the Menard circuit court which required a discussion on hereditary qualities of mind, natures, etc. Lincoln's mind was dwelling on his case, mine on something else; Lincoln all at once said, 'Billy, I'll tell you something, but keep it a secret while I

live. My mother was a bastard, was the daughter of a nobleman so
called of Virginia. My mother's mother was poor and credulous, etc.,
and she was shamefully taken advantage of by the man. My mother
inherited his qualities and I hers. All that I am or hope ever to be I
get from my mother, God bless her."

Dennis Hanks identified the mother of Nancy as Lucy Hanks,
later the wife of Henry Sparrow. The early biographers, including
Sandburg, agree with this identification. Nicolay and Hay state that
Nancy's mother was Lucy Hanks and name her sisters, the daughters
of Joseph Hanks.

Mrs. Caroline Hanks Hitchcock, whose book *Nancy Hanks* was
published in 1899, identified Nancy as the daughter of Joseph
Hanks, born in the same year of 1784 (the one called Nannie in our
novel). This is impossible since it is authenticated that this Nancy
Hanks married Levi Hall, not Thomas Lincoln, and was the mother
of the illegitimate Dennis Hanks.

Dr. William Barton, author of many Lincoln books during the
1920s, states that Nancy was the granddaughter of Joseph Hanks
and his wife Ann, whom he called Nannie. He assumes that Nancy's
mother was Joseph's daughter Lucy, though no Lucy is named in
Joseph's will, which mentions Elizabeth, Polly, and Nancy. In his
book *The Women Lincoln Loved* Barton explains this omission by
the supposition that Lucy had left the family after its arrival in Kentucky, having incurred her father's displeasure because of her moral
lapse.

Dr. Louis A. Warren, another eminent Lincoln authority, names
Nancy's parents as James Hanks and Lucy (Shipley) Hanks, her father having died before Joseph Hanks, who presumably was Nancy's
grandfather, came into Kentucky. However, he is unable to prove
that Joseph had a son named James. In his article, "The Shipley Ancestry of Lincoln's Mother," Warren gives evidence that descendants
of Robert Shipley testified that the mother of Nancy Hanks was a
sister of Rachel (Shipley) Berry, wife of Richard Berry, Sr. But there
seems to be no proof of a Lucy among the Shipley sisters except by
inference.

Dr. Adin Baber, author of many genealogical books including *The
Hanks Family of Virginia and Westward,* identifies the parents of
Nancy as the daughter of Abraham and Sarah Hanks, Abraham

being a brother of Joseph. Apparently, however, this Nancy married someone other than Thomas Lincoln.

A more recent student of Lincolniana presents an entirely different finding of Nancy's parents. While accepting Joseph and his wife as Nancy's grandparents on her father's side, he accords her a different set of grandparents on her mother's. Since these findings are as yet unpublished, I do not present them here.

Confronted with this multiplicity of theories, a novelist must choose one. While realizing that it has many objections, that it is only a theory, I chose to follow the earlier biographers, especially Barton. Though realizing that Herndon was not always accurate in his portrayal of events, I was unable to believe that he manufactured Lincoln's statement out of pure imagination.

J. Edward Murr in his comprehensive articles on "Lincoln in Indiana," states that in his conversations with residents of the region of Lincoln's boyhood "the mooted question as to the President's maternal ancestry was altogether in favor of the position taken by almost all of his earlier biographers, particularly by Herndon. . . . In every case when Lincoln's pioneer neighbors were asked as to the obscure origin of Nancy Hanks, the reply was invariably the same—that she was the daughter of Lucy Hanks, and a Virginian."

I followed Baber, Barton, Curtis, and others in their supposition that Joseph Hanks's wife was Nancy (Nannie), one of the Shipley sisters, though this is not proven. Since it is known that Nancy spent part of her girlhood in the home of Richard Berry, Sr., and his wife Rachel (Shipley) Berry, this seems at least a reasonable assumption. And since she also spent years with Elizabeth (Hanks) and Thomas Sparrow, so that she in fact was known as Nancy Sparrow, her relationship with the family of Joseph Hanks is well established.

Details of Nancy's life with the Berry family and of her courtship and marriage may be found not only in the biographies, especially in the Briggses' *Nancy Hanks Lincoln,* but also in Louis A. Warren's article "The Romance of Thomas Lincoln and Nancy Hanks," which also gives much information about Thomas' early life and family; in Warren's article "The Shipley Ancestry of Lincoln's Mother"; and in "The Lincolns, Hoosier Pioneers," all published by the Indiana Magazine of History.

The death of Thomas' father is related by Dennis Hanks in Hertz's *The Hidden Lincoln,* and in colloquial language by John Hall in

Gridley's *The Story of Abraham Lincoln,* and by Thomas himself in
Whipple's *The Story of Young Abraham Lincoln.*

Camp meetings such as the one depicted are effectively described
in the Briggses' *Nancy Hanks Lincoln,* as well as in other books illustrative of the times.

Details of life in Elizabethtown and the Lincoln connection with it
may be found especially in Samuel Haycraft's *History of Elizabethtown, Kentucky;* in R. Gerald McMurtry's *The Lincolns in Elizabethtown, Kentucky;* and in McMurtry's "Thomas Lincoln's Corner
Cupboards."

PART TWO: Since most of the events in this part are chronicled
in the Lincoln biographies or other books indicated in the bibliog-
raphy, it seems unnecessary to call attention to the specific sources of
each detail or incident.

An excellent description of the "milk-sick," which was the cause
of Nancy Hanks's death, is given in Philip D. Jordan's article "The
Death of Nancy Hanks Lincoln."

PART THREE: Details concerning the Bush family in Elizabethtown and Sally's courtship by Thomas Lincoln are well outlined by
Samuel Haycraft in his *History of Elizabethtown, Kentucky,* and by
Louis A. Warren in his article "Sarah Bush Lincoln, the Stepmother
of Abraham Lincoln," as well as in many of the biographies.

There is discrepancy among authorities as to the birth date of John
Davis Johnston, estimates varying from 1810 to 1815. In accordance
with Charles H. Coleman's Genealogical Tables, based on census reports, I have placed it in 1810, since this date seems more in har-
mony with his actions in later life. It is doubtful, for instance, that
Lincoln would have permitted a boy so much younger to engage in a
fight on his behalf with William Grigsby. Warren, however, may be
correct in placing him slightly younger. Authorities differ also as to
Matilda's birth date, Warren placing it in 1811, Coleman in 1809.

Many details of Sally's relationship with Abe during the early Indiana years are given in "Mrs. Thomas Lincoln's Statement" to William Herndon on September 8, 1865. This is included in full in
Hertz's *The Hidden Lincoln,* pp. 350–53.

One good source of material on the Little Pigeon Church in Indiana is John F. Cady's article, "The Religious Environment of Lincoln's Youth."

For biographies the best sources for the Indiana years are: Louis

A. Warren, *Lincoln's Youth, Indiana Years, 1816–1830;* Francis Marion Van Natter, *Lincoln's Boyhood, A Chronicle of his Indiana Years.* Among periodicals an invaluable resource is J. Edward Murr's articles, "Lincoln in Indiana." In Emanuel Hertz's *The Hidden Lincoln* there are recorded statements of many contemporaries: Dennis Hanks, S. A. Crawford, Elizabeth Crawford, John Hanks, Nat Grigsby, Joseph Richardson, as well as Mrs. Thomas Lincoln.

PART FOUR: Two books among the many biographies were of special value. Charles H. Coleman's *Abraham Lincoln and Coles County, Illinois* furnished invaluable resource materials for these years when Sally and the Thomas Lincoln family were living in Coles County. This section could not have been written as fully without its help. Eleanor Gridley in *The Story of Abraham Lincoln, or The Journey from the Log Cabin to the White House,* tells of her visit in 1891 to the site of the cabin in Coles County and her interviews with people who knew the Lincolns. She includes pictures of the old cabin where Sally spent her last years, Sally's cherished bureau, the old andirons brought from Kentucky, Nancy's soap kettle, Thomas' grindstone and drawing knife, Sally's teakettle, her spinning wheel and bedstead, and the only picture she ever had taken, late in life.

Bibliography

BOOKS AND PAMPHLETS

The American Humorists: Old Abe's Jokes. 1864.

Andrews, Mary Raymond Shipman. *The Counsel Assigned.* New York: Charles Scribner's, 1912.

Atkinson, Eleanor. *The Boyhood of Lincoln.* New York: McClure Co., 1908.

Baber, Adin. *The Hanks Family of Virginia and Westward.* Privately printed by the author, Kansas, Illinois, 1965. Sold exclusively by The Arthur H. Clark Co., Box 230, Glendale, Cal.

———. *Nancy Hanks, the Destined Mother of a President.* Kansas, Ill., 1963. Sold as above.

———. *Nancy Hanks of Undistinguished Families.* Kansas, Ill., 1960. Sold as above.

Bailey, Bernadine. *Abe Lincoln's Other Mother. The Story of Sarah Bush Lincoln.* New York: Messner, Inc.

Barton, William E. *The Life of Abraham Lincoln.* 2 vols. Indianapolis: Bobbs-Merrill, 1925.

———. *The Paternity of Abraham Lincoln.* New York: George H. Doran Co., 1920.

———. *The Women Lincoln Loved.* Indianapolis: Bobbs-Merrill Co., 1927.

Basler, Roy B. *The Lincoln Legend.* Boston and New York: Houghton Mifflin Co., 1935.

———. *Lincoln Literature.* Illinois State Historical Society, 1959.

Beveridge, Albert J. *Abraham Lincoln, 1809–1858*. Boston and New York: Houghton Mifflin Co., 1928.

Boyd, Lucinda. *The Sorrows of Nancy*. Cynthiana, Ky.: The Hobson Press, 1943.

Bradford, Gamaliel. *Wives* (Chapter on Mrs. Abraham Lincoln). New York: Harper and Bros., 1925.

Briggs, Harold and Ernestine B. *Nancy Hanks Lincoln. A Frontier Portrait*. New York: Bookman Associates, 1952.

Coleman, Charles H. *Abraham Lincoln and Coles County, Illinois*. New Brunswick, N.J.: Scarecrow Press, 1955.

Current, Richard N. *The Lincoln Nobody Knows*. American Century Series. New York: Hill and Wang, A Division of Farrar, Straus, and Giroux, 1977.

Curtis, William Elroy. *The True Abraham Lincoln*. Philadelphia and London: Lippincott, 1903.

Dictionary of American Biography, "Abraham Lincoln." New York: Charles Scribner's, 1928.

Dixon, Thomas. *A Man of the People*. D. Appleton-Century Co., 1920.

Donald, David. *The Folklore Lincoln*.

Esarey, Logan. *The Indiana Home*. Bloomington and London: Indiana University Press, 1953, 1976.

Frazier, Carl and Rosalie. *The Lincoln Country*. New York: Hastings House, 1963.

French, Marian. *Lincoln Heritage Trail Cook Book*. Williamsburg, Va.: Tory Hill Press, 1971.

Galleher, J. E. *Best Lincoln Stories Tersely Told*. Chicago: M. A. Donahue and Co., 1898.

Gore, J. Rogers. *The Boyhood of Abraham Lincoln*. (From the Spoken Narratives of Austin Gollaher). Indianapolis: Bobbs-Merrill Co., 1921.

Gridley, Eleanor. *The Story of Abraham Lincoln, or The Journey from the Log Cabin to the White House*. New York: Eaton and Mains, 1900.

Gross, Anthony. *Lincoln's Own Stories*. New York: Garden City Pub. Co., Inc., 1912.

Haycraft, Samuel. *History of Elizabethtown, Kentucky*. The Woman's Club of Elizabethtown, Kentucky. 1921 (written in 1869).

Herndon, William H. and Weik, Jesse W. *Abraham Lincoln.* New York: D. Appleton and Co., 1892.

——. *Herndon's Lincoln,* 3 vols. Springfield, Ill.: Herndon's Lincoln Publishing Co., 1921.

Hertz, Emanuel. *The Hidden Lincoln.* New York: Viking Press, 1938.

Hitchcock, Caroline Hanks. *Nancy Hanks.* New York: Doubleday and McClure, Co., 1899.

Hill, Frederick Trevor. *Lincoln, Emancipator of the Nation.* New York and London: D. Appleton and Co., 1928.

Holmes, Fred L. *Abraham Lincoln Traveled This Way, The Log Book of a Pilgrim to the Lincoln Country.* Boston: L. C. Page Co., 1930.

Howells, William Dean. *Life of Abraham Lincoln.* Life written in 1860 for the Campaign, corrected by Lincoln. Reprinted. Bloomington: Indiana University Press, 1960.

Hubbard, Elbert. *Abe Lincoln and Nancy Hanks.* New York: the Roycrofters, East Aurora Co., 1920.

Luthin, Reinhard H. *The Real Abraham Lincoln, A Complete One Volume History of his Life and Times.* Englewood Cliffs, N.J.: Prentice-Hall Inc., 1960.

McClure, Colonel Alexander K. *"Abe" Lincoln's Yarns and Stories. Complete Collection.* Copyright by Henry Neil, 1901.

McMeekin, Clark. *Old Kentucky Country.* New York: Duell, Sloan and Pearce, 1957.

McMurtry, Gerald. *The Lincolns in Elizabethtown, Kentucky.* Fort Wayne, Ind.: Lincolniana Publishers, 1932.

Mearns, David Chambers. *Largely Lincoln.* Introduction by Earl Schenck Myers. New York: St. Martin's Press, 1961.

Morgan, James. *Abraham Lincoln, the Boy and the Man.* New York: Grosset and Dunlap, 1908.

Nadal, E. S. *A Virginia Village.* Freeport, N.Y.: Books for Libraries Press, 1968.

Newcomb, Rexford. *In the Lincoln Country.* Philadelphia and London: J. B. Lippincott Co., 1928.

Newman, Ralph Geoffrey, ed. *Abraham Lincoln, His Story in His Own Words.* Garden City, N.Y.: Doubleday & Co., 1975.

Nichols, Clifton M. *Life of Abraham Lincoln,* being a biography of his life from Birth to his Assassination; also a record of his ancestors and a collection of anecdotes. New York: Mast, Crowell and Co., 1896.

Nicolay, John G. and Hay, John. *Life of Lincoln,* Vol. 1. New York: The Century Co., 1886 and 1890.

Rice, Wallace. *The Lincoln Year Book.* Chicago: A. C. McClurg and Co., 1908.

Rothschild, Alonzo. *Honest Abe, A Study in Integrity.* Boston and New York: Houghton Mifflin Co., 1917.

Sandburg, Carl. *Abe Lincoln Grows Up.* A Voyager Book. New York and London: Harcourt, Brace, Jovanovich, 1926, 1953.

——. *Abraham Lincoln. The Prairie Years and the War Years.* New York: Harcourt, Brace and Co., 1939.

——. *Lincoln Collector.* New York: Harcourt, Brace and Co., 1949.

Sherwood, Robert E. *Abe Lincoln in Illinois.* In *Abraham Lincoln, His Life, Work, and Character,* edited by Edward Wagenknecht (see below).

Singmaster, Elsie. *From Gettysburg, Stories of the Red Harvest and the Aftermath.* In *Abraham Lincoln, His Life, Work, and Character,* edited by Edward Wagenknecht (see below).

Sloan, Eric. *A Museum of Early American Tools.* New York: Ballantine Books, 1964.

Stephenson, Nathaniel Wright. *Lincoln, An Account of His Personal Life.* Indianapolis: Bobbs-Merrill Co., 1922.

——. Compiler and Annotator. *An Autobiography of Abraham Lincoln.* Indianapolis: Bobbs-Merrill, 1926.

Tarbell, Ida M. *Abraham Lincoln.* 2 vols. New York: Lincoln Memorial Association, 1895, 1900.

——. *In the Footsteps of Lincoln.* New York and London: Harper and Bros., 1924.

Thayer, William M. *The Pioneer Boy, and How He became President.* Boston: Walker, Wise, and Co., 1864.

——. *From Pioneer Home to the White House, Life of Abraham Lincoln, Boyhood, Youth, Manhood, Assassination, Death.* Boston: James H. Earle, 1887.

Thomas, Benjamin P. *Abraham Lincoln.* New York: Alfred A. Knopf, 1952.

——. *Portrait for Posterity.* New Brunswick, N.J.: Rutgers University Press, 1947.

Toulmin, Harry. *The Western Country in 1793. Reports on Ken-*

tucky and Virginia. San Marino, Calif.: Copyright by Henry E. Huntington Library, 1948.

Turner, Justin G. and Linda Levitt. *Mary Todd Lincoln, Her Life and Letters.* New York: Alfred A. Knopf, 1972.

Van Natter, Francis Marion. *Lincoln's Boyhood, A Chronicle of his Indiana Years.* Washington, D.C.: Public Affairs Press, 1963.

Wagenknecht, Edward, ed. *Abraham Lincoln, His Life, Work, and Character.* An Anthology of History and Biography, Fiction, Poetry, Drama, and Belles-Lettres. New York: Creative Age Press, 1947.

Warren, Louis A. *Lincoln's Parentage and Childhood: A History of the Kentucky Lincolns Supported by Documentary Evidence.* Indiana Historical Society, 1926; New York: The Century Company, 1926.

———. *Lincoln's Youth, Indiana Years, 1816–1830.* Indiana Historical Society, 1959.

Whipple, Wayne. *The Story of Young Abraham Lincoln.* Philadelphia: Henry Altemus Co., 1915, 1918.

PERIODICALS AND PAMPHLETS

Bailey, Bernadine and Walworth, Dorothy. "He Loved Me Truly. Story of Sally Lincoln." *Reader's Digest* 46: 27–31. Feb., 1945.

Cady, John F. "The Religious Environment of Lincoln's Youth." *Indiana Magazine of History* XXXII: 16–30. March, 1941.

Coleman, Charles H. "Lincoln's Lincoln Grandmother." Illinois State Historical Society 52 (1959).

Crockett, Margaret W. "The Mary Todd Lincoln That Abraham Lincoln Loved." *Yankee* 42: 104–110, 148–157. Feb., 1978.

Croy, Homer. "Lincoln's Teacher." About Mentor Graham. *Holiday* 19: 11–13. May, 1956.

Don Marquis. "No Matter What They Think." Fictional story of Abe's paper on religion. *Collier's, The National Weekly.* Quoted in Wagenknecht (see above).

Gorsline, Douglas, "The Clothes Lincoln Wore." *American Heritage* 8: 102, 103. August, 1957.

Gunderson, Robert G. "Reading Lincoln's Mail." *Indiana Magazine of History* 55: 379–392. June, 1959.

Hansen, Richard. "The Other Abraham." *Reader's Digest* 66: 52–54. Feb., 1952.

Jordan, Philip D. "The Death of Nancy Hanks Lincoln." *Indiana Magazine of History* XL No. 2: 103–110. June, 1944.

Kunhardt, Dorothy Meserve. "Lincoln's Lost Dog." *Life* 36: 83–84. Feb. 15, 1954.

——. Lincoln, Mrs. Thomas. Interview with William Herndon on September 8, 1865. From the Library of Congress. Also in Hertz (see above).

"Lincoln Had a Stepbrother." *Saturday Evening Post* 212: 26. Feb. 17, 1940.

Luthin, Reinhard H. "Fakes and Frauds in Lincoln Literature." Review of book by Earl Schenck Myers. *Saturday Review* 42: 15, 16. Feb. 14, 1959.

McMurtry, R. Gerald. "Thomas Lincoln's Corner Cupboards." *Antiques* 85: 206–208. Feb., 1964.

Morgan, Arthur E. "New Light on Lincoln's Boyhood." *Atlantic Monthly* 125, 1920.

——. "The Lincolns in Elizabethtown, Kentucky." Lincolniana Publishers, 1932.

Murr, J. Edward. "Lincoln in Indiana." *Indiana Magazine of History* XIII: 307–348, Dec., 1917; XIV: 148–182, Jan., 1918.

——. "Nancy Hanks' Son." *Time,* Oct. 27, 1941.

Randall, Ruth Painter. "Lincolns Were Good Neighbors." *New York Times Magazine,* Feb. 8, 1953. Pp. 10 f.

Rutledge, Archibald. "A Southerner Views Lincoln." *Scribner's Magazine* 83: 204–213. Feb., 1928. Also in Wagenknecht (see above).

Tobey, James A. "Life and Death in Lincoln's Time." *Hygeia-Today's Health* 28: 32–33. Feb., 1950.

Warren, Louis A. "Herndon's Contribution to Lincoln Mythology." *Indiana Magazine of History* XLI: 221–244. Sept., 1945.

——. "The Lincolns, Hoosier Pioneers." *Indiana Magazine of History* XXXVI: 251–264. Sept., 1942.

——. "The Romance of Thomas Lincoln and Nancy Hanks." *Indiana Magazine of History* XXX: 213–222. Sept., 1934.

——. "Sarah Bush Lincoln, The Stepmother of Abraham Lincoln." Reprinted from the Transactions of the Illinois State Historical Society. Danville, Ill.: Illinois Printing Co., 1926.

——. "The Shipley Ancestry of Lincoln's Mother." *Indiana Magazine of History* XXIX: 203–212. 1933.

Wheeler, Bruce E. "Lincoln and the Kirkham Grammar." *Hobbies* 47: 8, 9. Feb., 1943.

Wilson, William. "There I Grew Up." *American Heritage* 17: 30–32. Oct., 1966.

Woldman, Albert A. "Lincoln Never Said That." *Harper* 200: 70–74. May, 1950.

Zornow, William Frank. "Those Lincoln Legends." *American Mercury* 82: 76–77. Feb., 1956.

CHRISTIAN HERALD ASSOCIATION AND ITS MINISTRIES

CHRISTIAN HERALD ASSOCIATION, founded in 1878, publishes The Christian Herald Magazine, one of the leading interdenominational religious monthlies in America. Through its wide circulation, it brings inspiring articles and the latest news of religious developments to many families. From the magazine's pages came the initiative for CHRISTIAN HERALD CHILDREN and THE BOWERY MISSION, two individually supported not-for-profit corporations.

CHRISTIAN HERALD CHILDREN, established in 1894, is the name for a unique and dynamic ministry to disadvantaged children, offering hope and opportunities which would not otherwise be available for reasons of poverty and neglect. The goal is to develop each child's potential and to demonstrate Christian compassion and understanding to children in need.

Mont Lawn is a permanent camp located in Bushkill, Pennsylvania. It is the focal point of a ministry which provides a healthful "vacation with a purpose" to children who without it would be confined to the streets of the city. Up to 1000 children between the age of 7 and 11 come to Mont Lawn each year.

Christian Herald Children maintains year-round contact with children by means of a *City Youth Ministry.* Central to its philosophy is the belief that only through sustained relationships and demonstrated concern can individual lives be truly enriched. Special emphasis is on individual guidance, spiritual and family counseling and tutoring. This follow-up ministry to inner-city children culminates for many in financial assistance toward higher education and career counseling.

THE BOWERY MISSION, located at 227 Bowery, New York City, has since 1879 been reaching out to the lost men on the Bowery, offering them what could be their last chance to rebuild their lives. Every man is fed, clothed and ministered to. Countless numbers have entered the 90-day residential rehabilitation program at the Bowery Mission. A concentrated ministry of counseling, medical care, nutrition therapy, Bible study and Gospel services awakens a man to spiritual renewal within himself.

These ministries are supported solely by the voluntary contributions of individuals and by legacies and bequests. Contributions are tax deductible. Checks should be made out either to CHRISTIAN HERALD CHILDREN or to THE BOWERY MISSION.

Administrative Office: 40 Overlook Drive, Chappaqua, New York 10514
Telephone: (914) 769-9000